9/11 and A

Christians, Jews,

MW00479254

9/11 and American Empire
Christians, Jews, and Muslims Speak Out

Edited by Kevin Barrett, John B. Cobb, Jr.,
and Sandra B. Lubarsky

OLIVE
BRANCH
PRESS

An imprint of Interlink Publishing Group, Inc.
www.interlinkbooks.com

First published in 2007 by

OLIVE BRANCH PRESS
An imprint of Interlink Publishing Group, Inc.
46 Crosby Street, Northampton, Massachusetts 01060
www.interlinkbooks.com

Passages of Nafeez Mosaddeq Ahmed's essay, "Interrogating 'Terrorism': Muslim Problem or Covert Operations Nightmare?" were previously published in his work *The War on Truth: 9/11, Disinformation, and the Anatomy of Terrorism* (Northampton, MA: Olive Branch Press, 2005).

Library of Congress Cataloging-in-Publication Data
9/11 and American empire : Christians, Jews, and Muslims speak out /
edited by Kevin Barrett, John B. Cobb, Jr., and Sandra B. Lubarsky
ISBN-13: 978-1-56656-660-5
ISBN-10: 1-56656-660-6
volume II of
9/11 and American empire : intellectuals speak out /
edited by David Ray Griffin and Peter Dale Scott.
p. cm.
ISBN-13: 978-1-56656-659-9 (pbk.)
ISBN-10: 1-56656-659-2 (pbk.)
1. September 11 Terrorist Attacks, 2001. 2. War on Terrorism, 2001—Political aspects.
3. United States—Foreign relations—2001- 4. United States—Politics and government—
2001- I. Griffin, David Ray, 1939- II. Scott, Peter Dale. III. Title: Nine-eleven and American empire.
HV6432.7.A128 2006
973.931—dc22
2006014385

Printed and bound in the United States of America

Cover image © AP Wide World Photos

To request our complete 40-page full-color catalog,
please call us toll free at 1-800-238-LINK, visit our website at
www.interlinkbooks.com or write to Interlink Publishing
46 Crosby Street, Northampton, MA 01060

CONTENTS

Introduction

TOWARD AN INTERFAITH DIALOGUE ON 9/11 AND EMPIRE

Kevin Barrett, John B. Cobb, Jr.,
and Sandra B. Lubarsky

THIS BOOK IS ABOUT OUR NEED FOR TRUTH—ESPECIALLY IF THE TRUTH IS disturbing, uncomfortable, or even painful. This is a controversial thesis. Not everybody agrees that truth is a good thing. Some of the neoconservatives who currently have great influence in the administration were taught by Leo Strauss that there are times when rulers need to lie to their people.[1]

Secularist readers may find it ironic that this book's message— follow the truth wherever it leads—is being presented by religious people. More than a few contemporary intellectuals agree with Marx that religion is the opiate of the people. Though history is full of examples of religious leaders and followers who preferred comforting lies to jagged, gut-wrenching truths, the basic thrust of the great religions has been toward truth, not illusion. Taoism, Buddhism, and Hinduism all aim at unveiling the deeper truths to be found in and through the evanescent world of appearances. The three great monotheisms—Judaism, Christianity, and Islam— affirm the unity of God, who is the Truth, against what they see as the illusions of polytheism and of idolatries that, in recent times, have often taken the form of nationalism and racism.

In this age of pseudo-religious hysteria and deceit, we need to listen to those religious voices calling for an unshakable commitment to truth—including Marc Ellis, David Ray Griffin, Rosemary Radford Ruether, Faiz Khan, and the other contributors to this volume. It may be a matter of life and death. As we write this in late winter 2006 CE/1427 AH the prognosis for humanity looks bleak. If human beings continue to burn fossil fuels at an ever-increasing rate, we must expect climate collapse. And if nature saves us from destroying ourselves with fossil fuel, as the peak-oil theorists suggest it might, we still face social and economic crises of frightening proportions, a "civilizational collapse."[2]

The solution of our global problems will require collective, coordinated, morally driven action by people all over the world. We need massive redistribution of wealth, the development of new sources of energy while simultaneously reducing its consumption, the radical retooling of our infrastructure, a spiritual renewal that will bring an end to consumerism, and a sustainable agriculture.

The problems are obvious. Why, then, is so little being done to resolve them? Part of the answer is that such efforts as were being made a decade ago have been partly derailed by 9/11. 9/11 has redirected attention away from globally critical problems to a "war on terror" that seems designed to be permanent.

The 9/11 television spectacular was scripted in such a way as to incite hatred of Muslims. It concentrates our attention on the planes flying into two World Trade Center towers, said to be flown by Muslims, and ignores the many problems associated with this explanation, such as the eyewitness reports of explosions, the symmetrical collapse of the towers (and building 7) at near free-fall speed, the production of molten steel by fires that could not have conceivably even have weakened the steel, much less melted it, and the fact that fire has never before or since brought down a steel-framed building. One way to explain the almost complete lack of interest in challenging the official explanation is that any alternative explanation would place the blame not on Muslims, but rather on US government officials.

On the other hand, among those who do not believe the official story, many rush to blame "the Jews." The always latent anti-Judaism in Christian cultures comes to the surface in truly dangerous ways. Now, unfortunately, this anti-Judaism is joined in its eagerness to scapegoat Jews by new forms of anti-Jewish bigotry that are becoming increasingly common among Muslims.

The tendency of 9/11 to create enmity among the Abrahamic traditions increases the urgency for Christians, Jews and Muslims to take the lead in speaking out about 9/11. We must, as David Ray Griffin argues, return to the basic moral values of our faith traditions.[3] We must work together if our struggle is to succeed.

It is not just that our faith traditions teach us to seek truth and abhor injustice, lies, murder, and plunder. The main function of 9/11 has been to justify American imperialist claims and actions, whereas our traditions are profoundly anti-imperialist. We can and should invoke our anti-imperialist heritage as we join together to do battle with empire. Jews should remember that the highlight of Moses's achievements was that he led an anti-imperial insurrection in Egypt. Christians should remember that Jesus was put to death for being an agitator against the Roman Empire. Muslims should remember that the Prophet Muhammad led a successful insurrection against an oligarchic mini-empire in Mecca—and that his followers quickly brought down the two greatest empires of the day, Persia and Byzantium.

Our three great faith traditions implore us to take the side of truth-tellers against liars, of persecuted people against their persecutors, and of justice-seekers against power-mongers. All three traditions embrace the prophetic voice that calls for a critique of power and injustice.

9/11 incited interfaith hatred and provided official justification for imperial aggression. Our government has used the attacks to paralyze us with fear and make us more easily manipulated. The neoconservatives accept Machiavelli's dictum that "it is better for a ruler to be feared than loved," and they have used 9/11 to scare the population into giving up its civil liberties and allowing its children to be killed in a pointless, bungled, and exceedingly expensive war. Many of our secular friends who consider themselves political "radicals" have been paralyzed by 9/11. They are afraid to speak out, afraid of Muslims, afraid of the Protestant "religious right," afraid of peak oil and climate collapse, afraid to engage in serious protests, and afraid to take a hard look at what really happened on 9/11. The same is true of many Jews, Christians, and Muslims. Nevertheless, faith in God, in principle, and for many, in fact, does offer a cure for that paralysis.

Indeed, as religious people we are in a uniquely effective position to break down the fear that sustains empire. As heirs to the tradition of Middle Eastern monotheism, we have been given the ultimate antidote to fear: "Yea, though I walk through the valley of death, I will fear no evil, for Thou art with me." If we walk with God, we have no reason to fear. With that kind of faith one can "move mountains," and perhaps even seek the truth about what happened on 9/11.

If we do not succeed in piercing the 9/11 veil of denial, we will continue to be distracted by non-issues—by the alleged threat of terrorism, which the administration can intensify whenever it needs to direct attention away from its most obvious mistakes, and by the fabricated "clash of civilizations." We will continue to pour trillions of dollars into technology for killing people, and next to nothing into saving ourselves and the planet. If we take this road, we are a failed species.

Though our ethical ideals are similar, Christians, Jews, and Muslims face somewhat different challenges in the shared quest to come to terms with 9/11. Christians have an almost 1,400-year history of viewing Islam as a dangerous rival, and of viewing salvation as an exclusively Christian possession. The official story of the 9/11 attacks plays into this Islamophobic chauvinism. For Christians, questioning the official account is made harder by the fact that Christianity has been on the wane, at least in Europe, for at least two centuries or more, whereas Islam is now undergoing something of a renaissance, both demographically and in terms of the intensity of faith shown by its followers. Many Christians prefer to view this intensity of faith as fanaticism and therefore favor the official account that holds that fanatical, suicidal Muslims took over the planes and flew them into the Twin Towers and the Pentagon.

Jews, for their part, have equally seductive reasons for accepting the official story. The rise of Islam, demographic trends, and the fact that the Muslim Middle East holds most of the world's best energy reserves combine to inspire existential fears for the future of the state of Israel. 9/11 triggered the massive use of American military force against Israel's enemies, which is why the right-wing extremist Benjamin Netanyahu viewed it as a godsend.

Muslims, unfortunately, are also guilty of 9/11 denial. The biggest cause of what Faiz Khan calls the "ghastly silence" of Muslims is fear.[4] The relentless media onslaught aimed at convincing us that any Muslim who offends the US administration is likely to be whisked away to a CIA prison has done its work. Far from being extremists motivated to dangerous or suicidal deeds by a burning faith in the rewards of paradise, the vast majority of Muslims are simply ordinary people with jobs to hold down and children to take care of. They suspect, rightly or wrongly, that speaking out for 9/11 truth could win them a one-way ticket to Guantanamo. Many American Muslims, especially immigrants, have little confidence in the American promise of constitutional liberty and freedom of speech, especially after the Bush administration's post-9/11 assaults on civil liberties and on

Muslims. To Muslims who are aware of horrendous US-supported repression abroad, the murder of thousands of citizens to start a war does not seem entirely out of character for American leaders. And Muslims in academia, for whom freedom of speech is not entirely illusory, feel compelled to embrace the prevailing orthodoxy in order to maintain job security and cordial relations with their colleagues, administrations, and students.

Though Christians, Jews, and Muslims all have reasons to remain silent, they have better reasons for speaking out. Christianity's ethical ideals militate so strongly in favor of truth, justice, and the oppressed that it is shocking that more Christians have not joined the theologians in this volume in calling for 9/11 truth. Indeed, the continued silence of Christians in the face of the 9/11 deception threatens to rob the faith of its moral legitimacy.

Although Christians, as representatives of the dominant tradition, have the major responsibility to seek the truth, Jews and Muslims also have powerful reasons to do so. The truth may implicate some Jews in the events along with many Christians, but it will count against the wholesale blaming of "the Jews." American imperialism is not a Jewish plot! Muslims can only gain as a group from a more accurate understanding of what actually occurred.

Learning the truth about 9/11, however, is not primarily for the sake of one religious community or another. It is for the sake of the American people and, indeed, the people of the world. The truth is likely to be painful, but basing our actions and our policies on lies will be vastly more costly. As religious people we believe that "truth will set us free." We who have edited this book, along with all who have contributed to it and many more, seek that freedom.

The three editors each took responsibility for soliciting essays from members of their religious traditions: Cobb, Christian; Lubarsky, Jewish; and Barrett, Muslim. None of us take responsibility for everything said by all the authors belonging to our own religious communities, nor for all that is said by the others. In some instances we find ourselves uncomfortable with what the members of other faiths have to say. However, we believe that we need to hear the opinions of others and the language in which they are expressed, even if we are offended by them, in order to attain a basis for honest dialogue and for cooperation in our shared quest for truth.

This book offers myriad voices from persons who share little more than, on the one hand, a concern that the truth about 9/11 be learned and made public, and, on the other, a commitment to an Abrahamic faith. With regard to 9/11, some of the contributors are fully convinced that the present administration orchestrated the attacks. Others only agree that the official account is unsatisfactory and that a serious effort needs to be made to find the truth. Still others are chiefly critical of the way the administration has used 9/11. With regard to the faith traditions, the typical perspectives of Christians, Jews, and Muslims also differ. This is partly a matter of traditional beliefs, but in this book the history of Christian vilification and persecution of Jews, of Muslim resentment of Zionism, and of the public association of Islam with terrorism are more important.

We have stressed previously that believers in all three traditions have reason to speak out for the sake of truth and the future of the earth. We have also stressed that members of these traditions are related to 9/11 in different ways. Since Muslims are publicly and officially blamed for the event, their reasons for contesting the offical story we have been told are particularly poignant. The reader will see how these differences are expressed in the chapters that follow.

We would like this dialogue to continue and develop. To that end, we will be inviting the contributors to respond to any or all of their fellow contributors, or to issues raised by this book, at a special page on the Muslim-Jewish-Christian Alliance for 9/11 Truth website: mujca.com/newbook.htm. We invite you to join in the conversation and will post selected reader responses.

Sandra Lubarsky and John B. Cobb, Jr. want to express their appreciation to Kevin Barrett for the primary leadership he has taken in this whole project and in writing this introduction, as well as in the larger effort to bring out the truth about 9/11.

1

THE EVIL THAT RESULTS FROM ERRONEOUS BELIEFS

John B. Cobb, Jr.

MOST AMERICANS FIND IT DIFFICULT, IF NOT IMPOSSIBLE, TO BELIEVE THAT responsible members of the administration could have been involved in 9/11. The attacks on the World Trade Center and the Pentagon have been portrayed as so heinous that people suppose that only extraordinarily vicious people could have perpetrated them. Americans can imagine that there are Arabs who are sufficiently vicious to do so, but they do not want to believe that any Americans are that evil. Above all, they do not want to believe that anyone who participates in the US government could be involved.

These beliefs provide a shield against inquiring into what really did take place on that day and how the attacks could have been so successful. Most Americans are prepared to accept the official explanation, whatever it may be, as long as all the blame is placed on foreigners, especially Muslims. They like to be assured that Americans played only virtuous roles. This requires believing that many Americans behaved extremely incompetently, even absurdly, and that none of those who did so have lost their jobs or even been demoted as a result. But this can be overlooked, since one trusts the authorities to take care of such matters.

Perhaps my being a Christian theologian has something to do with adopting a quite different perspective on these matters. From my perspective, there is no reason to suppose that those who planned and executed this attack were vicious. From their own point of view and that of their supporters, they were heroes. It is all too easy to forget that those who are called terrorists generally understand themselves as freedom fighters. A recent case is that of those who won Israel's freedom from Great Britain. These freedom fighters believe the cause for which they are fighting is worth both dying and killing for. Many agree with them.

That there are diverse views of which cause is worth killing and dying for is easy to see if we adopt the perspective of Osama bin Laden. In a video attributed to him, he has told us why he attacked us. Firstly, we support Zionism, which, while viewed by many Jews as salvific and part of God's providential plan, is experienced by many Arabs as an unmitigated evil. Without any consultation with the Arabs, the West gave Jews the right to seize Arab land, drive out most of the population, and then make second-class citizens of the remainder. Jews have taken over more and more land and reduced the political situation of Arabs on the West Bank and in Gaza to that of the colonized and their economic condition to near destitution. Those Arabs who resist are called terrorists and are imprisoned and sometimes tortured. Arab homes are demolished and Arab orchards are uprooted. None of this could have taken place without the support of the United States.

Secondly, the United States has troops on the sacred soil of Saudi Arabia. This is a sign of its imperial nature and a deep humiliation of the Saudi Arabs. It is also a sacrilege against the holy places of Islam. American economic and military power is such that there can be no direct resistance by patriotic Saudis or devoted Muslims. Further, the United States has corrupted the government of Saudi Arabia so that its national policies support American colonialism and imperialism. But there are ways of making American crimes against the Arab people costly. The World Trade Center represents American economic power and its oppressive role in the world. The Pentagon represents American military power. To attack these centers is to engage in the only kind of resistance that is open to Saudi Arabians.

I am not arguing that this is an accurate analysis of all that has happened. I could just as easily present the story from the point of view of Zionist Jews who see the establishment of a Jewish homeland as crucial to the very survival of the Jewish people in a Jew-hating world, and also view Israel as having acted with remarkable restraint, given the refusal of many Arabs to recognize the legitimacy of the state of Israel and the terrorist attacks upon its people by Palestinians. I am asserting that it is not difficult to understand that some Saudi Arabians would see the United States in this way. No more viciousness is required to think this way or to act on these views than for the American government to justify maintaining military bases in Saudi Arabia and supporting Israel's basic policies in relation to the Palestinian people.

Similarly, it is not vicious to adopt, and to act on, the views that have been articulated and published by the neoconservatives in the United States. In their vision, the United States is the global bastion of democracy and justice. Those parts of the world that share basic American practices and virtues are orderly and peaceful and make a good life possible for their people. But much of the world is still living under the rule of corrupt authoritarian governments. The mission of the United States is to extend democracy and personal freedom throughout the world. Now that the greatest threat to democracy, the Soviet Union, has collapsed, the time has come to realize the possibilities of the American century.

From this perspective, it is clear that to achieve an orderly and peaceful world of democratic nations, it is necessary that there be no center of power elsewhere capable of challenging the United States. Nuclear arms must be limited to the United States and its close allies. Also, the United States must have massive military superiority on land, in the sea, in the air, and in space. This requires increased military expenditures. It also requires that the American people support the use of American power to enforce a Pax Americana. The United States must not be inhibited by world opinion, the United Nations, or international treaties. It must be free to use its power to implement its policies.

Clearly, in order both to maintain its standard of living and to attain full global hegemony, the United States must control the world's oil. As oil becomes scarce in relation to global demand, the importance of this policy increases. The major resources the United States must secure, in addition to Saudi Arabia, are in Iraq, the Caspian Basin, and Iran.

Much of US policy since the fall of the Soviet Empire can be explained by this vision of the American role. However, administrations prior to the present one were more concerned to work with allies and make use of international institutions. They were willing to tolerate authoritarian governments hostile to the United States as long as they posed no threat to its security. Hence, although much of the action of the present administration has been continuous with that of its predecessors, the influence of the full neoconservative ideology is far more marked.

Now, let us take the next step. If one is deeply committed to the neoconservative vision, one will view the chief obstacle to its implementation to be public opinion in the United States. Most

Americans support foreign wars only if they are persuaded that other nations threaten the United States. They like America to be powerful, but they do not favor trying to control the whole world. They do not want to make the sacrifices needed to implement the neoconservative vision. In particular, most young Americans do not want to serve in the armed forces. Only under extreme circumstances will the American people support a draft.

What is required to gain the support of the American people for a far more costly and aggressive foreign policy? The answer is simple: We must be attacked. It must be a dramatic and serious attack. Americans must also be persuaded that this attack is not a single event to be punished and forgotten, but a part of a long-term threat to which they must be prepared to respond indefinitely. If those policies that are needed for the good of the world and of the United States cannot be sold to the American people on their merits, then there must be an attack upon us. An attack on the World Trade Center and the Pentagon would galvanize American public opinion and make it possible for the government to take those steps that are required for it to fulfill its mission. This will be costly in civilian lives and property, but, from the neoconservative perspective, these costs are trivial when measured against the benefits.

The point here, of course, is that virtuous people in positions of power in the United States government, employing their best judgments, could well come to this conclusion. That they would collude in enabling the attack to take place and preventing any serious investigation is, therefore, fully understandable. Whether this happened is, of course, a different question. Until and unless these suspicions are genuinely investigated, we can only speculate.

On the factual question of who did what when, a theologian as theologian has no better answer than anyone else. The question is one of evidence. However, it requires less evidence to establish the occurrence of a plausible event than of a radically implausible one. For example, in proving the case against one suspected of murder, establishing a motive plays a large role. Once we are clear that leading figures in the administration wanted something like the events of 9/11 to occur, indeed, that they considered it crucial that something of this sort happen, the theory that they permitted or even orchestrated it deserves serious consideration.

Serious consideration quickly reveals that there is in fact a great deal of evidence of complicity on the part of leading figures in the administration. At the present state of the investigation, none of this evidence is decisive. It is always possible to imagine other scenarios. However, the absence of decisive evidence results from the fact that the administration has blocked any serious investigation. This does not reduce the plausibility of the theory that there is much the administration wishes to conceal.

We should be clear that there is nothing vicious about this cover-up either. Once people decide that a particular action is needed for the sake of the nation and the world, the fact that it is illegal and politically unacceptable is no reason to avoid it. But its illegality is a reason to be very secretive and to use the power of the government to deceive the public and prevent the truth from being known.

What then is the virtuous response to a situation in which there seems to be a justifiable suspicion that governmental leaders may have engaged in massive illegal acts and concealed them from the public? The answer depends on the basic convictions of the one who responds. I will schematically suggest several possibilities.

Some people share the beliefs described above, which may have led to this collusion with, or even orchestration of, an attack upon the United States. They believe that the invasion and conquest of Afghanistan, together with the establishment of long-term American presence in the Caspian region, was needed. They also believe that the conquest of Iraq was essential to American well-being and to the realization of a Pax Americana or an American global empire. And to them it seems that the sacrifice of personal liberties involved in the PATRIOT Act improves the situation, making it easier to maintain governmental control over the American people. From this point of view, the administration should be strongly supported in covering up the successful operation called 9/11.

For others, American patriotism is primary. They tend to the view "America right or wrong!" The United States needs, accordingly, to maintain its national power and reputation. Especially with respect to any feature of our national life that has international ramifications, we should rally around the president as our commander in chief. We need to present a unified face to the world. People in this group may not approve of the acts of which some figures in the administration are suspected, but they do not want any investigation. Those acts are water over the dam. For those who hold these views, our task now is to move ahead in safeguarding American interests.

A third group is equally patriotic, but it understands patriotism in a different way: Our nation was founded on certain principles, and only when it is held to these principles can it flourish. Ours is a government of laws rather than of people. There are ways to put forward different proposals for foreign policy and to win support for them. But there is no justification for manipulating public opinion through deception as a basis for implementing policies that the people do not support on their merits. Leaders in the government should be held to especially high standards of moral and legal conduct. If, in fact, there is evidence of collusion with the attackers on 9/11, this should be thoroughly investigated and any found guilty should be prosecuted. However, most of those in this group refuse to believe that any responsible US government official would have engaged in a crime of this magnitude. Since, for them, obedience to the moral and positive law is so central to virtue, they find it difficult to imagine that others would engage in such an extreme violation of that law. They would support an investigation only if the evidence of guilt were overwhelming. For the most part, they are more critical of the accusers than of those suspected of involvement. The result is that they support the acceptance of the official theory and oppose the investigations apart from which the overwhelming evidence they demand cannot be obtained.

A fourth group consists of those who view world affairs in Machiavellian light. They find it quite likely that members of the present administration have committed a variety of crimes in order to gain and maintain power and to implement their policies. They do not exclude the events of 9/11 from this list. They recognize that Roosevelt may have tricked us into World War II and that Johnson lied us into the expansion of the Vietnam conflict. They see no reason to doubt that the current administration has been still more manipulative and deceptive. But they view those who expose such crimes as equally politically motivated and, should they gain power, equally likely to commit crimes. They are not against exposing the crimes of those now in power, but they do not expect any great gain from doing so. They see the law as functioning more as an instrument of power than of justice.

A fifth group is deeply opposed to the neoconservative ideology. Part of the opposition is the extent to which that ideology explicitly justifies deception and trickery in the interest of what is viewed as necessary governmental actions. But the opposition is also both to the goal of American empire and to the means of attaining it: unilateral action and indifference to international law and institutions. It is also to the militarization of society and the reduction of personal liberties. This group would like to punish the administration for leading us into unnecessary and destructive wars, especially for doing so through deceit. For the members of this group the goal is to amass a coalition of those opposed to current policy sufficient to defeat the Republican Party in the next elections. For this they believe that they need to maintain a moderate image. Even if they have little doubt that some members of the administration are capable of the sort of acts of which they are suspected, they do not regard it as politically prudent to raise such issues.

There are, also, however, those who believe that it is of great importance to learn the truth. The Christian faith as I understand it calls me to stand in this position. We believe that since the official account does not hold water and there are many unanswered questions, a genuine inquiry is urgently called for. In addition to the conviction that truth is inherently superior to falsehood, there are several practical reasons for this position.

First, currently much of our policy and practice is based on theories about the cause of 9/11 that are highly doubtful. For example, the administration has persuaded most of the population that al-Qaeda is entirely responsible for what happened. This was used as a justification for regime change in Afghanistan and influenced the acceptance by the American people of the invasion of Iraq. It currently provides a context for consideration of an attack on Iran as well. It leads to support of Israeli violence against Palestinians and attacks on Lebanon.

Despite some cautious statements on the part of the administration, the official theory has stimulated broad suspicion of Muslims as individuals and of Muslim nations. It has justified changes in the law that allow for government interference in religious affairs, an interference thus far exercised chiefly in relation to Islam. More broadly, it has allowed for the loss of civil liberties by Muslims and even the torture of Muslim prisoners. It has reduced the protection of all Americans from arbitrary governmental actions. It has concentrated power in the presidency, weakening the system of checks and balances.

If in fact 9/11 was a false-flag operation, it is obvious that few of these actions are justified. In this case, billions of dollars have been misspent, and tens of thousands of lives have been lost without justification. The fabric of our democracy has been seriously injured without reason. In planning for the future we will judge that the likelihood of future acts of terrorism of this sort does not loom so large. We will select different principles as the basis for our foreign policy. We can adopt a more balanced view of those who in various parts of the world consider themselves as freedom fighters but who are defined by governments as terrorists. Justification for the reduction of civil liberties and torture of prisoners will largely disappear. The general level of suspicion of our Muslim neighbors should be greatly reduced.

Our primary response should be to find ways to implement our system of checks and balances more effectively, to prevent the concentration of power in a few hands that makes it possible for such events to occur. It would also be appropriate to rethink the role of false-flag operations in other countries and, indeed, our whole quest for global hegemony. If the system of governmental secrecy functions primarily to prevent us from knowing the truth about our rulers, we should work to open up government to greater transparency.

Second, the public knowledge that the administration lies to us as a matter of course creates a profoundly unhealthy climate. The culture of corruption in Congress is matched by a culture of deceit in the administration. There have been half-hearted efforts to expose and condemn a few of these deceptions. But they have not gone far. The focus on whether some law has been broken usually becomes narrow and technical, whereas the issue is not as much the law as the basic relation of the government to the people.

Deception about 9/11, assuming there has been such, is by far the most important. A serious effort to learn the truth would clear the air in a very basic way. Today we live in a Kafkaesque society. Confidence in its structures and democratic functioning is badly eroded. Much else is needed, but an honest investigation into who was responsible for what on 9/11 would probably do more to restore confidence in the integrity of our political system than any other one action.

Thus far the only Americans who have been punished for what happened on 9/11 have been whistleblowers and those who tried to prevent the attacks. The only lesson that has been taught is to go along with authority. If we learn the truth about 9/11, we will expose wrongdoing and apply the law. We may even honor some who have tried to tell the truth at great personal cost. The lessons we teach future generations will be quite different.

I wish that the Christian churches adopted this commitment to truth. Regretfully, their members subscribe to all of the six positions just identified. The majority do not seek the truth. Those leaders who would like to lead the church in the pursuit of truth are warned by past occasions when the Protestant leadership moved forward without the support of most of the members. Meanwhile, few pastors encourage serious grappling with such questions in their congregations. In the more liberal churches where some pastors would like to do this, the fear of accelerating membership loss is too strong. Accordingly, I know that the Christian contribution to seeking the truth will come only from individuals and perhaps eventually from a few rare congregations.

I write, nevertheless, as a Christian theologian. This leads me to view other people in terms of their theologies or ideologies. I believe that most of the evils in the world result from erroneous or inadequate belief systems rather than from personal viciousness. There are sociopaths and sadists, and their actions are often appalling. But the evil caused by them is minor when set against the background of the massive horrors of history.

There are many people who are neither sociopaths nor sadists, whose concerns extend little beyond their personal interests. Some of them have adopted an ideology that holds that there are no valid moral principles transcending the quest for achieving personal goals. Some are persuaded that society as a whole functions best when each member seeks individual gain. The selfishness that results certainly does harm, since selfish people often ignore the consequences of their actions for others. Because the beliefs and ideologies that support this self-centeredness are growing in acceptance in our society, those who disagree must certainly find ways of confronting them effectively. But calling self-centered people vicious does not help. In any case, they are not those who have done most harm in history.

The massive evils of history have resulted from acting on belief systems. Most of the most damaging systems have been ethnocentric or nationalist. Members of one tribe or city-state believe that the interests of their tribe deserve attention even at the expense of the interests of other tribes. Nations gain part of their sense of well-being by triumphing over other nations. In recent times the causes of enormous conflict and suffering have also included political and economic ideologies.

For the most part religion has intensified these conflicts.

Nations call on their people to sacrifice for national glory partly on the grounds of their supposed religious superiority or the threats to their religious convictions that come from other ethnic groups. In these cases national and religious feelings merge. Much of this still occurs today.

Religious loyalties can also be an independent cause of conflict and mutual destruction. This is especially true of the Abrahamic traditions, and among them Christianity has played the largest role in causing historical evils. Once it gained power, it persecuted those who did not accept it. It organized a series of so-called crusades against the Muslim rulers of the Holy Land, resulting in hundreds of thousands of deaths. These crusades also initiated the worst stage of the religious persecution of Jews, culminating in the twentieth century in the Holocaust. In addition, Christians fought Christians over doctrinal differences. Christian teaching played a role in the genocide of Native Americans in North America and in the effort to eradicate the cultures of those who survived. It also supported the slaughter of alleged witches in Europe and the American colonies and the enslavement and pitiless exploitation of Africans.

No absolutes can be drawn about the relation of means and ends. Terrible things are sometimes necessary in order to prevent still more terrible things. But we need to recognize that the terrible things we do will have their own terrible consequences. We should engage in them only as what is truly a last resort and then with every possible safeguard to minimize the evil that they cause.

These cautions about means and ends, which we Christians have learned from our own mistakes, are highly relevant to other groups today. Both terrorists and governments widely seem to neglect this hard-learned wisdom. Such wisdom would almost certainly have prevented 9/11, wherever responsibility for this event may lie. This would certainly be the case if 9/11 is, as the official account would have it, the work of Muslim extremists. If, as I suspect, neoconservative ideology contributed to what happened on 9/11, it applies to those who have adopted this mode of thought as well.

A third reason that we need to know the truth about 9/11 is that in the absence of such knowledge it is hard to bring Christian wisdom, or any wisdom, to bear upon it. Nevertheless, I will proceed on the hypothesis of neoconservative involvement, recognizing that, without a thorough and open-minded investigation, it remains only a hypothesis. Even if it turns out that their thinking did not contribute in any direct way to 9/11, it is clear that their policies often need correction by this wisdom.

The point is that even those who genuinely believe that American hegemony would be good for both the nation and the world should beware of employing terrible means in pursuit of that goal. If pursuit of that goal requires much horror, that is sufficient reason for abandoning it. The means we use for purposes that we sincerely believe to be good have their own independent consequences that are likely to overwhelm the desired goals. The destruction wreaked on 9/11 has had many unanticipated consequences. However idealistic the goals may be, Christians should challenge the acceptability of using means of this sort to attain them. We should do so not condescendingly from a position of virtue, but out of our painful acknowledgment of the many crimes we have ourselves committed and condoned because we supposed that our noble ends justified them and even the horrible consequences that have in fact resulted.

We believe that the lessons Christians have learned painfully over the centuries are important for today. We are impressed by those who have learned them and developed means that are consonant with the ends sought. Gandhi, King, and Mandela stand out. All of history is full of ambiguities, but the results of the revolutions effected by these men are far less ambiguous than those of other historical changes that depended on the violence of war and terrorism.

As my third reason for seeking the truth about 9/11 I have argued that even if the attacks were carried out for what was, in the minds of the perpetrators, a good cause, they were profoundly wrong. We need to know whom to indict for that wrong. I am speaking here of a theological or at least a theoretical indictment. I suspect that this indictment is properly directed to the neoconservatives, but without a responsible investigation of the truth, the public argument cannot proceed.

Nevertheless, on the basis of the hypothesis that neo-conservative beliefs and ideals have some responsibility for 9/11 and the cover-up that has followed, I will indicate my substantive disagreements with them. I disagree with the neoconservatives' assessment of American virtue. We have yet to attain a genuine democracy ourselves. Indeed, we are moving away from authentic rule by the people. Today we are more a plutocracy than a democracy. Around the world the United States exploits the forms of democracy to gain control of the economies of other peoples. When this does not work, we overthrow even democratically elected governments. American global hegemony gained in these ways can never result in a genuinely democratic world.

Not only the pursuit of power but also its achievement has a strong tendency to corrupt those who wield it. The events of 9/11 express such corruption. The subsequent use of those events have also been corrupt. The "war on terror" generates terrorists so as to justify still more expenditure, militarization, and reduction of civil liberties at home as well as aggressive actions abroad. Even the realization of an ideal Pax Americana could not justify all this.

But from a Christian perspective a Pax Americana is, in any case, an inherently false ideal, what we theologians call an idol. An idol is a limited good treated as an ultimate one. There are certainly good features of American society for which I am personally very grateful. Causing other nations to be more like us in some respects would, in many cases, benefit them. But taking these limited goods and viewing them as an ultimate good is idolatrous. It leads to a great exaggeration of their goodness and to obliviousness to the many evils that are associated with them. It justifies actions that are horrendous and whose grave evil profoundly taints any positive achievements.

If our goal should not be a Pax Americana, what should it be? Christians certainly do not all agree on the answer. My judgment is that we should work toward a world in which there is increasing global governance in which all the peoples of the world participate. We should expand international law and increase the ability of global institutions to enforce it. But I am equally interested in the traditional Catholic principle of subsidiarity. That means that self-government should be exercised as locally as possible. We should not take actions at the global level with respect to problems that could be dealt with regionally or locally. Further, power should move upward from the people to governmental institutions and from local governments to national and global ones. We should take seriously the sovereignty of the people. Higher levels of government should interfere with lower ones only to ensure that all people are included in the local communities, that is, recognized as full participants, and that none act to the serious detriment of their neighbors.

A major obstacle to localism today is the globalization of the economy. Local communities, even nations, in many instances, have little control over their economies and thus lack any significant control over their own lives. When local government is dependent on distant corporations for the well-being of its people, the result cannot be considered self-government.

There are, however, good reasons to think that economic globalization is fragile. It now encounters enormous popular opposition, an opposition that is beginning to shape the policies of more governments as well. It depends on large US consumption, which is sustained only by enormous and growing debt. It is based on a petroleum economy that makes the cost of shipping goods great distances small. And it produces goods in ways that generate global warming and other ecological catastrophes. This is not sustainable. At some point creditors will cease to lend more money to the United States at low interest rates. We are already at or near peak oil, while demand globally continues to rise. The consequences of global warming will become unacceptable even to the economic elite.

Catastrophes can be slowed, mitigated, and survived, if not prevented, by moving toward local production of essential goods. There are already moves in that direction. If we view the world in the widest perspective, as those who believe in God are called to do, encouraging moves toward localism economically and politically seems far more valuable and positive than attempting to impose American domination on resistant peoples.

Better than authoritarian control of the world by one nation is global government that gives voice to many peoples. Better than concentrating power in such a government is distributing power, with respect to matters that do not require control at the global level, to more local regions. The model that commends itself to me, for both economic and political organization, is that of communities of communities of communities.

This is not a fanciful idea. Europe has given us a model of a community of national communities. There is always a tension between those who wish to keep their national identity and self-determination important and those who move toward erasing national boundaries in favor of sovereignty at the continental level. I am personally glad that the most recent moves in the latter direction failed. My vision requires that the nations also be communities of communities with as much power exercised locally as possible. European countries represent this kind of federalism to varying degrees. And, of course, my vision requires that Europe be a good citizen of the world community, developing and obeying international law and supporting and strengthening global institutions. To some extent this is already true.

Europe has by far gone the farthest along the path to that kind of order to which I believe we should be committed as Christians. But it is not impossible that other regions of the world move in somewhat similar directions. The support of the United States for this kind of development, instead of for economic globalization and US hegemony, could lead to a far better world than that envisioned by the neoconservatives.

This debate about the form of global order we should be seeking may seem quite different from the issue of seeking the truth about 9/11. However, they are related. Earlier I described a way of viewing the world that could have functioned to justify neoconservative idealists' facilitation of the events of 9/11. Many found the neoconservative vision convincing because of the lack of alternative visions of a desirable world order available in the public sphere. Most groups other than the neoconservatives, including, in general, the Christian churches, took the existing situation largely for granted and limited themselves to modest proposals for improve-ment here and there. Only the neoconservatives propounded a powerful vision of the great accomplishments possible for our nation if only we were willing to pay the price.

In Proverbs we are told that where there is no vision, the people perish. At a minimum we can say that where there is no vision, people lose interest in the wider scene and attend to their local interests only. We who disagree with the neoconservatives bear a heavy responsibility for having provided no vision. The neocon-servatives did provide one. They won hearts and minds. Sadly, we must say that when the vision is idolatrous, the people perish even faster than when there is no vision. The neoconservative vision is profoundly idolatrous. It may have provided the justification for the killing that occurred on 9/11. It certainly contributed to the far greater slaughter that has occurred in Afghanistan and Iraq.

The best way to undermine this idolatrous vision and the terrible means employed to realize it will be to expose both its erroneous assumptions and its horrible consequences to the light of day. The most effective focus of such exposure will be on the role of members of the administration in the attack upon us. A genuine investigation is of utmost importance.

Should a genuine investigation exonerate all governmental

figures, that, too, would be a great gain. We might still attend to other lies and deceptions in which some of them have participated and which are already part of the public record. But we would limit our criticisms to their known acts rather than to hypothesized ones. For having suspected them of involvement in 9/11 we would then owe them an apology. However, as long as the government blocks every move toward a genuine investigation, our suspicions will continue, and we will not cease to imagine scenarios that implicate leaders in our government in heinous crimes. We need to know the truth.

2

FALSE-FLAG OPERATIONS, 9/11, AND THE NEW ROME: A CHRISTIAN PERSPECTIVE

David Ray Griffin

IN THIS ESSAY, I OFFER A CHRISTIAN CRITIQUE OF THE AMERICAN EMPIRE IN light of the attacks of 9/11. Such a critique, however, presupposes a discussion of 9/11 itself, especially the question of who was responsible for the attacks. The official theory is that the attacks were planned and carried out entirely by Arab Muslims. The main alternative theory is that 9/11 was a "false-flag" attack, orchestrated by forces within the US government who made it appear to be the work of Arab Muslims.

Originally, a false-flag attack was one in which the attackers, perhaps in ships, literally showed the flag of an enemy country, so that it would be blamed. But the expression has come to be used for any attack made to appear to be the work of some country, party, or group other than that to which the attackers themselves belong.

The evidence that the attacks of 9/11 were false-flag attacks— orchestrated, at least in part, to marshal support for a "war on terror" against Muslims and Arabs—is very strong. However, many Americans who encounter this idea reject it on *a priori* grounds, thereby refusing even to examine the evidence. The most prominent *a priori* assumption is that America's political and military leaders simply would not commit such a heinous act.

I will begin by showing that there is ample historical evidence to reject this assumption. I will then summarize some of the most persuasive evidence that 9/11 itself was a false-flag operation, orchestrated to expand the American empire. In the final section, I will discuss the question of how Christians in America should respond to the realization that our country is the "new Rome."

I. False-Flag Operations

The idea that 9/11 was a false-flag attack, carried out by members of our own government, becomes more conceivable once one knows something about false-flag operations prior to 9/11. This section first provides some examples of (1) false-flag attacks carried out by other countries, (2) false accusations by the US government to start wars, and (3) US-sponsored attacks on innocent citizens in friendly countries. It then describes (4) a Pentagon plan for the US government to attack its own citizens as a pretext for war.

False-Flag Operations by Other Countries

The Mukden Incident: In the early decades of the twentieth century, Japan, hoping to establish economic self-sufficiency, was exploiting resource-rich Manchuria. The chief instrument of this exploitation was the South Manchuria Railway. In 1930, Chiang Kai-shek's increasingly successful effort to unify China caused Japanese leaders to fear that their position in Manchuria was threatened.

On September 18, 1931, Japanese army officers secretly blew up a portion of the railway's tracks near the Chinese military base in Mukden. Then, blaming the sabotage on Chinese solders, the Japanese army used this incident as a pretext for taking control of all of Manchuria. This military operation is considered by many historians to be the beginning of World War II. Therefore, the Mukden incident—which the Chinese call 9/18—was one of the most important false-flag incidents of the twentieth century.[1]

The Reichstag Fire: An equally fateful false-flag operation was the burning of the Berlin Reichstag, which was the home of Germany's parliament, on the night of February 27, 1933. The fire—which occurred less than a month after the Nazis took power—is now known to be have been orchestrated by Hermann Göring, the president of the Reichstag, and Joseph Göbbels, Hitler's propaganda minister, who had the fire started by members of the SA (Storm Troops).

The Nazis then blamed the arson on the German Communist Party, claiming that the fire was intended to be the signal for a Communist uprising. The only evidence the Nazis presented for this claim was the "discovery" on the site of Marinus van der Lubbe, a feeble-minded left-wing radical from Holland, who had evidently been brought to the site by the SA troops.[2]

The Reichstag fire then became "the excuse for a hitherto unparalleled persecution of Communist and Social Democratic

workers, intellectuals and party leaders."[3] Thousands of people
allied with the workers' movement were arrested; all left-wing
newspapers were shut down; and two so-called fire decrees
annulled civil rights provided by the constitution of the Weimar
Republic. These decrees "formed the pseudo-legal basis for the
entire Nazi dictatorship."[4]

Operation Himmler: Nazi Germany attacked Poland on the morning
of September 1, 1939. In Hitler's speech to the Reichstag later that
day, he referred to 21 "border incidents" of the previous night in
which Polish troops had allegedly initiated hostilities. The attack
on Poland was hence presented as a defensive necessity. But this
attack had been planned long before. The Nazis only needed a
pretext, so that the war would not be strongly opposed by the
German people and, they hoped, other nations.

After Heinrich Himmler came up with the basic idea for the
pretext, the task of planning and directing it was assigned to
Reinhard Heydrich (who would later be centrally involved in the
"final solution") and Heinrich Müller, the head of the Gestapo. The
plan, dubbed "Operation Himmler," was to have members of the
Gestapo and the Security Service, dressed as Poles, stage various
raids near the Polish–German border on the night of August 31.

The plan in some cases was to take some German convicts,
dress them as Poles, give them fatal injections, take them to the
sites, shoot them, then leave them there as proof that they had
been killed while attacking German troops.

The most famous of these raids was the Gleiwitz incident,
which was headed by Alfred Naujocks (who later testified about all
this at Nuremberg). Naujocks had one of the convicts, who had
been injected and shot, delivered to the German radio station at
Gleiwitz. Then he and his men seized the station, broadcast a
message in Polish urging Poles to attack Germans, and left. The
body of the dead convict, "discovered" shortly thereafter, was used
as proof that an attack by Poles had occurred.

The invasion of Poland on September 1 was the beginning of
World War II; France and the United Kingdom declared war on
Germany two days later.[5]

These three false-flag operations—the Reichstag Fire, the
Mukden Incident, and Operation Himmler—were all crucial events
on the road to World War II. The fact that this war caused millions

of deaths and enormous suffering illustrates how important it is that false-flag operations be exposed before the true perpetrators can use them as pretexts for carrying out their designs.

Many Americans, to be sure, may agree with this principle while assuming that US leaders would never engage in such deadly deceit. But this assumption is contradicted by the historical record.

US Wars Based on False Charges of Enemy Aggression
American leaders have in several cases knowingly used false charges of enemy aggression to start a war. I will look at four examples.

The Mexican–American War: One factor in the background to the Mexican-American War of 1846–1848 was a border dispute between Mexico and the Republic of Texas, after the latter had won its independence in 1836. According to Mexico, the border was marked by the Nueces River, whereas the Texans placed the border much farther south, at the Rio Grande.

Another factor was American expansionism, especially that of President James Polk. Although he was mainly interested in acquiring California, Polk had committed himself to annexing Texas, promising to support its border claim. In 1846, after being rebuffed in his attempt to purchase California, Polk ordered the US army to build a fort on the Rio Grande, about 150 miles south of what Mexico considered the border. Facing humiliation as the only alternative, Mexico reportedly initiated hostilities. When the good news reached Polk, he told Congress that Mexico had "shed American blood upon the American soil." Polk's claim that Mexico had been the aggressor was called "the sheerest deception" by a congressman named Abraham Lincoln.[6]

In any case, Mexico, being out-gunned, signed a peace treaty in 1848, ceding away what is now California, Arizona, Nevada, New Mexico, Utah, and part of Colorado. In compensation, the US government paid $15 million, which was a paltry sum even in those days (the US would later offer Spain $100 million for Cuba). The United States, in other words, used the trumped-up war to steal about half of Mexico.[7]

The Spanish–Cuban–American War: Through the nineteenth century, US business, military, and political leaders lusted after Cuba, wanting to make this richly endowed island part of America's commercial system.[8] They had, accordingly, supported Spain's continued sovereignty over Cuba, not wanting Cuba to be liberated until the United States was ready to take it over.[9] During the Cubans' war of liberation in the 1890s, the United States refused to loan money or sell arms to them.[10] By 1898, however, it appeared that the Cubans might win anyway.[11] The administration of President William McKinley decided, against the wishes of the Cuban leaders, to intervene.[12]

In preparation, McKinley sent, without invitation, the battleship USS *Maine* to Havana Harbor. A few weeks later, it blew up and sank, killing some 260 men. Although Theodore Roosevelt, then assistant secretary of the navy, accused Spain of "an act of dirty treachery,"[13] Washington knew that the last thing the Spanish wanted was for America to have an excuse to enter the war. But US newspapers inflamed the American public with the charge that Spain was responsible. The national slogan became "Remember the Maine, to hell with Spain." McKinley took advantage of this situation to get Congress to appropriate money for the war.[14]

Some critics of US foreign policy have argued that the Maine was blown up by Americans themselves, which would make this incident a classic false-flag operation. But no clear evidence to support this charge has emerged. An investigation by the Navy in 1976 concluded that the explosion was probably an accident resulting from ammunition stored too close to the engine. Whatever the real cause, however, US leaders knowingly used a false accusation to enter the war in order to take control of Cuba and other Spanish colonies.

The US War in the Philippines: The most important reason to go to war against Spain, from the point of view of US imperialists such as Roosevelt, was to take control of the Philippine Isles, partly for their own sake, partly as a stepping stone to the fabled China market.[15] The United States quickly overpowered the Spanish forces and then, at the peace talks, demanded and obtained the entire Philippine archipelago for the tiny sum of $20 million. The Filipinos, however, were not party to this agreement and claimed independence. This meant that to control this island nation, the United States would have to go to war against the Filipinos, who had just recently been their allies against Spain.

In January of 1899, General Arthur MacArthur—father of

Douglas MacArthur—ordered all Filipino soldiers out of a village they had occupied for several months. Another US general set up a sentry at a position in this disputed area known as the "pipeline," ordering the men to fire on any intruders. On the evening of February 4, the sentries were approached by four Filipino soldiers— who were probably drunk and unarmed—and opened fire on them. US troops, having been prepared for this "pipeline incident," then fired on Filipino positions for the next six hours. Few shots were fired in return by the Filipinos, but the war was on.

The US secretary of war, giving the official version of what happened, said: "On the night of February 4th..., an army of Tagalogs... attacked, in vastly superior numbers, our little army... and after a desperate and bloody fight was repulsed in every direction." This statement was part of a more general "propaganda offensive to prove that the Filipino army started the war."

Years later, MacArthur and three US officers who had been on the scene confessed that the whole battle was prearranged and that American troops had fired first.[16] By then, however, it did not matter much. The Philippines lost 250,000 people in this war— which was so dreadful that the usually ironic William James was provoked to say: "God damn the US for its vile conduct in the Philippine Isles."[17]

The Vietnam War: In June of 1964, advisors of President Lyndon Johnson discussed escalating the war in Vietnam by bombing North Vietnam. Pointing out that this escalation would require a congressional resolution, they counseled that without some "drastic change in the situation to point to," such as an "armed attack" by the North Vietnamese, it would be hard to get this resolution. Shortly thereafter, a clandestine operation known as OPLAN 34A was formulated.[18]

In mid-July, the US destroyer *Maddox* was sent to the Gulf of Tonkin to carry out electronic espionage. On July 30, South Vietnamese gunboats, with American advisers, made commando raids against North Vietnamese islands in the gulf.[19] Then on August 2, the *Maddox* cruised near North Vietnamese islands that were under attack by the South Vietnamese gunboats. Three patrol boats of the North Vietnamese, who rightly believed that the *Maddox* and the gunboats were part of one operation, charged repeatedly at the *Maddox*, veering off at the last moment. The *Maddox* then opened fire on them. The gunboats fired torpedoes in return, but missed. On August 3, Rusk sent a cable saying: "We believe that present Op Plan 34 A activities are beginning to rattle Hanoi."[20]

On the night of August 4, the *Maddox* and another destroyer fired their huge guns for several hours, having evidently been told by their sonarmen that torpedoes were headed at them. But no torpedoes hit them. A naval commander flying directly over the destroyers saw "nothing but black sea and American firepower." Commodore Herrick of the *Maddox*, realizing he might have been firing at nothing, sent a radio message saying: "Review of action makes many reported contacts and torpedoes fired appear very doubtful." The next morning, nevertheless, US troops were given orders to "retaliate" against North Vietnamese targets. At the same time, President Johnson was telling congressional leaders that the North Vietnamese had made "unprovoked attacks" against American ships in international waters.[21]

Secretary of Defense Robert McNamara, when asked by Congress if we had done anything to provoke the attacks, declared that the attacks were "deliberate and unprovoked" against a ship on "routine patrol in international waters." When he was asked whether there was a connection between the *Maddox* and the South Vietnamese commando raids, he said: "Our Navy was not associated with, was not aware of, any South Vietnamese actions."[22]

Congress, accepting these lies, passed the Tonkin Gulf Resolution, which authorized the president "to take all necessary measures to repel any armed attack against the forces of the United States" and to help South Vietnam defend its freedom.[23] With that blank check in hand, the Johnson administration soon initiated a full-scale war, which would go on for another eight years and result in the deaths of over 58,000 Americans and some two million Vietnamese.

False-Flag Attacks in Europe

Some Americans, being confronted with the preceding evidence of the willingness of US leaders to provoke and lie about incidents to justify going to war, might reply: "I grant that American leaders have done such things to enemies, but they would not deliberately kill citizens of friendly countries for political reasons." That assumption, however, would be false. In a 2005 book entitled *NATO's Secret Armies: Operation Gladio and Terrorism in Western*

Europe, Swiss historian Daniele Ganser has extensively documented the fact that during the Cold War, the United States sponsored false-flag terrorist incidents in many countries of Western Europe in order to discredit Communists.

In 1947, the Truman administration successfully sponsored the National Security Act, which created the Central Intelligence Agency (CIA) and its boss, the National Security Council (NSC). Existing primarily to prevent the victory of Communist parties in European elections, the NSC and its CIA first targeted Italy. Directive NSC 4-A ordered the CIA to undertake covert activities to prevent a victory by the Communists in the 1948 elections. After these operations succeeded, directive NSC 10/2 created the Office of Policy Coordination, which was authorized to carry out covert operations in all countries in the world. Such operations were to include "propaganda; economic warfare; preventive direction action, including sabotage [and] demolition...; subversion against hostile states, including assistance to underground resistance movements, guerrillas... and anti-Communist elements."[24]

With the creation in 1949 of the North Atlantic Treaty Organization (NATO), these operations came to be coordinated by a secret unit within NATO called the Clandestine Planning Committee (CPC), which was guided primarily by the CIA and the Pentagon. (US control was guaranteed by the fact that NATO's Supreme Commander would always be an American general.) When NATO was expelled from France in 1966 by President Charles de Gaulle, it moved to Brussels, Belgium. But the real headquarters—of NATO in general and the CPC in particular— remained in the Pentagon.[25]

These operations involved the creation of secret armies, comprised of members of the extreme right. (In Germany, for example, they included former members of Hitler's SS.[26]) They were officially called "stay-behind armies," since their official function was, in the case of a Soviet invasion of Western Europe, to stay behind enemy lines, thereby being in position to mobilize a resistance movement against the occupiers. No such invasion ever occurred, of course, so these secret armies never played this role. They only engaged in terrorism and other forms of subversion, which, insofar as they have been officially admitted, have been portrayed as secondary operations. It is not clear, however, that the United States ever believed that there would be a Soviet invasion. All of the so-called stay-behind armies may have from the first, as some critics have charged, been created entirely to do battle against domestic opponents, with the stay-behind function serving simply as a cover story.[27]

Although these right-wing armies engaged in many kinds of operations, including coups, I will focus here entirely on false-flag operations, giving examples from four countries.

Italy: The Italian secret army, which came to be called Gladio, and other right-wing extremists with which Gladio linked up, had together been waging a secret war since the end of World War II. But from 1969 to 1974, during the presidency of Richard Nixon, these operations became much more violent and included many false-flag attacks.

On December 12, 1969, four bombs exploded in Rome and in Milan's Piazza Fontana, killing 16 people and injuring another 80. This attack, known as the Piazza Fontana massacre, was blamed on the left by the military secret service, which destroyed evidence (a bomb that had failed to go off), then planted bomb parts in a leftist editor's villa.[28]

In 1972, some members of Italy's paramilitary police were set up to be killed by a car bomb near Peteano. An anonymous caller implicated a Communist group called the Red Brigades, after which some 200 Communists were arrested.[29]

In 1978, after the Communist Party had won an unprecedented number of seats in parliament, Prime Minister Aldo Moro decided, against the strongly stated wishes of Washington, that he had to include them in his government. Before he could do so, he was kidnapped and murdered. The Red Brigades were again blamed.

The deadliest attack in Italy occurred in 1980, when a massive explosion at the Bologna railway station killed 85 people and wounded another 200.[30]

For over a decade, the Italian public believed that Communists had committed these atrocities.[31] However, Italian authorities, beginning in 1984 with an investigation of the Peteano incident, discovered that these crimes were actually orchestrated by right-wing forces. Judge Felice Casson, who spearheaded the investigation, later said: "the Peteano attack is part of what has been called 'the strategy of tension'... to create tension within the country to promote conservative, reactionary social and political tendencies."[32] This interpretation was later confirmed by a member of the extreme right-wing organization Ordine Nuovo, who confessed to having planted the Peteano bomb, adding: "You had to attack civilians, the people, women, children, innocent people.... The reason was... to force these people, the Italian public, to turn to the State to ask for greater security. This is the political logic that lies behind all the massacres and the bombings."[33]

In 1990, Judge Casson discovered documents revealing the existence of Gladio and its connection to NATO and the United States. The truth of these discoveries was then confirmed by Prime Minister Giulio Andreotti, who emphasized the responsibility of the White House.[34]

In 2000, a parliamentary committee to study Operation Gladio concluded that "those massacres... had been organized or... supported by men... linked to the structures of United States intelligence." This conclusion was confirmed in 2001 by General Giandelio Maletti, former head of Italian counterintelligence, who said of the Piazza Fontana massacre: "The CIA, following the directives of its government, wanted to create an Italian nationalism capable of halting what it saw as a slide to the left." It seemed to him, he added, that to achieve this goal, "the Americans would do anything."[35]

One of the things the Pentagon evidently did was to have its own secret service, the Defense Intelligence Agency (DIA), prepare an instruction book, called Field Manual 30-31 (FM 30-31), for Gladio and NATO's other secret armies.[36] This manual came with two "supplements," entitled simply A and B. Supplement B, dated March 18, 1970, came to be known as the "Westmoreland Manual," because it contained the signature of General William Westmoreland, who, after commanding US military operations in Vietnam, served as US Army chief of staff from 1968 to 1972.

This Westmoreland Manual instructed these armies to carry out acts of violence, then blame them on Communists, and also to infiltrate left-wing organizations, then encourage them to use violence. Through these means, Supplement B says, "US army intelligence [will] have the means of launching special operations which will convince Host Country Governments and public opinion of the reality of the insurgent danger." However, the manual continues: "These special operations must remain strictly secret.... [T]he involvement of the US Army in the internal affairs of an allied country... shall not become known under any circumstances."[37]

The existence of FM 30-31 first became publicly known in 1973, when a Turkish newspaper announced that one of its journalists had come into possession of it. Although this journalist soon disappeared, never to be heard from again, the manual was translated into Turkish in 1975, after which it became known it Spain and Italy.

In 2006, after Ganser's book appeared, the US Department of State claimed that Supplement B was a Soviet forgery. Its evidence for this claim, however, is extremely weak, consisting merely of the claim that "Field Manual 30-31B... was exposed as a 'total fabrication' in February 1980 hearings before the US House of Representatives Permanent Select Committee on Intelligence."[38] The State Department does not reveal whether this was a conclusion reached by the committee as a whole or simply a statement of someone testifying at the hearings. It also does not mention the discovery of the document in Turkey and the disappearance of the journalist who discovered it. It does not mention that Ganser, rather than being oblivious to the claim that Supplement B was a forgery, pointed out that this claim had been made by Michael Ledeen (who has worked at the Pentagon, the National Security Council, and the Department of State, was involved in the Iran-Contra Affair, and was earlier allegedly involved in Operation Gladio). And it does not mention that Ganser presents two strong pieces of evidence against that claim. First, when Ray Cline, former CIA deputy director of intelligence, was asked about FM 30-31B in a BBC-aired film about Gladio produced by investigative journalist Allan Francovich, Cline said: "I suspect it is an authentic document. I don't doubt it. I never saw it but it's the kind of special forces military operations that are described." Second, when Licio Gelli, the leader of one of Italy's anti-Communist organizations, was asked in the same film how he came into possession of the document, he replied: "The CIA gave it to me."[39]

The State Department, in spite of providing such a weak defense of the claim that FM 30-31B was a Soviet forgery, then used that claim to support its more sweeping conclusion that the idea "that West European 'stay-behind' networks engaged in terrorism... at US instigation" is "not true." That conclusion would not follow, however, even if the State Department had made a good case for its allegation that FM 30-31B is a forgery, because Ganser's conclusion rests on far more than this document, as we have already seen and will further see below.[40]

France: After World War II, the French Communist Party (PCF) was very popular, due to the leading role it had played in the resistance against the fascist Vichy regime, which had collaborated with the Nazis. These Vichy collaborators in military and business circles were frightened by the prospect that the PCF might come to power. The United States shared this fear.[41]

US fears increased in 1946, when national elections showed the PCF to be the strongest party. As a result, Ganser says, "Washington and the US secret service were convinced that the PCF had to be attacked and defeated in a secret war."[42] The resulting strategy, known as "Plan Bleu," was "to escalate the already tense political climate in France by committing acts of terror, blame them on the left, and thus create suitable conditions for [a] coup d'état." There was reportedly even a plan to assassinate former President Charles de Gaulle to increase public resentment.[43]

This secret plan was exposed in 1947 by the French Socialist party, then in power, before it could be carried out. But this exposure did not end the secret war. It was carried on by a new anti-Communist secret army, code-named "Rose des Vents"—a reference to NATO's star-shaped symbol.[44]

Although France experienced its share of violence, it evidently did not suffer the kinds of false-flag attacks experienced by other countries from the late 1960s through the 1980s, perhaps because in 1966 de Gaulle expelled NATO and its covert agents from France.[45] France did, nevertheless, contribute to those attacks.

An especially important person in this respect was Yves Guerain Serac, who was recruited by the CIA. In 1962, Serac went to Portugal, where he created the Aginter Press, a front for a secret CIA-sponsored army. Aginter Press set up training camps to teach bomb terrorism and other kinds of clandestine operations. Between 1967 and 1968, for example, some of its agents went to Rome to teach the use of explosives to members of Avanguardia Nazionale, one of the right-wing organizations behind the Piazza Fontana massacre in 1969.

Serac also became influential through his writings. Describing how to target a democratic state that is insufficiently anti-Communist, Serac wrote: "The destruction of the state must be carried out as much as possible under the cover of 'Communist activities'.... [W]e must... demonstrate the weakness of the present legal apparatus.... Popular opinion must be polarized in such a way, that we are being presented as the only instrument capable of saving the nation."[46] As this statement shows, Serac explicitly advocated false-flag operations to turn the public to the right.

The Pentagon's involvement in the French and Italian secret armies is revealed in a 1952 top-secret memorandum of the US Joint Chiefs of Staff entitled "Operation Demagnetize." It laid out ways in which "political, paramilitary and psychological operations" are to be used "to reduce... the danger that Communism could gain strength in Italy and France and endanger the interests of the United States in the two countries." (Note that in this memo, intended to remain secret, there is nothing about protecting democracy or the freedom of the French and Italian peoples; the only concern is "the interests of the United States.") This memo added that "the limitation of the strength of the Communists in Italy and France is a top priority objective," which is "to be reached by the employment of all means"—a standard phrase to refer to the use of violence.

Turkey: In Turkey, the CIA and the Pentagon used a secret army that had been set up by Colonel Alparsan Türks, a Nazi collaborator. This army, known as Counter-Guerrilla, was composed largely of fascists.[47]

One of the most active periods for Counter-Guerrilla was "the terror of the 1970s," during which some 5,000 people were killed, most of whom were identified with the political left. The attacks suddenly came to an end in 1980 after a military coup, planned by the CIA, which gave the presidency to General Kenan Evren, the head of Counter-Guerrilla. The terror of the 1970s, a right-wing extremist on trial later said, had been a strategy to bring Evren and the military right to power.[48]

In the 1990s, the Turkish people learned that this secret army was funded by the CIA and run by NATO—which means, of course, by the Pentagon.[49] A book written by a former paramilitary commander who had battled the PKK—the organization fighting for an independent Kurdish state—revealed that Counter-Guerrilla had run false-flag operations. In order to turn Kurds against the PKK, he reported, Counter-Guerilla troops would dress up as PKK fighters and attack Kurdish villages, then engage in rapes and random executions.[50]

Belgium: In the 1980s, Belgium suffered a terrifying series of terrorist attacks known as the Brabant massacres. (Brabant is the geographic area around Brussels, where NATO has been headquartered since 1966.) The attacks usually occurred at shopping areas, especially supermarkets. In November of 1985, for example, three hooded men got out of their car and started firing at shoppers with a pump-action shotgun. Eight people were killed. "A husband and wife and their 14-year-old daughter were finished off in cold blood.... Another father and his nine-year-old daughter were killed in their car trying to flee." Between 1982 and 1985, there were 16 such attacks, which "reduced Belgium to a state of panic."[51]

Although the responsibility for the Brabant Massacres remained a mystery for many years, evidence later surfaced that they were carried out by a neo-Nazi organization known as Westland New Post (WNP). Michel Libert, a former WNP member, confirmed in 1992 that from 1982 to 1985, it was his job to scout out supermarkets, seeing if they had any protection that could interfere with WNP's operations. Libert's orders came from WNP commander Paul Latinus, who was paid by the Pentagon's DIA. A Belgian journalist reports that when he asked Latinus who had asked him to set up the WNP, he said: "American military secret services."[52]

With regard to the motivation behind the massacres, a member of WNP later said that the plan was to "make the population believe that these terrorist attempts were done by the Left."[53] A report issued by the Belgian parliament in 1990 said that the Brabant killings were "part of a conspiracy to destabilize Belgium's democratic regime, possibly to prepare the ground for a right-wing coup."[54]

Following the exposure of Operation Gladio in Italy in 1990, the discovery that other NATO countries had similar clandestine units became a major scandal in Europe (although it was scarcely mentioned in the US media). NATO has officially denied the whole story, but in 1990 Secretary General Manfred Wörner reportedly confirmed to the NATO ambassadors that "the military command of the allied forces—Supreme Headquarters Allied Powers Europe (SHAPE)—coordinated the activities of the 'Gladio Network.'"[55] One member of the European Parliament, speaking about this secret network, was especially incensed by "the fact that it was set up by the CIA and NATO which, while purporting to defend democracy were actually undermining it and using it for their own nefarious purposes." Another member said: "I should like to protest most strongly against the fact that the American military, whether through SHAPE, NATO or the CIA, think they can interfere in what is our democratic right."[56]

As these revelations show, the assumption that US military leaders would not sponsor the killing of innocent civilians in allied countries for political purposes is false. Some Americans, however, might grant this and still assume that our military leaders would not run false-flag operations that would kill fellow Americans. This assumption has, however, been disproved by the discovery of Operation Northwoods.

Operation Northwoods

Early in 1962, the Joint Chiefs of Staff presented President John Kennedy with a plan, called Operation Northwoods, describing "pretexts which would provide justification for US military intervention in Cuba." Exemplifying the "strategy of tension" that was being used by the Pentagon in Europe, this document advocated "a period of heightened US–Cuban tensions which place the United States in the position of suffering justifiable grievances." This plan would make the world ready for US intervention "by developing the international image of the Cuban government as rash and irresponsible, and as an alarming and unpredictable threat to the peace of the Western Hemisphere."[57]

The document then suggests several possible actions that would help create this image, such as a "Communist Cuban terror campaign in the Miami area... and even in Washington." One of the possibilities was what the Joint Chiefs called a "Remember the Maine" incident: "We could blow up a US ship in Guantánamo Bay and blame Cuba." Accordingly, this false-flag operation, devised by the Pentagon's military leaders, would have involved killing American citizens. President Kennedy did not approve this plan, but who can say that some other person in the oval office, such as Richard Nixon, would not have done so?

II. 9/11 as a False-Flag Operation

The facts discussed thus far undermine the main *a priori* reason for not examining the evidence that 9/11 was an inside job—namely, the assumption that American political and military leaders simply would not orchestrate murderous false-flag operations. When the official story and the relevant evidence are examined apart from that assumption, they provide many signs that 9/11 was such an operation.

The Alleged Hijackers

Central members of the Bush administration, including Dick Cheney and Donald Rumsfeld, came into office intent on attacking Iraq, an Arab nation.[58] The Bush administration had also been planning an attack on Afghanistan, a Muslim nation, for several months prior to 9/11.[59] The official story, by crediting the attacks to an Arab Muslim organization headquartered in Afghanistan, provided a basis for both wars—not a legal basis, to be sure, but an emotional basis sufficient to marshal support from a majority of the American people and their representatives in Congress. There are, however, many problems with this official story.

Not Devout Muslims: The alleged hijackers are portrayed in the official story as devout Muslims, ready to meet their maker. Mohamed Atta, called the ringleader, is said by *The 9/11 Commission Report* to have become very religious, even "fanatically so."[60] Some journalists, however, found that he loved cocaine, alcohol, gambling, pork, and lap dances. Moreover, according to an editorial in the *Wall Street Journal,* not only Atta but several of the other men indulged such tastes in Las Vegas.[61] But the 9/11 Commission, ignoring these reports, professed to have no idea why these men met in Las Vegas several times.[62] This is only one of over a hundred issues on which the Commission distorted or simply omitted evidence contradicting the official story.[63]

Names Not on Flight Manifests: Another problem is that, although we are told that four or five of the alleged hijackers were on each of the four flights, the flight manifests that have been released have no Arab names on them.[64] *The 9/11 Commission Report* simply omits any mention of this problem.

Planted Evidence? Just as evidence was sometimes planted in the European operations to convince the public that the attacks were carried out by Communists, it appears that evidence was planted to convince the public that the 9/11 attacks were carried out by the alleged hijackers.

One such example involves the alleged discovery of two of Mohamed Atta's bags, which supposedly did not get loaded onto Flight 11 because his commuter flight from Portland, Maine, was late. These bags contained flight simulation manuals for Boeing airplanes, a copy of the Qur'an, a religious cassette tape, a note to other hijackers about mental preparation, and Atta's passport and will.[65]

But this story is riddled with problems. First, there was, as even the 9/11 Commission points out, a full hour between the arrival of Atta's commuter flight and the departure of Flight 11,[66] so there is no explanation as to why his bags would have been left behind. Second, Atta, after already being in Boston on September 10, drove up to Portland and stayed overnight, hence making the early morning commuter flight necessary. Since that commuter flight might have been delayed, why would he have taken the risk of missing Flight 11? The 9/11 Commission admits that it has no answer.[67] Third, if Atta was planning to fly into the World Trade Center, why would he have taken his will? The whole episode appears to have been set up by someone so that Atta's luggage with the incriminating contents would be "found."[68]

The Legend of Osama bin Laden

Part and parcel of the official story about the Arab Muslim hijackers is that they, as members of al-Qaeda, were under the influence of Osama bin Laden (OBL), who had become America's archenemy. There are also many problems in this part of the story.

First, in June 2001, when OBL was already America's "most wanted" criminal, he reportedly spent two weeks in the American Hospital in Dubai, where he was visited by the local CIA agent.[69]

Second, it is claimed that Osama had become a "black sheep," estranged from the rest of the bin Laden family (some members of which had been closely involved with the Bush family). There are reports, however, that family members visited him at the hospital in Dubai and also came to Afghanistan to attend his son's wedding.[70]

Third, after 9/11, when America was reportedly trying to get OBL "dead or alive," the US military evidently allowed him to escape on at least four occasions, the last one being the "battle of Tora Bora," which the London *Telegraph* labeled "a grand charade."[71]

Fourth, the Bush administration promised to provide a white paper with proof that the attacks had been planned by OBL, but this paper was never produced. Also, although the Taliban said that it would hand OBL over if the United States presented evidence of his involvement in 9/11, Bush refused to provide any evidence.[72]

Fifth, two weeks after 9/11, OBL denied any involvement in the attacks. The Bush administration, however, claims that bin Laden did admit responsibility in a video allegedly found in Afghanistan two months later. But the man in this video has much darker skin, fuller cheeks, and a broader nose than the OBL of all the other videos, including one broadcast on al-Jazeera only six weeks later.[73] We again seem to have planted evidence.

The Destruction of the World Trade Center

According to the official explanation of the destruction of the World Trade Center, the buildings collapsed primarily from their fires—plus, in the case of the Twin Towers, the impact of the airplanes and, in the case of Building 7, some alleged structural damage caused by debris from the towers. It was, accordingly, the attacks by the two airplanes that brought down the three buildings. But this explanation faces several formidable problems.

First, the fires in these three buildings were not very big, very hot, or very long-lasting, compared with fires in some steel-frame highrises that did not induce collapse. In 1991, for example, a fire in Philadelphia burned for eighteen hours, and in 2004, a fire in Caracas burned for seventeen hours. But neither of these fires resulted in even a partial collapse, let alone a total collapse.[74] By contrast, the WTC's north and south towers burned only 102 and 56 minutes, respectively, before they collapsed. Building 7, which was not hit by a plane, had fires on only a few floors, according to some witnesses[75] and all the photographic evidence.[76]

Second, total collapses of steel-frame high-rise buildings have never, either before or after 9/11, been brought about by fire alone, or fire combined with externally produced structural damage. All such collapses have been caused by explosives in the procedure known as "controlled demolition."

Third, the collapses of these three buildings all manifested many standard features of controlled demolition, such as: sudden onset (whereas steel, if weakened by fire, would gradually begin to sag); straight-down collapse (as opposed to falling over); collapse at virtually free-fall speed (indicating that the lower floors were offering little if any resistance); total collapse (indicating that the massive steel columns in the core of each building had been sliced into many pieces—which is what explosives do in controlled demolitions); the production of molten steel;[77] and the occurrence of multiple explosions, as reported by dozens of people—including journalists, police officers, WTC employees, emergency medical workers, and firefighters.[78] The official theory cannot explain one, let alone all, of these features—at least, as physicist Steven Jones has pointed out, without violating several basic laws of physics.[79] But the theory of controlled demolition easily explains them all.

These facts contradict the idea that al-Qaeda terrorists were responsible. They could not have obtained access to the buildings for all the hours it would have taken to plant the explosives (although agents of the Bush-Cheney administration could have gotten such access, given the fact that Marvin Bush and Wirt Walker III—the president's brother and cousin, respectively—were principals of the company in charge of security for the WTC).[80] Al-Qaeda terrorists would also not have had the courtesy to ensure that the buildings came straight down, rather than falling over onto other buildings.

Also relevant is the fact that evidence was destroyed. An examination of the buildings' steel beams and columns could have shown whether explosives had been used to slice them. But virtually all of the steel was sold to scrap dealers, trucked away, and sent to Asia to be melted down, and all this was done under the supervision of federal officials.

Evidence was also apparently planted. While we were being told that the jet-fuel fires in the towers were big enough and hot enough to weaken steel, we were also told that the passport of one of the hijackers on Flight 11 was found.[81]

The Strike on the Pentagon

According to the official account, the Pentagon was struck by AA Flight 77, under the control of al-Qaeda hijacker Hani Hanjour. This part of the official story is also challenged by many facts. First, Flight 77 allegedly, after making a U-turn in the Midwest, flew back to Washington undetected for 40 minutes, even though the US military, which by then clearly knew that hijacked airliners were being used as weapons, has the best radar system in the world, one which, it brags, "does not miss anything occurring in North American airspace."[82]

Second, the aircraft, in order to hit the west wing, reportedly executed a 270-degree downward spiral, which according to some pilots would have been impossible for a Boeing 757 even with an expert pilot. Hanjour, moreover, was known as "a terrible pilot," who could not even fly a small airplane.[83]

Third, how could a pilot as poor as Hanjour have even found his way back to Washington without guidance from the ground?

Fourth, terrorists brilliant enough to get through the US military's defense system would not have struck the Pentagon's west wing, for many reasons: It had been reinforced, so the damage was less severe than a strike anywhere else would have been; it was still being renovated, so relatively few people were there; and the secretary of defense and all the top brass, whom terrorists would presumably have wanted to kill, were in the east wing.

Fifth, there is considerable evidence that the aircraft that struck the Pentagon was not even a Boeing 757. For one thing, unlike the strikes on the Twin Towers, the strike on the Pentagon did not create a detectable seismic signal.[84] Also, the kind of damage and debris that would have been produced by the impact of a Boeing 757 were not produced by the strike on the Pentagon, according to both eyewitnesses[85] and photographs.[86] Former pilot Ralph Omholt, discussing the photographic evidence, writes: "[T]here is no doubt that a plane did not hit the Pentagon. There is no hole big enough to swallow a 757.... There was no tail, no wings; no damage consistent with a B-757 'crash.'"[87]

Evidence was again destroyed. Shortly after the strike, government agents picked up debris from the Pentagon in front of the impact site, put it in a large container, and carried it off.[88] Shortly thereafter the entire lawn was covered with dirt and gravel, so that any remaining forensic evidence was literally covered up.[89] Finally, the videos from security cameras on nearby buildings, which would show what really hit the Pentagon, were immediately confiscated by FBI agents.[90] The Department of Justice has refused to release them and the 9/11 Commission did not use its subpoena power to force it to do so.[91]

Evidence again appears to have been planted. One example: A video frame, allegedly taken by a surveillance camera at Dulles Airport in Washington, DC, supposedly shows alleged hijacker Khalid al-Mihdhar going through a checkpoint shortly before Flight 77 took off. But whereas a typical security video indicates the time, the location, and the camera, there are no such indications on this video frame. A second example: Proof that Flight 77 was hijacked and heading back toward Washington was allegedly provided in a phone call from passenger Barbara Olson to her husband, attorney Ted Olson. But no evidence has been provided for the occurrence of this call except the claim of Ted Olson, who works for the Bush-Cheney administration.

Conclusion: Motive, Means, and Opportunity

For these and other reasons, it can be concluded that 9/11 was simply one more in a long series of false-flag operations, albeit evidently the biggest and deadliest one thus far. In a criminal trial, the prosecution must prove that the defendant had the necessary motivation, means, and opportunity to commit the crime. Members of al-Qaeda had neither the means nor the opportunity to defeat the US military defense system, strike the Pentagon, or bring down the World Trade Center. The US government, with its military organization and intelligence agencies, had the means, the opportunity, and a long history of practice to orchestrate the attacks along with the destruction and planting of evidence. But what about motive?

According to the official account, the attacks were carried out by Arab Muslims who "hate our freedoms"—a rather implausible explanation. Much more likely is the supposition that the attacks were orchestrated, like many previous false-flag attacks, by US agents as a pretext for a war to expand the American empire—a worldwide "war on terror" to replace the previous "war on Communism." I pointed out earlier that the United States already had plans to attack Afghanistan and Iraq. Further motives will be mentioned in the next section, which asks how Christians in America should respond to the realization, especially in the light of 9/11, that our country has become the new Rome.

III. Christians in the New Rome

To understand what it means to call America the new Rome, it is necessary to know something about the Roman Empire.

The Roman Empire

Rome liked to portray its empire as a Pax Romana. One of its emperors even assumed the title "Pacifier of the World."[92] But this pacification was achieved by means of overwhelming military might, which the Romans used ruthlessly. As a Caledonian chieftain at the time put it, the Romans "rob, butcher, plunder, and call it 'empire'; and where they make desolation, they call it 'peace.'"[93]

The Romans used their overwhelming power not merely to conquer but also to terrorize and intimidate. When the Roman legions were sent on expeditions, says Susan Mattern in her study of Rome's imperial strategy, their main mission was "to punish, to avenge, and to terrify," thereby inducing a psychological state of "awe and terror" in others.[94] "What mattered most [to the Roman elite]," she adds, "was how the empire [was] perceived by foreigners and subjects.... Terror and vengeance were instruments for maintaining the empire's image."[95]

One of Rome's terrorist tactics was crucifixion. The victims of this tactic were displayed in prominent places for all to see.[96] As one Roman put it: "Whenever we crucify the condemned, the most crowded roads are chosen, where the most people can see and be moved by this terror. For penalties relate not so much to retribution as to their exemplary effect."[97]

These methods proved effective. By the time of the birth of Jesus, Rome had subjected most of the known earth to its rule, and the goal of Augustus Caesar was "to conquer what remained."[98]

America as the New Rome

Throughout most of the twentieth century, the idea that America was anything like Rome was disavowed by all respectable commentators. To say that America had an empire was virtually a sure sign that one was a left-wing critic of US foreign policy.[99]

This attitude, however, changed with the end of the Cold War. In 1990, columnist Charles Krauthammer, in an essay called "The Unipolar Moment," pointed out that the world now had "a single dominant power."[100] In 1999, continuing on the theme of unipolarity, he exuded that "America bestrides the world like a colossus."[101] In 2000, Richard Haass advocated an "Imperial America."[102] It was only after the US response to 9/11, however, that talk of the American empire became commonplace. In 2002, Krauthammer, commenting on this trend, said: "People are coming out of the closet on the word 'empire.'"[103]

This new discussion of America's empire inevitably brought comparisons with Rome. Krauthammer bragged that America is "no mere international citizen" but "the dominant power in the world, more dominant than any since Rome."[104] A British article entitled "Is America the New Rome?" said that "the word of the hour is empire" and "suddenly America is bearing its name."[105]

Most of this discussion by conservative—especially neocon-servative—writers portrayed the American empire as benign, even benevolent. In 1991, Ben Wattenberg wrote: "The American empire is not like earlier European imperialisms. We have sought neither wealth nor territory. Ours is an imperium of values."[106] In 1998, Robert Kagan described America as "The Benevolent Empire."[107] In 1999, Krauthammer explained that the reason that America's hegemony had not given rise to a coalition "to cut down the big guy" is that "American hegemony is... so benign."[108] In 2003, six weeks after the invasion of Iraq, Max Boot said that our hegemony had evoked no opposing coalition because "America isn't like the empires of old. It does not seek to enslave other peoples and steal their lands. It spreads freedom and opportunity."[109]

But one conservative author, Andrew Bacevich, dissented in his 2002 book *American Empire*. After referring to famous historian Charles Beard's statement, made in 1939, that "America is not to be Rome,"[110] Bacevich added: "The reality that Beard feared has come to pass: like it or not, America today is Rome."[111] Implicit in Bacevich's statement is the fact that America's behavior in creating and maintaining its empire has not been morally superior to Rome's. Pointing to the US military's aim "to achieve something approaching omnipotence,"[112] he ridicules the claim that such power "is by definition benign" in the hands of America because it "does not exploit or dominate but acts on behalf of purposes that look beyond mere self-interest."[113] The present mission of the Department of Defense, Bacevich adds, is "global power projection," with "defense per se figure[ing] as little more than an afterthought."[114]

A similar portrait is drawn by many others. Erstwhile conservative Chalmers Johnson says that the United States, being "something other than what it professed to be," is in reality "a military juggernaut intent on world domination."[115] Richard Falk agrees, writing of the Bush administration's "global domination project."[116] So does Noam Chomsky, subtitling a recent book *America's Quest for Global Dominance*.[117]

Ideas supportive of this quest have been central to key members of the Bush-Cheney administration. In 1992, Paul Wolfowitz, who would become deputy secretary of defense in this administration, and Lewis "Scooter" Libby, who would become Cheney's chief of staff, prepared a draft of the Pentagon's "Defense Planning Guidance." This document, which was prepared under the guidance of then Secretary of Defense Cheney, is described by Bacevich as "a blueprint for permanent American global hegemony."[118] Its central ideas reappeared in 2002 in *The National Security Strategy of the United States of America*. Asserting that "our best defense is a good offense" and that the United States will act against "emerging threats before they are fully formed," NSS 2002 introduced the doctrine of preventive warfare—attacking other countries before they pose an immediate threat.[119]

These ideas had already appeared in 2000 in *Rebuilding America's Defenses*, which was published by the Project for the New American Century, many of the founders of which became central figures in the Bush administration, including Cheney, Libby, and Wolfowitz. This document emphasizes the importance of getting greatly increased funding for the technological "revolution in military affairs," centering on the US Space Command, the purpose of which was spelled out in a 1997 document entitled "Vision for 2020."

Saying that the mission of the US Space Command is to "dominat[e]... space... to protect US interests and investment," this document added: "The globalization of the world economy... will continue with a widening between 'haves' and 'have-nots.'" In other words, as America's domination of the world economy increases, the poor will get still poorer, making them hate America all the more, so we need to have the means to keep them in line. This document supports Richard Falk's characterization of the global domination project as "an unprecedented exhibition of geopolitical greed at its worst."[120]

The aggressive purpose of the US Space Command's program is announced in the logo of one of its divisions: "In Your Face from Outer Space."[121] Although this program is usually called "missile defense," suggesting that its purpose is purely defensive, it really involves the weaponization of space for offensive purposes. As Lawrence Kaplan, one of the hawks who argued for an attack on Iraq, has admitted: "Missile defense isn't really meant to protect America. It's a tool for global domination."[122]

The programs of the US Space Command, along with the other parts of the technological transformation of the military envisaged in *Rebuilding America's Defenses*, will be tremendously expensive. The document, accordingly, predicted that the needed transformation would probably take a long time "absent some catastrophic and catalyzing event—like a new Pearl Harbor."[123]

9/11 was regarded as such an event. Immediately after the attacks, Henry Kissinger said that America should respond to them in the same way it had responded to the attack on Pearl Harbor.[124] President Bush himself reportedly wrote in his diary that evening: "The Pearl Harbor of the 21st century took place today."[125] Donald Rumsfeld stated that 9/11 created "the kind of opportunities that World War II offered, to refashion the world."[126]

The attacks of 9/11 had the desired effects. First, although the United States was already spending as much for military purposes as the rest of the world combined, the Pentagon's spending has increased over 50 percent since 9/11. Second, Congress gave the Bush administration a blank check to wage its pre-planned wars in Afghanistan and Iraq. Third, just as the Reichstag Fire allowed the Nazis to pass acts restricting the human rights of German citizens, 9/11 allowed the Bush-Cheney administration to pass the USA PATRIOT Act, which will allow the government to crack down on those who protest its imperialist policies too effectively.

One of the greatest propaganda feats of the Bush-Cheney administration has been to convince a great number of Americans that it is promoting Christian values. When US foreign policy is correctly understood, however, its completely anti-Christian nature is obvious. One dimension of this point was brought out by the placard asking, "Whom would Jesus bomb?" But the conflict runs even deeper. A foreign policy devoted to making the rich richer and the poor poorer is an anti-Christian foreign policy. A foreign policy based on military supremacy is an anti-Christian foreign policy. A foreign policy that involves the systematic use of torture is an anti-Christian foreign policy. A foreign policy aimed at global domination is an anti-Christian foreign policy.

This conclusion that recent US foreign policy is immoral and hence anti-Christian can be reached entirely apart from the question of 9/11 and previous false-flag operations, as illustrated by the writings of Bacevich, Chomsky, Falk, and Johnson. But the conclusion becomes even stronger when we realize that these operations are part and parcel of the global domination project. A government that obtains approval for its imperial wars by terrorizing its own citizens and lying is anti-Christian.

The Attitude of Jesus and Early Christians to Rome
America is indeed the new Rome, with a foreign policy that is

diametrically opposed to Christian faith and values. How should Christians in America respond to this realization? We can approach this question by asking about the attitude of Jesus and the early Christians toward the empire of their day.

Roman Rule in Palestine: At the time of Jesus, Palestine had been under Roman domination for almost a century.[127] Rome ruled through puppets—first Herod the Great, then Herod Antipas in Galilee and Pontius Pilate in Judea—and this rule was devastating.

Roman legions killed tens of thousands of people and enslaved many more. One of the most traumatic attacks was the burning of Sepphoris, only a few miles from Nazareth, near the time of Jesus' birth.[128] Some 2,000 rebels were crucified at about the same time.[129]

Besides killing and enslaving the Palestinians, the Romans taxed them severely, pushing many of them permanently into debt. By the time of Jesus, there was "a crisis of debt and dispossession that touched and transformed the lives of nearly every peasant family in Galilee."[130]

Roman rule also violated the religious sensibilities of the people. The Roman emperor was elevated to the status of deity, as shown by an inscription about Augustus Caesar, which said: "The most divine Caesar... who being sent to us and our descendants as Savior, has... become [god] manifest."[131] For Jews to have acknowledged Caesar would have been idolatry. And yet temples and cities were built in Palestine to honor him.[132] Also the high priests of the Temple, who were chosen by Rome, offered sacrifices in honor of the emperor and collected the tribute to Rome—which was regarded by the people as "a direct violation of the Mosaic laws against idolatry."[133] This issue of the tribute was, in fact, the most volatile of all, contributing to a revolt near the time of Jesus' birth, another revolt when Jesus was about ten years old, and the big Jewish revolt about 36 years after his death, which led to the destruction of Jerusalem and its Temple.[134]

Jesus and Empire: Given this situation, it would not be surprising if Jesus had opposed the Roman Empire. And indeed, Richard Horsley says, Jesus preached an "anti-imperial gospel."[135] I will give a few of Horsley's examples.

What we call "the Lord's Prayer" is a modification of the Kaddish, a prayer for the establishment of God's kingdom, which was recited regularly in Jewish synagogues. The central phrase of Jesus' prayer was, therefore, "thy kingdom come"—an abbreviation of the Kaddish's petition, "May God establish his kingdom in your lifetime." That Jesus was not talking about some exclusively otherworldly realm is shown by the next phrases: "thy will be done, on earth as it is in heaven." Thus, says Horsley, "God's activity was political and Jesus' preaching of that activity was political—with obvious implications for the 'imperial situation' then prevailing in Palestine." The reign of the Roman emperors was to be replaced by the reign of God, which would transform "the social-economic-political substance of human relations."[136]

The centrality of economic issues is shown by two other phrases in this prayer: the petition for "our daily bread" and the claim that we should "forgive our debtors"—an allusion to the fact that unjust and unforgiven debt regularly forced peasants into servitude to rich landlords (as reflected in the parable of the wicked tenants).[137]

Signs of even more direct opposition to Rome are provided by evidence that Jesus challenged the payment of the tribute to Rome,[138] that he challenged the payment of the Temple tax,[139] and that he created a disturbance in the Temple in protest of its system of collecting money from the people.[140]

That Jesus was regarded as a rebel against the empire is implied by the very fact that he was crucified. The death penalty could be authorized only by the Romans and crucifixion was an exclusively Roman manner of execution, used primarily for those regarded as challengers to Roman authority. "That Jesus was crucified by the Roman governor," summarizes Horsley, "stands as a vivid symbol of his historical relationship with the Roman imperial order."[141]

The Attitude of Early Christians: The opposition of Jesus and his early followers to the Roman empire has been obscured by the fact that the authors of the gospels, seeking to present the message of Jesus to serve the needs of the Christian movement 40 or more years later, made it appear to have been directed against "the Jews" rather than the Roman empire and those who collaborated with it. This strategy was carried out most fully and effectively by the author of Luke-Acts, which was written to convince Roman authorities that Christians were faithful subjects and to convince Christians that the continued existence of the empire would facilitate, not hinder, the coming of the Kingdom of God. For example, although Paul in reality, according to tradition, suffered the same fate at the hands of the Romans as did Jesus, the Book of Acts ends with Paul peacefully "proclaiming the kingdom of God... with complete freedom and without hindrance from anyone."[142]

A more accurate picture of the attitude of early Christians to the empire is provided in the final book of the New Testament, which portrays Rome as a dragon, symbolizing Satan.[143] Richard Horsley and Niel Silberman, partly on the basis of this book, say:

> [For the early Christians,] Rome was the Beast, the Harlot, the Dragon, Babylon, the Great Satan. They knew that Rome's empire was made possible not by divine order but by the acquisition of vast territories through the deadly violence of the Roman legions and the self-serving acquiescence of their own local aristocracies.[144]

This failure of later Christians to understand the beginnings of their religion contributed to a fateful reversal: The most explicitly anti-imperial religious movement in history came to provide the religious foundation for the growth of empires even more extensive than Rome's.

How Should American Christians Respond?

Christians in America have been lulled into accepting or even supporting the American empire through several factors. One of these has been the failure to realize that Christianity began as an explicitly anti-imperial movement, which rightly considered the Roman empire to be antithetical to everything for which Jesus stood. A second factor has been the acceptance of the myth of American "exceptionalism," according to which America is free from the sins and weaknesses that led the nations of the Old World into corruption, war, and empire-building.[145] A third factor, closely related to the second, is the failure to understand that the political and military leaders of the United States have long been engaged in the project to create an all-inclusive empire—an empire no less self-serving, violent, and brutal than that of the Romans, the Spanish, the British, and the Soviets.

Any attempt at a complete answer to what Christians in America should do in response to the truth about the American empire would be very long. I would briefly suggest, however, two early steps that need to be taken. One would be simply to learn and expose the truth about the American empire in general and 9/11 in particular.

A second step would be to create a movement in the churches analogous to the Confessing Church, which was formed in Germany in 1934, after the Nazis attempted to make the church subservient to the state. Opposing the "German Christians," who supported the program of the National Socialists, the Confessing Church, in its famous Barmen declaration, rejected the attempt to make the church "an organ of the state."[146]

Religion involves, as Paul Tillich said, our ultimate concern or, as Josiah Royce more aptly put it, our ultimate loyalty. According to Christianity and other theistic religions, our ultimate loyalty should be to God, understood as the creator and lover of all human beings, indeed of all life whatsoever. Religion at its best leads us to transcend the human tendency to be concerned only with ourselves, or at most our tribe, in favor of concern for the welfare of all. Our Christian faith at its best would, therefore, lead us, both as individual Christians and as churches, to oppose the American empire in the name of God. As long as the church does not explicitly oppose this empire, it is, by its silence, a de facto supporter of it.[147]

3

SHATTERING ILLUSION

Carter Heyward

We starve
look at one another
short of breath
walking proudly
in our winter coats
wearing smells of laboratories
facing a dying nation
a moving paper fantasy
listening to the new told lies
the supreme visions
of lonely tunes.

—Gerome Ragni and James Rado, "The Flesh Failures/
Let the Sunshine In," from the musical *Hair*, 1969

I. A Christian-American Confession

Once upon a time, a long time ago to be honest, I not only believed that God was a kind and kingly sovereign in charge of the world, I also believed that the United States was in some special way a godly nation, a "people of God." Of course, we had done some evil things—the genocide of native peoples and the institution of slavery, to name two of the most egregious. But in spite of these particular and terrible wrongs, the people of the United States—including most of our leaders—were usually on God's side in matters of good and evil at home and abroad. This I believed when I was ten or eleven; or perhaps I harbored such naïveté into my mid-teens, but by the time I was fifteen or sixteen, I had begun to wake up.

In 1960, as a number of African nations were waging wars of independence, I turned fifteen. I remember these wars because I had a tenth-grade world history teacher, Miss Betty Smith, who encouraged kids to think about them. When I wrote in a term paper for Miss Smith that I didn't think it mattered so much whether the Congo (later Zaire) become "capitalist" or "communist" as long as the people had food, shelter, medical care, and education, she wrote back at the top of my paper: "Congratulations on an excellent paper, Carter! You are learning to think for yourself in a world in which few do." Little did I know that this lesson would be one of the most foundational in my life and that my teacher, Miss Betty Smith, would forever be one of my saints.

Soon after this, I began to take an interest in the civil rights movement, which was stirring intense reactions in the world around Charlotte, North Carolina. "Martin Luther King" was fast becoming a household phrase throughout the South and, in my home, it wasn't a bad phrase exactly but a little exotic. Dr. King and others in the movement were described over my family table as "well-meaning" and as "good people." But I was under the impression that my folks and most other "good white folks" thought the civil rights movement was a bit unrealistic about how fast social change can happen. The issue, I came to realize over time, was that most "good white folks," like my own family, were unnerved by social unrest of any sort, anything impolite or anyone "inviting trouble," as my father once said of Martin Luther King.

My parents were rather conservative politically, but neither was driven by either political or religious ideology. My mother had voted for Kennedy in 1960 and my father for Nixon, and it was perfectly clear to me that I was welcome to find my own place along the liberal–conservative spectrum in those days. That the place I took was about as far left as I could get without falling entirely out of the realm of reason inhabited by family and friends didn't surprise either of my parents or anyone who knew me. I wasn't perceived as especially weird, but rather as somewhat eccentric and smart and, therefore, as somewhat more susceptible to new ideas and even weird notions than most kids my age.

One of these weird notions was that God loves everyone as much as He (and "He" was still very much a "He" in those days) loves me and that the rest of the world is as important to God as the United States of America. I still believed that a loving God was basically in charge of the world, including the US. Like many liberal Christians, I assumed that God was working His purpose out. I also had concluded that we humans, including those of us in the US, weren't quite as godly as we often think we are. The civil rights movement had taught me that, and so would Vietnam.

By the late '60s and early '70s, as the United States became increasingly embroiled in Vietnam, along with many of my generation, I became increasingly troubled by the gulf between our national rhetoric of righteousness and our violent behavior, waged both at home and abroad against those whom we perceived, rightly or not, as our "enemies." Now, several decades later, many of us are clear that Abu Ghraib is neither the first, nor the most dreadful, image of US conduct in wartime. From Vietnam come haunting images of a naked girl, on fire with napalm, running down the street toward the camera; a South Vietnamese policeman summarily executing a young Vietcong soldier with a bullet to the head; and dead babies in the little hamlet called My Lai.

The civil rights era, and on its heels Vietnam, were moments not only of political radicalization for me but also the very beginning of a process of theological transformation. I was breaking out of a double illusion that a loving God is in charge of history and that He has tapped the Americans as His foot soldiers for freedom. But this was just the beginning of my awakening.

By the end of the Vietnam War, in 1975, when I was 30 years old, I would have insisted that, like other nations, the United States was a mixed bag, morally and politically, doing some good and some evil. I still clung to an illusion, however, of a nation that meant well, where intention meant more than impact. Of course, I figured, overzealous soldiers, like bad cops and racist governors, will always be a problem. But we as a people, we as a nation, try to do what is best and right for ourselves and others here at home and abroad. I held the same view of the church, by the way, in the mid-'70s, when I was immersed in the struggle for women's ordination. The church, like the nation, I believed, had a higher calling than what it embodied when it practiced racism, sexism, or violence of any form. And this higher call was from God, an ultimately powerful, and loving, being.

II. Disillusion and Shame

Fear shrinks us.
It tightens our muscles,
especially our heart.

It contorts our faces (and
gives us several of them).
It distorts our vision.

We see the world
as too big for us
and ourselves as
too small for
one another
and we turn
inward
seeking safe
space.[1]

The words "justice" and "love" go together, sometimes even as one word—"justice-love"[2]—signaling their inextricability and inseparability. But how can we speak seriously of either "justice" or "love" in a world in which neither seems possible except, if we're lucky, in very small pockets of our most personal lives? Are we to take seriously the holy men and women in our traditions who speak of justice-making and peace as sacred work? What are we to make of the Jewish and Christian prophets and of the women and men of other religious and spiritual traditions who speak of neighbor-love and social justice as rooted and grounded in the love and justice of God? And how do we live honest, truthful lives in a social order constructed on lies and distortions of truth? Is it possible to live beyond illusion in this world? How do we get beyond the illusions designed to shield us from the truths of our own lives, faith traditions, and national agendas?

September 11, 2001, is one of the most challenging and emblematic moments in US history because it so dramatically rivets our attention to illusions of our life together, and also to our efforts to move beyond these illusions in order to speak and hear the truth together as a people.

9/11 pretty much shattered whatever small pieces were left of my Christian-American illusions of a deity in charge of history and a nation working with that deity. The issues surrounding 9/11—some we know, or think we do; others, more mysterious (even perhaps devious)—invite us to think anew and freshly about our world and our lives. Theologically, 9/11 compels us to think differently than before about God and the world, including our most personal lives.

It is not that the events of September 11 were all that earth-shaking from a global perspective. Far greater tragedies are almost the daily fare of countless people and creatures on earth. But what came down with the Twin Towers—and what is shaking us up and will for many years to come—was, I believe, the double illusion that God is necessarily both powerful and loving and that God somehow favors the people of any nation or religion.

These spiritual illusions crumbled with the World Trade Center and the Pentagon because these buildings and the planes that destroyed them represented the economic aspirations and military power of an omnipotent, know-it-all God. Whether Christian, Jewish, or Muslim, a know-it-all deity is one who destroys His enemies. To His friends, he is king and ruler. To His enemies, he is a terrorist. But He is one and the same omnipotent, if imaginary, being, who does not abide dissent or tolerate opposition and in whose realm there is no room for heretics or infidels. Be clear that the God of Islamic terrorists and of Christian fundamentalists here in the US is one and the same God. Bush and bin Laden are much closer in their spiritualities and economic aspirations than they seem to be in their politics.

9/11 was, perhaps, the most shocking single moment of my life. This was not because it was exceptional in the vast scope of human tragedy or military assault. As of mid-autumn 2006, after all, the US invasion has caused the deaths of more than 40,000 Iraqis, mostly civilians.[3] 9/11 was shocking, not because it involved the death of several thousand innocent people, a tragedy unfortunately not all that uncommon from a global perspective, but because it represented so dramatically, and so immediately for us in the US, a form of violent devastation that we as a nation heretofore had been spared.

As we now know, the leaders of the United States were not caught off guard by the events of the morning of September 11, 2001. We are not yet clear about what they knew or what they could have done to stop the attacks before they took place. But it is clear that quite a few of our national leaders, including Bush, had been warned of planes being used as missiles and, in fact, had been told that Osama bin Laden was engineering just such an attack. As other essays in this volume argue, it is also apparent that the Bush administration did little or nothing to stop it, either on or before 9/11.

David Ray Griffin, an esteemed process theologian and professor of theology emeritus from Claremont School of Theology in California, has produced two books that meticulously challenge the Bush administration and the official 9/11 Commission's version of what happened on that fateful September morning, and Griffin is not alone in pressing these questions.[4] Another careful and impressive critic of the official story of 9/11 is Nafeez Mosaddeq Ahmed, executive director of the Institute for Policy Research and Development in Brighton, UK. Ahmed cites Mohammad Heikal, former Egyptian foreign minister and "the Arab world's most respected political commentator," who raises serious questions about the Bush administration's version of what happened:

> Bin Laden does not have the capabilities for an operation of this [9/11] magnitude. When I hear Bush talking about al-Qaida as if was Nazi Germany or the communist party of the Soviet Union, I laugh, because I know what is there. Bin Laden has been under surveillance for years: every telephone call was monitored and al-Qaida has been penetrated by American intelligence, Pakistani intelligence, Saudi intelligence, Egyptian intelligence. They could not have kept secret an operation that required such a degree of organization and sophistication.[5]

Ahmed continues with a quote from the American Free Press's publication on December 4, 2001:

> Eckehardt Wertheback, former president of German's domestic intelligence service, *Verfassungsschutz*, notes that "the deathly precision" and "the magnitude of planning" behind the Sept. 11 attacks would have required "years of planning." An operation of this level of sophistication would need the "fixed frame" of a state intelligence organization, something not found in a "loose group" of terrorists like the one allegedly led by Mohammad Atta while he studied in Hamburg, Germany. Wertheback thus argues that the scale of the attacks indicates that they were a product of "state organized actions."[6]

As outrageous as the possibility that the US was involved in planning the attacks, it is almost as outrageous that the US government has been unwilling to investigate the attacks thoroughly and publicly. Most people who have followed the investigation probably assume that the 9/11 Commission did exactly that, but the commission was laboring under intense political and social pressure to contain its inquiry within boundaries that would be tolerable and thinkable to the American mainstream. Thus, in effect, the response of our government to 9/11 has been to stonewall the search for truth. And such stonewalling is not a new strategy in US foreign policy. During the last half of the twentieth century, the US secured its foreign policy on lies and cover-ups: for example, the 1954 coup in Guatemala that toppled Arbende, a democratically elected president whom the US didn't like; the 1973 coup in Chile that, with the help of Henry Kissinger and Richard Nixon, brought down Allende; and the 1990 so-called election in Nicaragua that ousted the socialist Sandinistas, thanks to the foreign policies set in place by Reagan and Bush Sr. Not to mention the role our government has played in helping put in place, or defend, totalitarian regimes in the Philippines, South Africa, Liberia, Egypt, Pakistan, Saudi Arabia, and of course Saddam Hussein's Iraq when, in the 1980s, it served our interests to be his friend. What these various contexts and events have in common—and what may well link them with 9/11—is their requirement that the truth of the United States' goals or the extent of US involvement be hidden from the US public. Also deeply implicit in virtually every one of these apparently diverse contexts is the United States' increasingly global and militarized capitalist agenda.

I do not believe that 9/11 was produced simply by a small cell of Muslim fundamentalists under instructions from a leader hiding out in Afghanistan. I suspect it was more complicated and that more people—including nations—were involved in the production of September 11, 2001, than we are likely to know any time soon, if ever. More important for the future of our world and nation, however, is the recognition—brilliantly assessed by Ahmed—that 9/11 was a consequence of the convergence in modern times of global capitalist design and US foreign policy.[7] That the targets of the attack represented capitalism and war-making made 9/11 shockingly emblematic of a global crisis that neither began on 9/11 nor will end with a "war on terrorism" in Afghanistan, Iraq, or anywhere else.

My question as a Christian feminist liberation theologian is: What religious beliefs shape such illusions—of the rightness of national, religious, and cultural omnipotence—and require us to accept them? What false god requires that we put aside our questions and bury our skepticisms of such fascistic theologies under the rubrics of faith and patriotism? What false god insists that we cease searching for truth and abdicate our anger with political leaders who lie to us and with liberal religious leaders who say and do nothing?

What god indeed? It is the illusion of a father who knows best, not only for us but for everyone. It is a spiritually contrived know-it-all who will do whatever it takes to win souls, stocks, and elections. I am speaking of the Lord made in the image of the men who aspire to acquire the oil, control the capital, and rule the world. These are Christians, Muslims, Jews, and other men who stride globally, their dutiful women smiling and, typically, a step behind, their children invited to speak only when spoken to and, when invited, speak only of those matters that will well serve their father-god. This is the god of my own childhood, the god of George W. Bush, and the god of Osama bin Laden. This god is an illusion, a vision built on lies and distortions. Today this illusion is shattering through the spiritualities and politics of liberal and liberation Christians, Muslims, Jews, and others around the world. And as the illusion breaks apart, it also is providing the spiritual energy of the violence being waged in the name of God against Muslims and in the name of Allah against Christians and Jews. The problem with 9/11 is not just the violence that occurred that day, but how religion was used to inspire and exploit that violence. The problem is that the leaders of the United States are justifying their behavior by faith in a god who is, in fact, a concoction of their own lust for power. And so their god rules—in relation to 9/11 and much that has happened since, including the waging of wars, tax cuts for the rich, assaults on women's procreative freedom and on gay/lesbian/ bisexual/transgender justice. All of this and more is justified by the administration's faith in a god of profit, pride, and patriarchal control.

The administration's faith in this oppressive illusion, strengthened immeasurably by our collective faith in the same, has generated two significant theo-ethical problems, with social, psychological, and political ramifications, affecting our lives from the national to the personal level.

(1) Disconnection and isolation. The people of the US, on the whole, have learned to see our country as standing pretty much alone. This way of looking and thinking about ourselves, bred by a number of forces in our nation's history, has lured us into a spiritual and political isolation, in which we have learned to see ourselves as the center of what is good, right, or best on this planet. The problem with the petition "God Bless America" is its implication that we are the only nation in the world that God would choose to bless or that God should favor us above and beyond the others.

(2) Despair and resignation. What may feel to many people like depression on a personal level is actually the result of a deep collective despair and resignation that leads to our shrinking

spiritually even as we become richer as a nation and fatter as a people. Over the years, in this depleted spirit, we have come to tolerate—more accurately, we have come to accept either as politically necessary or as simply inevitable—the lies and silences, the secrets and illusions, that underlie and undercut our nation's relationship with other nations and indeed with one another. Finally, we ourselves have become a people of lies and secrets. Hearing lies and living in the shadow of illusions, such as the one about weapons of mass destruction and a link between Iraq and al-Qaeda, we find ourselves passing them on to our children, who are off to fight for what they believe to be true.

The further we have moved from the events of 9/11, the more I have read, watched, discussed, and not discussed for fear of sounding like a conspiracy nut, the more completely disillusioned I have become in relation to both the Christian churches and the United States of America—far removed now from the ten-year-old who in the mid-1950s believed in a kind and kingly God and a nation blessed by God to lead the world.

So what now do I no longer believe? What illusions have, for this Christian-American, been shattered? I no longer believe the United States of America is a basically benign, well-meaning country. We as a nation are working actively against the God of love, God of justice, God of the poor. The Hurricane Katrina crisis of the fall of 2005 is emblematic of our spiritual poverty. I view our political system as inextricable from capitalist powerbrokers, and that what we hear from our government is bound up in greed, corruption, lies, and violence whenever it serves our interests.

I believe that this state of affairs is systemic and that it is nothing new. It is no more about George W. Bush than George Washington. What is new, however, is the global, advanced capitalist design of the problem and the extent to which military sophistication, telecommunication, and rapid travel are shaping our lives and decisions. That the powerbrokers of the United States have put, and kept, in power a president of such small moral and mental stature is exacerbating each and all of these challenges.

I believe that all of these forces—the aims and arrogance of advanced capitalism, the pride of US militarism, the rage of Islamic fundamentalists, the abilities of modern technology, and the dishonest and conniving character of American leadership—conspired to produce 9/11: the events leading up to it, the day itself, and the aftermath. I believe that, in ways yet to be revealed to us, the US government response to 9/11 was, and continues to be, untruthful. It is also clear to me that the 9/11 attacks were either directly or indirectly a result of the United States' lust for global dominion, all for the sake of advancing capitalism.

As John Cobb says elsewhere in this volume, US leaders may believe they're doing the right thing as they try to secure United States' global military and economic hegemony. The same could also be said of course of the young men who flew the planes into the buildings on 9/11, especially if they were—as the official story goes—acting on the basis of their own strong religious beliefs. What we are faced with on both sides of the "terrorist" conflict between the US and al-Qaeda are self-righteous men being driven by fundamentalist religious fervor, Christian or Muslim.

It is clear today that the US government is being actively shaped not only by capitalist power forces but also by the so-called Christian right. Our lives, as a nation, are being shaped by an unholy alliance of Christian fundamentalism and advanced capitalist pursuits. Hence, the Bush administration is sparing no effort to make sexism and heterosexism—foundations of the Christian right—cornerstones not only of how our private lives are organized—with men on top of women—but also how our public funds are allocated. We see this in our government's efforts to overturn abortion rights, to enforce the global "gag rule" against even speaking about abortion and procreative freedom, to support "abstinence only" policies in public schools and organizations, and to "defend" the civil institution marriage against the desires of gay men and lesbians to share in it.

Our hope is in our capacity to be ashamed. In order to be healed and liberated as a people, as Christian Americans, and as other Americans, we must be willing to live more truthful lives, which involves facing and acknowledging our collective shame.

Shame on us, the people, for resignation to the violence our nation is generating!

Shame on us for letting the story of 9/11 be wrapped in a "homeland security" shroud of lies, secrets, and silence!

Shame on our liberal churches and other religious organizations for abdicating our prophetic vocation and muting our voices in feckless efforts to keep the customers satisfied!

Shame on Christian, Jewish, Muslim, and other religious communities, left and right, for colluding mindlessly in the advance of global capitalism!

Shame on churches, synagogues, mosques, and other religious groups for their blatant sexism and heterosexism packaged as "the word of God"!

Shame on our national, state, and local governments for policies grounded in the fear, silencing, and subordination of independent women, homosexuals, and others whose lives defy heterosexist dogmas and customs!

Shame on us rich white people for our hostility and apathy toward people of color and poor people!

Shame on us all, people of the United States, across color, culture, and class lines for our disregard for the earth, waters, sky, and creatures!

Shame on us all for our own racist, classist, and environmental violence, so vividly unmasked here at home by Hurricane Katrina!

Shame on progressive—liberal, radical, feminist, queer, and other angry, left-wing—Christians for giving away the store to those on the right!

Shame on us all for not exercising our creativity and courage on behalf of a just and compassionate, truth-speaking and peace-building world, at home and abroad!

Shame on us, Christians and others, for letting fear mute our voices and turn our outrage into resignation!

It is time for such confession, people, for we have left undone those things which we ought to have done, and we have done those things which we ought not to have done... God, have mercy.

III. Beyond Illusion

when we betray or batter
lie to or deny, those whom we love,
we rip into the heart of God herself.

the only adequate response
you say, both yours and ours,
is a sorrow too deep for words,
and a renewed commitment.[8]

We liberal, progressive, and radical Christians can resign ourselves to the steady unraveling of our illusions, or we can face reality and confess our collusion with powers that be and our shame at this state of affairs. If we choose the latter path and decide to share in this hard spiritual work of healing and liberation, we will have to endure the coming apart of some of what we have held most dear and much that we have held simply because we did not know how to let it go. But we can learn to let go of these death-dealing illusions if we can accept our place on this planet and in this nation, as Christians or persons of other spiritual traditions. Each of us, and our people, our nation, our religious tradition, has a rightful place in the scheme of things. And our rightful place is neither too large nor too small. When we find our place—beyond illusion and beyond shame—we can get on with it, with grateful hearts and open minds.

But how will we move on in creative ways buoyed by gratitude, hope, and faith that will carry us beyond illusion and shame?

Here is what we will do, and we will do it together, in our families and communities, and in our spiritual and religious organizations. We will speak these words, or words like them, publicly, without apology. We will write them and preach them. We will film them and sing them. We will teach them and pass them on. We will be open to new lessons from those we may not have known before, and we will stay open to the new. We will use all the resources we can—our minds, our hands and feet, our circles of friends and colleagues, our networks of contacts, our particular talents, and our money—to press on, loudly and clearly, quietly and serenely, in the search for truth and the struggles for justice, peace, and compassion.

As we live, one day at a time, we will draw strength from one another's presence in the struggles we share. We will speak and sing gladly our gratitude for such opportunities to help restore some truth and justice to this nation, and to the larger world. And every day we will confess that we ourselves do not know it all, and do not have it all, and do not want it all.

Whatever we do, we will help each other cultivate sweet spirits of humility, patience, and compassion. At the same time, we will help each other learn how to express publicly our anger at lies and injustice in a spirit of steely, nonviolent determination.

We the people of the United States will lay to rest the illusions of our manifest destiny, of our being the leader of the free world, of our being best among the good, strongest among the strong, having most among the "haves," and of being most chosen and most blessed by a loving and omnipotent Christian God (or God of any one religious tradition) who has singled our nation or our religion out to save the world.

We will live beyond the lies and deceptions that have characterized our "Homeland Security" after 9/11—and which may, to some yet to be revealed extent, have given a pass to the planes on that fateful day. With our friends, we will move beyond the fear and hatred that fueled not only those planes but also our collective psyche as a nation, a fear and hatred being manufactured and manipulated by the administration, a fear and hatred that render mute those voices who seek to hold the president and Congress accountable.

We will stop apologizing for being liberal... queer: lesbian, gay, bisexual, transgender... socialists... communists... anarchists... left-wing... idealists... black, brown, red, yellow, white radicals... lovers of a Spirit who, in relation to those oppressed or downtrodden, includes rather than excludes, invites rather than condemns, welcomes rather than humiliates, heals rather than wounds.

We will be unashamed of our personal vulnerabilities and proud of our diversities of culture, color, sexuality, gender, and religion. We will be unapologetic in our respect for otherness of species as well as human cultures and religions. We will embody courage— heart—for learning how to build earth-community not only with other peoples but also with other species.

We will struggle, always and in every situation, to wage peace rather than war and will always seek alternatives to violence.

We will re-weave not an illusion but rather a dream of a people, ourselves, united not by fear or sameness, cynicism, or apathy, but by what we dare to love and the justice we dare to demand for ourselves and others, justice for all, justice all the time. We will give our best toward the realization of the dream.

We will try to keep ourselves in perspective, globally and personally, spiritually and politically, seeing ourselves and others as neither too small nor too big. We will be learning humility—to live lives more deeply grounded in common soil.

We will struggle to build a society and world, and to shape our cultures, communities, and religions so as to foster diversity and mutual respect, imagination, and creativity. We will think outside the box and we will root our spiritualities in an acceptance, rather than denial, of the greed, lies, and violence that threaten to undo us all— and in a shared commitment to the undoing of such evil through revolutionary and compassionate processes of social transformation.

We will move forward with arms open to the new, not shut tightly to protect ourselves. We will help each other break free of fear's stranglehold as we become people who believe wildly and passionately in something good.

We will practice living as people of a God whose love is Her vulnerability—Her openness—and in whose vulnerability is great transformative power for healing and change, both social and personal.

*

I was in my late thirties and early forties when the God/Father-who-knows-best really began to die for me. All of my life had been leading me up to this theological renunciation, including a wonderful study of the works of German theologian and martyr Dietrich Bonhoeffer in college ten to fifteen years earlier. But in the late '70s, I was introduced by a professor to the early works of the Holocaust survivor Elie Wiesel, which became a springboard for me into a theological—even more basically, a spiritual—transformation that would shape the rest of my life, work, and capacity to make a difference as a Christian theologian in the world.

My study of the early works of Elie Wiesel[9] led me beyond theism (belief in a God who acts in history), or rather, to a modified theism: I believe that God does indeed act in history; God not only "has" agency—that is, power to act; God is our agency, our power to act. This means that, in this world as we know it, God depends on our lives in history to shape a justice-loving world. In this sense, we are continually involved in "the redemption of God." For Christians, Jesus is our spiritual brother, friend, mentor, leader, guide through life, with us today and forever, showing us how "to god" and encouraging us to do so.

Peace and justice work in Central America in the 1980s and movements for diverse forms of justice would push me deeper into a confluence of "Christian atheism" (a term used by "Death of God" theologians in the 1960s and later by German Christian radical Dorothee Soelle[10]) with feminist liberation theology, which has been my primary theological arena for the past three decades. During this period, I have become ever more confident that—whether we name Him YHWH or Allah or experience Her as Sophia or Kwan Yin—if God is a loving force for goodness and mercy, then God is not omnipotent, but rather is a spiritual energy of yearning, urging, and singing for right mutual relation between and among all people on earth.

Even when confronted, as we are constantly, with violence

around us and among us, Christians are called—yes, beckoned by the power of love in history—to seek nonviolent ways of responding, so as to call forth the very best in even the very worst of our brothers and sisters.[11]

4

ELEMENTAL LOVE: TOWARD A COUNTER-APOCALYPTIC COALITION

Catherine Keller

People seem unable to understand love as a political concept.
—Michael Hardt and Antonio Negri

I. Love and War

Sometimes an outside view cuts through theological ambiguities. For instance, a new Jewish friend, never privy to any religious education, mentioned her perplexity about present US politics. "I know it sounds naïve," she noted, "but with all that wonderful love-talk of Jesus, Christians in this country seem to stand for hate and war." Of course I wince that "Christians" signifies conservative evangelicals, but I share her perplexity. Another non-theological thinker, Andrew Bacevich, a scholar of international relations and a Vietnam veteran, expresses a similar puzzlement: "Conservative Christians have conferred a presumptive moral palatability on any occasion on which the United States resorts to force." Reflecting on the legitimacy the National Association of Evangelicals has conferred upon our military imperialism since 9/11, he concludes that "were it not for the support offered by several tens of millions of evangelicals, militarism in this deeply and genuinely religious country becomes inconceivable."[1]

Given the unambiguous imperative of love in the gospels: how does Christian force so widely eclipse Christian love? How indeed does the underdog religion of love become the pretext for empire-building? How does the power of love flip into the love of power? Like many of us who belong to the minority voice of another, older, Christianity, I have lived with versions of this question for so long that it can seem naïve (well, of course, one responds, the religion of a colonized people converted the empire too early; or, power not only corrupts, it takes over...). Moreover, I am immersed in a vast ecumenical religious world with near zero support of, for instance, the invasion of Iraq. And yet progressive Christianity has so far failed to make a serious dent in Christian militarism. This essay considers the religious ferment of fear, hate, and violence that intoxicates so many American Christians. Its aim is not to denounce the religious right but to announce a more truly evangelical theology: a theology of love in times of empire.

Although some evangelicals are currently offering votes and legitimacy to the new American empire while others resist it, none would deny that a Christian involvement in national politics must conform to gospel values. However, there seems to be considerable confusion about what those gospel values in fact look like. This confusion is odd since, on this matter, Jesus leaves no room for doubt: the irreducible priority for a follower of his way would be the Great Commandment. Any Sunday School alum can recite it instantly: "Love the Lord your God with all your heart, and with all your soul, and with all your strength, and with all your mind; and your neighbor as yourself."[2] The Great Commandment is none other than Jesus' own interpretive citation of the love commandments of Lev 19:18 and Dt 6:5. It offers the crucial text for any investigation of the permutations and deformations of Christian love. Put more simply, it presents Jesus' nonnegotiable priority for Christian hermeneutics and action.

In order to develop the ancient and unfulfilled promise of this priority and of this claim, a specific evangelical perspective must be affirmed. There are three major senses of "evangelical." The oldest is based on the word *evangel*, gospel or "good news," and simply means gospel-based. The second, based in the Reformation as well as current German usage, signifies merely "Protestant." The third, often confused with "fundamentalism," refers to the recent, US-based phenomenon of a biblicist, "born-again" version of Christianity, often but by no means automatically yoked to right-wing politics. This essay operates within the two older meanings of the term—even as it seeks to engage the third. The first form can be considered obligatory for all Christians. The second is a matter of historical confession. The third is a modern phenomenon, even in its reactions against select elements of modernity. For a century and a half, it has been pulled into the orbit of an apocalyptic, tribulationist view of history, in which the battle between divine and satanic forces is coming to a head within our generation (whichever generation is preaching). The third form of "evangelical" (the quotes will distinguish it from the original form) has been especially prone to find signs of the end times in historical conflicts. In this it is less prone than mainstream Christianity to drift into a vague spiritual individualism. It takes the crises of modernity with utmost seriousness, and it attempts to turn the causes of fear into grounds of hope. But apocalyptic hope can mingle dangerously—and not at all evangelically—with politics.

The attack on the World Trade Center emblematizes this danger. David Ray Griffin also calls us to decode the signs of the times: indeed the attack seemed perfectly scripted to produce a fearful, furious, easily manipulated public. But rather than making God the author of a sinister conspiracy, he demands an investigation of those who had already been seeking cause for just this war and indeed for the development of a global empire.[3] Such a demand lies close to the prophetic tradition, with its founding mistrust of human superpower (whether Babylon or the Whore of Babylon!) But biblical prophecy has also been on the other side maneuvered into a justification of US empire. I am here, however, focusing on the spiritual tenor of that justification.

We cannot understand the successful manipulation of the 9/11 event—into a cause for war with a nation that had nothing to do with 9/11—as a mere effect of fear. The strange logic by which the al-Qaeda terrorists could be fused in the public imagination with the leadership of Iraq, which posed no ascertainable threat to the US, suggests not just fear, not just ignorance, but the effective production of a global Evil. Such an Enemy is not to be understood, not to be strategically isolated, resisted, or even defeated within history; this is an apocalyptic evil. Thus the president of the Southern Baptist convention announced that "the ultimate terrorist is Satan." Giving the "amen" to White House war-making rhetoric, he declared that "this is a war between Christians and the forces of evil, by whatever name they choose to use."[4] Such an Enemy transcends not only political fact, but also projected fear. Hate as a collective force must be stoked in order to keep it alive. Hate is the shadow cast by love, the effect of love gone toxic, turned into its opposite. There is much to be learned from studying how the apocalyptic orientation of much of Christianity serves as the toxin. If perfect love casts out fear, it is because "hate," as love's opposite, represents a certain kind of systematized fear, spliced with self-righteousness and thus rendered intractable. It is hate that translates fear into war.

Here I want to ask: how might love detoxify itself? All the progressive Christian rhetorics of peace, social justice, and liberation, and of structural change, have so far failed to transform the critical mass of Christianity. I believe that at the heart of our failure lies our embarrassment with Christian love.

Mainstream Christian political thought and action has for the last several decades privileged "justice" or "liberation." If love came into the theological picture at all (as for those seeking New Testament authorization of their struggles it was wont to do) it was immediately subordinated to the category of "social justice." Purged of personal or spiritual feeling—Christian "love" is not affect but action, we insisted—it became a clean-cut political virtue. Depending upon identities and ethnicities, it may have been permitted some free play in the dissident zones of sexuality— but even so, not as a reflection upon the New Testament agape, but as an oppositional eros. Nothing wrong with justice and its erotic edge, except inasmuch as the radical love-teaching itself evaporates. In the face of a mounting injustice, an injustice so global, systemic, and barely visible that it is not obviously injustice in most American eyes, more than the negative rhetoric of justice versus oppression is needed. In this context, it does seem that the political potential of love is coming again to the fore; that one encounters less of the automatic dismissal of love in favor of justice; that for the first time since the fading of Martin Luther King, Jr.'s radical love rhetoric, the Christian love teaching as the motive for justice may be coming into its own.

It may be no more from Christians than from secular progressive theorists and activists that an unfamiliar rhetoric of love started percolating up through the wailing websites and busy blogs, the humiliation and the fermentation, of the aftermath of the 2004 election.[5] As the political philosophers Michael Hardt and Antonio Negri suggest, people seem unable to understand love as a political concept. But Hardt and Negri's work is also a symptom of the shift toward a rhetoric of love. This pair of assertively secular analysts of the "postmodern Empire"—the sovereign hybrid of economic globalization and US militarization—reaches the following (startling) conclusion: "a concept of love is just what we need to grasp the constituent power of the multitude."[6] In their prior work *Empire*, these secular leftists had in fact arrived (in their final paragraph!) at the love-teaching of St. Francis of Assisi.[7] Perhaps their insistence on the positive force of love—indeed a love that in their work is drenched in iconic biblical associations—

can encourage religious progressives to develop our own theo-politics of love. This would be good news indeed.

II. Love Sentimental, Love Elemental

"It's fun to shoot some people." "You got guys who... ain't got no manhood left anyway. So it's a hell of a lot of fun to shoot them." Speaking out was Lt. Gen. James N. Mattis of the US Marine Corps. Chastened by his superior and inspiring reactions such as "How terrible! How insensitive!" Lieutenant General Mattis found a defender in the conservative Christian magazine *World* (February 26, 2005). Columnist Gene Edward Veith derides those who were shocked by the lieutenant general's call to have fun shooting and killing. Veith reminds readers that "there is a pleasure in battle... Excitement, exhilaration, and a fierce joy... go along with combat." Some soldiers testify to this pleasure; others feel very differently. Dr. Veith wants readers to appraise Mattis's pleasure in killing "from a Christian point of view." The question: "Should a Christian soldier take pleasure in killing people?" His answer: war-making is precisely the work of killing people, and "there is nothing wrong with enjoying one's work."[8]

Most evangelical Christians would abhor Dr. Veith's position: a little gospel alarm goes off. Love (uh, killing) the enemy? Yet perhaps we should not be so fast to judge. Veith touches an uncomfortable truth: if war unleashes a primal energy in some of its participants, a sporting excitation shared vicariously by many noncombatants back home ("war is a force that gives us meaning," after all) who would begrudge those who are doing our dirtiest work this pleasure? Doesn't public pleasure in vicarious violence support both Washington and Hollywood? So the predictable peace-making efforts of gospel-based Christians seem tired, lame, no fun. They lack elemental force. Virtue without the "vir"—the virile "manhood." No wonder Christendom has routinely, in the very name of the gospel, energized itself through violence. After all, the gospel contains the great world symbol of the vicarious benefits of violence: the cross, slick with the blood of its nonviolent victim. As the success of Mel Gibson's film "The Passion of the Christ" demonstrates, many Christians still assume that it is the very suffering, torture, and death of Jesus—rather than his love and his life—that saves us.[9] After the Constantinian conversion, the cross was wielded in defense, rather than defiance, of empire, and the blood of the Lamb would mingle with the gore of Christian wars: crusades and *conquistas*.

Neither progressive Christianity nor the secular left seems to have yet grasped the connection between passion and violence—in the craving for contact with elemental energies, open to chaos. The trick of Christian violence seems always to have been apocalypse: interpret the gospel in terms of the Book of Revelation, rather than vice versa. Then, with Jesus decked out as holy warrior, his word turned sword, the love commandment is oddly suspended; war becomes global; and absolute evil is answered by absolute war, illimitable global war as a God-blessed good.

Not coincidentally, then, the present imperial project requires the enthusiastic support of a wide band of activist Christians. For with the US's open-ended "war on terror"—its signifiers of "evil" floating freely across a spectrum of barely related enemies (from al-Qaeda to uncooperative dictators to home-front homosexuals and the ACLU)—US sovereignty seems, again, to require a religious legitimation. As Hardt and Negri argue, our situation seems to be once again "defined by the seventeenth century motto, *Cajus regio, ejus religio,* that is, the one who rules also determines religious faith—a dangerous and oppressive situation against which all the great modern movements of tolerance struggled."[10] So the new empire is postmodern not only in its disregard of modern boundaries, but also in its infidelity to its own constitutional secularism. It can thus call upon a purely apocalyptic notion of evil. "Posing the enemy as evil serves to make the enemy and the struggle against it absolute and thus outside of politics—evil is the enemy of all humanity."[11] In a sense, war is reduced to a police action within a boundless imperial space, even as the technologies of global destruction lend war an absolute, indeed "ontological dimension." Hardt and Negri offer in passing an all too apt metaphor: "The thinning of the war function and the thickening of the police function maintain the ontological stigmata of absolute annihilation": the threat of genocide and nuclear destruction.[12]

Eerily, this apocalyptically validated reorganization of planetary life sprang into action even as we crossed the threshold of a new millennium. Planned for decades by diligent neoconservatives in a difficult coalition with the religious right, it is managing to manipulate what we may call the apocalyptic unconscious of the nation.[13] In combination with the base—if not elemental—excitement of righteous violence versus "evil," it exercises an awesome mass appeal. This appeal is all the more wondrous for the willingness of so many sincere Christians to vote against their economic and ecological self-interest in the name of these "values." Can we appeal differently to that mass? Might a critical mass of this public morph into the force of resistance Hardt and Negri honorifically, and not accidentally echoing the biblical term, call the "multitude"?

A merely secular response to sacralized violence—such as appeals to tolerance, moderation, economic justice, general affluence, world peace—is likely to continue to fall flat with the crucial (swing-vote) population. Any effective answer will require the collaboration of a gospel-centered Christianity. And yet the "multitude," in its very Christianity, remains strangely deaf to the imperative priority of the gospel (perhaps then we have to do with, in Hardt and Negri's terminology, the "mob" or the "mass" and not the multitude). The unmistakable priority of the Great Commandment gospel seems hardly to register, even with such an avowedly evangelical national majority. And rendered most strikingly invisible is the very test case of that commandment: the love of the enemy.

Of course traditionally this latter imperative is usually read as a kind of call to exceptional personal virtue, meant only for the supererogation of the few, not required of Christians—something like celibacy. Love of the enemy in its radicality is surely the polar opposite of the above "Christian perspective" on killing as good sport, but it doesn't budge the masses. They get the message that good Christians can leave loving the enemy to the saintly exceptions. For the supererogatory reading has rendered this practice unrealistic for most and merely private for a few. The entire spectrum of Christian love, from love of God to love of the "neighbor" as friend, as stranger, or as enemy, then appears as a rather vapid moralism, a bit of rhetorical excess, readily subordinated to non-gospel texts—which, in the fundamentalist heritage, means subordinated to John's Apocalypse. And tellingly, the only reference to love in the Apocalypse is coupled with punishment: God "rebukes and chastens" those He [sic] loves (3:19). Of all the New Testament texts, and most of the Old, it is indeed only the Book of Revelation that uses "hatred" as a virtue.[14] Martin Luther actually argued on such a basis that Revelation lacks the savor of the gospel, and should not be part of the Bible. I am, however, not trying to redesign the canon.

The point is that apocalypse is not gospel. It cannot therefore form the basis for a legitimately evangelical Christianity. Apocalypse should be ordered to the ends of the gospel—not vice versa. When apocalypse is mistaken for gospel, "love" gets deprived of the priority that Jesus assigned it. And then, with alarming ease, love gets subordinated to such non-gospel yet supposedly "evangelical" priorities as opposition to abortion and same-sex unions, not to mention war and patriotism. Is this just because nationalism easily trumps religion, especially in times of war—and almost always has? Sure, but such an answer begs the question. Why does such a clear gospel priority lack traction for a critical mass of committed Christians? Is it perhaps that "Christian love" lacks the elemental force of Christian violence?

If liberal Christianity, like liberal politics, has largely failed to grasp the connection between violence and the elemental, it has left the playing field of passionate intensity to the right. This is not without irony. The right, with its rhetoric of conservative order, has learned to manipulate that margin of chaos that accompanies change. And the apocalyptic imagination channels the excitement through its vision of an "Evil" that can only be countered by all-out holy violence. In Revelation, the whore's imperialism of war is ultimately countered precisely not by love but by messianic terror— the holy war directed against the superpower of its day. In an excruciating historical irony, the messianic warrior, arguably the most clearly anti-imperial figure of the ancient world, became the great defender of various Christian empires—Holy Roman, Spanish, British, and now, truly apocalyptic in its weaponry, American. So the current religio-political right channels the excitation of apocalypse— minus the gospel of love. And the nice Jesus of the mainline is helpless in the face of it.

If love lacks political currency it is not just because it undermines the politics of friend versus foe; it is not just that it might inhibit personal or national self-defense. It is also because love has not been learned in ways that vitalize—bring life—to human relations in the first place. It seems to dampen down the spirit of adventure and "fun"; its agape seems to repress eros; indeed it has vast power to demean those already degraded even further, to encourage in the vulnerable a cringing acquiescence in abuse, and in the powerful, a condescending disengagement (the two faces of what Nietzsche called *ressentiment*).

Yet if it is read in its evangelical—gospel—context, it may evince another potential altogether, a potency not sentimental but elemental.

III. Love out of Bounds

The invocation to love one's enemy is found within the gospel of Matthew in the first great address of Jesus to "the multitudes": the Sermon on the Mount. It is not a counsel of personal morality; it is a call to the widest possible public. And Jesus does not offer it in the form of a commandment, as though adding to the Great Commandment. It is not an imperative to take an extreme or self-sacrificial position: rather—and this is so important, and so routinely ignored—it is offered as an argument against an extreme: "you have heard that it was said, 'You shall love your neighbor and hate your enemy'" (Mt 5:43).

Where would the *ochloi* (the people) have heard this said? Nothing like it occurs within Jewish scripture. Where it does occur, it may have held considerable interest for these specifically Galilean multitudes: in the Dead Sea Scrolls, the text of the Qumran community with which Jesus' old mentor John the Baptist was associated.[15] So then Jesus' utterance directly counters apocalypse, at least in the form of an intensified apocalyptic dualism of good and evil that had emerged in the intertestamental period, as a response to debilitating occupation by a foreign empire. There was no more politically and subversively coded symbolism in the ancient world than this apocalypticism of the children of light versus the children of darkness. In the Christian apocalypse, the evil would be identified directly with the imperial city Babylon (Rome).

The gospel, however, counsels instead: "I say to you, love your enemies and pray for those who persecute you" (Mt 5:44). This proposal must be read not as a new law, and not as a counsel of self-sacrificial or saintly extremity, but as a theo-political strategy: if it is radical to love one's enemy, it is because it counters the radicalism of cosmic dualism. Apocalypse has proven tempting and suicidal for oppressed people (like the community at Qumran)—and irresistible to Christian aggressor-states. We are observing its effects in the hands of yet another empire today. So Jesus' logion can only be read as an alternative theo-politics—a politics of love, directed not to the few but to the multitude. Rather than construing the enemy as pure evil, to be defeated by the righteous force with whom "we" are identified, the enemy must be "loved," "prayed for"—which is precisely not to say admired, accepted, or obeyed, but rather relativized, i.e., understood in relation to ourselves. This love humanizes the enemy: makes me recall the enemy's humanity and calls the enemy to notice mine—and if direct contact would be lethal, prayerful indirection provides a good alternative! It demands understanding. Yet we hear routine denunciations of any attempt to understand Islamic extremists, as though "to understand" means to condone, to acquiesce, or to justify. This refusal to understand refuses a more basic religious insight: we are all interdependent members of the same species; the enemy is no more purely evil than "we" are purely good. But when the official policy is one of extermination, understanding— sliding as it does toward love—becomes subversion.

Jesus' love-preaching is a lure cast out to the multitude, an attempt to create mass movement, to shift the course of history: beginning where each member of the multitude can, no matter how powerless, always begin—in self-transformation, the activation of our singular gifts. But this preaching is not, as so much of the church has mistakenly thought, fulfilled in individual spiritual trans- formation. This address to the *ochloi* on love was a wild strategy for a new world. Not accidentally, there is resonance in Hardt and Negri's call to the postmodern multitude: "Become different than you are! These singularities act in common and thus form a new race, that is, a politically coordinated subjectivity that the multitude produces. The primary decision made by the multitude is really the decision to create a new race, or rather, a new humanity."[16] This new humanity can only take place within the space opened up by the deconstruction of apocalypse—otherwise all primal force is sucked and circulated between the poles of good and evil, draining human, creaturely interdependence of its vitality, burning up hope in the fantasy of annihilation. Thus the humanization of the enemy is indispensable to any progressive politics: otherwise our humanity remains divided against itself.

For it is then no less than the creation that is called upon as the interpretive context of this radical love: "so that you may be children of your Father in heaven, for he makes his sun rise on the evil and on the good, and sends rain on the righteous and on the unrighteous" (Mt 5:45). How shall we read this elemental gesture, inscribing upon divine love the signs of nonhuman nature? Again the critique of apocalyptic "righteousness" is unmistakable. But more, infinitely more, is at play than a specific debate: this utter excess of divine love, disturbingly amoral in its natural expression, is being invoked as the ground of an alternative theo-politics. The tradition has often taken this to be the inscrutable omnipotence of the creator at play, maintaining all of life. But this distance is not Jesus' point at all; he is teaching the way to intimacy with God, the way to be God's sons and daughters.

To be children of God is to take part in a creation-sustaining, indiscriminate love; to be sons and daughters of God is to practice this solar radiance, this fertilizing downpour. The rain of God that drenches all: this is a metaphor of boundless inclusivity. (It does not hate the sinner or the sin—those final meanings of our lives will all get sorted out later, after the lives, in the end, finally, separating wheat from tares—none of our business; not even, for now, God's business.) But does it render meaningless all moral striving, all resistance to oppression, all distinctions of good and evil, just and unjust? Not at all. It renders them relative to each other. But this is no moral relativism. On the contrary, it is lifting up as the moral imperative the practice of this streaming agape.

In emulation of this nondiscriminating generosity, this sheer excess, this gift of agape, we may reclaim our likeness to God. This is not a trivial claim, nor one readily reconciled with an Augustinian or Reformation theology of the sin-shattered *imago dei*. "Be perfect as your heavenly Father is perfect"—an outsized demand, no doubt a rhetorical hyperbole, but not to be confused in context with moral perfectionism aimed at heavenly reward. This love is rewarding; it is its own reward, not just as means but also as the end of human existence. I do not "love" now so that then I can pig out in solipsistic heavenly bliss in the end. The rewarding end of love is precisely that of the consummation of love, a release of our individuality into the eternal life of boundless Love. Its "perfection," *teleion*, a concept meaning wholeness, ripeness, maturity, is suggestive of the realization of the telos, hence in this context eschatological. This eschatology does not aim out of the world but into it and through it—like the rain and the sun. These natural processes are not mere figures of speech; they remind us of the living material matrix that nurtures and holds us, the creation of which we are creaturely elements.

Elemental love is charged with the energies of non-human nature—for our human interactions take place within the living, vulnerable, and shifting ecologies of the creation. A love and a spirituality abstracted from its cosmos is not only self-defeating but self-deceiving. Elementality resists sentimentality inasmuch as it opens us to the complex, multiplying interdependencies of our shared social and material lives.

"The multitude" potentially names such a complex inter-dependence. The collapse of moral dualism, ethnic purity, or identity politics in progressive politics opens up the elemental space for the "self-transformation, hybridization, and miscegenation" of the multitude.[17] In the elementality of love, the traditional opposition of agape and eros collapses. Traditionally, only an agapic one-way love, not passionate desire, can be divine. A politics of love will take place only in a reclamation of gospel agape in its inseparability from the elemental creatureliness of eros. God desires; God desires passionately. Biblically, there is no basis for making God's love into some condescension that loves us only for our sake. Covenant is the very heart of reciprocity amid asymmetry: the creation in all its messy, material interdependency matters to God. But surely the indiscriminate generosity is wildly and unconditionally for our sake too, for the sake of all of us creatures—that is, the whole of the creation. For "God so loved the world" that Jesus as the very flesh and child of God invites us to (re)join the family of creation: in the creation of a new kind of humanity. "When love is conceived politically, then, this creation of a new humanity is the ultimate act of love." Indeed, Hardt and Negri even allude to the passionate elementality in the Song of Songs (6:8), lifting it—startlingly—beyond the mere interplay between intimate eroticism and allegory of faith, into its theo-political potentiality: "both God's love of humanity and humanity's love of God are expressed and incarnated in the common material project of the multitude. We need to recover today this material and political sense of love, a love as strong as death."[18]

In this forcefield, this creativity, crackles and flows an energy otherwise channeled into the sick righteousness of violence. As love therefore, with its elemental, nonhuman dynamism, it must test and strengthen itself on the inhumanity of the enemy as well as the obstreperousness of the neighbor. Its release is the counterforce of the new creation, the counterapocalypse that begins in a nonhuman excess of generosity, a boundlessness of passion.

IV. Postmodern Agape

But if agape, the primary word for love in the gospel, expresses a passionate excess, what remains of the classic distinction of agape and eros—between a unilateral donation to another and a desire for the other? The generosity of agape is conventionally and unfortunately construed as a one-way grace; eros desires something back from the other, desires the desire of the other, and drives toward reciprocal exchange. The gospel does not make such a distinction. Feminist theology has been at pains to counter the condescending power dynamics of the traditional agapic model, seeking to liberate a more embodied eros.[19] However, for our particular form of the evangelical, we cannot write off agapic generosity. We can, however, refuse its construal as a unilateral love and indeed an omnipotent act. Unilateral power is incapable of love. The notion of a sovereign grace breeds the politics of Christian unilateralism and leads to the apocalyptic exchange of love for power. But there remains a distinction we cannot lose. It comes coded in the radicality of enemy-love and elemental passion. It is this: the agapic gesture initiates. It takes upon itself the risk of initiation.

Within an alienated, oppressive status quo, where our interdependence with all human and nonhuman creatures has been occluded by the concept of sin, someone has to start the transformation. Someone has to begin to be different. Someone has to break the cycle of friend/foe polaritizations. At any given moment, in any given deadlock, someone, some agent, must take the chance of novelty. So to initiate is to risk but not to seek self-sacrifice. The risk of agape is the initiation of love: it involves a one-way gesture, a direction of flow. This is not unilateralism of love or politics: this is the initiation of reciprocity. For the initiation is invitation.

Only as elemental love does the gospel priority of agape have the chance of its *kairos*—its incarnation, its enfleshment in history. As Hardt and Negri write in their different but not Christ-free context, "We need to learn what this flesh can do." They cite Merleau-Ponty, reminding us that "the flesh is not matter, is not mind, is not substance. To designate it we should need the old term 'element,' in the sense it was used to speak of water, air, earth, and fire.' The flesh of the multitude is pure potential, an unformed life force, and in this sense an element of social being, aimed constantly at the fullness of life."[20]

In the elemental Spirit of this flesh, loosening itself from the bounded bodies of its own failed ecclesiologies and politics, another *ekklesia* lives, has perhaps always lived, and may yet, as it never has, come into its own—in time to serve a politics that this time we will not seek to apocalypticize and control. With critical gratitude, it will engage the heritage of a secular enlightenment, which has its own roots in millenialist-progressive forms of the apocalypse. A strong distinction of religion from the state—even when no pristine separation has ever been possible—enables not only the survival of democracy but by the same token, of progressive Christianity. By contrast, the assault on the boundary between church and state threatens the church itself—in case by church we still mean the communal embodiment of the gospel. The spirit of Christ has barely survived the power politics of officially and unofficially Christian states. And the specter of the most global empire in history lying with a loveless fundamentalism tempts one with new visions of the whore and the beast gloating in their bed of power. However, we do not need any new progressive apocalypticism to come and trump again the fierce first stirrings of a postmodern politics of love.

If now, perhaps out of desperation, religious and secular moderates, liberals and progressives begin to work with more discipline together, with persistence and insistence, we may move beyond the mere flare-ups of trendy resistance. A counter-apocalyptic coalition can emerge. Together, we experiment with the politics of a love whose shadow is not hate but vulnerability. Indeed it recognizes its partners in all who would share the fullness of life. It becomes possible to extend a positive force of love into the shadows of our collective future.

5

AMERICAN EMPIRE AND THE WAR
AGAINST EVIL

Rosemary Radford Ruether

THE UNITED STATES HAS EMERGED AS THE GREATEST SUPERPOWER IN HUMAN history. Its political, economic, military, and cultural power reaches more parts of the globe than any previous empire. In September, 2001, before the current war in Iraq, the United States military maintained 725 foreign bases in 37 different countries in all parts of the world.[1] Its military budget equaled the combined military budgets of the rest of the countries of the world. The Roman empire, the Chinese empire, the Islamic empire at their heights of power were parochial compared to the global reach of the United States. The critical question that confronts Americans and the peoples of the rest of the nations of the planet is how benign or destructive is this massive American power.

The United States has long entertained a sense of itself as unique and divinely chosen to be a model for the rest of the world. Our Puritan ancestors in the Massachusetts Bay Colony spoke of their settlement as a "city on a hill" called to be a beacon of light for all humanity. Nineteenth-century US expansionists claimed we had a "manifest destiny" to spread across the continent and into the Caribbean and Pacific islands, exhibiting to the world the superiority of our civic virtue and democratic institutions.

This ideology of American goodness and greatness, however, has often been countered by voices of prophetic critique who have pointed out our glaring failures and called us to repentance and renewed fidelity to the principles of "liberty and justice for all" as the heart of our civic creed. John Winthrop in 1630 warned that we could become cursed rather than blessed if we "played falsely with our God" and failed to exemplify the virtues to which we pretended.[2] Martin Luther King confronted us with the sorry history of slavery and racism and exhorted us to realize an American Dream betrayed to our African-American populace.

Having first emancipated itself from the British empire in the late eighteenth century, the United States began to follow in the footsteps of that empire in the nineteenth century. With the Monroe Doctrine we staked our claims to rival British power in the Americas. After buying up or conquering French and Mexican territories within the continental US, we put our feet on the path of empire with the Spanish-American War in 1898. Claiming to intervene as liberators, the US blocked and suppressed independence movements that were well underway in Cuba and the Philippines, to substitute our own colonial control for that of the displaced Spanish. With the doctrine of Manifest Destiny, we swept across the continent, pushing aside the American Indians and taking most of their land.

Repeated military interventions in the first half of the twentieth century in Caribbean and Central American nations, such as Haiti, the Dominican Republic, and Nicaragua, showed our determination to prevent any independent political or economic development in what we defined as our "backyard." In the second half of the twentieth century this interventionism would become global, with major wars and coups in Korea, Vietnam, Guatemala, Nicaragua, Chile, and elsewhere, wrapped in the flag of anti-communism.

The end of the World War II saw the collapse of the colonial empires of Britain, Holland, and France, as these nations were forced to rebuild national economies shattered by the war. The United States, as the nation whose own national economy had been unscathed by the war, emerged as the defender of the Western capitalist world against the rival communist bloc. This rivalry was defined not simply as political and economic, but as ideological and even theological. The term "godless communism" turned this power struggle into a crusade of good against evil, God against godlessness. The US defined itself as God's representative to defend a divinely blessed "American way of life" and to extend it to the rest of the world against its diabolical enemies.

From the '50s through the '80s this American hegemonic power was seen as relatively benign by our European allies and by those elites around the world who benefited from our power. Deeper anti-Americanism surfaced among those who aspired to "national liberation" from American-led neocolonialism. But efforts to shake free of this power and to foster alternative paths to development were undermined and defeated by a combination of economic strangulation through world financial institutions, embargo by the US, and either direct or surrogate military intervention.

All of these methods were brought to bear to destroy the Sandinista revolution in Nicaragua in the 1980s, crushing the bold experiments in popular education and health and a mixed democratic socialist model of society, rendering this tiny nation more impoverished than before. As one American supporter of the revolution put it to me in Managua "they had to destroy the threat of a good example," i.e., the danger that an alternative way of development through democratic socialism might actually work to improve people's lives.

Although the Soviet Union was defined as our *bête noir*, its military power, economic aid, and ideological influence operated to create a certain global balance of power in the '60s to the '80s. The US developed strategies of multilateral cooperation with our allies, collaboration in international treaties, and forms of assistance designed to show that the capitalist mode of development was superior to that of socialism, even while doing everything possible to prevent actual successes of the socialist path. In the late '80s, however, it became evident that the Soviet Union was about to collapse and break up into its constituent nations. The USSR was economically exhausted by a $300 billion military budget that rivaled that of the US but constituted twelve percent of its GNP, in contrast to the US military budget, which was only six percent of its GNP. It could no longer hold together an alliance and form of government that had become distasteful to most of its people.

With the collapse of the Soviet Union, US hegemonic militarism faced a crisis of legitimacy. Without communism as its enemy, its vast military budget and role as policeman of the world was in danger of losing its rationale. Many Americans began to speak of a "peace dividend," anticipating a scaling back of the huge Cold War military budget by half. They hoped to free large sums to rebuild the infrastructure of US society, such as roads and bridges; to re-fund schools; and to rethink matters such as national health care insurance. Alarmed by such talk, the Pentagon began to cast its eyes across the globe for new enemies. It defined a military strategy as one that must be ready to fight "two wars at once," and lumped together remaining pockets of communism with militant Muslim nations as the enemies. In a precursor of George W. Bush's "axis of evil," it listed Cuba, North Korea, Libya, Iraq, and Iran as the evil enemies that we must be ready to fight.

A new alliance of the Christian right—with its wars on gays, feminists, and reproductive rights— with national security and free-trade neoconservatives who believed in American military and economic supremacy, had emerged in the Reagan years. This alliance seemed to be somewhat in retreat with the 1990s victory of Bill Clinton, who sought to capture a middle ground of American politics that included moderate concern for social welfare at home and humanitarian international alliances abroad. But the weakness of this centrist vision, as well as his personal peccadilloes, laid the ground for a new victory of the Christian fundamentalist–national security state alliance with the non-election of George W. Bush in 2000. This alliance of the neoconservatives and the Christian right would sweep Bush to victory in the 2004 election, again with some unanswered questions on the rigging of voting machines in key states, such as Ohio.

The hard-right ideologues of this Bush "team," such as Dick Cheney, Donald Rumsfeld, and Paul Wolfowitz, had already laid the ideological ground in the mid-'90s for a different vision of the American future. With no international rival for hegemonic power, they believed the way was clear for the US to seize control of the whole world, eliminating not only any actual rivals but any potential rivals to American power. This new imperial dream would demand not a scaling down but a vast increase of the American military budget, dwarfing the military budgets of the rest of the nations of the world. America was to have absolute military predominance, both to intervene militarily in any nation that threatened it, even before any attack had actually been mounted, and also to defend itself against any missiles that might be directed at our national territory.

But the authors of this strategy of American imperial expansion feared that Americans lacked the will for such adventures. In a 2000 document called *Rebuilding America's Defenses*, the Project for a New American Century (PNAC) opined that we needed a "New Pearl Harbor": that is, an attack by an outside force that would generate a paroxysm of fear and hatred and thus create the national will for such a military expansion, a prediction that would eerily come true on September 11, 2001.[3]

Several critics, including process theologian David Ray Griffin, in his 2004 book *The New Pearl Harbor: Troubling Questions about the Bush Administration and 9/11*, have accumulated a large amount of evidence to support the thesis that the Bush administration had considerable advance information on the coming attack on September 11 and decided to facilitate it happening in order to create the desired crisis. The major media has chosen to ignore these findings, treating them as an unsubstantiated "conspiracy theory." But careful examination of the data gathered by Griffin reveals that his case is impressive.

A great deal of very specific knowledge of the planned attacks was known more than six weeks before the attacks. Questions also surround the failure to intervene to prevent the attacks on 9/11, suggesting that the military had been given orders to "stand down." There are also questions about the actual nature of the plane that hit the Pentagon, which does not seem to have been the Boeing 757, as well as whether the planes that hit the upper levels of the Twin Towers could have caused the towers' collapse without explosives planted in the buildings. Finally there is the extensive evidence of continual cover-ups and denial of information during the subsequent investigation.[4]

All this points, in my opinion, to some level of US government complicity with the attacks themselves. What is unquestionable, however, is that the attacks were immediately seized upon by the Bush administration to leap forward in its plans for global dominance. Leaders of the administration, such as Donald Rumsfeld and Condoleezza Rice, reveal their mentality in frequent references to the attacks as an "opportunity" to "remake the world." We know now that demands to respond by invading Iraq were made within a day of the attacks, despite lack of any evidence of Saddam Hussein's involvement. It was only with difficulty that such war proponents were persuaded to pursue the attack on Afghanistan first and then build the case for the invasion of Iraq. There is no doubt that the Bush administration continues to profit enormously by cloaking its imperialist aggression in the guise of a war on "terrorism" on behalf of American security.

In the 1990s such plans for greatly expanded American empire had been impeded by new efforts to withdraw from international engagement. Conservative "realists" believed that with absolute military predominance, US collaboration in multilateral alliances to curb civil wars abroad, heal diseases, and prevent environmental degradation could be discarded as not serving our "national interest." In his 2000 campaign for the presidency, George W. Bush himself disparaged US involvement in "nation building" and pledged to withdraw from such engagements.

There was also a concerted attack by conservatives on "big government," both federal government projects that nationalized funding and standards of social welfare and also the United Nations as a potential "world government" that might lessen absolute US sovereignty. Any kind of international law against violations of human rights that might possibly be applied to US personnel or its allies, such as Israel's Sharon or Chile's Pinochet, was seen as an intolerable affront to our national autonomy.

When George W. Bush came to power in 2000, he quickly showed his alignment with the neoconservative view of unilateral and militarist American power. In rapid succession he curbed US contributions to international family planning, rejected American participation in the Kyoto climate treaty, dismantled international arms control treaties, and rejected the jurisdiction of the World Court for any crimes that might involve the US. But this policy direction gained a new rationale with the terrorist attacks on the two major symbols of American military and economic power, the Pentagon and the World Trade Center, on September 11, 2001.

9/11 gave the Bush administration the new global enemy it needed to justify its global imperial strategy. "Terrorism" became the new incarnation of evil. The fight against terrorism was defined not as a collaborative effort to defend all victimized people against non-state violence, but rather as a world war without end to be fought with the most advanced military technology, including nuclear weapons. This was to be directed not primarily against the small enclaves of terrorists, but against the nations that "harbored them."

But such armaments of all-out war, designed to combat other nation-states, are a completely ineffective tool for catching "terrorists" who are by definition stateless, who slip across borders and are more likely to gather in Northern Germany and London than in Baghdad. Indeed, as the July 2005 bombings in London have shown, there is a whole new generation of home-grown terrorists, who grew up places such as Leeds, England and learned their ideas and skills on the Internet. After four years of the "war against terrorism" there is little evidence that such groups have diminished. On the contrary, especially with the occupation and resulting chaos in Iraq, it is clear that we are creating the incitement for new recruits all over the world.

By designating its global imperial strategy as a war against terrorism, the Bush regime assured itself of both a bipartisan consensus and popular support, while denouncing any critics of these policies as incipient traitors and collaborators with "terrorists."

With such a war against terrorism projected as virtually endless, the far-right ideologues sought to make their power permanent and irreversible in the US and across the world. Thus it is no surprise that, having pushed over the Taliban regime that supported the al-Qaeda network in Afghanistan (without apprehending its leaders), the Bush administration quickly set its sights on what had already been defined as its larger goal; namely, Iraq.

Iraq was the major target for US supremacists for two reasons: it has vast supplies of oil, and it represented unfinished business from the Gulf War of 1990 for US dominance over the Middle East. Iraq represented a challenge to the imperial hegemony of the US and its client state Israel over the region. Even though his fabled weapons of mass destruction evidently did not exist at the time of the US invasion of Iraq, Saddam Hussein represented at his heights of power in the 1980s an aspiration to leadership in the Arab world.

Though Iraq was deeply weakened and impoverished under international sanctions in the 1990s, Hussein continued to thumb his nose at American demands for control. To smash his remaining power and to reshape Iraq according to our imperial demands became a main objective of both ideological and military–economic US supremacists. Although the initial conquest of Iraq was relatively easy, and the hunt for its fugitive leader finally netted him from an underground hiding place eight months later, Iraq today shows little evidence of becoming that showplace of American benevolence that we promised. Basic utilities of electricity, water, gas, and phone service still have not been adequately restored even in the capital city, much less throughout the country.

The occupying American army in its endless search for dissidents, in house to house searches that invariably kill and injure passersby as much or more than activists, in bombing raids that destroy whole cities, shows itself mainly adept at hardening the anger and hostility of ordinary Iraqis at our continued presence. The occupation has also become a bonanza for big government contractors, such as Halliburton and its subsidiary Kellogg, Brown, and Root, who have literally wasted billions of dollars, much of it Iraqi money earmarked for reconstruction, in schemes of private enrichment.[5]

Yet the designs of world hegemonic power that underlie this crusade against Iraq are, more than ever, clothed in the vestments of absolute moral righteousness. Saddam Hussein was depicted as a diabolic plotter who threatened the national security of the United States and the whole world. Even though his military budget was a pittance compared with that of the United States (in 2001 it was $1.4 billion, compared to the almost $500 billion that funds the American military machine), his weapons were depicted as threatening to overwhelm those of the United States.

His evil treatment of his own people and his neighbors was undoubtedly worthy of criticism, but the rhetoric used to denounce these evils conceals the fact that many of these crimes were committed when he was an ally of the United States and with the connivance of the very critics who now attack him. In the 1980s Donald Rumsfeld was shaking Saddam Hussein's hand and promising him our everlasting support. In the 1990s when we decided to depose him he became the global Devil. The plans for war against Iraq were depicted as one more episode in an apocalyptic drama of good against evil, the angels of Light against the forces of Darkness, America, God's chosen people, against God's enemies.

Juan Stam, a Puerto Rican pastor and theologian, has analyzed George W. Bush's religious rhetoric and found that it weaves together two types of language. One of these is the language of apocalyptic warfare, the war of good against evil, which absolutizes the US as good against our enemies as the epitome of evil. The second language is messianism. America in general and George W. Bush in particular are depicted as messianic agents of God in combating evil and establishing good throughout the world.

This language was exemplified at its extreme in speeches made by General William Boykin, a conservative Christian charged with the hunt for Osama bin Laden. In speeches to his religious constituency, Boykin declared that America is an object of hate by other nations because we are uniquely a "Christian nation." He went on to claim that our "spiritual enemy can only be conquered when we confront them in the name of God." Muslims, by contrast, he believes worship an "idol" and not the true God. Boykin then opined that God had put George W. Bush in the White House at this time. "We are an army of God raised up for such a time as this." In effect George W. Bush is God's elect Messiah put in power to lead the apocalyptic warfare of God's angels against the demonic power in the last days. Although the Pentagon distanced itself from Boykin's rhetoric, it did nothing to actually counteract it.

This language creeps continually into White House declarations of their identity and role. Neoconservatives Richard Perle and David Frum titled their 2003 book *The End of Evil: How to Win the War on Terror.* In her recently released "New Pentagon

Papers," former military intelligence officer Karen Kwiatkowski reveals the atmosphere of extreme fanaticism that took over Pentagon intelligence policy just before the invasion of Iraq, suppressing accurate information on the Middle East. She writes

> I saw a dead philosophy—Cold War anti-communism and neo-imperialism—walking the corridors of the Pentagon. It wore the clothing of counter-terrorism and spoke the language of a holy war between good and evil. The evil was recognized by the leadership to be resident mainly in the Middle East and articulated by Islamic clerics and radicals. But there were other enemies within, anyone who dared voice any skepticism about their grand plans.

I would add to this analysis of holy war language by suggesting that the Bush administration alternates between two different rhetorics, designed to appeal to two different audiences. One is the religious rhetoric of apocalyptic messianism designed to appeal to the religious right supporters of the regime. The other is a co-optation of liberal progressive language that speaks of America invading Afghanistan and then Iraq to "liberate" their people from oppressive tyrants, to bring them freedom, democracy, and, of course, the American way of life, namely the free market. For Americans affronted by the first rhetoric, it is hoped that they will be reassured that our true intentions are expressed by the second kind of language.

What we have here is a fallacious but long-standing ploy in American political language; namely, the equation of political freedom with a neoliberal ideology of the "free market." But the free market has nothing to do with social and political freedom and flourishes quite well in dictatorships of the right or left. Basically what neoliberals mean by the free market is the right of mega- corporations to batter down any restrictions on their ability to monopolize the world's markets, preventing small nations from protecting their national production and subsidizing health care, education, and basic commodities for the poorer classes. What our presence in Iraq means economically is a wholesale sell-off of Iraqi resources to favored American corporations such as Halliburton. This is veiled behind arguments that such corporations are simply the best and most efficient means to do the "job" of rebuilding Iraq, although the exact nature of such "rebuilding" in Iraq has not yet become clear. So far it seems to have little to do with actually making daily life more livable for Iraqis.

What are we to say about the emergence of America as a superpower in the first decade of the twenty-first century? Is it a force primarily for human good or for evil? It is my belief that the direction charted by the Bush administration to direct American power toward global empire is a disaster both for the world and for the American people itself. It means dismantling many of the fragile structures of international cooperation designed to curb militarism and to foster social welfare, environmental health, and peace. It has further enflamed hatred in general and against the United States in particular, both in the Islamic world and much of the developing world and also antagonized many in Europe who have come to see the United States as a kind of "rogue nation." In a poll taken in the European Economic Union nations in December 2003, Europeans declared that Israel and the United States were the primary threats to world peace.

This imperial agenda is also further distorting the US economy, delaying any reinvestment in needed infrastructure, education, health, and social welfare. The whole world, and finally ourselves, will be impoverished, both morally and economically, by this wrong-headed drive for imperial power. Above all, it must be questioned for its idolatrous moral absolutism, for its claims to represent good against evil, God against the Devil, resisting any critique of its own power. Not only critics from Muslim and developing nations, but also our European allies are deeply offended by this rhetoric and direction of American power.

The Christian churches have a responsibility here to challenge the misuse of religious language for imperial power. To posit the United States as the representative of absolute moral righteousness against absolute evil violates the basic principles of Christian theology, which understand that all humans are flawed and all are in need of divine grace and self-critical repentance. To speak of any nation and its leader as messianic is the opposite of Christian faith in Jesus Christ as crucified Lord who unmasks the power of empires and stands with the poor of the world. Christian churches and theologians, in allowing Christianity to be used by the neocon-servatives for their imperial plans, have failed to do their theological work in protecting the authentic vision of Christian faith and challenging its counterfeits.

Ideally, Christian churches should make such a critique of the misuse of religious language in concert with Jewish and Muslim colleagues who also have a stake in questioning such abuse of religion. This language not only falsifies Christianity, but it seeks to split Christians and Jews from Muslims, who are being set up as the demonic adversaries of this messianic crusade. Christians, Jews, and Muslims need to stand together to make clear that the word Allah is the word for God in the Arabic language shared by all Arabic-speaking peoples, Christians, Jews, and Muslims. The three peoples of the Abrahamic faith share a common faith in the same God. If there is an idol to be denounced, it is the idolatrous appropriation of language for God into the sacralization of oppressive military and economic power.

Christians and all people of faith and good will also need to stand together to unmask the misuse of liberal and liberationist language about "freedom," "democracy," and "liberation" to cover up blatant invasions and occupations of other countries in order to control their economic resources, as well as to repress critics at home. The basic religious and ethical stances of biblical faith, shared by Jews, Christians, and Muslims, is to stand with the oppressed and impoverished peoples of the world against every empire. The American empire, no less than the Roman empire, needs to be challenged by a religious vision that calls for "good news to the poor, the liberation of the captives, the setting at liberty of those who are oppressed" (Luke 4:18).

Finally and most basically, the American people themselves must challenge a domestic and foreign policy that guts our own traditions of democracy, human rights, and prophetic self-critique. We need a new generation of prophets to arise to denounce the misuse of American might for blatant power mongering and self-enrichment of the super-rich. Even more, we need new prophets who will redefine how America can become simply one nation among others in a world community that together seeks "liberty and justice for all."

6

TERRIBLE FEARS, TERRIBLE DESIRES: A JEWISH RESPONSE TO 9/11

Sandra B. Lubarsky

CLEARLY 9/11 IS AN AMERICAN ISSUE, A GLOBAL ISSUE, AND A POLITICAL issue. It is also a specifically Jewish issue and American Jews need to respond to 9/11 as Jews and not simply as Americans. In what follows, I will consider why and how the events and consequences of 9/11 have significance for religious communities in general and the Jewish community in particular and how Jews might begin to grapple with this complicated legacy.

I. Identity, Memory, and Master Narratives

Every decade since the late 1600s, the residents of Ober-ammergau, Germany have performed the Passion of Jesus, keeping the vow made by their ancestors who were spared from the plague. Until recently, the play depicted Jews as "Christ-killers," dressed Judas in yellow to call up associations with cowardice and with the yellow Stars of David that Jews have been forced to wear, and outfitted Caiaphas in a hat shaped like devil's horns. Four times, the mob at Jesus' trial was scripted to shout "His blood be on us and on our children." When Hitler viewed the play in 1934 he said, "It is vital that the Passion play be continued at Oberammergau; for never has the menace of Jewry been so convincingly portrayed as in this presentation of what happened in the time of the Romans. There one sees Pontius Pilate, a Roman racially and intellectually so superior, that he stands out like a firm, clean rock in the middle of the whole muck and mire of Jewry."[1]

Central to the making of traditions, religious and otherwise, is the telling and retelling of sacred stories. These stories shape and secure the general worldview that defines a tradition. Master narratives serve as shorthand that orients and legitimates a way of life.[2] They are attached to seasonal periods and calendar dates and repeated in ritual form so that memory is invested with emotional alacrity. Indeed, master narratives often become a part of the tacit knowledge on which societies are built. The Exodus from Egypt, the crucifixion and resurrection of Jesus, and the life story of Muhammad constitute the master narratives of Judaism, Christianity, and Islam.

In addition to their psychological power, master narratives stake out epistemological truths. They claim to be historically accurate even as they often include testimony regarding miraculous events. In the modern age, of course, the epistemological assertions made by Judaism, Christianity, and Islam have been closely scrutinized. Scholars have brought to bear all the tools of critical and historical exegesis, archaeology, philology, and psychology on master stories. These inquiries have most often been undertaken out of a desire to know if the systems in which we have placed our faith have been worthy mediators of reality. We have been compelled to know whether we have rightly understood traditional claims, rightly grasped original intentions, rightly assessed our place in the world, and rightly comprehended the consequences of our traditions. What has been revealed has often been painful for believers, sometimes casting their allegiance into doubt. But it has also helped some people to correct errors in their religious paths and others to find alternatives that might help their traditions to grow and flourish under vastly different historical conditions.

It is partly because of the impact of master stories on individual psyches and community identities—and on an accompanying sense of historical mission—that they must be subject to a perennial critique, both from within and without. The performance of the Passion story in Oberammergau has been subject to such critique, based on its association with violence against Jewish communities. Beginning in the 1980s, in response to Jewish and Christian criticisms, the play has been revised. The yellow robe and horned hat have been discarded; the Jewishness of Jesus is now acknowledged; the blood curse is no longer spoken; the condemnation of Jesus is no longer presented as a unanimous Jewish position. With these changes, it becomes possible to tell this central Christian narrative without inciting anti-Jewish emotion.

The Bush administration and all Americans are presently involved in the shaping of a story that has the potential to be as dangerous to the entire world as the Oberammergau Passion plays were to the Jewish community. The story follows the shape of other central narratives, beginning in vulnerability and aiming toward a resolution in which the original vulnerability is overcome by an increase in power. The 9/11 narrative is linked to a larger narrative, which features America as the foremost bearer of democracy, individual rights, and human decency, fortified by a superior economic system. On 9/11, innocent citizens of this model of civilization were targeted, attacked, and murdered, victims of four remarkably successful hijackings. They were murdered by nineteen Muslim men, representatives of a part of the world that rejects modernity, secularism, and democracy, and remains wedded to an unremediated, irrational religious tradition. According to this narrative, 9/11 is the result of a religion that seeks world domination, acting on behalf of a god who rewards fanaticism. The "war on terror" is a war that Americans neither started nor deserved. But it is one we intend to finish, not simply out of respect to those who died on 9/11 or in order to protect American soil from future violations, but for the sake of the security and stability of the entire world order. Indeed, it is assumed that this story will end in victory because, although Americans were the innocent victims of 9/11, we are also citizens of the most powerful nation in the world, not about to be undermined by a loose scrabble of Muslim extremists. This war will make it clear that the power of democracy trumps all other power. America will win out because America is a democratic country, harboring the purest of hopes that all nations will some day embrace this way of life.

This rendition of the American master narrative is invoked repeatedly by President George Bush, and for a large number of Americans it suffices as good reason for the US war on Iraq. It is a story told both to validate and exonerate one group of people over another, and to legitimize the use of force. It is a story that makes capable use of its emotional content. "Early on," writes Nikki Stern, whose husband was killed on 9/11, "the idea took hold that the deaths of nearly 3,000 people represented something larger than personal grief. Our loved ones were 'heroes' whose lives were sacrificed to the concept of freedom."[3] And yet it is a story that, upon close examination, appears to require the kind of faith that, with regard to religious traditions, necessitates considerable interpretive effort. Anyone who has read David Ray Griffin's work detailing the explanatory lapses of the 9/11 Commission cannot help noting that the 9/11 narrative involves a number of events that might qualify as secular "miracles." The symmetrical freefall of the Twin Towers and WTC 7 is visually the most phenomenal. The fact that no fighter jets intercepted the hijacked planes seems a miracle of absence. And what is to be made of the Boeing 757 that crashed into the Pentagon, undetected by the sophisticated radar and anti-aircraft systems that protect this central defense headquarters?

The 9/11 story that has emerged lays claim to being what the Jewish theologian Emil Fackenheim has called a "root experience": a public event of such magnitude that it reshapes our understanding of the past, present, and future.[4] The claim that "Everything changed with 9/11" is an indication of its status as an orienting event. And like a biblical orienting event, it has come to us with narrative gaps as challenging as if the story had been pieced together from fragments of ancient text.

But it would be a mistake to believe that the events of 9/11 are akin to the scraps of Qumran. The horrors of 9/11 were captured on video. Survivors and rescuers, highly skilled experts, and an enormity of information all exist. Those of us who understand the power of orienting events and master narratives cannot allow this story to be so carelessly told. Too much has been wagered on it. It has been the de facto pretext for the invasion of Afghanistan and Iraq and it has yielded great harm. These consequences alone compel the kind of close and honest scrutiny that we have given other master narratives. We who know the chief sins of master narratives—the power of truth transformed into the power of power; the enthusiasm and confidence that declare one way, a single key, a path that is more narrow than straight—must pore over this 9/11 story, exposing its offenses and failings, before we can accept whatever truth it conveys.

The course of Jewish history in Europe attests to the harm that can result from false or prejudiced readings of history. And surely no good can come of incomplete or inadequate accounts or from unnatural silences and absences. Memory works hard to tell a seamless story about who we are and where we ought to be heading, but that story can be made false by that which is either unknown or willfully denied. Like family secrets, national transgressions corrupt identity, destiny, and relations for years to come.

While master narratives serve as conduits for cultural power, they are themselves often stories about power and power relationships, designed to lessen human vulnerability. So, for example, the Exodus entails a radical reversal of power: those who were slaves not only become free but regain their status as a chosen people. In Christianity's central narrative, a similar reversal of power takes place: the one who is crucified, powerless to withstand the violence of those who misunderstood him, is revealed to be the redemptive messiah whose death overcomes death itself. The story of Muhammad's illiteracy has a similar twist: one who could not read becomes the recipient of the most beautiful and powerful truth of all. Indeed the master narratives of the three religions of the West can be read as narratives that move from seeming incapacity to revealed mastery, from limited to vastly increased power, from persecution to victory.

The 9/11 story also begins in vulnerability to "reckless aggression" and moves, by means of "shock and awe," to overcome insecurity and fear and ensure inviolability. It has become a story used to explain the extension of America's reach in the world. But master stories need not be interpreted simply as stories about victory. Indeed, Jews, Muslims, and Christians, aware of the danger and inadequacy of reading their central narratives as battle tales, have added interpretive depth to their stories so that they become lessons in sensitivity and responsibility. So, for example, the heart of the Passover story is not the victory of the Israelites over the Pharaoh and his taskmasters but the establishment of a covenantal relationship with God at Sinai. The Passover becomes a story that reminds us of our vulnerability—"you were slaves in Egypt" and "strangers" in a strange land. On the basis of this memory is built a system of obligation for the welfare of the other. Likewise, Christians have maintained that the core lesson of the Passion is that agape—selflessness, making oneself entirely vulnerable—is the ideal form of relationship. And Islam instructs its followers to understand that the greatest strength is in submission to God. For many Jews, Muslims, and Christians, it is a misreading of the text to seek invulnerability and to gain it through the use of aggression and brute force. Vulnerability is not to be overcome, but rather recognized as part of the human condition, a part that makes us open to each other and to God.

Since 9/11, people feel radically vulnerable. Americans feel weakened, exposed, and fearful; Muslims worldwide feel a heightened sense of anxiety, alienation, and foreboding; among

Jews there is apprehension and increased consternation. The Chilean novelist Isabel Allende once told an interviewer that, unlike Americans, most people know that they live in a world over which they have little control. "Our challenge," she said, "is to live with dignity despite our lack of control." The master narratives of our traditions can help us to do so, both by teaching us lessons in sensitivity and by exposing the new American narrative as a story bereft of wisdom.

II. Terrible Desires and Alternative Narratives

There is an alternative story being told by some in the American secular community and in the worldwide Muslim community. The central motif of this story is that 9/11 would never have happened were it not for the American support of Israel. A secondary theme is that Zionists were actually responsible for the bombing of the towers or that Israeli spies knew it would happen but failed to share their knowledge with US agents. A development on these themes is that the invading American forces in Iraq are tools of Zionism. Many of those who offer this story identify themselves as 9/11 truth seekers. But the fact is that this alternative story is based less on the desire to seek truth than it is on a set of pernicious assumptions that parallel classic anti-Semitic charges.

Sadly, according to the Anti-Defamation League, the theory of Jewish or Israeli involvement in 9/11 is widely accepted in the Arab world and by a majority of Muslims.[5] According to this version, Jews/Israelis had the most to gain from an attack on the towers if such an attack could be made to look as though it was carried out by Muslims. Because of the Jewish lobby and the close relations between Israel and the US, Jews/Israelis were able to plan and carry out the attack. Because of Jewish control of the media, the real story of Jewish villainy has not surfaced. As the deputy editor of the Egyptian government daily *Al-Gumhouriyya* explained:

> We also find a heavy blackout by America regarding the results of the investigations into the September 11 events. So far it has published no conclusions, and has not told us who the real perpetrator of these events is, as revealed by the investigations. Since America knows very well that the Jews and Mossad are behind these events, it will never declare the results of the

investigations. This is so as not to anger its ally Israel and in order to evade the evil of these Jews and of the Zionist lobby that infiltrates and rules the decision-makers in America. In addition, the ongoing blaming of the Arabs and Muslims gives America justification to escalate and develop this wild attack on the Muslims, even though it is an imaginary charge not grounded in reality.[6]

Others involved in seeking the truth about 9/11 argue that since the true account has been repressed by the US government, it is likely that the truth behind other major world events has also been distorted. If there is one big lie—the 9/11 "story"—it is likely that there are other lies. Most notably, the accuracy of historical accounts of the Holocaust has been questioned. Why would the Holocaust be the primary candidate for reassessment? What is the relationship between Holocaust history and suspicions surrounding the official version of 9/11? For those who hold that Israel's existence is a scandal, it is a temptation to underplay the horrors of the Holocaust. For if the evils of the Holocaust were fiction, so too the victimization of the Jews and any necessity there may be for the State of Israel. The argument goes as follows: Jewish Zionists are responsible for the worst act of terrorism ever experienced on American soil, motivated by a desire to control not only Israel but America as well. These same Jewish Zionists have inflated their own history of suffering. They are not the victims they have claimed to be; indeed, their power has made victims of others. The two allegations—of Jewish responsibility for 9/11 and of the "big lie" of the Holocaust—serve a single objective, together constituting an argument against the ongoing Jewish and Zionist claim to a national homeland in Israel.

Seeking truth is fraught with difficulties, even when we admit that there is no simple, singular truth that sits like a pearl in a shell, awaiting the lucky diver. Instead truth is interwoven in the worldviews that clothe and comfort us in our search for meaning. And so, facts can be made into fiction, knitted into a narrative that is part of a deeper, unspoken narrative. When the author of "Planet Quo," an anti-Zionist website, asserts that "it is not anti-Semitic to criticize the policies of the state of Israel," he is right. But when he goes on to say that the neocons in Washington operate in service of "but one flag—the flag of the state of Israel" and when he characterizes Jack Abramoff first and foremost as a Zionist and not simply as a deeply corrupt individual who did the bidding of many masters, the subterranean narrative of anti-Semitism begins to surface.[7] Though "Planet Quo" insists that his criticism of Israel is "the moral duty of those who believe in truth, decency, justice and peace," in fact, those values serve instead as a kind of formulaic incantation for an anti-Semitic brew.

Throughout Western history, major dislocating events have often led to an increase in anti-Semitism. It is an expression of the terrible desires that arise during periods of fear and vulnerability—the wish that someone else, some other group, religion, ethnicity, or nation, is responsible for whatever monstrous action has occurred. When the Murrah Federal Building in Oklahoma was bombed, many Americans leapt to the assumption that it was the work of non-Christian foreigners. Muslims were the first accused. And now we see a similar "terrible desire" among Muslims, many of whom claim that Jews or Zionists were responsible for 9/11. "It is a skill we learn early, the art of inventing stories to explain away the fearful sacred strangeness of the world," writes the novelist William Kittredge. "Storytelling and make-believe, like war and agriculture, are among the arts of self-defense."[8] The fact that 9/11 has given rise to "terrible desires"—imposing collective responsibility and heightening anti-Judaism in some cases and anti-Islamism in others—is a consequence that deserves serious attention from religious communities.

It is possible that we may learn, at some point, that there was Israeli involvement in 9/11, though it is much more likely that the principal actors were US citizens motivated by an arrogant notion of what is "best" for the US or for themselves. Still, that possibility raises in me the terrible desire that it never be true, for I fear the consequences it might have on American attitudes toward Judaism and Israel. The fragile tolerance that holds between secularists and those who maintain religious commitments, the bewilderment that even now characterizes relations of many non-Jews to Jews, and the complicated resentments harbored by some toward Jews and their Holocaust memories—resentments interlaced with guilt—make me fearful of what might happen, were Jewish or Israeli involvement in 9/11 established. As a Jew, I understand the terrible fears and desires that cause many Muslims to want to distance their religion from terrorism and to wish that others were culpable.

It is a sign of the asymmetry of power relations that Jews and

Muslims share a sense of vulnerability. After the Oklahoma bombing, after Timothy McVeigh was arrested, Wolf Blitzer of CNN continued to insist that "there is still a possibility that there could have been some sort of connection to Middle East terrorism. One law enforcement source tells me that there's a possibility that they [the white supremacists] may have been contracted out as freelancers to go out and rent this truck that was used in the bombing."[9] There is still a possibility. Aren't these words that reveal a terrible desire on the part of the dominant culture, words that heighten vulnerability?

The path toward 9/11 truth can be treacherous. Amid so many terrible desires, when so many issues of identity are at stake, truth-telling can become truth-denying. Such is the case for those who in their call for 9/11 truth give serious hearing to revisionist Holocaust historians and make too much of Jewish or Israeli "influence" on world politics, American media, or the system of global economics. Anti-Semitic assertions must be recognized as utterly inappropriate to the 9/11 inquiry. The same holds true for anti-Islamic assertions that characterize 1.3 billion Muslims as part of a terrorizing civilization that clashes with Western culture. Anti-Semitic and anti-Islamic statements must be named for what they are: ideological constructs rooted in terrible desires. Jews are not responsible for the ills of the world. Neither are Muslims. The ills of the world surpass the making of one people. Certainly responsibility falls far more at the feet of those with more, rather than less, power. (And hence the desire to exaggerate the power of those who become the object of terrible desire.) Those who seek the truth of 9/11 must be on guard against narratives of "self-defense" in which the vulnerability of others is increased. Most likely, such narratives reveal only a weakness for easy answers, a desire to mitigate one's own culpability, and a susceptibility to the kinds of conspiracies that move us further away from truth.

III. Shaping a Spiritual Commons: Interfaith Obligations

For Jews and other religious minorities, the establishment of a secular sphere was one of the great blessings of modernity, conferring citizenship and enabling participation in the larger social and political order. The separation of religion and state was supposed to lead to the creation of a neutral arena, devoid of the influence of organized religion. Religion would be a private activity, kept separate from public life. Of course this division between public and private, state and religion, was never realized in such a tidy form. In some cases, the privatization of religion simply led to its precipitous decline, thus diminishing its role as a counterbalance to secularism. In other cases, particularly in regard to evangelical Christianity in the US, the relationship between religious and secular realms has been one of protracted opposition.

The Enlightenment solution to religious oppression was to separate religion and public life, religious and non-religious values, and religious and secular power. As with other dualisms, this relationship has proved inadequate. The post-9/11 period calls us on to consider other ways to configure the relationship between the secular and religious and to think anew about the role that religion and religious traditions can play in the public arena.

Those of us who are engaged in religious traditions know that our deepest commitments are not constrained by the separation of religious life from public life. We seek coherence between meaning systems and a comprehensive understanding of experience. This requires that religion not isolate itself from politics or science or economics, but lead us to search for ways to make sense of our traditions in relation to modern forms of knowledge—and vice versa.

The great Jewish theologian Abraham Joshua Heschel knew the impossibility of "religion without indignation at political evils."[10] In 1963, as the civil rights movement gained momentum, he sent President John F. Kennedy a telegram in response to an invitation to discuss the "Negro problem":

> Please demand of religious leaders personal involvement not just solemn declaration. We forfeit the right to worship God as long as we continue to humiliate Negroes. Church synagogues have failed. They must repent. Ask of religious leaders to call for national repentance and personal sacrifice. Let religious leaders donate one month's salary toward fund for Negro housing and education. I propose that you Mr. President declare state of moral emergency. A Marshall Plan for aid to Negroes is becoming a necessity. The hour calls for high moral grandeur and spiritual audacity.[11]

Are we, post 9/11, in a "state of moral emergency"? Doesn't religious integrity demand that those of us who act out of moral and spiritual traditions concern ourselves with promoting and protecting life? Otherwise, don't we also stand accused of having "forfeited the right to worship God?" The mantra that "9/11 changed everything" is a ruse for permitting preemptive war, disregarding human rights, compromising personal freedoms. Religious people of all traditions must expose it for what it is and they must assert that concern and care for one another, and especially for the vulnerable, is not subject to historical digression.

Religion simply cannot detach itself from the moral and spiritual demands of the day. Where there is the possibility of preventing evil or aiding the vulnerable, religion must enter the discussion. The notion of a "spiritual commons," akin to the notions of an environmental and public commons, may help us to do so. The environmental commons includes the air we breathe, the soils that nurture our food, the great seas and oceans, the diversity of plant seeds, the water that flows without regard for national boundaries. The public commons includes language and the knowledge base developed by generations, public squares and neighborhoods, folk music and traditional arts, indeed "anything not owned but shared in common."[12] To speak of a spiritual commons is not to disassociate spirituality from these other life-affirming structures, but to highlight a dimension of both in which relationality becomes a moral imperative. "Adam, where art thou?" "Cain, where is Abel thy brother?" These are God's questions to us all and they carry with them an expectation that we will serve as witnesses to each other. "Are we all brothers or not?" responded Mdm. Trocmé of the French town of Le Chambon, when asked why she became a rescuer during World War II.[13] The spiritual commons is the site of collective responsibility.

A recent *Washington Post* survey found that 46 percent of Americans have a negative view of Muslims.[14] As participants in the spiritual commons we must ask ourselves what our responsibility is in regard to this disclosure. In a spiritual commons, this view of Muslims is not a problem for the Muslim community alone; it is a problem for us all. In solidarity with those who are at risk and out of our own responsibility for their increased vulnerability, we are obligated to address this issue as Jews and Christians.

In the face of terrible fears and terrible desires, membership in the spiritual commons calls for ensuring that responsibility and compassion remain in the public domain. Because the Danes refused to distinguish between Danish Jews and foreign Jews, refused to give in to distorting stereotypes, they were able to save the lives of almost all Jews in their country. Rescue literature makes it clear that high levels of empathy, strong value systems, and networks of care and responsibility were key features of rescue activity. Moreover, people who became rescuers reported that their parents didn't speak negatively about Jews, while those who were bystanders recall growing up with stereotypes. We honor rescuers because they did what our various religious traditions call on us to do: to act with fearlessness in regard to the care of life.

The ecologist Aldo Leopold's evocative guidelines for a sustainable ecosystem have relevance to a spiritual commons: "A thing is right when it tends to preserve the integrity, stability, and beauty of the biotic community. It is wrong when it tends otherwise."[15] To this we can add Wendell Berry's insistence that a good and sustainable society is one in which "no tender, vulnerable thing has to be sacrificed."[16] This requires that we serve as each other's witnesses as we strive to fulfill the moral precepts of our religious and spiritual traditions. We aid and abet one another and we act as each other's rescuers. We say "no" to stereotyping, to scapegoating, to ignoring the plight of others, to increasing suffering, to unrestrained power. We say "yes" to the prophetic tradition of justice and compassion, to "moral grandeur and spiritual audacity." 9/11 is not a root experience for Jews, nor should it be one for any American. It is however, a historical event that calls us to remain vigilant in seeking truth on behalf of justice and practicing loving-kindness as a rejoinder to power.

AFTER 9/11: THE STRUGGLE TO REDEFINE JEWISH IDENTITY

Marc H. Ellis

IT MAY BE TRUE THAT THE WORLD IS IN A PERPETUAL CRISIS, A "STATE OF emergency," as the Jewish philosopher and literary critic Walter Benjamin wrote during the Nazi era. It may also be true that our traditions and identities are always at an end point, evolving, dying, seemingly reborn. Claims of continuity in tradition, identity, and faith are therefore always suspect. A Jew of the fifteenth century is quite different than a Jew of the first century or, for that matter, the twenty-first.

Yet even in this discontinuity there are aspects of an associative spectrum, hence the struggle in each generation to define what it means to be Jewish—or Christian, Muslim, or Hindu. Why would we struggle so mightily, with so much emotion and suffering, if the affirmation of a particular identity were unimportant? How can I articulate the meaning of the struggle to be faithful as a Jew if something of great importance is not at stake?

So if the perpetual crisis in continuity and identity is punctuated by particular crises, perhaps these crises are what bind the larger structures of religious and communal definitions. If that is the case, thought and action within our particular lifetime are what link us to the generations that came before us, and those to follow. Though we cannot know how our particular fidelity to the present moment will play out in the long run, just as those who came before us could not predict our present circumstances, this moment is what we are left with, and it is now, at this time, that we make our distinctive contribution.

There is no question that contemporary Jewish identity is framed around the events of the Holocaust and the founding of Israel, and it is within and around these events that Jewish fidelity is lived out in our time. There is a general agreement with such a sensibility, so much so that Jewish religiosity today is impossible to understand without these two reference points. Some have even speculated that the Holocaust and Israel are the touchstones of a new religion, one that is paradoxically both continuous and discontinuous with the Judaism that came before.[1]

Yet surely there is no return to this earlier Judaism. Since that time, an unexpected and as yet unacknowledged force has become part of the Jewish future. Within the narrative of the Holocaust and Israel, the Palestinian people loom large, their presence as part of Jewish history assured. Seen for the most part as foreign and threatening, culturally and politically, by mainstream Jewish thought, that very definition fails to grasp the more subversive role that the Palestinians play. For Jews, Palestinians are the "other" that is within, challenging the very notions of Jewish identity found within the structures and institutions that interpret the Holocaust and Israel.[2]

On Constantinian Judaism, Progressive Jews, and Jews of Conscience

What does the displacement and suffering of the Palestinians mean within the narrative of the United States Holocaust Memorial Museum? Surely, the Holocaust and the ethnic cleansing of Palestinians during the creation of the state of Israel in 1948 are two separate events. Yet the memory of the Holocaust and what has been done in its name cannot be considered today without also remembering the tragedy that befell the Palestinians. So too when the memory of the Holocaust is invoked as a symbol of Jewish innocence then and now, the plight of the Palestinians remains before us, though in mainstream discourse the very mention of the Palestinians with regard to the Holocaust and Israel is seen as inappropriate, even blasphemous. Since the force of this discourse is so powerful, we hardly even ask whose story we are asserting. Is Jewish discourse, or even the mainstream discourse of the West, the only one available or permissible? Surely Palestinian discourse sees the question differently, and much of the world in fact questions Jewish empowerment in Israel and the use of the Holocaust to avoid accountability for the present actions of the state of Israel.

Mainstream Jewish discourse labels these other narratives anti-Semitic. Is this the case always and everywhere? Perhaps these are differing understandings that need to be taken into account as a critique of a now-powerful community that seeks, like all powerful communities, to hide aggression under the cloak of innocence.

There are Jews as well who see the historic and ongoing plight of the Palestinians as part of defining Jewish identity. They join an ever-broadening narrative that speaks truth to power. Who are these Jews and what do they say to the crisis confronting us as a people?

We need to distinguish among three broad trends in Jewish life.

First is the emergence and consolidation of a Constantinian Judaism; that is, a Jewishness in league with the state and power. Constantinian Judaism, much like Constantinian Christianity and Constantinian Islam, uses religion and history to buttress positions and policies that further an in-group advantage and dispense injustice to others under the guise of innocence and redemption. Here religion and identity are in the service of the state and power; in the twenty-first century, mainstream Jewish institutions serve the American and Israeli states. Here the Holocaust and Israel are seen as cornerstones of Jewish identity and projections of Jewish ascendancy and common human decency. Any critical under-standing of either event or how the events are used inside or outside of Jewish life is considered akin to treason or blasphemy. Included within Constantinian Judaism are the mainstream Orthodox, Conservative, and Reform denominational structures, the seminaries that serve these denominations, the Anti-Defamation League and Holocaust memorial structures and outreach, and many university Holocaust and Jewish Studies programs.

Second is the broadening progressive movement within Jewish life. In the main, this movement is known as Jewish renewal and seeks to reinvigorate Judaism and Jewish life through modern understandings of religion and ritual, and stands for justice and peace within Jewish life and beyond. Jewish renewal seeks to broaden understanding of both the Holocaust and the state of Israel, reaching out to others and dissenting against the unjust use of power in Jewish and non-Jewish hands. Even with this attempt to move beyond the Constantinian Jewish establishment, Jewish renewal frames its arguments within Jewish mainstream understandings and thus limits the scope of dissent. In short, Jewish renewal has argued that the Holocaust mandated the creation of the state of Israel and that the mistakes of the post-

1967 Israeli occupation of the West Bank and Gaza need to be corrected with the establishment of a Palestinian state. Whereas Constantinian Judaism does not admit the validity of Palestinian aspirations, progressive Jews do, albeit in a very limited way that blunts the breakthrough they purport to seek and raises questions about the integrity of their efforts. In short, it is helpful to see progressive Jews and Jewish renewal as the left wing of Constantinian Judaism, assenting to Jewish ascendancy while critiquing certain aspects of it. Though Palestinians are present in the thought of Jewish progressives, they are secondary and a certain paternalism is present. Included among progressive Jews and Jewish renewal is the Israeli group Peace Now, the American progressive journal *Tikkun*, Rabbis for Human Rights, and aspects of Jewish denominational and university life.

Third is the small but growing minority of Jews of conscience. These Jews are breaking with Constantinian Judaism and Jewish renewal as aspects of Jewish life that do not meet the crisis before the Jewish people in the twenty-first century. For Jews of conscience, the very limitations of the critique of Israeli and American power increasingly place Jews within the context of power structures that cannot be reformed, and if reformed will continue the present injustices. Jews of conscience believe that a new prophetic paradigm, picking up from the old, is needed and that conscience is the guiding force to a reclaiming of aspects of the Jewish past, at the same time providing a new openness to the world. In the critique of unjust power, especially when wielded by Jews in the name of Jewish history, the Holocaust and Israel are placed in a new perspective and the Palestinians, having their own perspective, aspirations, and destiny, are now linked to the Jewish particularity of the future. Jews of conscience see an integrated future where Jews and Palestinians live across and within borders together, in equality and dignity. But first a reckoning with Jewish history is in order and a confession to the Palestinian people is forthcoming. This also means that the Holocaust is to be used as a bridge to all those suffering injustice rather than a blunt instrument of unaccountability. Israel is not our redemption, and it acts, too often and increasingly, like any other nation-state. Jews of conscience are fragmented and, for the most part, without established and named groups.

We need to pause for a moment on this understanding of Jews of conscience. They are on the fringe of Jewish life and yet they may hold the key for the future. The narrative of the Holocaust and Israel has been central to Jewish life for the last decades—Israel's ascendancy facilitated and assured by the 1967 war—replacing, almost in whole cloth, an already disintegrating rabbinic system of thought and practice. Though the rabbinic survives and is even experiencing a renewal of sorts today, its entire sensibility is now permeated by the narrative of the Holocaust and the state of Israel—even and especially when it pretends to transcend these historical events. Here I refer to the revival of various forms of Orthodoxy, including those who practice a form of settler Judaism on the one hand, and, on the other, those in the academy who form programs of Jewish studies around ancient texts and their interpretation that seek specifically to bypass the questions of the Holocaust and Israel.[3]

All of these understandings of Judaism have ties with the past and represent innovations that are specific to our time and culture. Progressive Jews linger in parts of the Orthodox and textual renewal and attempt to deal with the Holocaust and Israel at the same time. It is their tie to the latter understandings—what they consider to be authentic to Judaism—that seems to limit their ability to address the contemporary crisis. In a sense there is a competition to define or redefine the Jewish establishment by dissenting groups that live within an overall pattern of Jewish ascendancy. In sum, they live in the shadow of Constantinian Judaism, benefiting from its reach and affluence, all the while disputing its claim of univocal representation of Jewish history and life.

Jews of conscience understand that tinkering with the rabbinic system or attempting to transcend the crisis of Israel/Palestine—and the subsequent effect this has on the public carrying forth of the memory of the Holocaust—is futile. It simply means that Constantinian Judaism will continue its consolidation of power and representation, no matter the cries of dissent; in fact, it calls into question the seriousness of those cries. If the framework of allowable dissent dooms that dissent from the outset, can it be seen as serious in intent?

Jews of Conscience and the Rebirth of the Prophetic

The battle within Constantinian Judaism acquiesces—no matter the articulation against it—to its victory. Simply stated, that victory assigns to Judaism and Jewish life a power, affluence, and status—

a sustainable one I believe—unknown before in Jewish history. It also means alignments with other powerful groupings and ideologies, generally gathered under the rubric of neoconservatism, and a distancing from religious and ethnic communities—the vast majority of the world's population—on a permanent basis. In essence, the promotion and assertion of Jewish particularity on the world scene, again unprecedented in Jewish history, means a newly empowered separation from the rest of the world. Thus Constantinian Judaism offers a break in the type of separation Jews experience, this time the haves rather than the have-nots. The wager is simple: by joining the powerful in the world we will be protected against the less powerful, thus avoiding repetition of the darker days of Jewish history.

All of this may seem to be political rather than theological and thus mixing categories that have their own space and validity. Even when considering the two as one, the force of our criticism might still be limited. Even if we really wanted to, could we change the direction that Constantinian Judaism is taking us in? After our history of suffering and struggle, is it appropriate to suggest that our new-found power, flawed and often built upon the labor and exploitation of others, should be jettisoned? Can we honestly ask, indeed demand, that the power so often denied and with such horrendous consequences be relinquished? And relinquished to whom?

It may be that the proposed split between the political and theological is resolved within the question of identity: what does it mean to be Jewish? It has certainly never meant a strict separation between the political and the theological or a sense that history should or can be transcended. Elements of Constantinianism are present in Jewish history but never as defining ones; they are always critiqued, especially as consolidations of power take place. This critique is leveled at powers that are foreign and oppressive to Jews and to those within the Jewish community who seek to establish the essence of Jewish life as power, status, and wealth.

In short, Jewish identity has been variously defined but never celebrated for any length of time within the structures of the state, especially when those structures are built on the oppression of others, Jew or non-Jew. Obviously I am speaking of the prophetic here, but not simply the canonical prophets; the Torah itself is filled with these countercurrents. The Torah can stand alone as defining the Israelite and subsequent Jewish unease with unadulterated power. This is the very tradition that has surfaced periodically throughout Jewish history and is found today among Jews of conscience.[4]

But what can the prophetic mean today in light of the Holocaust and Israel? The prophetic is always under assault; the rabbis feared it and today Holocaust theologians and even many progressive Jews who invoke it do so with such constraints that reform is the reality rather than transformation. Also, the academic critique and institutional framework that emanates from Holocaust and Jewish studies and from Jewish institutional life almost mocks the limitations of the biblical prophetic. There are reasons for this: the ancient prophetic is too particular, patriarchal, and often violent in its imagery; the nineteenth- and twentieth-century Jewish prophetic, with its themes of revolution, Marxism, and anarchism, is seen as too universal, even self-hating and often misguided.

Yet with all of the critique and even within a time of empowerment and status and after the cataclysm of Holocaust—with the very celebration of Jewish survival and assertion of innocence in the air—is it really possible to articulate and sustain a Jewish identity without the pursuit of justice, and therefore a continuing critique of injustice, even and especially when it is entrenched at the very heart of Jewish life? The many books written about the Jewish covenant cannot hide the fact that today violence resides at its very heart. In this way we are becoming almost exactly what we once suffered under and fought against and thus in our practice at least we have adopted the Constantinian Christianity we so deride.

It is not a question of hypocrisy—that is always with us—but rather one of direction. If we lie about our position in the world to the generation that comes after us and seek to cover over the deep contradictions in our practice of Jewish life, can we expect a mature identification with Judaism and Jewish life from our children? If we teach and promulgate a sense of Jewish life to non-Jews that is clearly false and that falsity is easily accessible in the mainstream media, should we expect respect, or the feeling that Jewish commentators and thinkers are themselves undermining tolerance toward Jews and Judaism?

The tangle deepens. Anti-Semitism, a reality throughout Jewish history, remains. Yet the constant attention to that reality—even exaggeration, where almost every comment about Jewish and Israeli power is seen in this light—is seen correctly as a covering over of a distinct and concrete set of policies that further injustice. Clearly, some non-Jews still have difficulty separating the real and the mythic in descriptions of Jewish behavior. It is also true that many Jews have the same difficulty, glossing over the particular for the mythic, thereby collapsing the real with the mythic.

Is there a time in Jewish history when Jews and non-Jews alike dealt with Jews and Judaism in their complexity and flawed humanity? Even in Jewish and Christian renewal the mythic is emphasized, flowery language surrounding affirmation and critique. One thinks here of Michael Lerner and Arthur Waskow as leaders of Jewish renewal. Their significant contributions to Jewish life are limited by their special pleading, their strained, almost New Age mysticism and by their assertion of a Jewish particularity that, if seen within the context of global spirituality, seems less and less particular in a Jewish sense.

Christians fare little better in their understanding of Jews and Judaism. Sinking under the weight of their own history, Jews, once demonized, have gained, through a romanticization of the Hebrew Bible, the Jewish return to the land, and Holocaust commentators such as Elie Wiesel, a renewed lease on life. Even progressive Christians, African Americans, and feminists, for example, fall into this trap. One looks in vain for the critical words about Jewish ascendancy in politics, economy, and public discourse from James Cone, Cornell West, Elisabeth Schussler-Fiorenza, and Carter Heyward.[5]

Do those Christians who speak and write about Christian complicity in the Holocaust, who sit on boards of Holocaust memorials and make special pleas to the institutional life of the churches for repentance of the sin of anti-Semitism, speak truth to Jewish power? Do they seek to be honest about Christianity and Judaism, Christian and Jewish life? Or do they simply ride the wave of Jewish celebration? Where will they be when that wave comes to an end?

September 11 and the Question of Jewish Identity

After the violence of 9/11, with the subsequent increase in American and Israeli violence in Iraq and the Palestinian territories, these questions are rendered still more urgent. The drumbeat of war as protection against terrorism and anti-Semitism, now linked in the American and Israeli "defense" of civilization, reigns on college campuses and in the ecumenical and political discourse in America.

Again, how are Jews to find their own voice here, initially overwhelmed by the narrative of the Holocaust and Israel, and when both events seem to begin to fade in time and intensity, the issue of anti-Semitism again comes to the fore? The function of these understandings is to make it increasingly difficult to see the world as anything but dangerous for Jews.[6]

Yet whatever the dangers, Jews exist in the world, and the question is what path individual Jews, the community, and Jewish discourse will take. In a time of empowerment, the question is not only whether empowerment is important, but how we can pursue an interdependent life in which all are invited and included. Can the Jewish prophetic encourage this path? Is the Jewish prophetic alone here, chastened by history and contemporary life? Or does the Jewish prophetic exist within a complex of prophetic calls, all in some ways dependent for their origin on the Judaic, but also now independent with their own charisma?

Perhaps in the exercise of the prophetic, Jews are less alone than when the assertion of Jewish particularity is exercised as a power over others. Or perhaps those who live the prophetic are equally alone or joined in a broader particularity that is both contextual and transcends context. Is this the road that Jews of conscience travel today, exercising Jewish particularity by handing it over and then finding it again within a new expanded community?

Though it was voiced with alarming consistency in the days following 9/11, it has become a cliché now that after 9/11 everything changed. In fact the trajectory, at least within the context of Israel and the internal Jewish struggle, has remained constant. The re-invasion of Palestinian territory on the West Bank and Gaza after 9/11, widely supported by the Jewish establishment and with only muted dissent by many progressive Jews, has now been followed by an Israeli withdrawal from the Gaza Strip.

Yet historically and in the present the invasion and withdrawal are linked together, as two ends of a policy of expansion of Israel, containment of Palestinians, and encirclement of Palestine. This, coupled with the construction of the Wall, has the effect of sealing the fate of Palestinians and Palestine. Thus, Palestinian assertions and protest notwithstanding, the time of the two-state solution offered by moderate Palestinians and embraced by parts of the Constantinian and progressive Jewish establishment is effectively over.

Though advocacy groups hold fast to their own ideas about a just solution to the Israeli–Palestinian conflict, mostly inherited from the 1970s and 1980s, the facts on the ground have long since made them obsolete. Why then hold fast to proposed solutions that are denied by the facts on the ground and that everyone, at least in more sober moments, knows will never be achieved? Is it simply a diversion, again demonstrating that Constantinian Judaism and the progressive Jewish community are actually one and the same?

The similarities should not lead to a simplification of the complexity of the internal struggle of the Jewish community. There is a civil war within the Jewish world that predates 9/11; the framework remains the same afterward. Yet the relative quiescence of Jewish dissenters, a phenomenon that has been building over the years, reached a new level in recent times. Some of this has to do with the tremendous losses suffered by progressive Jews over the last decades, tied to the aging of those who began to protest Israeli power during the 1980s in response to the war in Lebanon. Also, the continual violent assault perpetrated by the Jewish establishment against these dissenters, as well as the violent assault that progressive Jews have waged against those to the left of them, smatterings of whom have emerged as Jews of conscience, likewise continues to eviscerate the Jewish progressive community. Thus the internal violence of group against group, all using the litmus test of Jewish identification for their own ends, has weakened the numbers and ideas of those who might have traversed the difficult terrain of post-Holocaust Jewish identity.

Yet the overwhelming factor is the reality of power and its ability to create and maintain political and territorial boundaries. Israel, with the help of the Holocaust narrative in the United States and the consolidation of Constantinian Judaism, has made any critique fall on deaf ears in the public realm and within the mainstream Jewish community itself. Whatever has been said, proposed, or cried out in anguish has been swept aside by the success of power on the ground. This has been true with regard to Palestinian resistance and leadership as well. Whatever can be said about the failures of both, does anyone really think the outcome of the Israeli-Palestinian conflict would be significantly different if

Palestinian resistance and leadership had been better prepared and more efficacious?

In the broad scope of the historical moment, with the imbalance of power between the industrialized and developing worlds, the internal problem of the Arab and Muslim worlds, the ascendancy of European and American power, and the cause of Jews taken up by the West—which in the twentieth century very nearly annihilated the Jewish people—the Palestinian cause seems lost from the beginning. Certainly the geopolitical realities and historical events of the twentieth century give pause to those who see the defeat of the Palestinians as simply caused by their own limitations and malfeasance. It also means that the self-criticism of Jewish dissent for its own failures must be placed in context as well. 9/11 is simply another factor in the ascendancy of Jews in the United States and Israel in the Middle East, concurrent with loss of ground in Palestine.

Yet 9/11 may also signal a sea-change in the perception of Jews by non-Jews and a reevaluation of Jewish identity by those Jews who cannot argue their Jewishness simply from a position of dominance. In the first days after 9/11, the question of Israel and its place in American foreign policy was broached in the mainstream media. For a long time, Israel was seen as an alliance that promised only benefits to the American people, both ideologically as a democracy in the Middle East and as an ally in an oil-rich and often unstable part of the world. The link between American support for Israel and hostility toward America in the international arena was unknown to most Americans before 9/11; that terror on American soil could result from such a connection came home forcibly in the days following the attack. Whatever the merits of the argument linking America's support for Israel as part of a holy war against Islam, more than a few Americans asked the question of whether the ability to make such an argument was worth the price of American blood.

Though this issue quickly disappeared from the American media discussion, the question itself was a breakthrough of sorts. After all, America's support for Israel has largely gone unquestioned, and if raised at all, the question was seen as untoward, outside the mainstream, and anti-Semitic. Jews, especially those Jews who had tried, for the most part unsuccessfully, to raise a critical voice on the Israeli–Palestinian conflict on a national scope, were surprised to hear this discussion in public. The context was hardly anticipated, and in the long run, the discussion proved to be counterproductive.

The surprise remained. Could the breakthrough to a more rational discussion of Israel/Palestine occur only in a moment of national hysteria? Because that moment contained the seeds of other wars, first in Afghanistan and then Iraq and all under the umbrella of a global war on terror, the initial questions surrounding the American alliance with Israel were submerged in a tightening of bonds between the two—in foreign policy initiatives but also in the public perception—so that the questions disappeared as soon as they arose.

Yet, as at other flash points in the history of Israel—the Lebanon war and the suppression of the first Palestinian uprising in 1988 are examples—the chipping away at the narrative of Israel as innocent and redemptive continued. Too, the quick end of the initial questioning also increased the sense that the case for a just peace between the Israelis and Palestinians would be decided by power rather than moral argument. In fact, a sense among many dissident Jews was that the case was already closed. Why then fight a victory that would not be reversed, and in a world of such volatility why fight a losing battle that could become a suicidal one, where the arguments for justice became twisted with the desire for revenge?

So the Jewish progressive movement continued to atrophy and splinter. On the one hand, Jews who saw the fight as futile and dangerous and whose commitments in the first place were of reform rather than radical questioning drifted away from the issue. Other Jews, more serious in outlook and critical sensibilities, took a different path. Thus the birth of Jews of conscience. For these Jews the occupation of Palestine had become more or less complete. The re-invasion of Palestinian territory, the building of the Wall, and the ever-expanding settlement population were simply tactics within an overall strategic plan. That plan—the conquest of as much of Palestine with the least number of Palestinians—had been outlined in the years previous to the 1967 war; in fact the beginning can be traced to the creation of Israel itself with the ethnic cleansing of Palestinians from what became the state of Israel. Step by step, no matter the outcry of Palestinians, some international bodies, and Jewish dissenters, the cleansing of Palestinians proceeds.[7]

In the aftermath of 9/11 the question was starkly posed: since the occupation is irreversible, what position do Jews of conscience, indeed anyone working on behalf of the Palestinians, take now? What is to be done? For some Jews of conscience, the stands taken and solutions proposed had to dovetail with the official Palestinian positions. These positions—a two-state solution with Palestine comprised of Gaza, the West Bank, and East Jerusalem—remained static and were increasingly out of touch with the realities on the ground. Of course many Palestinians, including much of the leadership of the Palestinian Authority, knew that these were simply bargaining positions for the appearance of dignity and political legitimacy. Some Palestinians recognized the futility of such a static understanding but were afraid, literally and figuratively, of announcing that the dream of a Palestinian state, a real state with a geopolitical and cultural base to succeed in the family of nations, had disappeared.

Jewish progressives have never recognized the full legitimacy of the Palestinians. In fact, Jewish progressives constantly speak for the Palestinians, limiting their arguments and perspectives, in effect truncating their discourse to fit the level acceptable to Jews. It is as though the Palestinians are unable to speak for themselves, chart their own course, and criticize Israelis, the Constantinian Jewish establishment, and progressive Jews in their own language and categories. Can the Palestinians accuse world Jewry, as a collective, and without signaling exceptions, of a program of ethnic cleansing that rivals other colonial and settler movements in history? Can Palestinians assert that historic anti-Semitism and the Holocaust have no claim on them and that the entire Israeli project, at least from their perspective, is illegitimate?[8]

After 9/11, these questions registered anew. Could Jews of conscience be free of accepted Jewish understandings and Palestinian slogans/programs? In doing so, could Jews of conscience negotiate the complexities of Jewish and Palestinian identity, leaving others to define themselves and initiating a new self-definition?

Toward a Post-9/11 Jewish–Palestinian Solidarity

9/11 did not change everything, but it did accelerate both the displacement of the Palestinians and the self-awareness of Jews of conscience. Now, as 9/11 fades in time and relevance, the continuity in policy and scope, the very complicity in the diminishment of Palestine, is more clearly recognizable.

The progressive solidarity of Jews and Palestinians, working toward a two-state solution for their own reasons—for Jews an attempt to reclaim a self-defined innocence within Jewish empowerment, for Palestinians a desperate attempt to secure their own survival—exists today only in worn and tattered slogans. In the next years it will be jettisoned, especially if a Palestinian state, truncated, without Jerusalem and contiguous viable borders, does emerge. Will victory then be declared by progressive Jews and Palestinians?

Many questions are raised here. If the situation was reversed, if Jews and Palestinians changed places, would Jews limit their arguments about territory and statehood as Palestinians are now expected to? Would Jews declare victory if the Jewish state were declared after its inhabitants had been cleansed from most of their homeland, surrounded by walls, and denied their political, cultural, and economic capital? What kind of solidarity would Jews expect in this situation?

There exists a solidarity within Israel/Palestine between Jews and Palestinians and between Jews and Palestinians in the diaspora. A continual crossing of borders and boundaries in politics, culture, and history is required so that the political distinctions generated and enshrined on the ground in Israel/Palestine are treated as superficial, artificially imposed boundaries resulting from a stage of European/American and Middle Eastern history that is tangible and time-bound. The boundaries are real in the sense that they need to be transgressed while their reality is subverted by that very transgression.

This is politics in another key, a deeper politics that may, in the long run, be more efficacious. Just as 9/11 may over time facilitate the integration of Muslims in American society, thus having the opposite effect of the immediate isolation the Islamic community experiences, the crossing of boundaries within and outside of Israel/Palestine by Jews and Palestinians may ultimately render imposed borders meaningless. Working together as one, with the mutual understanding of equality and dignity, operating as though all have the same citizenship rights and obligations, the distinctions that separate Jews and Palestinians will diminish.

This will happen for a variety of reasons. The splintering of both Israeli and Palestinian society as well as the increasing divisions within the Jewish community in America will force a reconsideration of national, ethnic, and religious differences. Is the moderately religious and secular Jew in Israel closer to the militant Orthodox settler, or to the moderately religious and secular Palestinian? Is this same Palestinian closer to the militantly religious Muslim or to his Jewish counterpart? The Americanization of Jews and Palestinians will also serve as a bridge to understandings that are overtly shared in the American experience and to other understandings that bind Jews and Muslims in their historically shared experiences, many of them instructive in mutual tolerance. This includes a shared history in Palestine before the creation of Israel.

Over the last decades, the experience of Jews and Palestinians of conscience has already yielded significant gains that bode well for the future. The narrative of the founding of Israel, accepted by most Jews and a majority of the citizens of Europe and America, a narrative that sees the Jewish community in Palestine as innocent and beleaguered in its struggle to create a state—the same narrative positing the Arab struggle against that creation as testifying to their belligerence, anti-Semitism, and lack of civilization—has been transformed.

Today there is no serious dispute about the complex history of the formation of Israel. Among others, Israeli historians have confirmed and extended, in great and meticulous detail, the longstanding Palestinian version of their displacement, including the massacres and ethnic cleansing of Arab Palestinians. Even the causes of the 1967 war, an explosive catalyst for support of Israel among Jews and others in the West and a foundational support for what was once narrated by Israel and its supporters as a forced benign occupation, is undergoing a complex revision.

At the same time, and intimately connected with these new historical understandings, the history of the annexation and expansion of Jerusalem and the occupation of the West Bank and Gaza is also undergoing revision. Though denied at the outset, it seems that the occupation of Jerusalem, the West Bank, and Gaza was part of an overall plan to settle these regions with Jews and to displace the Palestinians who lived there, including the Palestinian refugees who were earlier cleansed from what became Israel. It is because of these revisions that the Israeli withdrawal from Gaza is not being accepted at face value—as an Israeli retreat—but instead is seen as a strategic move to jettison part of the settler movement in order to consolidate the larger and more important settlements in Jerusalem and the West Bank.

This is the theme of Rafi Segal and Eyal Weizman's *A Civilian Occupation: The Politics of Israeli Architecture*. In short, Segal and Weizman, along with the many contributors to the collection, see the Israeli military occupation of Jerusalem and the West Bank as the matrix from which civilian planners and contractors, aided and abetted by governmental bureaucracy, can permanently change the Palestinian landscape into an Israeli one. Further, the settlement expansion into East Jerusalem and the West Bank is continuous with the initial Jewish settlements in what became Israel in 1948.[9]

Since the pre-state Jewish population was primarily concentrated on the Mediterranean coast, the newly enlarged state, now virtually emptied of Palestinian Arabs, was, from an Israeli perspective, in need of settlement. The challenge of the newfound state was to settle the interior, and this it did—in virtually the same way that it settled the newly emptied interior of the West Bank after the 1967 war. To see this continuity is to understand the un-announced, continuous policy behind the announced "war against Israel" and "protection against terrorism" policies that have "forced" Israel to extend, maintain, and now, through the Wall, make permanent the conquest of Palestinian land. 9/11 was simply another event that allowed a furthering of the overall project.

Again, the question is posed: If the occupation is not primarily military in nature, or if the military simply protects a permanent civilian occupation in which all sectors of Israeli society participate and benefit—from contractors, architects, government officials, teachers, medical personnel, and alike; in short, the settlements as normal towns and cities that function more or less like any Israeli population center—how is dissent to be organized?

This revision of dissent is mandated by the historical revision of Israel's founding: the founding and continuing expansion of Israel are not necessitated by war or opposition of the neighboring states, rather they are the planned formation and expansion of the state in a strategic and viable way that is already permanent. In a sense, the combination of historical revisionism in the founding and post-1967 analysis of Israel makes it more difficult to see a way beyond the present situation. In many ways, the conclusion is that the Palestinians are, more or less, permanently displaced. Palestine has been lost.

What can a Jewish–Palestinian solidarity mean in light of the permanent civilian occupation of Jerusalem and the West Bank?

Again, long-range thinking and acting are essential. Permanence is always qualified and, over time, assimilation of identities and cultures the norm. Though this assimilation will happen in the diaspora among Jews and Palestinians in the West, and thus become a force for bridging differences in Israel/Palestine, the physical room for that trend to become concrete will have diminished significantly. Much like the Native American experience in America, where the story of Native displacement is now accepted as part of the American historical narrative and where assimilation of many Native Americans has taken place, the unassimilated population dwells on reservations in dire straits and is forced to trade on a culture, through tourism to museums and casinos, that is barely alive. As the Jewish and Palestinian diasporas flourish through assimilation and boundary-crossing, is the fate of Palestinians in Palestine akin to that of the Native Americans?

9/11 and its aftermath will help define and redefine this Jewish–Palestinian solidarity as long as the longer view is kept in mind. Many elements and events will intervene in the coming years, and the unexpected, an interruption of the continuity of Israeli expansion and Palestinian displacement, cannot be dismissed as fantasy or hopeful thinking.

How will such a change in the balance of Israeli–Palestinian power affect the American empire? Will the completion of the Wall and the constant unrest in the Arab and Muslim world toward Israel and American foreign policy one day move America toward a more even-handed approach? To continue on as empire, will America make a deal with other powers that will be premised on a sharing of the land of Israel/Palestine?

In the shadow of 9/11, the way forward is preparation for a future that will arrive one day, a future where Jews and Palestinians live in equality and peace. An evolving Jewish–Palestinian solidarity prepares for that future.

8

SPIRITUAL COMMUNITY IN THE POST-9/11 WORLD: A JEWISH PERSPECTIVE

Tamar Frankiel

AT OUR SHABBAT TABLE ONE FRIDAY NIGHT, A YOUNG HASIDIC MAN ASKED us about something that had been bothering him:

> You know, it seems to me that many people are teaching a view of life where the primary motivation for doing good is what's going to happen in the hereafter. They warn about punishment—how long you'll burn, roast, or boil—and occasionally promise rewards for good behavior. I'm not arguing that it's not true, but according to the way I was educated, this isn't the best way to motivate people. I learned that a person should want to do what's right because that's what God wanted, in order to "make a dwelling place [for God]" in this world.

I commented, as the fish was passed around the table, that this reminded me of a certain philosophical approach I'd been studying, which discussed different kinds of power. Real power doesn't come from threatening people with bombs and missiles, knives and bullets. Nor does it come from shouting and ordering people around or trying to make them afraid, whether in this life or the hereafter. That is only indirect power, because it affects our bodies and/or our emotions, and only then our decision-making. Direct power comes from presenting shared experience and hopes, inspiring another person with a vision of ideals to be achieved. This is like what the Hasidic masters call "words from the heart that penetrate the heart."

When I inject philosophical comments into a Shabbat discussion, it's not unusual to find people suddenly discovering a reason to congregate in the kitchen, or turning to their neighbor to ask about their upcoming vacation. But this time, no one left or turned away. People nodded. I was surprised—enough that I asked my daughter later whether she thought people understood what I said. "Sure," she said, "it's right in line with what Mendel was talking about." She confirmed what I had suspected: the Hasidic way of thinking runs parallel, in important ways, to process philosophy. Despite—or perhaps because of—its fascinating mystical heritage, Hasidism took an important turn in its view of human nature.

So I come to this paper informed in part by process philosophy, especially David Ray Griffin's work, and in part by Hasidut, which I have been exploring for some twenty-five years as part of my intellectual journey and spiritual practice. I am not going to argue that the two philosophies are completely consonant—their terminologies as well as historical contexts are too different for that. Also, respect for earlier masters—particularly for Maimonides—weighs heavily on the greatest of Hasidic thinkers. Nevertheless, I want to suggest that indigenous resources in Judaism allow us to approach our current problems in a way that is profoundly helpful. Not least of its virtues is that because Hasidism was a movement geared toward ordinary people, it phrases its insights in simpler terms than we find in process (or most other) philosophies.

Power, Ideas, and Polarization

A major issue of the post-9/11 world situation is that of managing and sharing power in a multitude of diverse communities. Military, economic, and technological power are constant concerns, whether because of the war in Iraq, the oil cartels' management of resources, or piracy of computer technology. The power of ideas and ideologies is equally important, as well as the media that convey those ideas, from the *New York Times* to al-Jazeera. In all these communities, power relations are delicate and constantly changing, and in most societies the management and exchange of power is subtle and complex.

Some thirty-five years ago the anthropologist Kenelm Burridge wrote a book entitled *New Heaven, New Earth*, in which he explored what happens when a long-evolved, complex system of social power is confronted by a new "measure of man" (Burridge wrote before the increased concern over gendered language). In most of the Pacific island societies he studied, the new measures of humanity were brought by Europeans, who literally measured in terms of money. Complex measures were replaced by simple, often polarized, categories—you have access to money or you don't; you have a lot of money or very little. Often, the shift created new religious movements, including "messianic" figures who could negotiate the new situation.

I think of Burridge's work because what seems to have happened since 9/11—though its historical roots are far deeper than 2001—is a new or sharper polarization. After two hundred years of industrial capitalism and an increasingly complex system of banking, finance, and exchange; after a worldwide explosion of consumerism and a materialistic approach to life unprecedented in human history; after transformations of societies ranging from socialist and communist experiments to dictatorships by Western-educated heads of clans, a new proclamation emerged. Representatives of one purported "world"—radical Islam, claiming to represent all true Muslims—dramatically attacked representatives of another, "the West," by slaughtering workers at the World Trade Center. The perpetrators of the attack were attempting to reshape, with their dramatic act (actually the latest in a series of international terrorist attacks on innocents which began with the Munich Olympics in 1972), the measure of man. Implicitly, they denied the complexity of the world situation and proclaimed their leader, Osama bin Laden, as the bearer of truth, while the West (and Israel) were the carriers of evil. Most disturbingly, alienated from the values of the sanctity of life preached by most religions, they focused on the martyr/murderer as the ideal, a person devoted to his vision of God and fearless of death. In the face of death, money and material resources are, of course, irrelevant.

The world seemed suddenly simple. For the average American, the choice was also hauntingly biblical: "I have set before you life and death, blessings and curses. Now choose life..." (Deut. 30:19). Radical Islamists soon were being portrayed as promoting a culture of death, while Americans and their allies were waving the banner of life. Many Christians and Jews firmly set their faces against this Islam, called "fundamentalist" or "radical." But, of course, the situation is not so simple as the polarities would suggest. Many people live primarily secular lives and are not willing to put themselves at the service of a religious vision of any kind. Moreover, "choosing life" means something different to various communities within American society, as we can readily observe from our graphic slogans of "pro-choice" or "pro-life."

Ideologies of polarization, and acts that attempt to demonstrate the power of those ideologies, are attempts to simplify a complex situation, to rally around a "new measure of man," while the enemy has an obsolete or corrupt version of what it is to be human. Since 9/11, a great deal of the American government's communication with its people has been devoted to trying to convince us that we have such an enemy—even though, in our globalized society, there is no clearly "external" enemy any more. Speeches identifying enemies have ranged from terrorism, radical Islam, and Iraqi weapons of mass destruction to Asian economies and the Asian bird flu. Eventually people do recognize that such finger-pointing often leads to a wild goose chase. But even more importantly, the social reality is that those labeled as potential "enemies" are as much "in here" as "out there." Your Muslim neighbor might go to a radical mosque or might not. Your Chinese client might do business in Taiwan or Beijing or both. Immigration along the Mexican border triply illustrates the problem—legal and illegal immigrants, families on both sides of the border, children of illegal immigrants who, born on this side, are American citizens.

Even the contrast between competing ideologies is overdrawn. For example, we are often treated to a contrast between individualistic, democratic ideals and more collectively based ideals such as the clan structure of some Arab (or non-Arab) societies, where family and clan honor (or its opposite, shame) take precedence over Western values of achievement. It is true that "honor killings" of women who have been raped and murders of "collaborators" runs contrary not only to Western ethics but to most codes of justice. But we should beware of painting the two sides black or white. Honor codes still hold sway in some sub-communities, for example the US military, where loyalty to group norms and an honorable death (sacrifice for others) supersedes individual self-fulfillment. Nor are Muslim societies the only ones without democratic forms of government.

What does seem to be the case is that Western-influenced democracies have a greater tolerance for discussion and examination of societal norms without the discussants suffering sanctions—and that is why we can examine all these matters here. However, the willingness even of academics to ostracize colleagues because of political actions of their governments—as happened in Britian against Israeli colleagues and institutions—shows that the emotions that underlie polarization run deep in human nature.[11]

In truth, the "enemy" is polarization itself. The first step in greater spiritual consciousness is recommitting to a nondualistic view of the world, on every level. In our political and social discourse, this means rejecting "us vs. them" arguments. Most of us are very much invested in being right and proving the other person wrong. This is the intellectual face of polarization and our media constantly promotes it, under the guise of "hardball" debates.

In contrast, let us recall our Hasidic friend's straightforward statements. Confronted with the dogma of afterlife punishment, he first of all said, "I'm not arguing that it's not true, but..." How long has it been since someone prefaced their comment with the humility of "I'm not arguing. I'm not claiming that what you said isn't true"? We are, of course, engaged in a search for truth, and we have the obligation to make sure that the process of inquiry remains open and that claims are backed by evidence. But let us not begin by assuming that we have the corner on truth. Even more importantly, we must remember the fundamental question around which we unconsciously polarize: How to put forward a new measure of humanity? How do we formulate the ideal aims for our society and individuals, and actualize them? This will lead us to a richer and more sensitive formulation of any positions we take.

Coercion and Persuasion

Our Hasid said that a system based on fear of punishment "isn't the best way to motivate people." Theoretically, Western liberalism agrees with this. Drop capital punishment; substitute rehabilitation of criminals. Use educational incentives rather than grades that seem to highlight failures. However, this approach has two flaws: first, it fails to deal with the fact that most people revert, under the slightest pressure, to the reptilian brain's instinct, which says "survive at all costs!" If you've done something wrong, escape is far better than accepting responsibility—admitting guilt and paying one's debt to society. If you haven't studied, it's easier to cheat and try not to get caught than to do the lesson again. An ethical sense of duty can easily be overridden.

Second, it's much easier to see when others are acting reptilian than when we are doing it ourselves. We often use "reward and punishment," which are forms of coercion, in milder ways. A good example is the boycott. We think of the boycott as being good in a potentially oppressive economic situation because it's a nonviolent alternative. Yet, even though it does not use physical force, it is confrontational and causes suffering to innocent people, such as workers whose jobs are jeopardized by a boycott. Another example is the recent use by churches of policies of divestment against Israel. Besides the arrogance of taking action against Israel while the government was disengaging from occupied territory— giving up land even with no reciprocal agreement from the other side—divestment is a technique of coercion that necessarily affects the livelihood of innocent people. That is not to say that boycotts, divestments, and the like are always unethical; but we should not pretend they are non-coercive. They still rely on pressure in the physical realm rather than the spiritual.

Boycotts have been best used as demonstrations of power by those previously presumed powerless, as when Cesar Chavez thirty years ago led a boycott of California grapes. This was promoted by the workers themselves (not concocted by a well-meaning outside group) and was followed by tough negotiations—a non-coercive form of action. Similarly, the civil rights movement of the 1950s and 1960s used protests and sit-ins effectively in concert with legal, electoral, and negotiating efforts. In other words, confrontation effectively stopped the reptilian dynamic, and from there people could move to a higher level.

We know, intellectually, that negotiation and persuasion are the best approaches to resolving differences. Yet even educated people—in whom the neocortexes are presumably functioning well—can resort to name-calling and worse when they feel ineffective. We need only witness the reactions of liberal Christian communities in face of the recent rise of conservative evangelicalism, or Reform Judaism as the Orthodox population swells. When survival (i.e., philanthropic donations) are at stake, we simply "forget" that we are contributing to an ethic of coercion and reinforcing polarization. The alternative of non-coercion necessarily requires deep communication, which demands nuance, subtlety, deep investigation of self and other. It is time-consuming and indirect, with no quick fixes. But it has a higher value, and ultimately a greater power, in the long run.

The higher value and greater power come from motivation toward an ideal future. Process philosophy, like Hasidic thought, holds that people are best motivated by non-coercive means; in both cases, the holding forth of an ideal is the primary motivation. According to David Ray Griffin, Whitehead held that God acts in the creative process, in concert with humanity, by presenting "ideal aims" for us to prehend and bring forth into actuality: "The worldly actual occasions prehend God... thereby feeling the relevant divine aims. Because God entertains those aims with the subjective form of appetition that they be actualized, the worldly occasions... feel those aims sympathetically, thereby with an intial urge to actualize them."[12] This is God's persuasive power, and God's mode of action is "always the mode of persuasion."[13]

In Hasidism, the ideal is "making a dwelling place" for God in each person and in community. For each individual, this is activated both by study, in which a person can come to understand God's purpose and one's own role in the divine design, and by the practice of *mitzvot* (commandments) that manifest God's will in this world. One of the mysteries of this approach is how it is that the practice of *mitzvot* helps a person develop. On the surface, many of the practices seem to be, at worst, rote actions, or at best, beautiful traditions. I would suggest, borrowing from process language, that it is through these practices that one comes to "feel the relevant divine aims." In a non-intellectual fashion, by doing things with one's physical body, a person may begin to resonate with higher purposes. An individual's sense of unity of purpose affects the organs, perhaps even the cells and molecules, "all the way down."

If persuasion is the divine mode of action, then ideally, if we are living in *imitatio dei*, our primary activity should be presenting ideals to others, ideals that appeal to them and that they can actualize in their lives. Presumably, this would be true for communities as well as individuals. God, however, has a considerable advantage over most of us. S/He knows what ideals are appropriate for each of us, and each community, at any given instant, what will be truly appealing at our present level and what is beyond our scope. Then we can exercise our free choice among aims, all of them realizable. Some possible aims are not new, but simply repeat our old patterns, while others will produce more creativity and beneficence in the world.

An important Jewish thinker of the twentieth century, Rabbi Eliyahu Dessler, described this unique tailoring of God's aims for a person as the point of free choice ("bechira-point"). A person brought up in an inner-city ghetto will have a different bechira-point than a person raised in a refined, educated way with a strong family structure. For the youth of the ghetto, it may never occur to him not to shoplift; his bechira-point may be whether or not he will use a weapon to commit robbery. For a person who has learned from youth not to steal, it might never occur to him that shoplifting is even a choice—he just doesn't do it. Whether to cheat on income tax, however, might be his bechira-point. God knows all these details about each person's life.[14]

Those examples are negative—what we traditionally have called "sins." The same is true, however, with positive development in education, morality, and awareness. The ghetto youth may never dream of being a heart surgeon, as the son of a doctor might, but still he is presented with ideal aims at his level: first to get through high school without dropping out, then to attend community college; to get a job and keep it; and in that way continue to grow. As he enters into new communities, new moral choices will present themselves and old temptations will usually fall away. His awareness of the world, and of more options, will grow. This is the sort of gradual process we all engage in, and in spiritual growth the same dynamic occurs, in interaction with God's persuasive presentation of these aims.

From this it is relatively straightforward that our job, within our communities and in relation to other communities, is to discover the ideal aims that will motivate ourselves and others toward a better outcome. However, it is not so easy to understand and practice persuasion. During the process of writing this essay, I heard a public radio program on the torture of prisoners. One of the interviewees, a former interrogator, described how he related to prisoners. He said he preferred to describe his procedures not as manipulation or pressure, but as persuasion: "You have to get to know the prisoner, get inside his head, and figure out what will motivate him to tell you what you want to know."

What is the difference between this kind of persuasion and a more benevolent kind? In the torture situation, the "persuader" has an agenda. He wants a certain result according to his own needs and wishes, in this case the revealing of information useful for military operations or security. Most of the time, when we are trying to persuade a person, we have our own ideas of the appropriate outcome at the forefront. If we are acting in *imitatio dei*, on the other hand, we want to persuade the person to actualize what is best for him/herself and for the largest possible scope of good outcomes.

What can we do in the many cases where different communities do not agree on fundamental values? Or where their strategies for reaching negotiated agreements do not follow our usual way of working? To take an example from social situations, we may all agree that persuasion is better than coercion and competition; but what constitutes manipulative, or psychologically coercive, behavior? Some people grow up in a "bargaining" culture, where not revealing one's true position is an important part of the game. To an American who grew up in a society where prices are fixed, being thrown into a bargaining situation can be extremely confusing. Many Americans end up feeling manipulated after the simplest purchase at a *shuk* (Middle Eastern market). The requirement to argue over prices is difficult enough, but how does one also accommodate the emotional communications of the other party, which affect every bargaining move? Even in democratic countries, the idea that there can be a "win-win" position is a relatively new idea. Usually it is assumed that the majority wins and the minority just has to tolerate being the underdog until it can one day become part of the majority. The minority is temporarily "coerced" in the name of the greater part of the community. In a relatively balanced democracy, the situation is tolerable even if, as Winston Churchill is supposed to have said, "democracy is the worst form of government except all those other forms that have been tried from time to time." Perhaps we live coerced and coercing more than we want to admit.

Persuasion and Inter-inclusion

Perhaps there are more dimensions of social process to consider in order to understand persuasion properly. Let us review. Our Hasidic friend suggested that the way to make change happen is not to frighten people but to find a better way to motivate them. From the perspective of process philosophy, as in Hasidic thought, the only authentic motivation is an ideal, one which is felt (prehended) as something that promises to engage one's fullest self. In trying to apply this to social life, we explored the realities of coercion and persuasion. That led us to ask how much knowledge we actually have of another person's (or community's) best outcomes, and how much our own agendas interfere with the ideal aim, which is to help each person or community reach their own highest potential. And we ended in something of a bind. It seems nearly impossible to interact with a person or community with whom one disagrees without introducing some element of coercion, manipulation, or similar effort to impose one's own agenda on the other.

Faced with this reality, some have proposed that the only way to persuade is to become a model. Following this line of thinking, you don't try to persuade anyone to change anything, just be the best person you can and eventually the light of your life will inspire others around you. A truly radiant being changes the world as a candle lights a dark room. This is self-evidently a non-coercive means of persuasion. In the popular mind (not necessarily in theology or philosophy), this resonates with many religious ideas. It can sound like an *imitatio dei*, particularly in tune with a Christian view of God as incarnating in an individual as the "perfect man." This underlies the popular view that the way to decide something is to ask, "What would Jesus do?" The idea of the exemplary model also resonates with the Hindu avatar or the Buddhist arhat or bodhisattva. God sends individuals to inspire us (Jesus or Krishna), or individuals achieve what we all would wish to achieve (the Buddha; in Judaism the patriarchs and matriarchs), and we follow their examples.

This seems to cohere with a general ideal that we are each to become the fullest example of humanity that we can be, and our communities should be the fullest examples of human communities that they can be. Our friend put this succinctly in saying that the truest motivation for good action is what God wants, namely that we "make a dwelling place [for God] in this world." The context for this interesting phrase is centuries of interpretation of a biblical command that Moses was to transmit to the Israelites: "Let them make me a sanctuary, that I may dwell among them" (Exodus 25:8). Literally, the commandment was to build the portable desert sanctuary; but metaphorically and spiritually, it has been understood in Hasidic literature to mean that the entire world is to be made fit for the Divine to dwell within. As individuals, as communities, and as the complex human organism we call the "human race," we are to become vessels for Divine light. So if we have examples of people radiating Divine light, we should be able to echo their example, "follow in their footsteps," and do the same ourselves. Eventually, we'll all be perfect beings in which God can dwell.

Attractive as these ideas are, they are problematic, from both the Hasidic and process viewpoints. The "radiant being" model suggests that some people have more light, and if we hang out with light-filled beings, we too will learn to radiate light. We haven't solved our problems yet because there just aren't enough people who are filled with light. There's not enough "light"—not enough clarity, not enough brilliant thinking, an insufficient quantity of radiant beings. However, I would argue this is the wrong way of putting the issue. We have had clarity, brilliance, and radiance in every generation. We have had profound religious leaders, superb thinkers, and stellar examples of high-quality, ethical living. Even the war-torn twentieth century produced such remarkable individuals as Martin Luther King Jr., Mohandas Gandhi, and Mother Theresa, who thought, meditated, and prayed deeply, who carried a universalistic vision and inspired millions to follow; many other unsung religious heroes did the same.

Moreover, the idea of imitating another person violates the Jewish idea that each person has a unique soul and a distinctive mission on earth, and therefore the ideals presented must be suited to her own situation. Neither the exemplary model generalized as a "perfect [hu]man" nor a particularized guru or teacher can do this.

Process philosophy and Hasidism both clarify the issue: The "model" and "imitator" are treated as monads whose mode of interaction is unclear. If the model is not persuading (because that might become coercion), and if the imitator is not precisely imitating (because that is impossible if they are unique beings), what is going on between the two?

Only if we revise this model to be dynamic and deeply relational can it approach what we need, and it may require that we formulate our intuitive notion of what persuasion is. In terms of Hasidism, we need an "inter-inclusive" model, wherein each person is seen as a facet of the Infinite Light, and each is illuminating the other. Rabbi Yitzchak Ginsburgh, a modern interpreter of classic Hasidic thought, puts it as follows:

> In the present order, at least in its idealized form, the creative forces God used and uses to create and sustain the world act in harmony, each taking into consideration the personality of all the others. This is made possible by the fact that they exhibit inter-inclusion, that is, each creative force possesses within its own internal makeup something of all the others.[15]

This means that one is not the model and the other the imitator; rather, they refract the same light differently at any given moment.

In terms of process philosophy, the dynamic between them is one of participating in feeling, in the Whiteheadian sense of that term; that is, both prehend with desire God's aims. The "exemplary model" doesn't "exhibit" ideals in an abstract form, but activates them with feeling and desire inherent in her prehension of them, and that same information-with-desire is present to the "imitator." Reciprocally, the "model" grasps the life course of the "imitator," the similarities and differences they have, and is able to convey a shared sense of being on the same trajectory, toward the Divine aims. To put it in more limited, but more famililar, psychological terms, an exemplary model works for us if we feel the model-person cares for us, knows us, and sees us in all or many dimensions, and if in return we feel a connection to what that person is actualizing in her life.

The Hasidic parallel is that of the "rebbe" who, contrary to popular conceptions, does not dictate what his followers must do, but understands inwardly the situation of each person and presents the ideals toward which each must strive in a way that makes sense and is realizable. It is said that the Hasidic masters— the great rebbes who were precious guides to their followers— would not answer a question until they could find the place in their hearts, or the memories in their cells, where they had experienced exactly the same situation as the other person. Then they could truly empathize. Yet at the same time, the Hasidic master was relatively egoless; that is, he no longer had attachment to what had happened to him personally. His own story was utterly unimportant to him. Therefore, when the rebbe found that place in himself that grasped the other person's feelings, he could respond with a clarity that the person seeking help could not muster, and could help the other person see potential for change. Thus his insight was directly empowering of the other. (Of course, this model is not always realized in every person called "rebbe," but there are numerous authentic accounts of this kind of interaction between leader and follower.) This marks the essential difference between the popular conception of the "radiant being" or "ideal man" and an authentically persuasive model.

This may help us correct our common-sense ideas about the process of persuasion. Persuasion in the process sense is not a straightforward rational process where you present me with incontrovertible evidence that you are right, and I am persuaded by information that I did not have before. That process of discernment is, to be sure, important in dealing with our shared reality; I do not want to act on incorrect or partial information if better is available. Persuasion, however, is something different: a presentation of aims in a way in which their desirability is felt and shared.

The root of "persuasion" is etymologically akin to the Latin word *suavis*, which means "sweet." When we share an ideal, our picture of future reality is sweetened. Remarkably, this is akin to a Hasidic concept. In spiritual growth, one repeatedly goes through stages that involve humbling one's ego and separating oneself from one's ties to the past. The final step is "sweetening," when clarity of perspective is achieved and wholeness becomes apparent.[16] Persuasion is the sweet taste of wholeness in our felt and shared reality.

Light and Vessels

Rabbi Isaac Luria, known as the Ari, was the most famous Jewish mystic of the last five hundred years, if not of all time, and his work is foundational for Hasidism as well as for other modern traditions of Jewish mysticism.[17] His account of what happened in the creation of the universe is that in the beginning God created "Light" and "Vessels." The vessels were the forms that would hold the energy of creation in sufficient stability that the world could unfold. However, when God poured the divine light into the vessels, they shattered—they were unable to hold the light. Since then, the world as we know it is composed of sparks of light enclosed in shards of the vessels, darker husks that prevent the light from emerging. It is our task to "raise the sparks"—to liberate the light so that it can be seen.

This story tells us that there's already enough light—in fact, endless light pervades the entire universe at every moment—but the vessels were a difficult thing even for the Creator of the Universe. On the one hand, the vessels had to be strong. On the other, if they were too rigid, they would burst. In the imagery of this story, the latter is what happened. The Ari taught that each of the original vessels was pure and perfect in itself, but none had any way of sharing its power with the others. That rigidity, the lack of inter-inclusion, was what caused the shattering. Paradoxically, that apparently purer world was called the World of Tohu, meaning chaos (from Genesis 1:2, "the earth was tohu va-vohu, formless and void"). Monads with no relationship have no real shape, no organic form.

The metaphor is apt for our situation: religious and political communities have usually represented "vessels" that are gross, thick, and rigid. Instead of being able to convey the light, they have concealed it, each within its own boundaries. On the other hand, when we have tried to create communities with more permeable boundaries, they rarely last. For example, mass movements, such as Gandhi's and King's, inspire many but their effect in the long run is the memory of a powerful street drama, portraying an attractive ideal but with limited ability to contain the light. The declining effectiveness of large marches and protests is fallout from a sociological form that was unable to hold the ideal.

What creates a strong yet flexible communal vessel? What enables the divine light to be held in stable form and radiated into the world? We have already suggested some components. We must avoid dualism in our thinking and polarization in our speech and action. This also means not needing to be right and remaining open to information from all sources. Second, we must abstain from coercive action and manipulation. Third, we must develop new ways of sharing ideals, in light of our new understanding of the power and significance of persuasion.

This is the most difficult and subtle part, for it requires us not only to understand but to practice a view of the world that is largely unfamiliar. It requires that we listen and commu-nicate within an entirely new frame of reference. We must assume that we all have access to the mind of God and to each other, if only we can listen. As David Ray Griffin puts it:

> We are directly perceiving the minds of others all the time, so that those moments in which people have what are normally termed "telepathic experiences" would be special only in the sense that the ongoing prehensions of the other minds in question had, for some reason, momentarily risen to the level of conscious awareness. The same principle would imply that if there is a divine actuality, it would implant aspects of itself in all human experiences, which would mean that we would actually be perceiving God all the time.[18]

Divine and human feelings (in the larger Whiteheadian sense of prehensions, not just emotions) are aspects of the field of non-local information instantaneously grasped, from our knowing of our bodies to the radiations from the universe.[19] Most of the time we are filtering out the vast amounts of non-local information available to us. Occasionally a useful piece of information rises to the surface of consciousness from these pre-conscious perceptions, and we call it "intuition." Our requirement now is that we become attuned to larger and larger fields of information, so that we indeed participate in a shared felt reality.

Examining Differences

But what does this mean when we are confronted with communities who are NOT committed to a model of non-coercive persuasion? In early 2006, we watched with dismay as people were killed in riots over the publication of caricatures of the prophet Muhammad. We may have been speaking of being nonjudgmental and overcoming polarity, yet lives were being snuffed out. Are our familiar Western psychological frames of reference, with emphasis on listening, empathy, and inclusion, simply ineffective in the face of the complex interactions of societies with different values? This has, indeed, been the moral critique of liberalism from the conservative right: Are there no lines that cannot be crossed, no rules that cannot be bent in the name of inclusiveness, tolerance, and development of potential? Are there no moral absolutes? In the face of a vicious form of street drama, are we impotent?

Whitehead recognized that despite the ideal of persuasion, social reality requires force in certain circumstances. We use force when we pull a child back from the curb, or when we arrest a thief and take him to jail. The presumption is that not everyone is in alignment with ideal aims; many, perhaps most of us most of the time, pursue more selfish goals. When our acts in pursuit of selfish aims interfere with the greater good, institutions such as the police, army, and court are necessary. In a healthy society, the long-term aim is, through moral education, to sensitize individuals to the welfare of others, so that we will actually come to desire the greater good, and eventually our desires for our own welfare will coincide with the welfare of all entities. This moral education is paralleled in Hasidic thought by the desire for transformation, so that each person will want to "make a dwelling place for God" on earth. In the Jewish daily prayer, the prayer asking for the destruction of the wicked is interpreted to mean that wickedness be destroyed and that those who desire evil will have their desires transformed.

That hope is messianic. In the meantime, law and its accompanying coercion are and must continue to be an important part of our social framework. Indeed, the cosmological framework of process philosophy assumes that God initially determined that there would be certain physical laws governing the universe, and we can assume that similarly, certain moral principles would be appropriate. As Griffin has pointed out, the moral laws, even when set forth in scripture, are not written in stone as literally applicable for every occasion. Jewish tradition agrees, and the result is the vast literature of Mishna, Talmud, codes, and responsa which discuss and respond to particular situations in terms of the general laws set forth in the Torah. Among those laws are certain near-absolutes such as do not murder, and one of its obvious, and almost universally accepted, exceptions is self-defense.

Violations of the inherent moral laws of our world, which are so sacred as to be enshrined in most of the world's religious traditions, require responses that may be quite harsh because, if allowed to continue, they undermine civilization itself, including the entire process of moral education and sensiti-zation. This is the job of the political and legal authorities and those who execute laws and sanctions. In modern Western societies, religious communities are voluntary and officially non-political, so they do not wield those indirect powers of physical coercion. (They are, however, social bodies with their own inner dynamic, so they may function in emotionally coercive, i.e., manipulative, ways.) The primary mission of religious and spiritual communities is not, then, to participate in actual sanctions or to become involved in polarized debate (though as individual citizens we may choose to do so). Rather, it is to recover a sense of the high purpose of human life and civilization itself.

The near and present danger is that continued atrocities desensitize even people of high moral caliber, so that we are no longer shocked by suicide bombings or other attacks on the innocent. We are no longer horrified at assaults on civil liberties, tyranny, or ethnic and religious hatred. A parallel from American history might be Northerners' attitudes toward Southern slavery in the early nine-teenth century. Despite the known horrors, including racism, violence, rape, and destruction of families, it was accepted as something "they" did "down there." Only gradually over decades, and only when other factors played a part, did the North's moral conscience awaken sufficiently to agree to confront the evils of slavery.

Similarly, we are in danger of allowing basic principles of civilized living to deteriorate out of presumed respect for other cultures and compassion for those who have suffered. In reality, we are responding only to the most strident among the hundreds of thousands of suffering human beings on the planet. We must find ways to interact compassionately with others, without giving up our own basic principles.

In particular, we must honor our own traditions and, in humility and gratitude, recognize that the achievements of Western ethics, human dignity, tolerance, and democratic thinking are genuine achievements. We have been able to create vessels that hold a certain kind of light, which we must protect. Moreover, while trying to understand other cultures, we must recognize honestly that the liberal tradition's unwillingness to use coercion is not always matched in other societies—and of course conservatives in Western societies are quite willing to use coercion in certain circumstances, as discussed in other essays in this collection. Using the idea of the bechira-point, the point of free will, that we discussed earlier, we can see that Western societies have created the potential for building certain ethical foundations, certain assumptions, that enable us to choose non-coercive actions. Not everyone is at that point. This creates an inherent ethical dilemma: to what extent can we honor and respect groups that do not share non-coercive values? This same question underlies issues such as freedom of speech for those who would take away freedom of speech, tolerance for those who espouse intolerance (e.g., neo-Nazis). But it is only an extension of the principle that one cannot allow free use of weapons to those who use weapons to commit crimes. Therefore, liberal as we might wish to be toward others, we must remember that compassionate understanding of others' positions does not justify overthrowing our hard-won ethical foundations. For example, we cannot condone terrorism or violence against noncombatants under any guise; we cannot condone random destruction of property in the name of protest against offense.

Only by maintaining the level we have achieved can we be offered the opportunity to achieve more. Our wish to achieve a humane global society must be accompanied by a seriousness of purpose that will not allow previous achievements to be undermined.

Power and Prophecy

At the same time, it must be admitted that our calling is difficult. We wield the power of ideals only, through what Abraham Joshua Heschel called the prophetic voice. The voices of ancient prophets did provide, in many ways, the foundations for our ethics today, so we can take from that an inspiration to go forward. But we now need to set our feet firmly on the prophetic path.

What do we know about prophecy? Certainly, the phenomenon of prophecy was the origin of religion in the West. Prophets were rooted in history, and thus were guardians of the people's memory. Moreover, they had to cultivate a relationship to God within, according to rabbinic sources, a context of emotional and physical stability. Prophecy could not happen in a state of anxiety or depression; prophets had to be grounded in joy. This was necessary because their mission was to gaze into and through the world, understanding events from the point of view of God's concern for the human enterprise. From this point of view, they could speak of the Divine vision.[20] They could, as our Hasidic friend said using the words spoken by God to the greatest prophet, Moses, describe what had to be done to "make a dwelling place for God" in this world.

Can we plan for and develop prophets today? In ancient times, it seems that visionaries simply emerged, almost as though the pressure of the times made them bubble up to the surface, articulating what everyone needed and no one else could say. Even in our own time, visionaries seem to have popped out of nowhere, declaring like Dr. King, "I have a dream!" In other eras, societies have lived on hope for a new visionary, searching for the Messiah and wishing "if only he would come," but nothing happened.

Decades of work by historians and anthropologists have shown that "messianic" individuals were one among many experiments in new "models of man." We also know that the apparently random appearances of prophets in ancient times were often grounded in schools of prophecy, with their own meditative techniques. The conditions for and the development of prophets and visionaries were likely neither random or miraculous. I believe we are now, tentatively, able to elucidate the relevant processes more consciously, and to build them into our personal and communal development.

Prophets and sages and mystics emerged from intense spiritual communities, and, as leaders, transcended their immediate community to sharpen the vision. In our time, as we develop a greater ability to share a felt reality, we can work in groups much more effectively so that prophecy will arise not just from one but from many.[21] The details of spiritual group development are beyond the scope of this paper. The main principles are (1) the recognition that each of us is inter-included in everyone else, so each holds part of the vision, and each is a "persuader" of all; and (2) spiritual practice that develops listening, empathy, and intuition for relating to others. Then our groups can hold forth their part of the larger vision, with the hope of each contributing to all.

The importance of renewing our vision cannot be overestimated. "Making a dwelling place for God" in this world has too often been translated into building institutions rather than portable sanctuaries for holiness. Once built, each institution becomes a historic preservation site that no one can modify. None of the light from other sources can penetrate, and eventually the light that inspired the original development dims. But this is in contradiction to God's work. God, according to the Jewish prayer book as well as process philosophy, is continually creating the world: "In His goodness He renews every day continuously the work of creation." Making God comfortable in a world in which God is continually offering new options is not easy; there's a lot of news to keep up with. But that is precisely why we must be open, expansive, and inter-inclusive. Our collective prophetic voice, speaking from its place at the edge of the advancing universe, is the only hope for inspiring a new model of being human. "Would that all the Lord's people were prophets and the Lord would put his Spirit on them!" exclaimed Moses (Numbers 11:29).

Here, then, is the question for each of our religious communities in this post-9/11 world: Who wants to build a world where Divine love, order, and creativity are welcome? Who wants to be part of a group that will, in the name of love, hold themselves to impeccability of ethics and continuous rededication to higher values? Who wants to study and learn on a level that demands clarity of thought and openness of mind, so that light can enter, even from unexpected places? Who wants to commit to the joy and discipline of spiritual practice, practicing the new measure of humanity? Who wants to live in a new world—a small one at first, but expanding as new visions penetrate our dense reality? And to those who answer "I do!", ask them to take the following vows:

I am willing to abandon dualistic and polarized thinking;

I am willing to stop arguing to prove myself right;

I am willing to abandon coercion and manipulation; to establish the ethic of a new humanity;

I am willing to scrutinize my beliefs to make sure they are aligned with the highest ideals, and throw away anything that isn't;

I am willing to use reason to examine evidence but not to rationalize;

I am willing to embrace a bigger picture of reality than I have ever imagined before, to liberate the intellect of a new humanity;

I am willing to learn to listen deeply, without agendas;

I am willing to let myself intuit the larger whole in which we all participate;

I am willing to learn to feel with a distant sufferer as much as I do my own child, and about my cranky neighbor as much as a distant sufferer, to expand the heart of a new humanity.

Power and Love

Ultimately, those who would manipulate us through indirect power—bombs and guns, oil and uranium, torture and terror—will succeed only in creating resistance that will eventually overthrow them. Ultimately, says Jewish tradition, God's purposes and designs will win out (and every blade of grass will be enlightened), for persuasive power, with its sweet and gentle tugging at our heartstrings, is the greatest power of all.

Yet Jewish thought insists that human beings have an important role to play; we can hurry things along, at the very least. The Zohar proclaims that God awaits the "arousal from below" to instigate Divine desire, and the Hasidic masters tell us that God will "obey" a saintly person's "decree."

Our power is limited only by our willingness to share it. We began our analysis by saying that the management and sharing of power is a crucial issue in the post-9/11 world. We followed that line of thinking into the Jewish mystical tradition, which observes that a major flaw in creation resulted from the lack of ability to share power and powers. We pointed out further that any kind of influence that is not generated from a shared prehension of ideals has the potential to be manipulative and coercive. Truly ethical behavior, therefore, must be rooted in empathy and in visions developed in common. This in turn led us back to our own communities, where we need to begin the sharing of power, of ideals, of hearts.

Ultimately, we cannot function as healthy human beings unless we do this. Rabbi Isaac Luria was correct: unless the vessels are open and flowing, exchanging their powers with one another, they shatter. Or, to paraphrase Abraham Joshua Heschel, unless a person becomes more than human, s/he is less than human. After 9/11, we are challenged to open ourselves to yet broader expanses of human and Divine experience, even as we mourn the continued existence of that which is repulsive and destructive. But only when we open to the whole span of experience available to us, can we become truly Human, as we are meant to be.

9

9/11 AND AMERICAN EMPIRE: SOME JEWISH QUESTIONS & ANSWERS

Roger S. Gottlieb

You shall not oppress your neighbor nor rob them. You shall not stand idle while your neighbor bleeds.
—Lev. 19:13, 16

We are Israel, Adonai, when we proclaim You the God of freedom, as did our ancestors on the shores of the sea.
—Rabbi Harvey Fields, 1965, after participating in the Montgomery civil rights march

You shall destroy all the peoples that the Lord your God delivers to you, showing them no pity... you shall obliterate their name from under the heavens: no man shall stand up to you, until you have wiped them out.
—Deut. 7:16, 24

WE HAVE BEEN TOLD THAT THE COORDINATED TERRORIST ATTACK OF 9/11 is the defining event of our time.[1] Our collective sorrow for the thousands of innocent victims and their families, and our legitimate rage at this terrible violation of basic human decency, has been channeled into support for a new foreign policy doctrine that justifies preemptive American military action anytime our government suspects a threat to national security—and into a "clash of civilizations" in which the US and its allies represent freedom, democracy, goodness, and God's will. Our enemy, we have been told by the Bush regime, is the very embodiment of evil, seeking to destroy by any means necessary the very foundations of democratic civilization. But since our enemies are not rooted in any particular country, instead organized in small, disconnected splinter cells, they cannot be defeated in national war. Therefore, lest the terrorists win, we are obligated to wage permanent war on a number of fronts.

On the other side of this bitter struggle, violent Islamic fundamentalism has its own reasons for endless conflict. Its leaders cite the invasion of Iraq, US threats to Arab national autonomy in the Middle East and assaults on Muslims throughout the world, military aid to Israel (which has no right to exist), complicity in hundreds of thousands of deaths from sanctions against Iraq, and the export of a godless, licentious culture that conflicts with Muslim civilization. To those Muslims unimpressed by what the US says of itself, "fighting for democratic values" simply masks the pursuit of oil justified by hypocritical moralizing. Violent Muslim fundamentalists, suicide bombers, and terrorists also believe that God is on their side, and they too see themselves in a fight to the death.[2]

As an American, a Jew, a human being, and a leftist, I stand in opposition to and cannot support either of these dark antagonists.

For a start, I view the US account of its present foreign policy in the historical context of countless other justifications of an aggressive anti-democratic foreign policy. From the Spanish-American war to anti-democratic interventions in Latin America and the Middle East, our policies have typically tended toward the maintenance and expansion of a militarily, economically, and culturally hegemonic system of global capitalism. Our vaunted love of democracy has not kept us from supporting dictators—as we supported Saddam Hussein. Our opposition to terrorism has not kept us from training and arming them—as we did with Osama bin Laden. Our embrace of democracy at home has often coexisted with a brutal, unprincipled foreign policy. At present, the American empire's enormous wealth and power are matched by an unprecedented destructiveness. The environmental consequences of global capitalist expansion alone are responsible for millions of deaths, widespread poverty, long-term decline in environmental health, and the fastest and largest extinction of species of the last 70 million years.[3] We also find increased gaps between rich and poor, genocide of indigenous peoples, and a catastrophically irresponsible waste of money on armaments and addictive consumerism.[4]

Yet in the conflict between the United States and violent Islamic fundamentalism, we face an adversary that is a grave threat to a just and humane society.[5] From Iran to Pakistan, al-Qaeda to Muslim guerillas in Algeria, this movement has been fiercely committed to turning back the clock on democracy, women's rights, distinctions between church and state, and any kind of religious ecumenism—and will stop at nothing to accomplish its ends. Just as American empire is, I believe, a profound threat to human well-being, so is radical Islam's stated goal of theocratic world domination and willingness to murder anyone designated as an enemy, including Muslims of a different stripe. Its psychotic anti-Semitism conjures up terrifying images of Nazism reborn.

It seems we are confronted with two fiercely opposing forces, each of which has what it firmly believes are legitimate reasons to fear and hate the other. While this battle rages, concerns with poverty, ecology, moral development, human rights, and human fulfillment will be pushed (at best) to the back burner. If this conflict is to define our times, we face bleak prospects indeed.

How can reasonable, decent, and well-meaning Jews, Christians, and Muslims respond?

My first thought is that perhaps we really have nothing to say, and that saying nothing would be the most powerful and authentic response. Refusing to take sides, to join in the cacophony of self-righteousness and hate, implying that we will not be part of the madness even to the point of making what should be devastatingly obvious criticisms of both sides' addiction to violence, inability to empathize, naked justifications for capitalism, theocratic male power, and inexcusable waste of resources.

As attractive as this alternative might be, of course we cannot take it. If nothing else, we are American citizens: our tax dollars support the muscle behind American empire and our standards of living benefit from it. As Christians and Jews we must say what it means to be attacked for our religion. If we are devout Muslims we must say what we think about these actions done in our name. Like it or not, silence often appears as tacit consent. If our faiths cannot tell us what to say about terrorism and empire, of what use are they?

When asked about her view of the Israeli–Palestinian conflict, my teenage daughter Anna, cutting through decades of violence and hundreds of thousands of pages of analysis, said only, "It's a shame, just a damn shame."

While we will move beyond Anna's painfully concise judgment, it is perhaps the best place to start. For like the Israeli–Palestinian conflict, the conflict between global capitalism and Islamic fundamentalism is also a terrible shame. As religious people we should not shy away from the obvious, since in a complex time the obvious, as necessary as it is, may be lost. Perhaps then we should begin not with analysis and outrage, programs and calls to action, but with a clear expression of the deep grief that, I suspect, haunts us all. The lives lost on 9/11— including those of the murderers—were a terrible waste. Each person who died began life in innocence, each had unique gifts that could have been used to make life better for the earth community. And what the American empire is doing—with the cooperation and support of economic and military elites in the rest of the world—is also a great tragedy. Religion, at least as I understand it, must help us mourn all these losses.

Now we must get into the messy details, find the demons there, and try to root at least some of them out.

I will do my part of that enormous task as a Jew, one whose Jewishness has been shaped by (and which has shaped) radical politics, spiritual seeking, and ecological concern. The specifically Jewish resources I can call on to help me include theological writings from Genesis to Elie Wiesel, to be sure, but also what might be called Jewish historical experience and distinct (though certainly not in all ways unique) sensibility. Exile, homelessness, persecution, and newborn nationalism have formed Jewishness as much as any tractate of the Talmud. These factors have led to a perplexing two-sided sensibility of empathy for victims and fear of annihilation; a universally oriented perspective that seeks the coming of the messianic age for everyone on earth; a constricted self-protection that believes that history has made it clear we can only trust ourselves; and a commitment to compassion for human weakness and a sense that absolute evil must be opposed with everything we have.

Defined in this way, what can I say as a Jew about 9/11 and American empire, something that is not simply a repeat of secular political and moral analysis? What does being Jewish help me to say that I might not be able to say otherwise?

To begin, for me Judaism is about a direct confrontation with moral responsibility. God's challenge to the Israelites is all too clear on this point: "This day I call heaven and earth as witnesses against you that I have set before you life and death, blessings and curses. Now choose life, so that you and your children may live" (Deut. 30:19). For Judaism (as I suspect for Christianity and Islam as well), the bedrock of moral life is the human capacity to ally with life or death, blessings or curses. It is not, as for instance it is for Buddhism or Plato, about knowledge.[6] We can know everything there is to know and still do the wrong thing—that is what moral choice means.

But this element of moral choice is not simply about taking responsibility for challenging other people's moral failings—to stand up to US foreign policy, the machinations of the global ruling class, or religious fanatics—but to be critical of oneself: both individually and as a group. From Isaiah's ringing denunciation of Jewish spiritual hypocrisy[7] to the traditional idea that a Jew is supposed to spend more than a month in moral self-examination before he or she prays for forgiveness on the Day of Atonement, Jews are reminded that there is no guarantee that Jews will be better than anyone else, or that the Covenant removes us from the possibility of moral failure. The Covenant, rather, places an increased responsibility on us, without ever promising that we will keep it (in fact, rather, with frequent warnings that we won't!).

Despite the fact that the exodus from Egypt is a central historical moment for the Torah, in a paradoxical moral teaching, the Torah sees Egyptians and Jews as to some extent interchangeable. To put it another way: it is empathetically motivated moral conduct ("Always remember that you were slaves in Egypt" is a frequent justification for a moral rule) that makes one a Jew rather than an Egyptian, and not simply the vagaries of birth. That is why the same adverb used to describe the Egyptian treatment of the Jews ("The Egyptians ruthlessly imposed upon the Israelites" [Exodus 1:13]) is employed in laws instructing Jews how to treat poverty-stricken Jewish workers ("You shall not rule over him ruthlessly..." [Lev. 25:43]). The Exodus narrative defines two fundamental ethical roles—that of slave and that of master. But once the yoke has been removed from his neck, anyone can then act like a master; and once masters give up their oppressive role, they must be treated fairly: "You shall not abhor an Egyptian, for you were a stranger in his land" (Deut. 23:8).

In that spirit, and before I confront other critically important concerns, I as a Jew must first ask: What is there from my tradition that contributes to our tragic global calamities?[8]

The answer is neither hard to find nor easy to take. There is a strain of self-righteous violence that runs through Judaism from the earliest texts to the present day, a celebration of our physical and cultural triumph over those who threaten us or who simply stand in our way. From Moses' instructions at the end of Deuteronomy to kill the Canaanites and destroy their holy places to the grisly depictions of Israelite triumph in Joshua to the West Bank settlers who (with tacit or overt support from "religious" authorities) burn down olive groves and terrorize Palestinians, this strain darkens the moral radiance of my tradition. If as a Jew I can take pride in the Jewish invention of the Sabbath, longstanding concern with personal morality and social justice, and visionary spiritual insights, I must be willing to confront the dark side of Judaism as well.

The first specifically Jewish response to "9/11 and American empire" then, is not to point the finger at George W. Bush, Dick Cheney, Halliburton, or Osama bin Laden, but to examine ourselves and see to what extent some part of our tradition may be part of what is wrong, to use our own tradition in order to criticize our own tradition.[9] Cautiously, but honestly, we need to ask: How much does Jewish tradition contribute to the goal of annihilating the enemy, or to seeing whole groups as less worthy of life or God's love than ourselves, or of seeing ourselves as having a special prerogative to take what we want? Does the US's presumption that it has a seemingly natural right to Middle East oil echo in some way the biblical guarantee that the Jews get the Promised Land, whatever the other inhabitants of the area might have to say about it? Does al-Qaeda's certainty of God's blessing on violent conquest reflect some of Islam's roots in the books of Joshua or Judges? Can such roots also be found mirrored in the assumptions of the religious right that the US has a unique relation with God—and thus unique prerogatives in world politics? Such questions may be especially poignant for a Jew, since as the oldest of the Abrahamic faiths we may have set the tone for what followed. Yet as our religious offspring have long reached cultural adulthood, they must take responsibility for what they have done with the original teaching. Christian-justified colonialist genocides and mullah-sanctioned Islamic wars are the responsibility of

Christians and Muslims. Thus this Jewish question is one that Christians and Muslims need to put to themselves as well. All of us need to know if we are carrying within ourselves or our institutions that part of the Abrahamic legacy that celebrates collective violence.

If there are, as Rabbi Michael Lerner has said, "two voices in Torah"[10]—one that repeats a message of violent conflict and oppression and one that teaches care, humility, and compassion—it is up to us to separate those voices out and join our own words and actions with one rather than the other. And this includes speaking up in our own religious communities when fear or a false sense of entitlement prompts us to unthinkingly celebrate our own power and our triumph over the Other. It is at this point that we must remember that all human beings are made in the image of God, that part of what that sense of human identity means is that we are to be God's representatives on earth,[11] and that the God we seek to represent offers the following self-description: "The LORD, the LORD, the compassionate and gracious God, slow to anger, abounding in love and faithfulness, maintaining love to thousands, and forgiving wickedness, rebellion and sin" (Exodus 34:6–7).

At this point another Jew might say that if the Jewish experience has taught us anything, it is that sometimes the Other does take on a face that we cannot recognize, that no longer calls to us or engages us morally, but is simply the face of death—of them or of us.[12] There are Pharaohs—and Hitlers—in this world. Individuals, institutions, and even whole societies can be lost to morality, respect for life, and even sanity. In such cases, as in that of the Amalekites who attacked the Israelites from the rear after the escape from Egypt, compassion is replaced with a relentless, implacable opposition. When confronted in this way, the biblical call to care for the "widow, the stranger and the orphan," the Kabbalistic notion that each person is a divine spark who can only be unified with God after we repair the world, the spiritual gentleness that pervades Hasidic spiritual writing—all these must be suspended.

It is only with the deepest fear and trembling that we can decide how to apply these two mutually exclusive perspectives to our current dilemma. Are either—or both—al-Qaeda and American empire the contemporary analogues to Pharoah or to Hitler, or to some soulless bureaucratic ecocidal nightmare that can be anticipated only by an act of darkest imagination? Can the terrorist be reasoned with or appealed to? Can the World Bank or Exxon or Donald Rumsfeld or Wall Street? It is here that we need to remember the end of God's self-description cited above: "Yet God does not leave the guilty unpunished; God punishes the children and their children for the sins of the fathers to the third and fourth generation." And as long as God is silent, as God has been for so long, it may in fact be up to us to punish the guilty, to "blot out the memory of Amalek from under heaven" (Exodus 17:14).

Yet once again we must think—what would it mean to "blot out" the terrorist networks, since these networks are a fairly predictable outcome of a certain set of economic, social, cultural, and psychological conditions? What would it mean to "punish the guilty" for American empire, since "the guilty" includes literally millions of people whose actions are directly or tacitly condoned by hundreds of millions of other people in democratic nations? American empire and global terrorism stem from collective social processes, for example the evolution of global capitalism, world trade relations, the commodification of human relationships, failed modernizations, and destabilized traditional societies. Therefore we cannot "blot out" either side of the conflict at hand by defeating some small group.

How then are we to punish the guilty when responsibility is so widely shared?

Must we side with either al-Qaeda or the US government? In the face of so much reckless hate, must we put aside our quarrels with our leaders and support the "war against terror"? Or shall we say that after decades of murderous intervention throughout the world, the US is getting, if not what it deserves, at least what it should have expected? If both sides seem so evil, must we simply side with the greater against the lesser and hope that eventually, when number one is defeated, we can get around to number two?

At the risk of seeming wishy-washy, naive, unrealistic, or a fence-straddler, I will not side with either. And, I believe, at least some of Jewish tradition would take this stand with me. For Judaism is above all a religion of this earth. Whatever promises of a messiah are present in the tradition, whatever ideas of the resurrection of the actual bodies we have now, the Covenant between God and the patriarchs and Moses concerned continuity in historical time: a land of their own and a people as numerous as the stars in the sky. As a Jew then, I believe that my duty to the earth is to live as decent and human a life as I can, and that to do so I cannot allow the moral alternatives to be defined by others. Thus I refuse to choose between George W. and Osama, between the mad fanaticisms of the religious fundamentalists and soulless brutality of the globalizers.

Fortunately, this response also makes a kind of strategic sense. For if the only antagonists really were George W. and Osama, then it might make sense to support one over the other, to join in the patriarchal zero-sum game of might makes right, winner takes all, and "I'm holy—you're evil." If only one of these two individuals were going to run the world, then we would have to side with one or the other.

But neither the US president nor the top terrorist do anything by themselves. Everything they undertake depends on complex networks of immediate associates, advisors, generals, lieutenants, and foot soldiers; not to mention a much wider population of taxpayers, media support, and sympathetic popular opinion. No one can defeat the US militarily. Nor, given its decentralized and far-flung membership, can anyone defeat al-Qaeda. The task, then, is not our own jihad against either American imperialism or Islamic fundamentalism, aiming for some decisive victory. Rather, the only realistic plan is to try to lessen popular support for them—to change the minds of those who think either of these groups have the right ideas about what social life should be like.

If we are not about to overthrow the government and institute the messianic age (or at least a global society with a modicum of rationality and decency) through a great apocalyptic battle in which all the evildoers are blotted out, what is to be done?

To begin with, I think it is our continuing duty to reclaim, or at least contest, the public meaning of religion. This is a struggle with two fronts. On the one hand, we need to oppose the notion that religion—in the broad sense of large-scale frameworks of meaning and value—can ever be excluded from public life. Every time we decide to protect an endangered species rather than develop one more wetland into a mall, or define sex education as about mechanics rather than the sacredness of life force, or commit resources to the military over care for the elderly, we are making collective choices that necessarily depend on value perspectives for which there is no ultimately rational justification. The secular myth that seeking more money is rational while serving God is just a matter of (irrational) faith is itself just an ideological justification for one way of life, one framework of values, over another. While ministers should not have political power because of their religious status, and governments should not actively support the Episcopal Church over Quakers, our laws, policies, and budgets will always embody somebody's version of the central values that should guide human life.

Our second front, therefore, is to say what we think those values should be, and in so doing wrest the meaning of religion from those who would identify it with patriarchal, anthropocentric capitalism or patriarchal, anthropocentric fundamentalism. It is much less important to debate the place of religion in public life— whether we should have a "Christmas tree" or a "holiday tree"—than it is to challenge those who would reduce Christianity to having the clerk say "Merry Christmas" as he hands you your Visa card back, or who believe that religious passion entails crushing the unbelievers. If religion is central to our lives, and if we think society should be guided by at least some of its values, let us say how and why.

To take one example in the Jewish case: If the Talmud teaches reconciliation, humility, and peacefulness (and it does) or the great twentieth-century Jewish teachers Abraham Heschel, Martin Buber, and Arthur Waskow have pointed toward a respectful relation between Arabs and Jews, then it is the obligation of Jews who follow these Jewish teachings to make their case to other Jews, the American public, the US government, and Israel. Clearly the vicious Jew-haters who populate much of the terrorist world will not be convinced by anything we say or indeed by any change in Israeli policy whatsoever—but what about those who are not so fanatical? What about the Muslims who may be sympathetic to al-Qaeda precisely because they believe that US support of Israel would cheerfully consign the Palestinians to national oblivion forever? What about those who might well change their minds about Israel if Israel changed some of its policies?

In short, part of a religious reaction to the joint threats of terrorism and globalization is to offer a third alternative, in which peace, rational ecological policies, human rights, and a reasonable distribution of wealth and respect take a leading place. There is no doubt, I believe, that just as there are within all three major Western religions real justifications for narrow and violent group self-interest, there is also justification for the opposite. If we are picking and choosing from the tradition to find this justification, so are, for their part, the fundamentalists—whatever they may say about how orthodox they are.

We are different from them, it must be stressed, not because we are tolerant and they are not. It is, rather, because we are committed to different values and beliefs than they are. For instance, I personally do not care how anyone else prays to and talks about God (or doesn't), but I am not willing to compromise one bit on such issues as human rights, women's liberation, and aggressive militarism. If fundamentalists are committed to preserving patriarchal power, or the Defense Department to treating the interests of US citizens as naturally more important than those of the rest of the world, we will—both effectively and humanely, I hope—oppose them. If they think the way to make the world safe is through violence, we would rather actually sit down and talk things over. If they believe that religion should be imposed, we think a religion imposed has already admitted its own spiritual bankruptcy.

In short, as a (particular kind of) Jew I embrace a comprehensive and very particular moral and political vision. If this vision is informed by the history of socialist, feminist, and ecological movements, that does not make it any less Jewish. The idea that Leviticus or the Talmud could have all the answers on how to do God's work on earth in the twenty-first century makes about as much sense as thinking Isaiah could also tell us how to build the Rebbe's computer. And in any case, it is often extremely difficult to tell where religious ideas leave off and secular ones begin. Marx's vision of communism, as many have observed, has affinities with Jewish messianism. Claims to equal rights for all, others argue, make sense in a culture formed by the idea that everyone is made in the image of God.[13] Contemporary liberal Judaism certainly did not get the idea of women's liberation or environmentalism from within the Jewish tradition, though it can find support for both ideas once it has been taught to do so by feminists and environmentalists.[14] Certain forms of religion, no less than certain political movements, offer visions of a social life fundamentally altered in the direction of certain comprehensive and sweeping value commitments. Both religion and politics can be ways of making—and remaking—the world. It is not surprising, then, that at times their injunctions should coincide or their ideas should shape each other.[15]

Equally important to articulating a vision for social life that accepts neither the spiritless attachment to the "bottom line" nor a murderous pretension to holiness is actually to embody an alternate set of values. That is, as spiritually oriented religious people we should be able to demonstrate that we have something to offer that neither the terrorists nor the globalizers do.

First on the list, and in some ways in these days the most difficult, is to live out the idea that, as Anne Frank said, "Despite everything, I still believe that people are good at heart." While anyone who is not depressed these days probably hasn't been reading the newspaper, while a kind of madness seems to have swept the globe, if a teenager hiding in an attic to avoid genocide can have some hope for human beings, we can too.

As a Jew, I will maintain this hope (if I can!) without denial, joining my choice to communicate, to avoid demonization, and to openness to the Other with the knowledge that some people are not—or at least no longer—good at heart. As a Jew I cannot forget Hitler or Pharaoh and that while being "good at heart" is something we all come in with, we also develop, along the way, the capacity to become ruthless, morally blind, and murderous.

Embodying hope for humanity while never losing sight of our collective evil gives way to another paradox within which we must live. On the one hand, as Jews we have been told that while the world God created is "very good" (Genesis 1), it is nevertheless unfinished and imperfect. Humans therefore have been given the task of *tikkun olam*—repair and healing of the world. Translated into secular terms by generations of Jewish social activists, this has meant large-scale attempts—some clearly futile and some not—for large-scale social change. On the other hand, not unlike some of the teachings in other traditions,[16] we are also told in the Talmud that "We are not expected to finish the work" (though we are also expected to do some of it) and that "To save one person is to save the world."

I interpret this to mean that we must seek to heal the world's brokenness without desperation, fanaticism, or despair. We must do the work having no sense of whether or not we will succeed, or even make a dent in the evil we confront. We need to act without "attachment to results"—that is, without an ego-bound demand that we accomplish what we think is right. Ultimately, the world is much too large, complicated, and confusing for us to ever be certain that we have done so. Ultimately all we can control is our own effort and commitment.

Beyond embodying an emotional, spiritual, and political capacity to tolerate the paradox of compassionate concern in a world in which evil is all too real, we need to keep hope alive by manifesting our own capacity for joy. The world, as the eighteenth-century mystical founder of Hasidic Judaism put it, is "filled with miracles."[17] Because of these miracles—a bird in flight, a child's laughter, a comforting hand—it is a "mitzvah" (a religious obligation), as another Hasidic rebbe put it, "always to be joyful."[18] The history of Jewish persecution makes it fairly easy for us to attune to the world's pain. Even as disaffected a Jew as Woody Allen could remark that "the news that someone is starving somewhere could ruin my dinner." It is perhaps less easy for us to keep the miracles in mind and show some joy. Yet for Jews in particular, and—I believe—for any serious Christian or Muslim, it is to this that we are called: to bear witness to the world's suffering, to resist it as we can, and still to let everyone know that such witness does not exclude delight.

Indeed I believe that only in the context of awareness and resistance is real joy even possible, for otherwise we will be part of the evil or spend untold psychic energies in avoiding and denying it.[19] If all this sounds almost impossibly hard, it is. But then at the very least it gives us a spiritual task, against which we can measure ourselves, for a lifetime.

Any reader familiar with religious literature may at this point wonder: "There is nothing new here, and hasn't 9/11 changed everything?" My answer, in three words, is simple: yes and no. On the one hand, we live in a new political terrain, which includes both the worldwide terrorist network capable of such mad violence and the US government's mobilization, deceptions, and threats to our civic liberties. To cope with this situation requires a deep awareness of historically unprecedented threats, powers, and possibilities.

At the same time, however, I don't think we can really remember a time without moral struggle, resistance to evil, and the task of remaining faithful to a nearly impossible moral and spiritual vision. It is in that task that we find the basis of a meaningful, and even at times joyful, life. And nothing that the terrorists of whatever religion or nation can do will ever take that away.[20]

10

WHAT NEXT? WILL IT MAKE A DIFFERENCE IF WE SUCCEED IN EXPOSING 9/11 AS A FRAUD?

Rabbi Michael Lerner

I AM AN AGNOSTIC ON THE QUESTION OF WHAT HAPPENED ON 9/11. AS other authors in this collection have shown, there are huge holes in the official story and contradictions that suggest that we do not know the whole story.

I would not be surprised to learn that some branch of our government conspired either actively to promote or passively to allow the attack on 9/11. For those who watched the reactionary political uses made of this tragedy, it's easy to conjure up a variety of possible conspiratorial motives that would have led the president, the vice president, or some branch of the armed forces or CIA or FBI or other "security" forces to have passively or actively participated in a plot to re-credit militarism and war. We've learned enough about the subsequent ways that the Bush administration lied to the American public to no longer be shocked if there had been some active involvement by them in these deeds.

Neither would I be surprised if, when all the archives were opened and all the communications revealed, it turned out that there was some other non-conspiratorial explanation for elements of the story that currently seem to make no sense. I'm not an expert in physics or chemistry and am in no position to devise such explanations, but I wouldn't be surprised if someone could do so.

I am not, however, much of a fan of a politics that concentrates on conspiracy theories, even when there are real conspiracies. At one point in my life I thought that real conspiracies were a left-wing fantasy, and that sophisticated Marxists and other social theorists would not have reason to want to acknowledge the existence of such conspiracies against the left or against anyone else. But in 1970, I was one of the "Seattle Seven" indicted in a federal trial for "conspiracy and using the facilities of interstate commerce with the intent of inciting to riot," because of a demonstration I had organized to oppose the Vietnam war and support black liberation, which turned violent after police attacked the demonstrators. I soon learned that my organization, the Seattle Liberation Front, was totally infiltrated by police agents. Indeed, many of those most vociferous in denouncing me and other leaders for being "too timid" were actually paid FBI informants or members of various law enforcement agencies. When one such agent changed his mind and began to reveal his story of having been solicited by the FBI to try to engage us in violence that would have led to some of us being killed, I understood that conspiracies do sometimes happen—paid for by the US government.

But I also learned another lesson at the time: a movement is not always helped by putting a focus on government conspiracies. That focus leads people to believe that the major problems we face are those generated by evil people in powerful positions, not on something more systemic.

True, when we exposed Nixon on Watergate we managed to get him pushed out of office. But in so doing we also managed to validate the perception of many that he was the problem and that once he was gone, America could return to a new age of goodness, and politics could be safe in the hands of the politicians. "The system worked," we were told, and most people believed it.

In retrospect, I suspect that the focus on Nixon's conspiracy undermined our capacity to educate people to a far more important element in our society: the elites of wealth and power and their attempts to ensure American corporate dominance of the global markets, sometimes using force. While conspiracies were real under Nixon (I should know—I ended up in a federal penitentiary, not for the original charges but for the "contempt of court" charge leveled against me and co-defendants during the Seattle Seven trial), the focus on Watergate actually freed the ruling elites from having to give an account of how they— including the mainstream of the Democratic Party—had bought into assumptions about the world that led us into the Vietnam war.

I'm afraid that the focus on 9/11 conspiracies could have the same effect in American politics, even if the authors in this collection are, in the context of their discussions of 9/11, attempting a deeper critique. Democrats who share many of the same militaristic assumptions about the world as their Republican colleagues could easily use the exposures that may be produced in this process to show that there were a few evil or perverted people at the top of the Republican hierarchy, that Democrats shouldn't have been so trusting, but after all they had no reason to believe in foul play, and that in any event it is they who will bring the bad guys to justice (if that ever happens). It could play out like this: a reaffirmation of liberalism with all its limitations and willingness to support the militarist economy and global expansionism. But this result is not inevitable—if we prepare ourselves to think not only of how to expose the lies, but also how to frame the politics so that the systemic problems are exposed.

The major challenge facing those of us who want peace today is not only to show that there was a conspiracy against peace by some part of the government, but to uncover the underlying ideological consensus that leads people in both parties, including many who would never have dreamed of being part of any conspiracy, nevertheless to believe that violence and war are the means by which to achieve a world of peace.

In my new book, *The Left Hand of God: Taking Back Our Country from the Religious Right*, I present a Spiritual Covenant with Americans that provides a very different way to challenge the power of war- and violence-oriented ideologies. Instead of showing the evil intents of those who propose such ideologies, I provide an account of the fears that make those worldviews plausible to millions of Americans and then present an alternative, spiritually-based worldview that provides a coherent alternative. I argue for a strategy of generosity that would commit the US to lead the G8 countries to use five percent of the gross domestic product of each of those countries every year for the next twenty years, starting with the US, to eliminate global poverty, homelessness, hunger, inadequate education, and inadequate healthcare, and to repair the damage done to the global environment by 150 years of irresponsible forms of industrialization. Winning support for this kind of thinking requires a very different kind of argument and focus than asking whether the towers could have fallen as a result of strikes by airplanes.

One could argue that there is room for both conversations, and there is. In fact, the kind of psychic trauma that would happen were the charges of intentional involvement in 9/11 by the president, vice president, other high office holders, or our security apparatus ever proved in a court of law would almost certainly open up political space for a serious discussion of the kinds of radical changes I'm suggesting, especially regarding our approach to foreign policy and homeland security. Indeed, people might be open to establishing much more forceful checks and balances on the imperial presidency, reaffirming and even strengthening civil liberties protections that have been undermined by the PATRIOT Act and other policies of the Bush administration, securing democratic forms by eliminating the electoral college and establishing instant-runoff voting and fully publicly financed elections that forbid any direct or indirect contributions or support for campaigns or the parties that run them, establishing firm public control of electronic voting and of lobbying to ensure that money plays no role directly or indirectly in the process, and other measures to reclaim the democracy that has eroded since 9/11.

These are important changes that could be won if 9/11 lies are exposed, and for that reason I salute the people in this collection of articles who are doing an amazing job of examining what may prove to be one of the most perverse conspiracies in the history of democratic governments.

But my own experience in American politics leads me to believe that those who wish to expose the 9/11 conspiracy must simultaneously provide an alternative framework that includes the Spiritual Covenant and the specific suggestions for how to repair the damage done by these crimes, or else risk the debate being defined by media that are more concerned with proving the viability of the system than they are with changing it. They will certainly try to frame any future revelations within the conceptual arena of "see, the system is working to expose its own distortions" and to berate those who are seeking to "use this terrible tragedy for their own ends." We risk throwing one tyrant out of office only to find that the system of tyranny has actually survived and even been strengthened in the process. That is why the time is now, even as the courageous writers in this volume are still trying to obtain a forum for this important public discussion, for others of us to be developing a positive vision of what to do next once the details of what happened are exposed and those involved are being brought to trial. When that occurs, we must already be insisting on a broader response, and have ready our own clear and compelling vision of the kind of repair our society needs to prevent similar crimes in the future. Then we will have at least a slight chance of preventing the corporate media from turning this important discussion into another extravaganza that does more to increase viewership and readership than it does to spark a fundamental transformation that could preserve and enhance American democracy, and turn us from an empire of domination and fear to a force for kindness and genuine caring for all people on the planet.

11

INTERPRETING THE UNSPEAKABLE: THE MYTH OF 9/11

Kevin Barrett

9/11 IS MYTH, NOT HISTORY.

This suggestion will at first sound absurd. Did not actual events, terrible events, really happen on that day? Did not many people really die? Did the events of 9/11 not alter the course of history?

Certainly the awful destruction and suffering on that day were all too real. But the result was not to make or alter history, but to annihilate it and replace it with myth. Since September 11, 2001, we have been living after "the end of history"—though a rather different end from the one predicted by the repentant ex-neocon Fukuyama.[1]

History, like any other human construct, is not a given. Like myth, religion, ideology, and identity, history is an interpretive grid imposed upon events. More than other such constructs, history depends upon the skeptical sifting and winnowing of evidence to construct a believable narrative about the past. It is not simply a matter of "public presumptions... beliefs thought to be true... shared in common within the relevant political community" as Philip Zelikow, self-styled expert on the creation and maintenance of public myths, would have it.

Years before 9/11, Zelikow evinced an astoundingly prescient fascination with a coming "watershed event" of "catastrophic terrorism" that would "like Pearl Harbor... divide our past and future into a before and after."[2] Such were the credentials that brought him the position of Royal Mythographer and main author of *The 9/11 Commission Report*. One wonders, given the evidence that 9/11 was a hoax scripted to become a Zelikow-style "public myth," whether someone with Zelikow's areas of expertise did not write the obviously false "let's roll" heroic mini-myth of Flight 93, and indeed script the explosive demolition of the World Trade Center, without which the New Pearl Harbor would have been

2,000 deaths short of the old one, and manifestly inadequate as a trigger for the war that will not end in our lifetimes.[3]

This fearless and irreverent examination of evidence that separates history from "public myth" has been conspicuously absent from official discourse—journalistic, academic, judicial, and political—surrounding the events of 9/11. Corporate media outlets, in particular, have been gratuitously remiss in their duty to call attention to the embarrassingly abundant source data that undermine the official account of what transpired that day. Academics, who are supposed to be both more reflective and more analytical than journalists, and who are supposed to know their history—including the evidence that most of the wars America has fought have been triggered by contrived "incidents"—have been equally derelict of duty. Politicians, with a few courageous exceptions, have likewise been missing in action. The judicial system, too, has gone AWOL. And the farcically under-funded and under-mandated 9/11 Commission, whose creation the Bush administration frantically struggled for almost two years to prevent, and whose hobbled "investigation" it impeded at every turn, produced a blatantly mendacious narrative that pointedly failed to answer any of the real questions that have been raised. *The 9/11 Commission Report* is myth disguised as history, and its sham "documentation" appears, upon critical examination, as hilariously, insanely fantastical as the mad narrator's footnotes in Nabokov's *Pale Fire*.[4]

What does it mean to call the official account of 9/11 a myth? Why not simply call it a lie? That, of course, has been done. A tremendous amount of research has targeted the many holes in the standard account, and taken as a whole, this research has indeed proved that the official story is a lie.[5] But simply proving the "nineteen Arabs" fantasy a lie is not enough. We need to understand why the lie was told, why it has been so widely believed, how it has functioned historically and culturally, and how it can be annihilated and replaced by a better story. By better I do not simply mean truer or more accurate, but also more life-sustaining, since a true story that is death-dealing rather than life-sustaining is of no use to anyone.

Truth-versus-lies is a simple binary opposition. The richly ambivalent word "myth" takes up where "lie" leaves off. The disciplines contiguous with mythography, including folklore, psychoanalysis, literary criticism, and religious studies, are appropriate tools for the interpretation of 9/11. For that event, as it comes down to us mediated by culture, is less a historical happening than a peculiar intersection of fantastic tales, the sacred, and applied mass depth psychology. The study of myths and legends provides an excellent point of departure for any serious attempt to come to grips with this still-unspeakable object.

Myth and Mythography

Mythography, the study of myths and their meanings, was born out of a secularizing trend in Western universities and intellectual life in general. The word "myth," an ancient Greek term that described, among other things, its own culture's sacred narratives, was taken up by Christians and applied to the sacred narratives that Christians believed to be false, starting with those of the ancient Greeks and Romans. By extension, it came to mean "falsehood," as in "that's just a myth; that character is purely mythical."

In the nineteenth century, more and more European intellectuals came to doubt their own culture's Jewish and Christian sacred narratives, yet shied away from applying the new literary-historical critical approaches developed for other cultures' sacred narratives to their own. By the twentieth century, however, that taboo had been breached, and the Western intelligentsia no longer used its own Jewish and Christian sacred narratives as the touchstone of truth against which the falsity of other cultures' sacred stories could be measured. It has been argued that a new myth of progress, rationalism, and enlightenment had taken the place of the old Jewish and Christian mythology, and that this myth too went largely unquestioned until the rise of postmodern thought in the late twentieth century.

In today's folklore and anthropology departments, the term myth normally refers to a narrative—often a foundational one for a worldview or social order—that is considered both true and sacred by those who use it and believe in it.[6] The discipline of mythography seeks to understand sacred narrative from a perspective that goes beyond the naïve or unconscious acceptance of one's own sacred narrative as the touchstone for the interpretation of all others as something less than truth. How, then, can a religious believer do mythography? The very notion of scripture would seem to put a particular set of sacred narratives on a pedestal, bracket them off, and make them immune to mythographic analysis.

As a Muslim trained in mythography, I have been grappling with this problem for some time. My purpose in discussing it here is to answer the question: How can a believing and practicing Muslim be offering a mythographic analysis of 9/11—or any mythographic analysis of anything, for that matter?[7]

First, it must be said that Islam is an extremely scriptural religion—indeed, the ultimate scriptural religion in the view of Muslims themselves. The whole religion is based on belief that the Qur'an is literally the word of God, as received by the Prophet Muhammad, peace upon him. Scholars have tried to show, with a great deal of success, that the Bible is the product of many authors, which implies that if indeed there is only one God, the Bible must have been written by humans, perhaps in some or all cases under some form of divine inspiration. Such an approach does not work with the Qur'an. There is plainly a single consciousness responsible for the entire Qur'an as we have it today; no reason-able literary critic could assert that some parts of it appear to have been written by one hand, and others by another.[8] So we are left with the choice of imagining the Qur'an to have been authored by a single human author, presumably Muhammad of Mecca (the non-Muslim position) or viewing it as a divine product, as the Qur'an itself asserts.

As a Muslim, I embrace the latter position. I read the Qur'an as the word of God, as it asks to be read. In doing so, do I not undermine my credentials as a student of mythography? Am I not asserting that the Qur'an is the world's one and only genuine sacred narrative, immune from mythographic analysis, while all others are fair game, to be read in light of their confirmation or rejection of Qur'anic positions?

The answer is: yes and no. What I take to be the basic message of the Qur'an is quite straightforward and immune to the usual sorts of mythographic analysis. The Qur'an departs from the whole notion of myth as sacred narrative in part because it isn't really a narrative at all, but a compendium of poetic exhortation studded with narrative fragments that shine with wisdom like gleaming jewels, but which do not in themselves constitute a sacred narrative. (The closest thing Islam has to a sacred narrative is the Sira, or life of Muhammad, peace upon him, which does not really have a single canonical form and which occupies a marginal place in the corpus of Islamic scripture.)

The Qur'an exhorts us to be aware of and submit to the one

God, Lord of the worlds, the transcendent, ineffable, eternal creator, the absolutely Real (all else is relative) whose first two quasi-tangible qualities are mercy and compassion. This exhortation is primary; all the embedded and surrounding narratives are secondary, and, in my view at least, fair game for mythographic analysis. Indeed, the Qur'an comes to correct not just the erroneous myths that stem from human alteration of previous divinely revealed messages, but the whole process of taking a human-authored story for an absolute truth. The process of storytelling is inevitably contaminated (and in another sense enriched) by human desires, which are themselves bound up with the haughty, self-centered human ego. The stories we want to hear, and tell, are those that appeal to our desires and pander to our egos, not those that are good for us. The Qur'an overwhelms us with its magnificent language and offers the "true" versions of some of the earlier revelations that the Bible distorts—"true" in the sense that they are the God-authored ones that are good for us, that take us beyond our own fallible desires and egos.

For me, analyzing narratives from a Muslim point of view is a logical extension of literary studies, which in its classical form also seeks texts that are somehow good for us, such as Shakespeare and Balzac, and rejects those that are not, such as Horatio Alger and Mickey Spillane. The former, it is believed, hold the potential to raise us beyond our dumb brute egos into a realm of freedom and pure contemplation, while the latter feed and freeze those egos into a fixed, bestial, rapacious form. In fact, things are not quite that simple: moral and spiritual effects are produced by text-reader-context interaction, not text in a vacuum. One can read about evil so as to get better at avoiding it. And one can read a perfectly good text and derive corruption from it. (One of the twentieth century's worst writers and human beings, E. Howard Hunt, reportedly bought the rights to *Animal Farm* from Orwell's widow on behalf of the CIA, in order to make sure that any films of the book would be mere anti-Soviet propaganda—and in so doing showed he had learned nothing from Orwell except how to be more Orwellian.)[9]

Literary criticism, like literature itself, is basically moral critique that at its best rises to lofty spiritual heights. The whole modern literary industry is grounded in a debate about Christianity that arose in the nineteenth century, and whether we see literature as a substitute for traditional Christianity (Matthew Arnold and the whole tribe of secularizers), an exhortation to traditional Christianity (C. S. Lewis), or a gesture toward some alternative, estoteric religious vision (Blake and Bloom, symbolist-surrealist-Romantics), Western literature, as presently constituted, is the stepchild of Christianity. This is not necessarily a bad thing, even from a Muslim perspective. Christianity and Islam are quite similar universalized versions of Judaism, and they agree on most key points, with the areas of disagreement mostly being semantic and/or provisional.

Turning back to mythography, a subfield of literary studies and anthropology, we can see a parallel moral and spiritual debate taking place. The explosion of popular interest in myth in the sense of "other people's sacred stories," is symptomatic of a dissatisfied yearning on the part of intellectuals who have lost faith in Christianity.[10] Like the explosion of conversions to Buddhism, interest in New Age alternative spiritualities, and indeed the growing trend toward conversion to Islam, the popularity of such figures as Jung and Campbell shows that mythography is driven and energized by post-Christian culture's need to fill a certain religious void.

It was once thought that students of mythology could be scientific, neutral, and objective in their approach to other people's sacred stories. That naïve epistemology is now almost entirely defunct, replaced by a new paradigm that is sometimes called postmodern, but which extends beyond the bounds of that term to embrace almost all current methodologies, which require, in one form or another, the development of systematic self-awareness on the part of the student so that the mythographic/ethnographic product is framed as a self-conscious dialogue between two worldviews, rather than a monologic description of the other by a privileged observer.[11]

Thus a Muslim doing mythography simply needs to be clear about what that entails, and what assumptions are being brought to bear on the material. My own approach is built on ambivalence: Myths should be celebrated for their richness and beauty and occasional glimmerings of wisdom, while simultaneously deflated and deconstructed as idolatrous fantasies. Any myth that overwhelms its audience and demands to be a focal point of existence, an absolute, a touchstone, is idolatrous. Like anthropomorphized gods, human heroes presented for worship as if they were gods are idols. And idolatry, or *shirk*, is the first sin in Islam. Why? Because idols represent and reinforce unbalanced aspects of the *nafs*, the desiring ego, and turn our natural tendency for worship away from God and toward the self.[12] This is where Joseph Campbell reaches his limits of understanding. Campbell celebrates pagan mythologies and idols, arguing that human beings need to live for something beyond and greater than the self (correct) and that mythic heroes and similar idols offer a way to do that (often incorrect). Certainly such mythic heroes as the prophets of the Judeo-Christian-Islamic tradition, and presumably the thousands of other prophets who have come to other peoples, do offer models for enlightenment. But Campbell ignores the destructive potential of idolatry, evidenced by the cults of human sacrifice that are such a pervasive part of debased "religion" all over the world, as René Girard has persuasively shown.[13] Ultimately Campbell's moral-spiritual vision is blinded by his post-Catholic Romantic idealization of the exotic other, and a parallel rejection of that key dimension of religion, morality, and ethics, of which he was perhaps force-fed too much in Catholic school. His work, like so much of the other spiritual alternatives in American popular as well as academic culture, appeals to those who, for reasons of selfish desire, wish to reject the moral-ethical dimension of their monotheistic heritage.[14]

So let me lay my cards on the table: I am doing mythography as a rational moral critique grounded in the basic precepts of Islam. When I see a myth whose main function is to trigger and legitimize mass human sacrifice—like the myth of 9/11—I feel obliged to deconstruct and denounce it. So much more so in that the myth of 9/11, even more than others, is so transparently a human product, crafted by human hands in order to attain the basest and most illegitimate of human desires. Those who brought us the myth of 9/11 are pursuing what Richard Falk has called the "global domination project."[15] Citing the adage "power tends to corrupt, and absolute power corrupts absolutely," David Ray Griffin points out that the "tends to" in the first half of the phrase disappears in the second, underlining the point that power may conceivably be exercised responsibly while it is merely relative, but when absolute power is attained, the only possible result is absolute corruption.[16] The neo-conservative think tank Project for the New American Century (PNAC), which guides the Bush administration and had sixteen of its members appointed to administration posts, openly called for a "new Pearl Harbor" in September 2000 and boasts that its purpose is absolute global domination—that is, absolute power.[17] Indeed, those who already possess something akin to absolute power,

American-Atlanticist global economic and military hegemony, seek to make their power eternal and prevent any challengers from ever arising to make it less than absolute. The inevitable result of this situation, of course, is absolute corruption.

The Islamic antihero who is the avatar of such behavior is Pharoah, Moses's shadow antagonist.[18] Holding absolute worldly power, Pharoah imagines himself a god. The result is his utter destruction at every level: moral, spiritual, and worldly. One does not need prophetic powers to foresee a similar end for the architects of the global domination project.

9/11 as Satanic Parody of Sacred Narrative

As the preceding discussion makes clear, I am analyzing the myth of 9/11 from a morally engaged perspective. I see the official account of 9/11, and the death cult that has grown from it, as a satanic parody of sacred narrative. It is a shallow myth that was consciously scripted, not divinely revealed, to serve as the foundation for a cult of human sacrifice. In this it follows the function of foundational myths: to inaugurate and legitimize a particular social order.

One does not have to believe that the official story of 9/11 is false or evil to accept that it is a myth in the deep, scholarly sense of a sacred legitimizing narrative of origins. The scholarly approach to myth does not usually concern itself with whether a myth is true, false, or something else. Scholars of mythology, like those of literature, find such stories fascinating in part because they convey information in a way that is more powerfully profound and world-shaping than is possible in modes of discourse that foreground verifiable truth claims, such as scientific writing, journalism, nonfiction, biography, and historiography. (Those supposedly nonfictional forms, upon closer inspection, often turn out to be rich in mythography themselves, and it is usually the mythical element at least as much as the truth value that is responsible for their appeal.)

Though we can analyze the official story of 9/11 as a myth without concerning ourselves about whether or to what extent it is true, that does not mean that, in the final analysis, the truth of the story does not matter. That way lies nihilism—whether the vicious and mendacious nihilism of the neocons, avatars of the Big Lie, or the less pernicious nihilism of certain postmodern thinkers, who believe that truth is boring and passé. The truth does matter. Though the myth of 9/11 functions in about the same way whether nineteen extremist Muslim hijackers actually did it, or whether they were framed by intelligence agents working for the US high command, the question of whether and to what extent this myth was consciously authored, and by whom, is obviously relevant to its ultimate meaning. Roland Barthes, the first and greatest analyst of the mythologies of modern life, supposedly oversaw the death of the author: According to Barthes, the author's intended meaning is irrelevant to the meaning of her text.[19] This may be true for *Finnegan's Wake*, but not for 9/11. If we learn that the myth of 9/11 is false, a fictional creation intended to inaugurate an era of an endless "war on terror," the meaning that we draw from it, and the historical effect we create as we draw that meaning, will be quite different from what we would have drawn and done as true believers in an egregiously false myth.

Our analysis of the official story of 9/11 as a myth in the deep sense can also help us understand why so many people believe it, despite the existence of overwhelming evidence against it. The official tale in general, and the Kean-Zelikow novel in particular, is a terrific story. It is woven around a stunning mythic image, has an unbelievable cast of larger-than-life heroes and villains, hails its American audience by casting it on the side of the angels, exerts a strong yet subliminal sexual fascination, sustains itself through a powerful structural rhythm of tension (insecurity) and partial release, and forces itself upon us through repeated tellings around our modern tribal hearth until it is deeply ingrained in our consciousness. Questioning it begins to feel like sacrilege.[20]

In short, many Americans have accepted the official version of 9/11 simply because it is such a good story. And we love good stories, as every storyteller knows. Nobody wants to be awakened from the "storylistening trance," that pleasurable state evoked by a well-crafted narrative.[21] And if the awakening is a rude one—if the storyteller and his biggest heroes turn out to be vicious, cold-blooded murderers posing as our protectors, wielding the power of life and death over all of us with a murderous, cynical sneer—it may be less painful to remain half-asleep, dreaming the pleasant dreams that flicker evanescently from the television soma-dispenser.

The official story of 9/11 is not only a good story, but (on the surface, at least) it is a coherent one. The allegedly relevant facts are arranged in such a way that they appear to all fit together. Those who point out the existence of a massive body of evidence contradicting the official story cannot easily produce an equally coherent counternarrative to explain the event. They must admit that they don't know for sure whether there were any hijackings or not, whether occupied passenger planes or remotely guided dummy planes hit the buildings, who the relevant actors were and exactly what they did, and so on. All the critics of the official version can do is make educated guesses. And educated guesses are not as appealing as a tightly woven, thrilling narrative, with each of its threads apparently in place, and its myriad loose ends concealed.

Our examination of the myth of 9/11 must explore the ways that it is such a good story. The core of the official 9/11 story is its central mythic image: the collapse of the Twin Towers. Who will ever forget the sight of those massive, looming monuments exploding into dust and collapsing at free-fall speed? And though the sight itself was unforgettable, even on a nineteen-inch television screen, the major television networks, largely owned by defense contractors that would be lapping up 9/11's trillion-dollar windfall, made absolutely sure we wouldn't forget it, by running the same footage over... and over... and over. Cognitive psychologists tell us that the most effective way to transfer data into long-term memory is repetition, repetition, repetition. That is why the best way to learn a new acquaintance's name is to use it several times in quick succession.

The endless reruns of planes crashing into buildings, then buildings exploding and collapsing, did more than drive a message into the audience's long-term memory. It also created a powerful, irrational link between the plane crashes and the buildings' explosions and collapses. This is less a matter of logical inference of causality from chronology than an emotional linkage whose glue was the spectacular horror of the two events. Such irrational linkages, hardened into the illusion of logical causality, can be extremely difficult to deconstruct rationally, no matter how much evidence is produced showing that the crashes and collapses were physically unrelated. The perpetraitors[22] used misdirection, the central principle of stage magic, leading the audience to focus on the planes, and the horror-movie script of what allegedly transpired on board, while the buildings were actually brought down with explosives.[23]

The endlessly repeated crash–collapse footage served another purpose: It battered the viewer's psyche into horrified submission to authority. As we identified with the victims—and the harangue from American television channels reinforced that identification for US citizens by indoctrinating us with an "American victims–foreign attackers" dichotomy—we watched ourselves get murdered over and over and over. It was like an endless snuff film with ourselves as victims. And the worst part is that we were doing it to ourselves. I do not mean this just in the sense that our tax dollars paid the salaries of the politicians, military leaders, and covert operatives who carried out the atrocity. As television viewers, we could not turn away. We could not change the channel—after all, this was historic, and the same thing was on every channel. Few of us could summon up the courage to just turn the damned thing off.

We thus became complicit in our own endlessly repeated mass murder. By watching the atrocity again and again, we literally tortured ourselves. And self-torture, as the CIA has long known, is the most effective kind of torture. That is why the hooded figure from Abu Ghraib is standing with his hands straight out, trying to avoid moving: he is being tortured by electric shocks every time he moves.[24] As CIA interrogators know, it is possible to resist torture applied by another person. Create a situation in which the victim tortures herself, and she will quickly be reduced to jelly. The self-torture victim collapses into a state of extreme dissociation, in which her previous identity, her sense of herself in the world, is exploded. The self-torture victim is ready to be infantilized, taken under the wing of a substitute parent figure, and told what to do, think, say, feel, and believe.[25]

By battering us in this way, the perpetraitors, including our governmental, financial, and media elites, became our abusive parents. Like battered children, and the Winston Smith who loved Big Brother, we identified with our abusers. We blinded ourselves to the abuser's evil, and instead relinquished our souls to the very forces that battered us. We were collectively overwhelmed by a new socio-psychiatric disorder that might be termed ACS, Abused Citizens Syndrome.[26] And most of us entered a deep state of denial from which we have yet to emerge.

The coercive hypnotic power of this carefully scripted, endlessly reiterated disaster footage was immense. The images of planes hitting skyscrapers, and of skyscrapers collapsing, possess the kind of scope and power that makes them potent mythic icons. Humans have always dreamed of flight and trembled with fear and longing—look at Icarus! And the dream of trying to build a tower to the skies, and then watching it collapse into ruins, is to building what the dream of Icarus is to flying. The collapsing tower dream is the core image of the Babel myth. In fact, the parallels between 9/11 and the Babel myth are rather stunning. In the story of the Tower of Babel, the tower builders get their power from the gradual unification of humanity under a single language. On 9/11, the world was nearly united under a single language, English, in which the techno-economic discourse of global capitalism is expressed. The triumph of capitalist "democracy" would, according to the wildly and inexplicably popular neocon Fukuyama, bring the "end of history."[27] In fact, Fukuyama claimed, history had already ended; we just didn't realize it yet. The world was unified under the anglo-capitalist Tower of Babel, which was destined to reach the stars. Yet the hidden masters of this tyrannical globalization were being challenged by the anti-globalization movement, whose Islamist wing—because it rejects usury, holds fast to its religious tradition, and dwells atop most of the planet's remaining oil reserves—remains the biggest obstacle to one-world tyranny under Atlanticist domination.

On 9/11, the World Trade Center collapsed, blown up by the globalists themselves—and capitalist globalism collapsed with it.[28] Rabid neocon nationalism, laying bare the real forces behind so-called globalization, arose on the ruins of the towers, and in proclaiming an incipient American empire, the Bush administration set the stage for the confusion of nationalistic tongues that increasingly drives the world toward chaos. Fukuyama's report of history's death turned out to have been greatly exaggerated.

It is one of history's exquisite ironies that the architects of the 9/11 myth were trying to preserve the very empire they so efficiently destroyed. The US empire, and especially its Israeli outpost, were doomed in the medium-term anyway, with or without 9/11. Inexorable demographic and economic trends were working against them. The European Union was already bigger, both in population and GNP, than the United States, and Israel was losing its demographic race with the Palestinians it had always needed to expel as a precondition for an apartheid "Jewish state."[29] Peak oil was coming soon, and with it the empowerment of whoever controlled the remaining oil reserves—meaning the Arabs and Muslims. Meanwhile, China was shaping up as the superpower of the second half of the twenty-first century. The neocons, through their think tank PNAC, openly stated what seemed, to them, obvious: The US had a limited window of opportunity to shape the international environment, and it had better take advantage of its unmatched military power, the only card in its hand, while it still could. But US military might would only be fully unleashed, the PNAC neocons wrote, after "some galvanizing event like a new Pearl Harbor."[30] Without this new Pearl Harbor, Americans would not make the sacrifices—such as accepting widespread poverty, unemployment, the destruction of Social Security and the limitation or even end of their constitutional civil liberties—necessary for the US to put all its eggs in the military basket, and then lob those eggs at every imaginable potential adversary. Unfortunately for the US empire, these neocon strategists had not understood the point Charles Kupchan makes so forcefully in *The Vulnerability of Empire*: Empires fall when they make stupid, rash decisions, and those bad decisions are almost always driven by the same psychological factor: a fear of homeland vulnerability.[31] By killing over 2,700 Americans as they staged what was intended to be the inaugurating myth of the New American Century, the neocons spurred the US into a frenzy of pathological overextension, uniting the whole world, especially the energy-rich Islamic world, against America. Instead of preserving US power, they assured their empire of a much earlier, more violent, and complete demise than would have been the case had it merely faded slowly and wisely from its position as world hegemon.

Intended to kick off a New American Century of absolute domination, 9/11 now looks more like the beginning of the end of the American empire. In any case, it marks a transition. The core mythic image represents the explosive transition from one epoch, one state of being or non-being, to another. It separates the time and space we know from an earlier condition of chaos, void, or nonexistence. The best-known creation myth in Western culture, of course, is Genesis:

> In the beginning God created the heavens and the earth.
> —Now the earth had been wild and waste,
> darkness over the face of Ocean,
> breath of God hovering over the face of the waters—
> God said: Let there be light! And there was light.
> God saw the light: that it was good.
> God separated the light from the darkness.

God called the light: Day! And the darkness he called: Night!
There was evening, there was morning: one day... [32]

God goes on to separate waters from waters with a dome, creating heaven and seas; separates the seas from land; life from non-living matter; man from woman; and so on. Note the pattern: One big moment of creation, the birth of somethingness (heaven and earth) out of nothingness, is followed by lesser acts of creation by division. In each case, something chaotic or amorphous is divided, resulting in two less-amorphous entities, one of which is better, being less chaotic or amorphous than the other. Chaos is broken into light and darkness (light is better); the waters are broken into above and below, and those above (heaven) are better; dry earth is divided from the seas, and dry earth is better; plant life appears from the earth (life is better than mere earth); animals appear (an improvement over plants); and finally humans are created in God's own image, with men being better (less amorphous and chaotic) than women. This magnificent myth is a monument to the human ego: The process of creation that led to ME consisted of cutting chaos in two, discarding the worse half, and keeping the better half, until finally I was created in the image of God.

The Bible's creation myth is clearly derived from earlier Middle Eastern creation myths. The one preserved in the Gilgamesh epic posits a somewhat more violent sundering of chaos, in the person of the oceanic female, and the bloody carving out of the domain of (aggressive male) order. That aggressive male ego is then held up as the tribal norm.

The core mythic image of 9/11, the destruction of the WTC, is more like the Gilgamesh/Sumerian versions of creation than the one in Genesis. For one thing, it is ultra-violent. Thousands of human bodies are smashed, pulverized, and exploded into pieces. But unlike the Sumerian version, in which the primordial chaos goddess is dismembered by the male warrior hero, here the sacrificial victim is ambiguously gendered. The Towers, of course, are phallic symbols, and the American audience is invited to view their destruction as a kind of symbolic castration. Yet this symbolic castration of America is linked to the "our women are threatened" motif, perhaps the most powerful motivational myth available to those who wish to stimulate warlike behavior. The media propaganda machine worked overtime cranking out portrayals of Arabs and Muslims as vile sexist villains who abuse, oppress, and sexually exploit women. Thus the destruction of the Towers is blamed on these dark sexist villains who threaten womenfolk everywhere, and the image of the collapsing Towers made into a kind of rape. America, robbed of its two towering phalluses, is feminized, symbolically penetrated by gigantic, explosive airplanes ejaculating jet fuel, whose crews and passengers had already been penetrated by Arab-Muslim blades, box cutters that had somehow penetrated airport security. The image of a nation vulnerable to penetration is heightened by the story about the alleged "nineteen hijackers" who supposedly snuck into the country to do the dastardly deed. The sexualized nature of the attack seems to have been intended to trigger the erection of a pre-planned post-9/11 sex torture gulag, famously represented by that poor parody of Pasolini's *Salo* known as Abu Ghraib.

This violent, spectacular, sexually charged image separates "us", the forces of order, from "them", the forces of chaos and evil—a primal sundering that repeats the pattern of all creation myths, which cleave before from after, good from evil, day from night, inaugurating the whole social reality that the myth-participants and their descendants subsequently experience. "If you are not with us," George W. Bush famously warned, "you are against us." This bifurcation of the world into light and dark, white (Americans) and dark (Ay-rabs and Nee-groes), pure, unsullied Judeo-Christians and swarthy, sexually aggressive Muslims, repeats the pattern of earlier Euro-racist mythologizers, notably Adolf Hitler. Like Bush and the neocons, Hitler and the Nazis inaugurated their new era by destroying an architectural monument and blaming its destruction on their designated enemies, dusky-hued, sexually aggressive Semites whose penetration of the pure white homeland would have to be stopped by any means necessary. The new, post–Reichstag Fire world would be one of endless aggressive war. Bush's obsession with this idea of a whole new era of perpetual war, an era inaugurated by the destruction of an architectural monument, produced one of the most bizarre presidential Freudian slips in history. In a story that should have been headlined "Bush Threatens Submarine Attack on Clinton Presidential Library," Sidney Blumenthal described President Bush wandering beside the Arkansas River just after the opening ceremony of the Clinton Presidential Library:

...Bush appeared distracted, and glanced repeatedly at his watch. When he stopped to gaze at the river, where secret service agents were stationed in boats, the guide said: "Usually, you might see some bass fishermen out there." Bush replied: "A submarine could take this place out."

Was the president warning of an al-Qaeda submarine, sneaking undetected up the Mississippi, through the locks and dams of the Arkansas River, surfacing under the bridge to the twenty-first century to dispatch the Clinton library? Is that where Osama bin Laden is hiding?

Or was this a wishful paranoid fantasy of ubiquitous terrorism destroying Clinton's legacy with one blow? Or a projection of menace and messianism, with only Bush grasping the true danger, standing between submerged threat and civilization? Perhaps it was simply his way of saying he wouldn't build his library near water.[33]

As Blumenthal suggests, this scene drew a stark dividing line between America's past and its apparent future. The past, symbolized by the Clinton Presidential Library, is the pre-9/11 world, a world of literate presidents, libraries, buildings sitting peacefully beside a river. The future is Bush's fantasy of sending a nuclear submarine to destroy the Clinton library—to destroy the past order and erect a new order of war, terror, and fascism. As Bush put it in another telling Freudian slip, "They never stop thinking about new ways to harm our country and our people, and neither do we."[34] Along with blowing up American buildings, Bush also fantasizes about blowing up Social Security, international law, and the Constitution. Such fantasies would be harmless were he not in a position to realize them.

The Myth that Failed

One of the early epitaphs of Communism was "the God that Failed."[35] The attempt of the architects of 9/11 to create a mythical *sui generis* event, and found a whole new social order upon it, was a far more abject failure. Communism, after all, lasted well over half a century—from the Russian Revolution in 1917 to the fall of the Berlin Wall in 1989. But as I write, in the winter of 2006, the post-9/11 moment of flag-waving patriots exuding purity and righteousness as they march off blissfully to found a globe-conquering 100-year empire has already passed. In truth, it only lasted a couple of months. Launched by the media's Big Lies in the hours after the attacks, the New World Order petered out somewhere in the mountain snowfields of Afghanistan, when it grew obvious that the US high command had no interest in pursuing, much less apprehending, Osama bin Laden—that the whole thing had been a pipeline grab for Caspian Sea energy resources and geopolitical advantage.

The myth failed because it was phony. Real myths are organic, growing naturally out of a particular people's soil, shaped by thousands of hands, and bearing fruit that meets the needs of many generations. But this one was as plastic as the imploding petro-civilization whose terminal decline it hastened and highlighted.

Admittedly it was not the first plastic myth. We have been getting what passes for our mythology on celluloid for nearly a century, and those celluloid (now digital) artifacts, consciously crafted by the high-priest propagandists of Hollywood, are a poor imitation of the sacred narratives that sustain genuine civilizations. But 9/11 took the ersatz mythology of Hollywood, whose dominant tone is a realism designed to make the audience forget that it is watching an artifact, and made it a thousand times more putrid and death-dealing than the ugliest snuff film. By staging the on-camera murder of 2,752 unpaid extras in the most obscene special-effects extravaganza ever committed to film, the architects of 9/11 were counting on the very real suffering they inflicted to create what Roland Barthes calls "l'effet du réel"—the effect of the real, that certain *je ne sais quoi* that makes an audience suspend all critical judgment and forget that it is beholding an artifact.[36] Like the philosopher George Bataille, who wanted to stage a public human sacrifice in hopes of reawakening the religious emotions of which modern man had been deprived, the authors of 9/11 believed that the ritual murder of human beings would magically right the wrongs of a doomed civilization. They thought that this mass human sacrifice would create the "new Pearl Harbor" they called for in September 2000—a "galvanizing event" that would unleash a brave and virile imperial culture unafraid to send its children off to die overseas, believing they were fighting for goodness and justice.[37] And they apparently thought that mass murder was their best insurance against getting caught—that the very act of murdering 2,752 of the very citizens they had sworn to protect, in an act of treason against the Constitution they had sworn to defend, was so heinous that nobody would ever believe them capable of such a thing, no matter how much evidence they left behind.

This attempt to consciously craft a civilization-saving myth was remarkable for its audacity as well as its evil. Those of us trained in literature are inclined to admire the amazing energy and imagination that authors invest in their fictional creations, and there is something about the 9/11 myth that inspires this kind of awe—especially since it must have been the product of a number of minds, rather than a single evil genius.[38] Still, it has been said that the King James Bible is the only document written by committee that turned out any good, and the 9/11 myth will certainly never be viewed as the second such success. In the final analysis, considered as a work of art, it is blatantly bad—a horror movie in which you can see the strings attached to the monster's jaws as they snap at dime-store model airplanes.

The qualities implied by adjectives like false, shoddy, ersatz, plastic, fake, artificial, unreal, and so on, ultimately return us to the notion of the lie—the deliberately fabricated untruth. The myth of 9/11 has failed precisely because it is a lie. Had there been a real attack on 9/11 by real foreign terrorists who had outwitted a government that was really trying to prevent any such attacks, the resulting myth might not have failed. The nation might have rallied to a nationalist cause based on such a "true myth," rather as it did after the Japanese attack on Pearl Harbor.[39] But after 9/11, it wasn't just the perceptive minority that smelled a rat. I suspect that most, perhaps all, of the population knows at some level, whether consciously or unconsciously, that the whole 9/11 event exudes a potent whiff of rotten fakery. In many cases that knowledge remains thoroughly unconscious, blocked from awareness by the kind of wall of repression that Freud famously analyzed, along with the denial characteristic of abuse victims.

The main source of that repression and denial is clear: Nobody wants to believe that their own government willfully slaughters thousands of its own citizens and then lies through its teeth about it. Nobody wants to believe that the media we depend on for our information are that corrupt. Nobody wants to believe that things are quite that bad.

Another cause is hidden a bit deeper: We have erected a wall of repression around 9/11 because deep down inside, we experienced a powerful wave of forbidden pleasure at the destructive spectacle, akin to that described by Tom Robbins:

"Tell me, amigo," said Switters in a voice just loud enough to penetrate the fellow's earphones, "do you know why boom-boom movies are so popular? Do you know why young males, especially, love, simply love, to see things blown apart?"

The man stared blankly at Switters. He lifted his headset, but on one side only. "It's freedom," said Switters brightly. "Freedom from the material world. Subconsciously, people feel trapped by our culture's confining buildings and its relentless avalanche of consumer goods. So, when they watch all this shit being demolished in a totally irreverent and devil-may-care fashion, they experience the kind of release the Greeks used to get from their tragedies. The ecstasy of psychic liberation."[40]

Of course, there is a part of us that loves explosions and destruction even without reference to the burden of possessions. I remember the awed fascination I felt as a child while watching pictures of plane and train crashes on TV; such images are still staples of our popular culture, relentlessly purveyed in documentary and fictional disaster footage. On 9/11, the pleasure of such an extraordinary destructive spectacle was inadmissible to consciousness and unspeakable in polite company—thanks to the real human suffering that the operation's architects had included for that very purpose. A wall of repression, in the form of patriotic cant and mediated big lies, was immediately erected around the event. The repression of the horrific pleasure we all felt at watching those buildings fall stands as one of the least-discussed, least-understood, yet most obvious causes of the neurotic wall of denial that still stands, battered and tottering, around the reality of 9/11. Hypocrite voyeur—*mon semblable*—*mon frère*! Deep down inside we are still screaming "I am not on the side of those who did this!" as we go through with our increasingly empty, meaningless, repetitious, and unhappy neurotic behavior, while channeling our lust for still more explosive thrills toward the more socially acceptable alternative of "revenge against the evil-doers." Crush Kandahar! Bomb Baghdad! Torch Tehran! Nuke them all! Yet the neurotic veneer is wearing thin, and the primal scene—the father-government's explosive rape of the World Trade Center and of America—is starting to come back to us. Only its full exposure can offer a cure.

The widespread unconscious or pre-conscious awareness of 9/11's artificiality made it a stillborn myth. By the time of the Iraq invasion in spring 2003, a worldwide wave of revulsion had already arisen, based largely on a deeply felt but mostly inarticulate sense that something was rotten in Denmark. Thierry Meyssan's books had set publishing records in France, and the basic thrust of Meyssan's books had been endorsed by majorities in many parts of the world—including those parts the Bush administration was intent on invading, using the myth of 9/11 as its one-size-fits-all *raison d'être*.[41] The universal semi-awareness that 9/11 was a sham drove the global antiwar majority, just as a repressed understanding of the momentous threat posed by nuclear weapons drove the anti-nuclear-power movements of earlier decades. In both the case of 9/11 and that of nuclear weapons, the root of the problem was so awful that most people simply could not face it, but instead chose to struggle against a surface symptom in order to avoid the real issue.

A successful myth cannot be created from a deliberate lie. But in the end, the myth of 9/11 has failed not just because of its falseness: All myths take liberties with objective, empirical truth, though this one admittedly pushes untruth to an extreme. It has failed because it cannot provide the life-sustaining nourishment of story and symbol that we need. Successful myths, including those of the great religions, grow from the seed and soil of truth. In their highest embodiments, they are firmly rooted in the highest kind of truth, that currently unfashionable commodity known as ultimate truth or divine truth, and they offer their followers access to at least a taste of that ineffable gift. The myth of 9/11, however, offers nothing life-sustaining whatsoever. Its only conceivable legacy is an unending cycle of destruction, Cheney's war that will not end in our lifetimes.

To be sure sure, the myth of 9/11 attempts to whip up a life-sustaining brew of story and symbol. But what kind of life is it meant to sustain? The pre-scripted line "we were attacked by nefarious evil-doers, and we must not stop until the evil system responsible is destroyed" worked reasonably well for World War II, which targeted a palpable and genuinely evil enemy (Nazi Germany) that could be defeated in less than four years.

The myth of 9/11, however, does not offer a life-sustaining way to get through the historical mess we find ourselves in. That does not, of course, mean that it was never meant to. It was intended to set the American empire in stone for at least a hundred years, perhaps even to found a new, imperial 1000-year Reich like the one the Nazis dreamed of. It was meant to offer an unshakable legitimacy to a stepped-up regime of Anglo-American global domination. It was meant to overcome the resistance of the colonized, especially in such resource-rich regions as the Middle East, and to annex these regions as stable appendages of empire. In so doing, it was meant to achieve the geopolitically unsustainable feat of dominating Eurasia from an imperial center in the Western hemisphere during the critical civilizational turning point of peak oil.[42]

This project, of course, is impossible. Empires get their power from their economic-technological base, and the American empire was starting to totter well before the architects of 9/11 gave it a huge push designed to keep it upright—which only set it to tottering that much harder. The very impossibility of the project may well be responsible for the hallucinatory lies with which it was realized. The French have a saying, "il prend ses desires pour des réalités" (he mistakes his desires for realities), which applies nicely to the neocons. The neocons wish empires did not rise and fall for reasons beyond human power or comprehension. They wish they could control the process and forestall empire's end through a judicious application of illusion. They wish the erosion of America's economic-technological-productive base could somehow be ignored, and American imperial power sustained through lies and deceit even after the base is gone.

At a deeper level, I suspect that many of them at least partly believe their own lies, even though those lies were consciously crafted as lies to manipulate the masses. They have inadvertently hypnotized themselves into believing that America is the greatest place on earth and that whatever it does is right. They have conned themselves into believing that the brown-skinned followers of Muhammad are barbarians and fanatics whose lives are worth little and whose suffering hardly matters. Some of them may even have actually believed that there might have been a couple of irrelevant WMDs in Iraq somewhere, that the Iraqi people would welcome the American "liberators," and above all that nobody would dare speak up, ever, about the all-too-obvious lies surrounding the 9/11 operation. Indeed, a few of the less clever among them may actually believe the official 9/11 legend.

When people start to believe their own lies, they are usually in serious trouble. The neocons running the US empire on its eve of destruction are no exception. Their openly expressed scorn for those who indulge in "reality-based politics"—"we don't have time for reality, we're running an empire here!"—is beyond chutzpah, beyond hubris, beyond the pride that goeth before a fall. Such contempt for truth, for reality, is beyond tragic. It is insane.[43]

Such insanity is the natural product of a failed myth. Myths, after all, are the foundations of how people understand the world and act in it. Destroy someone's cherished myth, and you have destroyed their ability to cope with reality. How much more terrible, then, to have consciously participated in the invention of a myth, at the price of tremendous effort and energy and suffering and guilt, and then to watch the whole thing collapse before your eyes. The neocons, like the Nazis hunkering in their bunkers during the fall of Berlin, are in a pitiable situation, and one conducive to insanity. This, of course, makes them extremely dangerous—which may be one reason that so many apparently well-meaning liberals keep right on humoring them, especially about the big lie of 9/11.

In a larger sense, the failed myth of 9/11 is a synecdoche for the failed myth of America. The United States of America comes with a powerful built-in mythology, one that has sustained the Republic (more or less) for two centuries. The story about George Washington's cherry tree—"Father, I cannot tell a lie!"—may itself be a lie, but it expresses a quintessentially American reverence for truth. That reverence for truth, of course, now lies in tatters in the wake of 9/11. The founding myth of America is also profoundly anti-imperialistic: "We ragtag colonial subjects defeated imperial England and chased its troops out of our land! Hooray for anti-imperial revolution!" That too, of course, has been exploded by the neocon hyper-imperial project.

Above all, America is based upon the myth of freedom, which is linked to that of truth, as in the motto "the truth will set you free." Our whole history is one of a mythic quest for freedom: Freedom from the kings of Europe; freedom from religious repression; freedom from British colonial domination; freedom from the tyranny of an aristocracy; freedom to strike out for the territory when things get too oppressive. Then 9/11 came along with its pre-written PATRIOT Act, and our whole mythic history of freedom went up in flames.

The "neocon jobbers" blew up America's cherished foundational myth just as surely as they blew up the three World Trade Center towers. In their place, they intended to erect a new myth: The myth of 9/11, engine of the "war that will not end in our lifetime."[44] But the myth of 9/11 has failed utterly, and US imperial power is crumbling. We now find ourselves in an odd position: We are stuck between two myths that have exploded and collapsed in rubble. The old democratic myth has been destroyed, but the new 9/11-imperialist myth also collapsed almost as soon as it was built. We have nothing left to go on, no firm ground beneath our feet. We are in a liminal position, betwixt and between: The world behind us is gone, but the one the neocons put in front of us has collapsed of its own insubstantiality.

In a healthy culture, liminality is a brief stage, a rite of passage signaling the transition from one state to another: from the womb to the world (symbolized by baby showers and their equivalents), from childhood to adulthood (signified by events like bar mitzvahs), from bachelorhood to married life (symbolized by wedding rites), and ultimately from life to death (signified by funerals).[45] Those permanently stuck in a liminal realm, including Hamlet (who can't make the transition to adult/king by killing the pretender) and Ophelia (who can't speak her love and realize it through marriage) may be fascinating specimens, but ultimately they wind up doomed or insane.

We are stuck in the unspeakable and ripe for a talking cure. The taboo on the public expression of 9/11 truth must be shattered. We desperately need a 9/11 scandal and accompanying media feeding frenzy in the tradition of Watergate. Such an event would transfix the nation, exorcise its demons, save it from its true enemies, and restore our national moral, spiritual, political, and economic health.

The choice is ours. Will our culture survive the destruction of its old myth, and the failure of the ersatz replacement? Or will we degenerate into madness, culminating in a holocaust of post–peak oil cannibalism that will make the final scene of Hamlet look like a fairy tale happy ending?

No single new salvific myth will save us, so we had better salvage what we can of the old ones. Let us intone with T. S. Eliot, who knew something of liminality and wastelands: "These fragments I have shored against my ruins."[46] Eliot realized that modernity was unsustainable because it could not yield a viable myth. At this peak-oil post-9/11 moment, the truth of Eliot's position is growing clearer. After that orgy of destruction that some have called modernity, which others like James Kunstler have more accurately called the age of Petroleum Man, all that is left to us is the fragments of earlier myths.[47] Some of them, including the

American myth of constitutional freedom, and even more so the great religions, have much to offer us. It seems to me that these time-tested mythic systems offer the best hope for individuals faced with the wasteland the neocons have left in their wake. There are no atheists in foxholes, and the world we are entering is going to have a lot of foxholes. Whether we follow the architects of 9/11 and toss hand grenades between them, or recover our senses and toss packages of food, we will certainly not be a society, or a planet, of atheists.

And that, finally, is the significance of the failed myth of 9/11. A carefully designed ersatz-religious event, crafted by atheist neocons to dupe folks of good faith, has been exposed as a lie. The very magnitude of the lie, in its exposure, has created a massive gap, a huge yawning vacuum that only the greatest and largest of truths—the ultimate unities of God, the cosmos, humankind, and planet earth—will be able to fill.[48]

12

INTERROGATING "TERRORISM": MUSLIM PROBLEM OR COVERT OPERATIONS NIGHTMARE?

Nafeez Mosaddeq Ahmed

INTERNATIONAL TERRORISM HAS ROUTINELY BEEN UNDERSTOOD AS A phenomenon integrally linked to radical Islamism. After 9/11, this trend of thought, already prevalent in official circles, became the defining discourse of Western international relations, now permanently configured within the paradigm of the "war on terror."

So widespread is this notion that it has penetrated even the discourse of mainstream Islam itself. Thus, the respected moderate American Muslim cleric Hamza Yusuf declared after 9/11 that: "Islam has been hijacked by a discourse of anger and a rhetoric of rage."[1]

Consequently, much of the debate on the roots of international terrorism, both among Western policymakers and among Muslims themselves, concerns the role of Islam as an exploited ideological facilitating factor in the intensification of terrorist attacks around the world. Prominent Muslim commentators such as Ziauddin Sardar lamented after 9/11 that

> Muslims everywhere are in a deep state of denial. From Egypt to Malaysia, there is an aversion to seeing terrorism as a Muslim problem and a Muslim responsibility.... Terrorism is a Muslim problem... Saudi Arabia, Indonesia, Algeria, Bangladesh, Lebanon, Iran—there is hardly a Muslim country that is not plagued by terrorism.... Muslims have stubbornly refused to see terrorism as an internal problem. While the Muslim world has suffered, they have blamed everyone but themselves. It is always "the West", or the CIA, or "the Indians", or "the Zionists" hatching yet another conspiracy. This state of denial means Muslims are ill-equipped to deal with problems of endemic terrorism.[2]

A number of salient points can be derived here. Sardar, articulating a narrative very much supportive of Western officialdom's perspective on international terrorism, sees terrorism as ultimately a question of Muslim responsibility. The consequence of this for Muslims is that they should firstly lend their wholehearted support in principle to the West's fight against international terrorism, and secondly that they should manifest such support by routing out extremism within their own midst. Moreover, Sardar, once again echoing officialdom's perspective, supports President Bush's resounding *a priori* condemnation of "outrageous conspiracy theories concerning the attacks of September the 11th; malicious lies that attempt to shift the blame away from the terrorists, themselves, away from the guilty."[3] By implication, the guilty, then, are not merely the terrorists themselves, but Muslims as such for whom terrorism is an "internal problem" regarding which they persist in "denial."

This paradigm, however, is not based in an objective analysis of international terrorism itself. Indeed, it is devoid entirely of meaningful historical and empirical content. As such, it generally tends to generate two conventional forms of rebuttal, both of which are equally devoid of relevant historical and empirical analysis of the very phenomenon under discussion. The first comes from within Islam itself, and attempts to challenge the idea of using Islamic scripture—namely the Qur'an (considered to be the Word of God revealed to the Prophet Muhammad) and the Hadith (historical records of the Prophet's life, sayings, and actions)—that terrorism can be justified on its basis. Thus, it is argued that an authentic understanding of Islam delegitimizes terrorism. The second rebuttal comes from what might be amorphously described as the antiwar movement, and attempts to explore the dynamics of precisely why Muslims have developed the "internal problem" of terrorism. Those dynamics are found to be located precisely in a series of devastating historical conjunctures between the West and the Muslim world, proceeding for several centuries, whereby Western imperialism has subjugated predominantly Muslim regions of the Middle East and Central Asia. Events such as the 2003 Iraq War are considered to be merely extensions of this world-historical process.

The content of these rebuttals, on their own terms, is well documented and highly persuasive. However, in one simple way, they are exactly similar to the very argument that they attempt to refute, by failing to comprehend the reality of the phenomenon of international terrorism itself. As such, by refusing to confront this phenomenon directly, they inadvertently perpetuate the defactualization of analytical discourse that supports Western officialdom's bold equation of international terrorism with radical Islamism, and henceforth as a distinctly Muslim problem that needs to be dealt with by finding some sort of Muslim solution, even if that be a peaceful one.[4]

Therefore, my approach here will not be to pursue the arguments of conventional rebuttals to the paradigmatic perspective of the underpinnings of international terrorism, but rather to critique this paradigm on its own terms using a historical and empirical analysis.

My argument is not that there are no violent interpretations of Islam within the Muslim world that might be seen as endorsing terrorism. Of course there are. And my argument is not that the West's imperial role in the Muslim world should be ignored. Certainly, it should not. Rather, my argument is that when international terrorism is scrutinized impartially, scientifically, the conventional understanding of its supposed inextricable linkage with radical Islamism is fundamentally weakened in surprising ways.

The evidence that 9/11 was the result of a distinctly radical Islamist plan is highly questionable. The nature of "al-Qaeda" as a distinctly radical Islamist organization is also questionable. Finally, compelling evidence that identifiable groups involved in terrorist activity around the world are, in fact, manipulated on behalf of entirely non-Islamist Western geostrategic interests challenges the entire official narrative of the "war on terror."

I. Deconstructing the al-Qaeda–9/11 Mythology

9/11 and the Myth of Islamic Suicide Bombers

According to the official narrative, nineteen Muslim fundamentalists belonging to Osama bin Laden's al-Qaeda terrorist network hijacked four civilian planes on the morning of 9/11 and flew two into the World Trade Center and one into the Pentagon; the fourth, assumed to be on its way to Washington, DC, crashed in Pennsylvania. But this narrative, widely accepted by both proponents and critics of US imperial foreign policy, is problematic at its core: the very identities of the alleged hijackers.

It is now known that at least ten of the nineteen alleged

hijackers are alive, according to multiple, credible news accounts by the BBC, CNN, the *Telegraph*, the *Independent*, and other international media. As Jay Kolar observes, "at least ten of those named on the FBI's second and final list of 19 have turned up and been verified to be alive, with proof positive that at least one other 'hijacker', Ziad Jarrah, had his identity doubled, and therefore fabricated." Reviewing video evidence furnished by the government to support its narrative—including alleged footage of the hijackers at Dulles Airport and the infamous Osama bin Laden confession tape—Kolar finds them to be riddled with impossibilities and anomalies, and concludes that they are utterly unreliable at best, and downright forgeries at worst.[5]

The abject failure of the Bush administration and its key allies to substantiate its narrative of what happened on 9/11 with regard to the most basic issue of who perpetrated the terrorists attacks obviously raises fundamental questions about the official narrative as such. The failure can be summarized as follows: If the alleged hijackers identified by the FBI have now turned up alive, then we still do not know who, in reality, hijacked the aircraft on 9/11. And thus, the question of responsibility for the 9/11 attacks remains unanswered. Why has such a failure not been rectified, if the evidence exists? There are a number of possible explanations, the simplest of which is that the alleged hijackers were not, in fact, hijackers at all; or rather, that there were no Arab hijackers on board the planes. Another explanation is that there were hijackers, but that disclosing their real identities and the extent of the evidence of their connection to 9/11 might inevitably disclose a large number of related connections that would be deeply embarrassing, to say the least, for the US government. So we will not attempt to answer this question here. Suffice it to say that with the identities of the alleged hijackers not only in dispute, but essentially unknown, the core underpinning of the official narrative is vacuous; it is merely an unknown, a question.

Such questions extend to the very activities of the alleged hijackers as conventionally identified prior to 9/11. A variety of reports based on journalistic investigations and eyewitness testimonials provide a bizarre picture at odds with the conventional portrayal of the alleged hijackers as Islamic fundamentalists. Two of them, Mohamed Atta and Marwan al-Shehhi, visited the popular Woodland Park Resort Hotel in the Philippines several times between 1998 and 2000, according to numerous local residents and hotel workers, who recognized them from news photographs. They reportedly "drank whiskey with Philippine bargirls, dined at a restaurant that specializes in Middle Eastern cuisine and visited at least one of the local flight schools." Al-Shehhi threw a party with six or seven Arab friends in December 2000 at the hotel, according to former waitress Gina Marcelo. "They rented the open area by the swimming pool for 1,000 pesos," she recounts. "They drank Johnnie Walker Black Label whiskey and mineral water. They barbecued shrimp and onions. They came in big vehicles, and they had a lot of money. They all had girlfriends." But one big mistake they made was that unlike most foreign visitors, "[t]hey never tipped. If they did, I would not remember them so well." Victoria Brocoy, a chambermaid at the Woodland, recalls: "Many times I saw him let a girl go at the gate in the morning. It was always a different girl."[6]

According to US investigators, five of the hijackers, including Atta, al-Shehhi, Nawaq Alhazmi, Ziad Jarrah, and Hani Hanjour, visited Las Vegas at least six times between May and August 2001. The *San Francisco Chronicle* reports that here they "engaged in some decidedly un-Islamic sampling of prohibited pleasures in America's reputed capital of moral corrosion," including drinking alcohol, gambling, and visiting strip clubs.[7] As the *South Florida Sun Sentinel* observed, the hijackers' frequent debauchery was at odds with the most basic tenets of Islam:

> Three guys cavorting with lap dancers at the Pink Pony Nude Theater. Two others knocking back glasses of Stolichnaya and rum and Coke at a fish joint in Hollywood the weekend before committing suicide and mass murder. That might describe the behavior of several men who are suspects in Tuesday's terrorist attack [i.e., the alleged hijackers], but it is not a picture of devout Muslims, experts say. Let alone that of religious zealots in their final days on Earth.

For instance, Mahmoud Mustafa Ayoub, specialist in Islamic and Middle East studies and professor of religion at Temple University in Philadelphia, noted that the prohibition of alcohol, gambling, and sex outside marriage are Islam's most fundamental precepts: "It is incomprehensible that a person could drink and go to a strip bar one night, then kill themselves the next day in the name of Islam. People who would kill themselves for their faith would come from very strict Islamic ideology. Something here does not add up."[8]

Similar reports abound regarding other al-Qaeda terrorists connected to 9/11. Even the alleged 9/11 mastermind, al-Qaeda icon Khalid Shaikh Mohammed, reportedly "met associates in karaoke bars and giant go-go clubs filled with mirrors, flashing lights and bikini-clad dancers," according to evidence collected by Philippine investigators:

> He held meetings at four-star hotels. He took scuba-diving lessons at a coastal resort. When he wasn't engaged with the go-go dancers, he courted a Philippine dentist. Once, to impress her, he rented a helicopter and flew it over her office, then called her on his cell phone and told her to look up and wave.
>
> Mohammad's al-Qaeda associates engaged in much the same behavior. They had local girlfriends and held a drinking party "to celebrate the anniversary of the 1988 Pan Am Flight 103 explosion over Lockerbie, Scotland."[9]

Clearly, this pattern of debauchery is not by any standard commensurate with the strict requirements of al-Qaeda's brand of Islamic fundamentalism. As Professors Quintan Wiktorowicz and John Kaltner point out, al-Qaeda is

> a radical tendency within a broader Islamic movement known as the Salafi movement... The term Salafi is derived from the Arabic *salaf*, which means "to precede" and refers to the companions of the Prophet Muhammed. Because the *salaf* learned about Islam directly from the messenger of God, their example is an important illustration of piety and unadulterated religious practice. Salafis argue that centuries of syncretic cultural and popular religious rituals and interpretations distorted the purity of the message of God and that only by returning to the example of the Prophet and his companions can Muslims achieve salvation. The label "Salafi" is thus used to connote "proper" religious adherence and moral legitimacy, implying that alternative understandings are corrupt deviations from the straight path of Islam.

Thus, although there are various schools of thought within Salafism—including al-Qaeda's violent jihadist interpretation—they all emphasize and indeed attempt to derive their legitimacy from the Salafist goal of "piety and unadulterated religious practice" based directly on the piety and practice of the Prophet.[10]

In this context, the depraved conduct of the alleged 9/11 hijackers in terms of their routine violation of the most basic Islamic precepts contradicts al-Qaeda's strictly puritan Salafist philosophy.

The Takfir Paradigm

How to explain this anomaly? *Time* magazine reports that intelligence officials claim many al-Qaeda terrorists are "followers of an extremist Islamic ideology called Takfir wal Hijra (Anathema and Exile). That's bad news: by blending into host communities, Takfiris attempt to avoid suspicion. A French official says they come across as 'regular, fun-loving guys—but they'd slit your throat or bomb your building in a second.'" Another French official says that the goal of Takfir "is to blend into corrupt societies in order to plot attacks against them better. Members live together, will drink alcohol, eat during Ramadan, become smart dressers and ladies' men to show just how integrated they are."[11]

However, this depiction of al-Qaeda and Takfir wal Hijra is thoroughly inaccurate. Takfir wal Hijra was the title given to a radical Islamic movement also known as the Society of Muslims. The latter was founded in Egypt by Muslim Brotherhood member Shukri Mustafa after his release from prison in 1971. The group disintegrated after Mustafa was arrested and executed by the Egyptian government, but some of its followers went on to join other radical groups such as al-Jihad and/or fled to North Africa. Rather than attempting to integrate into modern society to carry out attacks as intelligence officials now claim, Takfiri ideology advocated the very opposite: "As contemporary society was infidel, he argued, Takfir would set up its own alternative community that would work, study and pray together.... Takfir declared that not only the regime but the society itself was infidel and under ex-communication. This entailed... a personal withdrawal from society." Even Takfir's rival radical Islamic group in Egypt, Jama'at al-Jihad, which means "the Society of Struggle," espoused such a harsh perspective of Islamic practice that it advocated as Islam's top priority "jihad against unbelievers—including 'Muslims' who did not observe the religion's requirements properly"—let alone endorsing in any manner a violation of those requirements.[12]

So extreme is Takfir's ideology that it sees bin Laden as not sufficiently Islamic in his violent approach. The *Sunday Times* reported a month after 9/11 that Takfir "regards Osama bin Laden as an infidel who has sold out." The group's members "have embarked on killing sprees in mosques against fellow Muslims in the belief that a pure Islamic state can be built only if the corrupt elements of the last one are wiped out." Takfir's enmity toward al-

Qaeda is based on the perception that Osama bin Laden is "excessively liberal." In 1995, four Takfir members attempted to assassinate bin Laden at his home in Khartoum. Takfiris continue to be "angered" at bin Laden's leadership of a "compromised jihad." According to the *Times*, "Takfir denounces all but those who copy the behaviour of the prophet Muhammad as infidels and promises to kill them." One senior Sudanese government source confirmed that Takfir "regard [bin Laden] as a sellout... the Takfir think that everything in contemporary Muslim society is corrupt and should be destroyed."[13]

Djamel Beghal and Kamel Daoudi—alleged UK-based terrorists arrested in September 2001 for plotting a series of spectacular terrorist assaults on Europe—were both supposed to be members of Takfir wal Hijra. But according to one Algerian in London who knew Beghal, integrating into Western culture by engaging in various acts of debauchery in violation of Islamic tenets was the last thing this alleged Takfiri would ever do: "Believe me, you do not want these people in your country... they will kill anybody, including their own family, if they are caught smoking or drinking."[14]

Thus, the new scenario being proposed by Western intelligence officials to explain the patently un-Islamic behavior of the 9/11 hijackers is largely incoherent. Despite claims to the contrary, Takfir wal Hijra is aggressively opposed to al-Qaeda, and its strict ideology is fundamentally incommensurate with the prospect of permitting defiance of Islamic rules under any circumstances. Furthermore, al-Qaeda is in turn staunchly opposed to Takfir. Therefore, the anomaly of the 9/11 hijackers persists: They clearly did not possess the conduct of hardened Islamic fundamentalists connected to al-Qaeda. So, who were they?

Al-Qaeda and the Myth of a Radical Islamist International Terrorist Organization

I will not attempt to answer the preceding question here. It suffices to point out that firstly, given that the names, faces, and identities of at least ten of the alleged hijackers belong to innocent, living individuals, the connection of the alleged 9/11 hijackers to the actual events of 9/11 is deeply questionable at best, and secondly, even assuming the validity of such a connection, the notion that the alleged hijackers were Islamist fundamentalists is simply unsustainable.

The problem is not isolated to these individuals believed to be members of bin Laden's international al-Qaeda terrorist network. The same questions can be addressed to al-Qaeda itself. Given that according to the official narrative, these individuals were members of an elite al-Qaeda cell, what does their un-Islamic conduct reveal about the real character of al-Qaeda? Two alleged hijackers— Mohamed Atta, who was reportedly leader of the cell, and Khalid al-Mihdhar, another elite member—were reportedly members of the Islamic Jihad group led by bin Laden's deputy, Ayman al-Zawahiri.[15] According to intelligence sources, "Atta and several others in the group" responsible for the attacks "met with senior Al Qaida leaders, most notably Ayman al-Zawahiri" in Afghanistan shortly before 9/11.[16] Thus, these distinctly un-Islamic characters had very close relationships to the senior leadership of al-Qaeda.

Other prominent members of al-Qaeda also reportedly behave in distinctly un-Islamic ways. The example of Syrian al-Qaeda leader Laui Sakra provides a case in point. Suspected of involvement in the November 2003 bombings of UK and Jewish targets in Istanbul that killed 63 people, Sakra was arrested in Diyarbakir, southeast Turkey.[17] Turkish officials said that Sakra is "one of the 5 most important key figures in al-Qaeda." By his own off-the-record account to police, "he knew Mohamed Atta" and had "provid[ed] money and passports." He also claimed involvement in the July 7, 2005, London bombings,[18] confessed to be in frequent contact with bin Laden, and admitted involvement in terrorist activity in the US, Britain, Egypt, Syria, and Algeria.[19] Citing further official revelations, the Turkish daily *Zaman* revealed that Sakra, like many of the alleged 9/11 hijackers, did not act in accordance with basic Islamic edicts. When Turkish Security Directorate officials told him that "he might perform his religious practices to have a better dialogue... and to gain his confidence," Sakra responded: "I do not pray. I also drink alcohol." Curiously, his fellow al-Qaeda detainees and underlings, Adnan Ersoz and Harun Ilhan, did "perform their religious practices." Police officials admitted that "such an attitude at the top-level of al-Qaeda was confusing."[20]

Sakra's story confirms the bizarre mixture of un-Islamic conduct penetrating the elite membership of al-Qaeda and the radical puritan exterior apparent in the use of Islamist language and symbols by its members. It is impossible to explain this within the parameters of the official narrative, which views al-Qaeda as one of the most militant elements of a radical Islamist tendency. In fact, the evidence perused so far fundamentally challenges the idea that al-Qaeda can be properly categorized as a genuinely Islamist entity. Other statements by Sakra further challenge the very idea of al-Qaeda as constituting an international organization in any meaningful sense, and throw further light on what might explain its duality between apparent fundamentalist Islamist and patently un-Islamic conduct. In his own words:

> Al-Qaeda organizes attacks sometimes without even reporting it to Bin Laden. For al-Qaeda is not structured like a terrorist organization. The militants have the operational initiative. There are groups organizing activities in the name of al-Qaeda. The second attack in London was organized by a group, which took initiative. Even Laden may not know about it.[21]

Sakra's description of al-Qaeda contradicts entirely the official narrative. But he went even further than that. *Zaman* reported incredulously the most surprising elements of Sakra's candid revelations during his four-day interrogation at Istanbul Anti-Terror Department Headquarters: "Amid the smoke from the fortuitous fire emerged the possibility that al-Qaeda may not be, strictly speaking, an organization but an element of an intelligence agency operation." As a result of Sakra's statements:

> Turkish intelligence specialists agree that there is no such organization as al-Qaeda. Rather, al-Qaeda is the name of a secret service operation. The concept "fighting terror" is the background of the "low-intensity-warfare" conducted in the mono-polar world order. The subject of this strategy of tension is named as "al-Qaeda."
>
> ... Sakra, the fifth most senior man in Osama bin Ladin's al-Qaeda... has been sought by the secret services since 2000. The US Central Intelligence Agency (CIA) interrogated him twice before. Following the interrogation CIA offered him employment. He also received a large sum of money by CIA... in 2000 the CIA passed intelligence about Sakra through a classified notice to Turkey, calling for the Turkish National Security Organization (MIT) to capture him. MIT caught Sakra in Turkey and interrogated him...
>
> Sakra was [later] sought and caught by Syrian al-Mukhabarat as well. Syria too offered him employment. Sakra eventually became a triple agent for the secret services... Turkish security officials, interrogating a senior al-Qaeda figure for the first time, were thoroughly confused about what they discovered about al-Qaeda. The prosecutor too was surprised.[22]

According to Sakra then, himself a paid CIA recruit, al-Qaeda is less a coherent centralized organization than a loose association of mujahideen often mobilized under the influence of Western secret services. His own lack of traditional Islamic piety at a senior level within al-Qaeda further discredits the widespread perception of al-Qaeda as a truly Islamist Salafist group.

Two key issues arise here—firstly the question of the manner in which al-Qaeda exists; and secondly, the question of Turkish intelligence's interpretation of al-Qaeda as integral to a "secret service operation" within a wider "strategy of tension."

As for the first issue, it is indeed difficult to identify any way in which al-Qaeda genuinely exists as a concrete international terrorist organization—or at all—as conventionally promulgated by Western government and security sources.

Award-winning filmmaker Adam Curtis in his series of BBC documentaries "The Power of Nightmares," went so far as to argue that al-Qaeda does not even have members, a leader, "sleeper cells," or even an overall strategy. As a concrete international organization "it barely exists at all, except as an idea about cleansing a corrupt world through religious violence."[23] Dr. Andrew Sike, a criminologist and forensic psychologist at the University of East London serving on the UN Roster of Terrorism Experts, similarly notes that al-Qaeda lacks "a clear hierarchy, military mindset and centralised command." At best, it constitutes a loose network of "affiliated groups sharing religious and ideological backgrounds, but which often interact sparingly." Al-Qaeda is less an organization than "a state of mind," encompassing "a wide range of members and followers who can differ dramatically from each other."[24]

Numerous other experts have thus questioned conventional portrayals of al-Qaeda, concluding that there is no solid evidence that it exists, let alone that it might function as an organized network. Conversely, mainstream studies that have endorsed such a perspective in support of the official narrative are profoundly flawed. Rohan Gunaratna's *Inside al-Qaeda*, for instance—widely acclaimed as the most comprehensive, authoritative, and well-documented analysis of al-Qaeda available—is consistently unreliable and inconsistent, to the point that the book's British publishers inserted a disclaimer in its edition cautioning readers to avoid interpreting its content as factual, but rather as "nothing other than a suggestion."[25]

This, of course, raises yet another question. If al-Qaeda does not exist in the conventional sense, then how does this fit with Sakra's description of al-Qaeda as a "secret service operation" operating within the parameters of a "strategy of tension"? The answer to this can be best sought in an examination of precisely what is denoted by what Turkish officials describe as "a strategy of tension." And to answer this, we must delve deeper into history to discover the roots of international terrorism in the Cold War.

International Terrorism: Ideological Framework, Covert Reality

International Terrorism as Ideological Construct

In the summer of 1979, a group of powerful elites from various countries gathered at an international conference in Jerusalem to promote and exploit the idea of "international terrorism." The forum, officially known as the Jerusalem Conference on International Terrorism (JCIT), was organized by Benjamin Netanyahu—now a former Israeli prime minister and minister of finance—on behalf of the Jonathan Institute. The institute was established in honor of the memory of Netanyahu's brother, Lt. Col. Jonathan Netanyahu, an Israeli officer killed by a stray bullet during the IDF raid on Entebbe.[26]

Over two decades ago, the JCIT established the ideological foundations for the "war on terror." The JCIT's defining theme was that international terrorism constituted an organized political movement whose ultimate origin was in the Soviet Union. All terrorist groups were ultimately products of, and could be traced back to, this single source, which—according to the JCIT—provided financial, military, and logistical assistance to disparate terrorist movements around the globe. The mortal danger to Western security and democracy posed by the worldwide scope of this international terrorist movement required an appropriate worldwide anti-terrorism offensive, consisting of the mutual coordination of Western military intelligence services.[27] The JCIT's findings served as the basis of the worldwide publication of hundreds of newspaper, think tank, and academic accounts of Soviet involvement in orchestrating an international terrorist network.

But as Philip Paull documents extensively in his master's thesis at San Francisco State University, the JCIT's own literature and use of source documentation was profoundly flawed. It heavily cited, for instance, statistics purporting to demonstrate a drastic ten-fold increase in incidents of international terrorism between 1968–1978—but as Paull shows, these figures were deliberately concocted and inflated, contradicting original CIA data illustrating a decline in terrorist incidents for the same period.[28] It also routinely relied on techniques of blatant disinformation, misquoting and misrepresenting Western intelligence reports, as well as recycling government-sponsored disinformation published in the mainstream media.[29] Paull thus concludes that the 1979 JCIT was:

> ... a successful propaganda operation... the entire notion of 'international terrorism' as promoted by the Jerusalem Conference rests on a faulty, dishonest, and ultimately corrupt information base.... The issue of international terrorism has little to do with fact, or with any objective legal definition of international terrorism. The issue, as promoted by the Jerusalem Conference and used by the Reagan administration, is an ideological and instrumental issue. It is the ideology, rather than the reality, that dominates US foreign policy today.[30]

The new ideology of "international terrorism" justified the Reagan administration's shift to "a renewed interventionist foreign policy," and legitimized a "new alliance between right-wing dictatorships everywhere" and the government. "These military dictatorships and repressive governments have long used the word 'terrorist' to characterize the opposition to their rule." Thus, the administration had moved to "legitimate their politics of state terrorism and repression," while also alleviating pressure for the reform of the intelligence community and opening the door for "aggressive and sometimes illegal intelligence action," in the course of fighting the international terrorist threat.[31]

The primary architects of the JCIT's "international terrorism" project were, reports Paull,

> present and former members of the Israeli and United States governments, new right politicians, high-ranking former United States and Israeli intelligence officers, the anti-détente, pro-cold war group associated with the policies of Senator Henry M. Jackson, a group of neoconservative journalists and intellectuals..., and reactionary British and French politicians and publicists.[32]

Individuals who participated included:
· Menachem Begin, then Prime Minister of Israel and former Irgun "terrorist,"
· Benzion Netanyahu, then Cornell University professor emeritus,
· Shimon Peres, then leader of the Israeli Labor Party,
· Gen. Chaim Herzog, former Israeli military intelligence chief,
· Maj. Gen. Meir Amit, former Israeli military intelligence chief,
· Lt. Gen. Aharon Yariv, former Israeli military intelligence chief,
· Maj. Gen. Schlomo Gazit, former Israeli military intelligence chief,
· Paul Johnson, former editor of the *New Statesman,*
· Honourable Sir Hugh Fraser, Conservative MP and former British undersecretary of state for colonies,
· Henry M. Jackson, influential right-wing senator from the state of Washington,
· Richard Pipes, a professor and Russian expert in President Reagan's National Security Council,
· Ray S. Cline, former deputy director for intelligence at the CIA,
· Maj. Gen. George J. Keegan, former US Air Force intelligence chief, and
· George H. W. Bush, former CIA director and then presidential candidate who later became president[33]

It is perhaps no coincidence that Bush Sr.'s son, President George W. Bush, has most effectively overseen the enforcement of an entire domestic and international American political program based principally on the ideology of "international terrorism." Noting the instrumental influence of the JCIT on US policy during the Reagan administration, reemerging with the George W. Bush administration, Diana Ralph rightly concludes that the new "war on terror" is "modelled on Islamophobic myths, policies, and political structures developed by the Israeli Likkud in 1979, to inspire popular support for US world conquest initiatives."[34]

Soviet Threat as Negligible

If the target of the US government's anti-terrorist program was not real, what was the government targeting? According to the late Richard Barnet, former state department aide to Assistant Secretary for War John McCloy, the inflation of Soviet-sponsored "international terrorism" was useful precisely for demonizing threats to the prevailing US-dominated capitalist economic system:

Even the word "communist" has been applied so liberally and so loosely to revolutionary or radical regimes that any government risks being so characterised if it adopts one or more of the following policies which the State Department finds distasteful: nationalisation of private industry, particularly foreign-owned corporations, radical land reform, autarchic trade policies, acceptance of Soviet or Chinese aid, insistence upon following an anti-American or non-aligned foreign policy, among others.[35]

This view is supported by the fact that there was no tangible, imminent Soviet threat to any of the regions subjected to aggressive US and Western military interventionism during the Cold War. Recently declassified top-secret British Foreign Office files, among other documents, establish this case decisively. These have been extensively examined by British historian Mark Curtis, former research fellow at the Royal Institute of International Affairs. A selection of the documents unearthed by Curtis is reviewed below.[36]

A December 1950 Foreign Office paper pointed out that "only three Middle Eastern countries... are exposed to direct Soviet attack." It went on to illustrate that such an attack was inconceivable. "Short of general war... an attack on Turkey is unlikely owing to the Western guarantees which she enjoys." As for Iran (Persia), "the Soviet government must be aware that any attack on her would carry a grave risk of general war, and it is more likely that Soviet efforts to gain control of Persia will be confined to propaganda, diplomatic and subversive activity." Regarding Afghanistan, "there is little danger of attack."[37]

Another document noted that "the Arab states are all orientated towards the West in varying degrees, opposed to communism and generally successful at present in minimizing or suppressing existing communist activities through restrictive measures." Rather, "ultra-nationalist elements may exercise greater influence and form a greater threat to maintenance of a pro-Western orientation."[38]

Regarding Africa, the State Department observed during 1950 that "'Black' Africa is orientated towards the non-Communist world. Communism has made no real progress in the area."[39] To the contrary, nationalism "constitutes the real force of the future in this area," according to Assistant Secretary of State McGhee.[40]

Concerning Asia, Kennan, then head of US Policy Planning Staff, affirmed that "the problem is not one primarily of Russians but of basic relations of Americans with Asiatics."[41] The State Department commented in 1950 that "in most of Southeast Asia there is no fear of communism as we understand it."[42]

The stark contrast between Western national security discourse and reality during the Cold War was also noted by the London *Guardian* reporting on newly declassified British government documents from 1968, including a pertinent analysis by the Foreign Office Joint Intelligence Committee, summarized as follows:

> The Soviet Union had no intention of launching a military attack on the West at the height of the Cold War, British military and intelligence chiefs privately believed, in stark contrast to what Western politicians and military leaders were saying in public about the "Soviet threat." "The Soviet Union will not deliberately start general war or even limited war in Europe," a briefing for the British chiefs of staff—marked Top Secret, UK Eyes Only, and headed The Threat: Soviet Aims and Intentions—declared in June 1968.[43]

The primary threat to Western interests was described in a 1952 Foreign Office study as "the problem of nationalism," which consisted of five key components parading themselves as "Communism": "(i) insistence on managing their own affairs without the means or ability to do so, including the dismissal of British advisers; (ii) expropriation of British assets; (iii) unilateral denunciation of treaties with the UK; (iv) ganging up against the UK (and the Western powers) in the United Nations."[44]

All this fundamentally contradicted Western national security discourse throughout the Cold War period. Indeed, this data suggests that there was negligible Soviet/Communist threat to the Middle East, "Black" Africa, North Africa, the Far East, South Asia, and Southeast Asia. This does not preclude that the Soviet Union posed a potential threat, which would explain the dynamics of the bipolar system. But countering Soviet expansionism was not the central galvanizing factor in Western national security strategy. The bipolar system functioned as a convenient framework for both superpowers to command and mobilize domestic politics and resources in the service of powerful vested interests.[45]

International Terrorism as Covert Operations Construct

International terrorism was not merely a construct of ideology, framed around the Soviet Union. It swiftly became a very real construct of Western covert operations. It is now well documented and no longer disputable that during the Cold War, high-level sections of the American, British, and Western European secret services participated in a sophisticated NATO-backed operation to engineer domestic terrorist attacks that were to be blamed on the Soviet Union. The objective was to galvanize public opinion against left-wing policies and parties, and ultimately to mobilize drastic anti-Communist policies at home and abroad, most of which were in fact designed to legitimize interventionism against nationalist independence movements throughout the South. The most authoritative study of this "strategy of tension," *NATO's Secret Armies*, is authored by Dr. Daniele Ganser, senior researcher at the Center for Security Studies in the Federal Institute of Technology, Zurich. Ganser's sources are unimpeachable: the transcripts of European parliamentary inquiries; the few secret documents that have been declassified; interviews with government, military, and intelligence officials, and so on.

The process was begun on the order of British Prime Minister Winston Churchill, who in July 1940 called for the establishment of a secret army to "set Europe ablaze by assisting resistance movements and carrying out subversive operations in enemy held territory."[46] By October 4, 1945, the British Chiefs of Staff and the Special Operations branch of MI6 directed the creation of a "skeleton network" capable of expansion either in war or to service clandestine operations abroad: "Priority was given in carrying out these tasks to countries likely to be overrun in the earliest stages of any conflict with the Soviet Union, but not as yet under Soviet domination."[47] In the ensuing years, Col. Gubbins's Special Operations branch of MI6 cooperated closely with Frank Wisner's CIA covert action department Office of Policy Coordination (OPC) on White House orders, and in turn coordinated US and UK Special Forces, to establish stay-behind secret armies across Western Europe.[48]

The program soon developed into a dangerous conglomerate of unaccountable covert operations controlled largely by clandestine structures operating as parallel subsections of the main intelligence services. Among the documents Ganser brings to attention is the classified Field Manual 30-31 (FM 30-31), with appendices FM 30-31A and FM 30-31B, authored by the Pentagon's Defense Intelligence Agency (DIA) to train thousands of stay-behind officers around the world. As Ganser observes: "FM 30-31 instructs the secret soldiers to carry out acts of violence in times of peace and then blame them on the Communist enemy in order to create a situation of fear and alertness. Alternatively, the secret soldiers are instructed to infiltrate the left-wing movements and then urge them to use violence." In the manual's own words:

> There may be times when Host Country Governments show passivity or indecision in the face of Communist subversion and according to the interpretation of the US secret services do not react with sufficient effectiveness... US army intelligence must have the means of launching special operations which will convince Host Country Governments and public opinion of the reality of the insurgent danger. To reach this aim US army intelligence should seek to penetrate the insurgency by means of agents on special assignment, with the task of forming special action groups among the most radical elements of the insurgency... In case it has not been possible to successfully infiltrate such agents into the leadership of the rebels it can be useful to instrumentalise extreme leftist organizations for one's own ends in order to achieve the above described targets... These special operations must remain strictly secret. Only those persons which are acting against the revolutionary uprising shall know of the involvement of the US Army...[49]

The existence of this secret operation exploded into public controversy in August 1990 when Italian Prime Minister Giulio Andreotti admitted the existence of "Gladio," a secret subsection of Italian military intelligence services, responsible for domestic bombings blamed on Italian Communists. Ganser documents in intricate detail how this subversive network, created by elements of US and UK intelligence services, orchestrated devastating waves of terrorist attacks blamed on the Soviet Union, not only in Italy, but also in Spain, Germany, France, Turkey, Greece, and throughout Western Europe. Despite a number of European parliamentary inquiries, a European Union resolution on the Gladio phenomenon, NATO's closed-door admissions to European ambassadors, confirmations of the international operation from senior CIA officials, and other damning documentary evidence, NATO, the CIA, and MI6 have together consistently declined to release their secret files on the matter.

This secret history demonstrates that in the absence of an existing mobilizing factor legitimizing the militarization of Western societies, military intelligence services took it upon themselves to manufacture, ideologically and operationally, a projected external threat of monolithic proportions. This was, then, the elemental ideological and operational structure of the Cold War:

1. Predominance of Western interests in the expansion and consolidation of a US-dominated capitalist world system;

2. Lack of a real Soviet threat sufficient to legitimize the militarization necessary to pursue those interests;

3. Ideological and operational construction by Western military intelligence services and policymakers of a projected external threat consisting of Soviet-directed "international terrorism."

The collapse of the Soviet Union entailed the collapse of this self-reinforcing structure, which was intrinsic to the policing of world order under US hegemony during the Cold War. Yet for the first time it opened the way for the projection of military power in theaters previously forbidden because of the possibility of Soviet reprisals. But to sustain such force projection required a new sort of threat projection, in which al-Qaeda was to play a crucial strategic role. Sakra's testimony as a leading al-Qaeda insider to the effect that al-Qaeda is a tool of a post–Cold War strategy of tension points to a startling and radical departure from the official narrative, and suggests that al-Qaeda plays a far more functional role in Western geostrategic imperatives than we are conventionally permitted to believe.

The Post–Cold War Strategy of Tension
The New Destabilization Doctrine

As early as June 1979—the same year the JCIT had established "international terrorism" as a defining ideological framework legitimizing the militarization of Western societies—the United States had already commenced covert operations in Afghanistan to exploit the potential for social conflict. According to Zbigniew Brzezinski, former national security adviser under the Carter administration, US involvement began long before the Soviet Union invaded Afghanistan on December 27, 1979.[50] According to *Jane's Defence Weekly*, "al-Qaeda" was created in 1988 "with US knowledge" by Osama bin Laden, a "conglomerate of quasi-independent Islamic terrorist cells" spanning "at least 26 countries."[51]

But conventional wisdom dictates that after the end of the Cold War and the collapse of the Soviet Union beginning in 1989, there was no longer any need for an alliance with the mujahideen. As such, Western military intelligence services broke away from their former proxies and severed their relationship with Osama bin Laden. This is simply false. The CIA had never envisaged that the operational scope of bin Laden's international al-Qaeda network would be restricted to Afghanistan alone. On the contrary, as one CIA analyst told Swiss television journalist Richard Labeviere— chief editor at Radio France International and author of *Dollars for Terror: The United States and Islam*:

> The policy of guiding the evolution of Islam and of helping them against our adversaries worked marvellously well in Afghanistan against the Red Army. The same doctrines can still be used to destabilize what remains of Russian power, and especially to counter the Chinese influence in Central Asia.[52]

Al-Qaeda operations were seen as integral to a new doctrine of covert destabilization, to be implemented in new theaters of operation strategically close to Russian and Chinese influence: namely, Eastern Europe, the Balkans, the Caucasus, and Central Asia.

A number of studies confirm in substantial detail this over-arching trajectory of al-Qaeda sponsorship in these regions in the post–Cold War period. Shortly after 9/11, for example, Michel Chossudovsky, professor of economics at the University of Ottawa, published a number of detailed analyses documenting US sponsorship of al-Qaeda in the Balkans and Caucasus, in relation to a number of conflicts, including Bosnia, Kosovo, and Macedonia. "The 'blowback' thesis is a fabrication," he concludes. "The evidence amply confirms that the CIA never severed its ties to the 'Islamic Militant Network.' Since the end of the Cold War, these covert intelligence links have not only been maintained, they have in fact become increasingly sophisticated," with new covert operations initiated in "Central Asia, the Caucasus and the Balkans," financed by "the Golden Crescent drug trade."[53]

Focusing on Central Asia, Peter Dale Scott, professor emeritus of English at the University of California, Berkeley, has unearthed considerable evidence of US sponsorship of al-Qaeda to accelerate the fragmentation of the Soviet Union and its successor republics, particularly in Azerbaijan. In his testimony to the US Congress in July 2005, Scott noted that for more than

> two decades the United States has engaged in energetic covert programs to secure US control over the Persian Gulf, and also to open up Central Asia for development by US oil companies...
>
> To this end, time after time, US covert operations in the region have used so-called "Arab Afghan" warriors as assets, the jihadis whom we loosely link with the name and leadership of al-

Qaeda. In country after country these "Arab Afghans" have been involved in trafficking Afghan heroin.... In short, the al-Qaeda terror network accused of the 9/11 attacks was supported and expanded by US intelligence programs and covert operations, both during and after the Soviet Afghan War.[54]

Ahmed Rashid, correspondent for the *Far Eastern Economic Review*, the *Daily Telegraph*, and the *Wall Street Journal*, documents the consistent US sponsorship of the Taliban—which was essentially equivalent to al-Qaeda's state-supported infrastructure—throughout the late 1990s through allies Saudi Arabia and Pakistan, to make the country safe for a UNOCAL pipeline project.[55] Rashid quotes a US diplomat commenting in 1997 on the new "free Afghanistan": "The Taliban will probably develop like the Saudis... There will be Aramco [consortium of oil companies controlling Saudi oil], pipelines, an emir, no parliament and lots of Sharia law. We can live with that."[56]

In all such cases, the operational imperative was to secure access routes to lucrative energy resources based largely in Central Asia and the Caspian Basin. My own research has attempted to extend these analyses worldwide, focusing on the detailed dynamics of American, British, and European connections with al-Qaeda in the Balkans, Central Asia, the Caucasus, the Middle East, North Africa, and the Asia-Pacific.[57]

A Case Study: Al-Qaeda in North Africa

In order to convey the manner in which this phenomenon occurs, we will focus here on the regional example of North Africa, which firstly furnishes the two principle operational modes by which covert Western sponsorship of al-Qaeda is achieved, and secondly clarifies the category of interests these modes are intended to secure. The first example, that of Algeria, provides data establishing a model of the indirect state-regional mode of sponsorship. The second example, that of Libya, provides data establishing a model of the direct human-network mode of sponsorship.

Algeria: State-Regional Node: The Armed Islamic Group (GIA) is an al-Qaeda–affiliated terrorist group in Algeria. The group was first "created in the house of the Muhajirin in 1989 in Peshawar." From here, on the border of Pakistan and Afghanistan, "the first hard core of 'Algerian Afghans' launched their terrorist campaign against Algeria." The al-Qaeda veterans of the Afghan war against the Soviets, "trained in the Afghan militias, returned to Algeria with the help of international networks, via Bosnia, Albania, Italy, France, Morocco or Sudan."[58] According to *Jane's Defence Weekly*, in the late 1980s between 400 and 1,000 Algerians who trained as bin Laden's mujahideen in Afghanistan joined various armed groups in Algeria. By January 1993, most of these groups united under the banner of the GIA.[59] The latter forged close links to al-Qaeda "in the early 1990s," reports the office of the attorney general in Australia, when the UK-based Abu Qatada "was designated by bin Laden as the spiritual adviser for Algerian groups including the GIA."[60] Afghan veteran Khamareddine Kherbane was close to both the GIA and al-Qaeda leaderships. Both the GIA and its sub-faction the Salafist Group for Preaching and Combat (GSPC) "developed ties with al-Qaeda early on." From 1997 to 1998, al-Qaeda achieved further "large-scale penetration of Algerian groups."[61] So far the total civilian death toll from the GIA massacres in Algeria amounts to nearly 150,000.[62] The GIA is also implicated in terrorist atrocities outside Algeria and has been "linked to terrorist attacks in Europe."[63] According to Algeria expert Stephen Cook of the Brookings Institute, "there are Algerian [terrorist] cells spread all over Europe, Canada, and the United States."[64]

British journalists John Sweeney and Leonard Doyle interviewed "'Yussuf-Joseph,' a career secret agent in Algeria's securite militaire until he defected to Britain." "Joseph," who spent fourteen years as an Algerian secret agent, had much to reveal about the reality of GIA terrorism. He told Sweeney and Doyle that "the bombs that outraged Paris in 1995—blamed on Muslim fanatics—were the handiwork of the Algerian secret service. They were part of a propaganda war aimed at galvanising French public opinion against the Islamists." The massacres in Algeria, blamed on the GIA, are "the work of secret police and army death squads.... The killing of many foreigners was organised by the secret police, not Islamic extremists." GIA terrorism is "orchestrated by two shadowy figures... Mohammed Mediane, codename 'Tewfik,' and General Smain Lamari, the most feared names in Algeria. They are, respectively, head of the Algerian secret service, the DRS, and its sub-department, the counter intelligence agency, the DCE." According to Joseph:

The GIA is a pure product of Smain's secret service. I used to read all the secret telexes. I know that the GIA has been infiltrated and manipulated by the government. The GIA has been completely turned by the government.... In 1992 Smain created a special group, L'Escadron de la Mort [the Squadron of Death]. One of its main missions to begin with was to kill officers, colonels. The death squads organise the massacres. If anyone inside the killing machine hesitates to torture or kill, they are automatically killed.... The FIS aren't doing the massacres.

As for the Paris bombings, Joseph reveals that Algerian secret agents sent by Smain organized "at least" two of the bombs in Paris in summer 1995. "The operation was run by Colonel Souames Mahmoud, alias Habib, head of the secret service at the Algerian embassy in Paris."[65] Joseph's testimony has been corroborated by the statements of numerous defectors from the Algerian secret services.[66]

Western intelligence agencies know far more than they have publicly conceded. In a remarkable report in the *Guardian*, Richard Norton-Taylor recorded that: "An unprecedented three-year terrorist case dramatically collapsed... when an MI5 informant refused to appear in court after evidence which senior ministers tried to suppress revealed that Algerian government forces were involved in atrocities against innocent civilians." The report refers to "secret documents showing British intelligence believed the Algerian government was involved in atrocities, contradicting the view the government was claiming in public." Attempting to suppress the evidence, three British Cabinet ministers—Jack Straw, Geoffrey Hoon, and the late Robin Cook—"signed public interest immunity certificates."[67]

The secret Foreign Office documents "were produced on the orders of the trial judge" eighteen months late. When they finally arrived, "they were in marked contrast to the government's publicly-stated view, expressed by the Foreign Office in 1998, that there was 'no credible, substantive evidence to confirm' allegations implicating Algerian government forces in atrocities." The documents, read in open court, revealed that according to Whitehall's Joint Intelligence Committee: "There is no firm evidence to rule out government manipulation or involvement in terrorist violence." According to one document: "Sources had privately said some of the killings of civilians were the responsibility of the Algerian security services." Another document from January 1997 cites a British source as follows:

"military security [in Algeria] would have... no scruples about killing innocent people.... My instincts remain that parts of the Algerian government would stop at nothing." Multiple documents "referred to the 'manipulation' of the GIA being used as a cover to carry out their own operations." A US intelligence report confirmed that "there was no evidence to link 1995 Paris bombings to Algerian militants." On the contrary, the US report indicates "that one killing at the time could have been ordered by the Algerian government." Crucially, a Whitehall document cites the danger to British government interests if this information becomes public—"if revealed," it warns, it "could open us to detailed questioning by NGOs and journalists."[68]

The Algerian junta–GIA–al-Qaeda terror nexus has received heavy Western financial assistance. In the late 1990s, the European Union released 60 million Euros—some $65 million—to the Algerian generals. The total loan package was worth 125 million Euros.[69] In June 2000, US-based international banks and investment houses such as Chase Manhattan visited Algiers, along with then Undersecretary of the Treasury Stuart Eizenstat. US private investments in Algeria were estimated at between $3.5 and $4 billion—almost entirely in oil and gas exploration and production.[70]

Algeria has the fifth largest reserves of natural gas in the world, and is the second largest gas exporter, with 130 trillion proven natural gas reserves. It ranks fourteenth for oil reserves, with official estimates at 9.2 billion barrels. Approximately 90 percent of Algeria's crude oil exports go to Western Europe, including Britain, France, Italy, Germany, the Netherlands, and Spain. Algeria's major trading partners are Italy, France, the United States, Germany, and Spain.[71]

John Cooley further reports the presence of "500 to 600 American engineers and technicians living and working behind barbed wire" in a collection of "protected gas and oil enclaves in Algeria." US commercial involvement in Algeria "began in earnest... in 1991." At the end of that year, the regime

> opened the energy sector on liberal terms to foreign investors and operators... About 30 oil and gas fields have been attributed to foreign companies since then. The main American firms involved, Arco, Exxon, Oryx, Anadarko, Mobil and Sun Oil received exploration permits, often in association with European firms like Agip, BP, Cepsa or the Korean group Daewoo.... The majority of oil and gas exports go to nearby Europe... the main clients in the late 1990s [being] France, Belgium, Spain and Italy.[72]

According to European intelligence sources, CIA meetings with Algerian Islamist leaders from 1993 to 1995 are responsible for the lack of terrorist attacks on US oil and agribusiness installations in Algeria.[73]

Libya: Human-Network Node: David Shayler worked for the international terrorism desk of MI5 for six years before resigning in 1997. In 1995, he obtained classified MI6 data detailing a covert British intelligence plan to assassinate Libyan Head of State Col. Muammar Qaddafi. MI6 paid over £100,000 to the al-Qaeda network in Libya to conduct the assassination. The operation failed. The al-Qaeda cell planted a bomb under the wrong car, killing six innocent Libyan civilians.[74] According to Shayler, the plot came to his attention in formal meetings with his MI6 colleagues. The *Observer*'s Martin Bright revealed that the said officers involved in the plot were "Richard Bartlett, who has previously only been known under the codename PT16 and had overall responsibility for the operation; and David Watson, codename PT16B." The latter was the MI6 handler for Libyan al-Qaeda operative "Tunworth," who was providing information from within the cell.[75] In a press release on the subject, Shayler observed:

> We need a statement from the Prime Minister and the Foreign Secretary clarifying the facts of this matter. In particular, we need to know how around £100,000 of taxpayers' money was used to fund the sort of Islamic Extremists who have connections to Osama bin Laden's al-Qaeda network. Did ministers give MI6 permission for this? By the time MI6 paid the group in late 1995 or early 1996, US investigators had already established that Bin Laden was implicated in the 1993 attack on the World Trade Centre. Given the timing and the close connections between Libyan and Egyptian Islamic Extremists, it may even have been used to fund the murder of British citizens in Luxor, Egypt in 1996.[76]

Shayler elaborated on these concerns in the *Observer*. The "real criminals," he argued, "are the British Government and the intelligence services. The Government has a duty to uphold the law. It cannot simply be ignored because crimes are carried out by friends of the Government." Given that innocent civilians were killed, "senior Ministers should, of course, have called in the police immediately.... The Government's failure to ensure that two MI6 officers are brought to justice for their part in planning a murder is what I would expect of despots and dictators."[77]

The British government completely denied the allegations. Then Foreign Secretary Robin Cook described Shayler's allegations as "pure fantasy."[78] However, the government soon accused Shayler of breaching the 1989 Official Secrets Act—his revelations were an alleged threat to British national security—and subsequently prosecuted him to prevent further publication of his information. Reporting on the upcoming trial in October 2002, the *Evening Standard* observed that

> Michael Tugendhat, QC, appearing for various national newspapers, is expected to argue that the Government has provided no evidence that national security will be threatened by the trial and will underline the importance of open justice... Shayler will be defending himself during the trial. He is expected to claim that British secret service agents paid up to £100,000 to al-Qaeda terrorists for an assassination attempt on Libyan leader Colonel Gadaffy in 1996. He is seeking permission to plead a defense of "necessity"—that he acted for the greater good by revealing wrongdoing by the security service.[79]

In further startling revelations supporting Shayler's allegations, the French intelligence experts Jean-Charles Brisard, adviser to President Chirac, and journalist Guillaume Dasquié documented that among the members of the Libyan al-Qaeda cell hired by MI6 to assassinate Col. Qaddafi was one of Osama bin Laden's most trusted lieutenants, Anas al-Liby. Anas al-Liby is on the FBI's list of "Most Wanted Terrorists" "in connection with the August 7, 1998, bombings of the United States Embassies in Dar es Salaam, Tanzania, and Nairobi, Kenya.... The Rewards For Justice Program, United States Department of State, is offering a reward of up to $25 million for information leading directly to the apprehension or conviction of Anas Al-Liby."[80] As *Observer* home affairs editor Martin Bright reported:

> British intelligence paid large sums of money to an al-Qaeda cell in Libya in a doomed attempt to assassinate Colonel Gadaffi in 1996 and thwarted early attempts to bring Osama bin Laden to justice. The latest claims of MI6 involvement with Libya's fearsome Islamic Fighting Group, which is connected to one of bin Laden's trusted lieutenants, will be embarrassing to the Government...
>
> The Libyan al-Qaeda cell included Anas al-Liby... He is wanted for his involvement in the African embassy bombings.

Al-Liby was with bin Laden in Sudan before the al-Qaeda leader returned to Afghanistan in 1996. Astonishingly, despite suspicions that he was a high-level al-Qaeda operative, al-Liby was given political asylum in Britain and lived in Manchester until May of 2000.

A police raid at al-Liby's Manchester accommodation discovered a 180-page al-Qaeda "manual for jihad" containing instructions for terrorist attacks.[81]

A Model of Covert Sponsorship: In the case of Algeria, the Algerian military regime constitutes a state-regional structure that is interpenetrated through direct military-intelligence liaisons with a domestic Islamist terrorist organization officially identified as an al-Qaeda network. This interpenetration acts as the catalyst through which Western financial, military, and intelligence assistance is provided through the state to the network. The entire relationship is sealed within the logic of Western interests in securing and controlling access to regional energy resources. The regime thus acts as a state-regional node by which the West sponsors a local al-Qaeda affiliate in order to protect geostrategic interests.

In contrast, in the case of Libya, there is no structural intermediary to facilitate the funneling of assistance between Western military intelligence services and a local terrorist network officially identified as an al-Qaeda network. Rather, Western financial and logistical intelligence support to the terrorist network is secured directly through immediate interpenetration between the intelligence service and the network, though the presence of double agent operatives. This relationship of direct interpenetration, a human-network node, provides the medium of control and the means of material assistance to al-Qaeda. In this case, although energy interests may have been an overall overriding factor in determining the general strategic direction of al-Qaeda sponsorship, the specific objective was an illegal assassination of a head of state considered, at that time, to be inimical to Western geostrategic interests.

Extensive empirical and historical data shows that the dual model established above applies differentially but consistently across the world's most strategic regions.[82] In all these regions, al-Qaeda destabilization programs consistently function—to this day—to guarantee US geostrategic imperatives. The extensive geographical scope and systematic temporal pattern of this operational symbiosis of US–al-Qaeda interests suggests that the strategy of tension is alive and well, but now in a sophisticated and elusive new form that yet largely conforms to the same self-reinforcing structure prevailing during the Cold War:

1. Predominance of Anglo-American interests in the expansion and consolidation of a US-dominated capitalist world system;

2. Lack of clearly identifiable regional threats sufficient to legitimize the militarization necessary to pursue those interests in those regions;

3. Ideological and operational construction by Western military intelligence services and policymakers of a projected external threat consisting of al-Qaeda–directed "international terrorism," used selectively and systematically as a tool of destabilization to secure specific regional interests.

This, of course, presents a fundamentally different picture of al-Qaeda than that of the official narrative. On the one hand, al-Qaeda as a coherent self-directed international entity barely exists in any meaningful sense. On the other, al-Qaeda as a euphemism for an ongoing US covert operations apparatus penetrating disparate Islamist groups, and extending the Cold War "strategy of tension" into the post–Cold War period, does exist.[83] This brings us to a much clearer understanding of the duality of al-Qaeda as a seemingly radical Islamist tendency, many of whose elite operatives and senior leaders are patently non-Islamic.

The reason for this ideological duality lies in its operational duality, in terms of its concocted exterior image as an organized network supposedly fighting against Western imperialism in the Muslim world, and in terms of its interior reality as a decentralized, disparate, amorphous association of mujahideen penetrated and manipulated on behalf of Western military intelligence interests. The strategy of tension—the demands of Western threat projection premised on legitimizing Western militarization—requires the former dimension, whereas the geostrategy of covert destabilization—a post–Cold War strategy that goes beyond the strategy of tension—is reliant on the latter dimension. In the post–Cold War period, al-Qaeda encapsulates not one but two US covert strategic doctrines: the strategy of tension and the doctrine of destabilization.

The Post-9/11 Destabilization Doctrine

There is compelling circumstantial evidence of the operation of the destabilization doctrine in the post-9/11 period. In a little noted but important article for the *Los Angeles Times*, US defense analyst William Arkin referred to a classified "outbrief" compiled by US Defense Secretary Donald Rumsfeld's Defense Science Board 2002 Summer Study on Special Operations and Joint Forces in Support of Countering Terrorism. The secret study—drafted to guide other Pentagon agencies—recommended the implementation of "new strategies, postures and organization" in fighting the "war on terror." The principal vehicle of these new methods is:

> ... a super-Intelligence Support Activity, an organization it dubs the Proactive, Preemptive Operations Group, (P2OG), to bring together CIA and military covert action, information warfare, intelligence, and cover and deception.

Among other things, this body would launch secret operations aimed at "stimulating reactions" among terrorists and states possessing weapons of mass destruction—that is, for instance, prodding terrorist cells into action and exposing themselves to "quick-response attacks by US forces."

Military intervention would be justified because such actions "would hold 'states/sub-state actors accountable' and 'signal to harboring states that their sovereignty will be at risk.'" The Proactive, Preemptive Operations Group (P2OG) is not an entirely unprecedented structure. Rather, its roots go back to the Intelligence Support Activity (ISA) established in 1981, which "fought in drug wars and counter-terror operations from the Middle East to South America," building a reputation for lawlessness. Throughout the 1990s, the ISA operated under different guises, and today is active under the code name "Gray Fox":

> Gray Fox's low-profile eavesdropping planes also fly without military markings. Working closely with Special Forces and the CIA, Gray Fox also places operatives inside hostile territory. In and around Afghanistan, Gray Fox was part of a secret sphere that included the CIA's paramilitary Special Activities Division and the Pentagon's Joint Special Operations Command. These commands and "white" Special Forces like the Green Berets, as well as Air Force combat controllers and commandos of eight different nations report to a mind-boggling array of new command cells and coordination units set up after Sept. 11.[84]

In other words, the P2OG merely expands an already existing apparatus for covert operations connected to terrorism. However, the language of the Defense Science Board clarifies that P2OG's primary purpose is to provoke terrorist groups into actually conducting anti-US operations in order permit a US military response. The board additionally proposes "tagging key terrorist figures with special chemicals so they can be tracked by laser anywhere on Earth" and "creating a 'red team' of particularly diabolical thinkers to plot imaginary terror attacks on the United States so the government can plan to thwart them." A key role for "an elite group of counter-terror operatives" would be "duping al Qaida into undertaking operations" and attempting to "stimulate terrorists into responding or moving operations." This will be facilitated by dramatic increases in urban warfare capabilities through "the development of a detailed database of most of the cities in the world... with GPS coordinates marking key structures and roads." This constantly updated database would "come together in a three-dimensional display showing buildings, including windows and doors, streets and alleys and underground passages, obstacles like power lines and key infrastructure like water and communications lines."[85]

The new Pentagon strategy then is ultimately "aimed at luring terrorists into committing acts of terrorism" as an integral part of fighting terrorism.[86] As journalist Chris Floyd wryly observes:

> Once they have sparked terrorists into action—by killing their family members? luring them with loot? fueling them with drugs? plying them with jihad propaganda? messing with their mamas? or with agents provocateurs, perhaps, who infiltrate groups then plan and direct the attacks themselves?—they can then take measures against the "states/sub-state actors accountable" for "harboring" the Rumsfeld-roused gangs.[87]

P2OG undoubtedly demonstrates that the strategy of tension continues to define the operational parameters of the "war on terror."

Applying the Doctrine in Iraq

This incestuous relationship between the West and its own alleged archenemy has continued well into the post-9/11 period, including apparently in Iraq. In November 2004, a joint statement was released on several Islamist websites on behalf of al-Qaeda's leader in Iraq, Abu Musab al-Zarqawi, and Saddam Hussein's old Ba'ath Party loyalists. Zarqawi's network had "joined other extremist Islamists and Saddam Hussein's old Baath party to threaten increased attacks on US-led forces." Zarqawi's group said they signed "the statement written by the Iraqi Baath party, not because we support the party or Saddam, but because it expresses the demands of resistance groups in Iraq."[88]

The statement formalized what had already been reported for a year—that, as post-Saddam Iraqi intelligence and US military officials told the *Sunday Times*: "al-Qaeda terrorists who have infiltrated Iraq from Saudi Arabia and other Arab countries have formed an alliance with former intelligence agents of Saddam Hussein to fight their common enemy, the American forces." Al-Qaeda leaders "recruit from the pool" of Saddam's former "security and intelligence officers who are unemployed and embittered by their loss of status." After vetting, "they begin al-Qaeda-style training, such as how to make remote-controlled bombs." Both Saudi Arabia and Pakistan appear to be integrally involved in the operation. "The alliance, known as Jaish Muhammad—the army of the prophet Muhammad—is believed to be responsible for increasingly sophisticated attacks on US soldiers." Jaish Muhammad is smuggling "millions of dollars, weapons and hundreds of Arab fighters across the desert border with Saudi Arabia."[89]

Pakistani military sources revealed in February 2005 that the "the US has... resolved to arm small militias backed by US troops and entrenched in the population" involved in the Iraqi insurgency. For the purpose, the US has secretly "procured Pakistan-manufactured weapons, including rifles, rocket-propelled grenade launchers, ammunition, rockets and other light weaponry." Consignments were bulk-loaded onto US military cargo aircraft at Chaklala Airbase arriving from and departing for Iraq. "The US-armed and supported militias in the south will comprise former members of the Ba'ath Party"—the same people recruited and trained by Zarqawi's al-Qaeda network in Iraq. A Pakistani military analyst familiar with strategic and proxy operations noted that US-made arms were not being supplied so as to conceal the role of US assistance. This was, indeed, the same policy behind US procurement of Pakistani arms to the mujahideen during the Cold War. He said:

> A similar strategy was adopted in Afghanistan during the initial few years of the anti-USSR resistance [the early 1980s] movement where guerrillas were supplied with Chinese-made AK-47 rifles [which were procured by Pakistan with US money], Egyptian and German-made G-3 rifles. Similarly, other arms, like anti-aircraft guns, short-range missiles and mortars, were also procured by the US from different countries and supplied to Pakistan, which handed them over to the guerrillas.

Military sources added that their destination was not the Iraqi security forces "because US arms would be given to them." Rather, the US is playing a double game to "head off" the threat of a "Shi'ite clergy-driven religious movement"—in other words, to exacerbate the deterioration of security by penetrating, manipulating, and arming the terrorist insurgency, thus legitimizing permanent Anglo-American military involvement in Iraq purportedly to promote security.[90]

It is thus plausible to conclude that "al-Qaeda" in Iraq actually designates yet another category of US covert operations. The insurgency appears to consist of two contradictory elements—a genuinely indigenous resistance movement, and a much smaller, insidious, alien element constituting operatives co-opted and sponsored by US military intelligence in coordination with key allied military intelligence services responsible for terrorist violence.

The endgame of this secret strategy is clearly the generation of destabilization, which is the classic and pre-eminent role al-Qaeda has played worldwide, consistently in service to Western military-strategic interests. Indeed, the plausibility of this view has not been lost on Iraqis, neither Sunnis nor Shi'ites. Sheikh Jawad al-Kalesi, the Shi'ite imam of the al-Kadhimiyah mosque in Baghdad, told *Le Monde*: "I don't think that Abu Musab al-Zarqawi exists as such. He's simply an invention by the occupiers to divide the people." Iraq's most powerful Sunni Arab religious authority, the Association of Muslim Scholars, concurs, condemning the call to arms against Shi'ites as a "very dangerous" phenomenon that "plays into the hands of the occupier who wants to split up the country and spark a sectarian war."[91]

Conclusions

The overall picture given here has not been designed to provide exhaustive answers to the questions raised at the outset, but to establish the existence of fatal anomalies in the official narrative, which ultimately defines international terrorism as a distinctly Muslim problem. Thus establishing the logically permissible boundaries of political debate, the official narrative purports to leave the world with only one logical alternative, a Muslim solution, or perhaps more accurately, a final solution targeted principally at Muslims and Islam.

The data discussed here undermines the credibility of this narrative in its most core assumptions. Not only are the identities of the alleged 9/11 hijackers in question, their status as Islamist fundamentalists is thoroughly problematic. As for al-Qaeda, not only is its organizational existence dubious, its continuing character as a radical tendency within the Islamist Salafist movement is implausible. The ephemeral and contradictory nature of what is conventionally labeled al-Qaeda is rooted in its ongoing utility to the Western covert operations apparatus. It is difficult in this context to justify the idea that there really is a "war on terror."

This counter-narrative, rooted in reliable documentation, strikes at the heart of the official narrative and challenges the entire paradigm of the "war on terror," not only as an accurate encapsulation of post-9/11 international relations, but also as a legitimate vehicle of Western domestic and foreign policies. As a discourse, it is discredited; as a policy regime, it is bankrupt.

This analysis has broad implications for understanding other anti-Western terrorist atrocities after 9/11. It can no longer be simply taken as given that terrorist attacks, officially blamed on Muslim extremists, are the consequence of a Muslim problem, implying that countering terrorism equates to "dealing" with Muslim communities. On the contrary, given the historic and contemporary role of Western powers in sponsoring terrorist networks officially identified as branches of al-Qaeda in key strategic regions, it would perhaps be prudent for scholars, journalists, and policymakers to embark on some serious soul-searching—starting at home—to uncover the fundamental sources of international terrorism within the arteries of Western financial and military power itself.

13

AMERICAN MUSLIMS AND 9/11 TRUTH: THE PARALYSIS OF DISCOURSE, THE INCOMPETENCE OF ACADEMIA, AND THE NEED FOR AN ACCURATE DIAGNOSIS

Faiz Khan

Ye who are conscious of God—If a fasiq[1] *comes with alarming news, make sure you verify their word, lest you afflict people out of your ignorance, and regret your actions.*
—Qur'an, Verse 49:6

At some point, silence before a lie becomes betrayal.
—Dr. Martin Luther King, Jr.

MOST AMERICAN MUSLIMS, BOTH LAY AND EDUCATED, HAD LOST THEIR WAY from the very start. However, for a few American minds of various religious persuasions—or no religious persuasion—from September 12, 2001, onward, the widely displayed "good Muslim–bad Muslim" dialectic just didn't cut it as an explanation of why the attacks of 9/11 occurred and succeeded. Their instincts served them well.

The surest sign of intellectual incompetence within the mass of 9/11 discourse is to blindly accept the limits that have been constructed in discussing the phenomenon, especially when this blind acceptance occurs in the face of clear and compelling evidence that the limits of discourse must be expanded to explain the operation and success of the attacks. Unfortunately, from September 12 onward there emerged a sustained yet unbelievably ludicrous mainstream explanation of the factors that produced 9/11, followed by a frantic inquiry of various people or groups that purportedly represented American Islam, asking how such an event could have been born of the nebulously frightful geographic and ideological Islamic world. I was one of those interviewed by various media outlets and others, and I quickly became silent because I came to the conclusion that the premise of the question, often asked by well-meaning journalists, was false and even deceitful: that the main cause of the 9/11 assaults and their success came from the Islamic world. As a medical doctor, my profession involves diagnostic reasoning and educating not only other doctors, but most importantly, the patients whom I serve ("doctor" etymologically comes from the latin *docere* plus *tor*, "one who teaches"). To answer questions, offer therapies, counsel, or elaborate explanations to them such that a deceitful or erroneous premise tacitly or explicitly is maintained in the response is first of all to become an agent of disinformation. In cases where lives are at stake—or in the case of interpreting 9/11 to a public yearning to understand the nature of such conflict—the consequences of endorsing deceit or error (consciously or ignorantly) are grave. Nevertheless, naively, yet predictably, the American Muslim scene performed its role by reeling onto the defensive and sucking the bait. Prominent Muslims busied themselves trying to explain "real Islam," distracted by and then swallowing the mainstream explanation of 9/11. Most completely neglected the grotesque inconsistencies and outright lies of the official story, which suggest that the success of the attacks had less to do with "militant Islam" and more to do with the inescapable fact that 9/11 was an inside job.

The "9/11 truth" thesis categorically rejects the mainstream thesis and asserts that the prime factor for the success of the criminal mission known as 9/11 did not come from the quarter known as "militant Islam," although the phenomenon known as "militant Islamic networks" may have played a partial role—the role of scapegoat and perhaps the role of patsy.

Moreover, the rise and popularization of these so-called militant Islamic networks—including their funding, the apparatus of their ideological propaganda, their logistical and material empowerment, and the relationships linking them to corporate-driven transnational covert operations that co-opt government infrastructure and policies of various nation states—these need to be seriously examined and boldly elucidated by anyone who cares at all about humanity. All authentic religions care deeply about humanity—as a Muslim, one is duty-bound to pursue this avenue of inquiry. The 9/11 truth thesis forces these issues onto the table.

Let me be clear about my opinion here, as it relates to the phenomenon of "militant Islamic networks," just in case the poorly trained minds I encounter all too frequently within the Islamic activist scene confuse my promotion of the 9/11 truth thesis with a denial on my part of the very real need to "clean out our own house" of the ills of militant Islamic networks. The usual response by those American Muslims who are mentally conditioned by the official 9/11 story is, "Let us point the finger inward on ourselves—shame on 'the Islamic world,' and these extremists among us. Let us root them out." This kind of accusatory, self-righteous indignation obstructs clear thinking. Such sentimental nonsense has no place in legitimate discourse.

So, to those who myopically conclude that remedying the forces behind 9/11, and even more broadly, the phenomenon of militant Islam, equates with reforming the Muslim world in whatever proposed fashion, I must say the following: I do not deny the reality of an ideological trend related to the so-called militant Islamic networks and the grave pathos that arises from this trend. Any sincere Muslim must be disgusted with the ideology that feeds this medley of "militant Islamic networks," most of which continue to receive tactical, logistical, and financial support from Western quarters, usually by proxy. The arms they use don't simply materialize—these "counterfeit religionists" have often been directly armed by Western governments that are themselves proxies for ideological and corporate agendas. I use the term counterfeit because 1) I am unsure of the origins of this "extremism in modern militant Islamic form" and 2) these militants openly preach and practice aggression, despite wearing the right costumes, using Arabic terms, and growing the beard to the specified length. Hence the term counterfeit, implying both *ersatz*-religious and counter-religious (the descriptive Islamic religious term in Arabic *dajaaliyyat* carries a meaning that reflects both counterfeit and counter-religious.)

Now, if I must use this term counterfeit, I must be fair: So-called American foreign policy is counterfeit American for the same reasons the policies of these militant networks are counterfeit Islamic, since the agendas and consequences of current US foreign policy lie squarely opposed to the principles enshrined in our American Constitution, as well as our American Declaration of Independence. I wish the term "American" would be dropped from the foreign policy that originates on Wall Street and is enacted through Washington, DC. For the sake of completeness, let me also speak clearly about the supposedly Islamic nation-states, because it takes more than cosmetics to function in accord with Shariah. The "Islamic Republics," in terms of their domestic and foreign policies, are no more in accord with the tenets of authentic Islam than Israel is in accord with the Sublime Way of Moses, authentic Judaism.

Getting back to 9/11 truth, we understand that militants exist who label themselves as "Islamists" and they are generally a most vile lot. But it is more than a stretch, indeed outright false, to conclude it was this bunch alone who brought the WTC down on 9/11. The crime of 9/11 was most definitely an inside job far more than it was an outside one.

Who's Doing the Talking Anyway?

Nearly all of those within the American Islamic community who were asked, or felt prompted to respond to the mainstream were, and are, for the most part, outside their areas of competence when it comes to explaining the crime of 9/11. From activists to religious scholars to academics, most have done far more harm than good through deluding themselves into believing that they are qualified to discuss the crime of 9/11. As I will explain, at best their input into the mainstream discourse elucidates only a small part of an equation. Only the entire equation and subsequent explanation, constructed appropriately, will begin to dismantle the official story. This means making use of a database far more extensive than that offered by the official story, and using minimal standards of intelligent inquiry and diagnostic reasoning. When those appointed as spokespeople of Islam in America begin to condemn the actions of radical Islamists, and correctly point out the counterfeit nature of the militant Islamic ideology, they are elucidating only a tiny portion of the equation. However, their comments and expositions, with their either tacit or explicit approval, are plugged into the official story—which is disastrous.

In this case, partial explanations are false explanations because they are presented to, or taken by, an audience as complete explanations. The numerous glaringly inconsistent aspects of the mainstream thesis are largely ignored by the self-appointed American Muslim leaders who use the mainstream thesis to "explain things" to the public—a public that is represented by media figures who turn to "American Islam" to ask "Why did your co-religionists do these things?" These spokespeople are either consciously or out of ignorance neglecting the evidence compiled by the 9/11 truth movement of the glaring inconsistencies in the official story. Such evidence would force them to modify their responses if they were honest in their analysis. Those who respond by limiting themselves to the mainstream thesis without assessing its legitimacy feel a terrible need to speak and comment prematurely without examining the facts of the case. One thing to note is that most "explicators of Islam and 9/11" who limit themselves to responding to the mainstream 9/11 thesis are basing their response on a thesis that is essentially false. They are incompetent responders; however, since the mainstream 9/11 explanatory thesis is layered with valid premises, this gives it, and those who respond within the false construct, a veneer of legitimacy.

We agree, as do the incompetent responders, with the following premises of the mainstream explanation of 9/11: Yes—Islamic militancy does exist; Yes—the third world does indeed hate American corporate-driven foreign policy and American corporate state-sponsored terror; Yes—there is tremendous bureaucratic obstruction and inefficiency in our national security apparatus, mainly at non-essential levels. From here, they would add: "But the actions of those terrorists led by their fanatical ringleader are not reflective of true Islam." The 9/11 truth movement would offer what has become its counter-thesis: "But if you think these were the factors responsible for 9/11—well, you got another think coming!"

Hence, at best, the mainstream thesis is full of accurate observations but false as an explanation of why 9/11 was successful. When American Muslims use a largely false thesis as a premise to respond, the explanations put forth are *a priori* prevented from digging deeper and uncovering the truth about why the 9/11 attacks occurred and succeeded. This is also dangerous because this hasty error leaves the real explanations uncovered and prevents us from facing the important conclusion that 9/11 was an inside job, a conclusion that would force a sincere individual to search for the guilty parties. Most individuals from the American Islamic activist and academic groups have utterly failed to address the issue of 9/11 truth.

Honest scholars remain silent when they are outside the limits of their competence; they are intelligent enough to refrain from comment. Anyone who would dare attempt to offer diagnoses or therapeutic interventions on the medical wards for a patient under my care while being unaware of the patient's database, would be immediately thrown off my team, not allowed to handle a living patient, and be forced to repeat the classroom portions of their medical education. Yet these various scholars, analysts, clergy, conflict resolution experts, and Islamists attempt to do just that—opine on matters which they have not reviewed carefully, and do so with an air of expertise. There seems to be a terrible need, or want, to speak by folks who don't possess the insight, qualifications, or discipline to adequately address this topic.

Perhaps an analogy is in order here to illustrate the gravity of the error. What would you think of a physician who addressed your cough and fever by explaining the afferent and efferent neural pathways of the laryngeal cough reflex as it relates to mucus production, and then proceeded to give you a great cough suppressant, but all the while missed the pneumonia? How about a physician who addressed the cough as above, and then elucidated the various interactions between your immune system and the invading microbes in the alveoli of your lungs, gave you a great cough suppressant and antibiotic for the pneumonia, but neglected to address the 30-pound weight loss accompanying your symptoms, thereby missing the cancerous lung tumor etiologically responsible for both the cough and pneumonia? Let us gloss over the question of what forces are at work in our above analogy that cause the doctor to miss these crucial diagnoses, or rather delude him into not entertaining these other diagnoses. What is clear, however, is that partial explanations are dangerous, and the MD in our example is guilty of serious incompetence. Pursuing the analogy further, if this were a primary care doctor, he ought to have deferred to the opinion of a lung specialist once he realized that his diagnoses were not adequate to explain the given symptoms, rather than maintaining his own ill-informed diagnosis.

To be intellectually honest in offering a diagnosis of why 9/11 occurred, what in the Good Lord's name are we doing building our explanations on foundations laid down by professors and academics, and even lay, semi-educated, or pseudo-educated scholars or commentators on Islam? I use the term pseudo-educated because the whole host of religionists, academics, and "policy studies majors" who have never worked in the realm of overt and covert geopolitical conflict don't really offer much and waste a lot of ink when they try to pose as authorities and analysts of geopolitical catastrophes and conflicts. To become competent analysts, they and anyone else interested in analyzing 9/11 should study geopolitics, especially the role of financial forces, covert operations, and elite criminality as key factors in the etiology of war.

To seek opinions from academic Islamologists in the case of 9/11 is analogous to looking for a Ph.D. lung physiologist for a friend stricken with cough and fever. In stark contrast to the Islamologists' irrelevancies are the opinions of experts in various disciplines that cover the following arenas: covert conflicts, the history of false-flag operations, espionage, demolition sciences, military response protocols, aviation, journalism, immigration policy, corporate financial money flow, the emergence and real world operations of militant Islamic networks, securities trading, and finally the governing dynamics of geopolitical warfare, which recurrently show that on levels known as "deep politics," nominal allegiances are completely subordinate to functional allegiances. In other words, functional allegiances may exist between nominally opposing parties due to a symbiosis based on mutual self-interest between upper-strata members of both groups. This self-interest is aimed at maintaining conflict in order to preserve elite hegemony—the common denominator of such hegemony being a desired distribution of some form of wealth, be it political, fiscal, or social wealth. In other words, two groups who are nominal enemies may at the upper policy-making level be functioning cooperatively to maintain tension and conflict. Specifically, on 9/11, it seems that allowing the enemy a blow, or more likely manufacturing the blow, fueled an agenda fruitful not only for the socio-economically and financially elite, but for all of us who are tied into this house-of-cards economy.

It would be wonderful to assemble such a panel of experts in genuinely relevant disciplines, who could then be consulted to shed light on the reality of 9/11. Until now, the only such efforts consist of those launched by academics and researchers allied with the 9/11 truth movement. If some members of such a panel happen to be experts on Islamic theology or Qur'anic exegesis, all the better, but Islam, even militant Islam, is a very small part of the picture of why the attacks occurred.

The lack of authority of those aforementioned academics who have elected to pontificate on the subject of 9/11 is beautifully illustrated by a scene from the 1985 Rodney Dangerfield comedy "Back to School." In this film, Rodney Dangerfield plays an elderly, self-made business tycoon. His character never got past high school, so he decides to enroll at the college where his son is studying, hoping to get closer to his son and complete his education. One of the most memorable scenes has Dangerfield's character sit through a lecture on business economics by a prestigious "expert" professor. The topic of the class is starting a business enterprise. After every statement the professor makes, Dangerfield cannot but comment on its incompleteness or outright falsity given the actual world of business. During one such interruption, the class actually begins to turn around away from the prestigious professor and his chalkboard and take notes on what Dangerfield elaborates: the reality of labor cost differentials, political implications of securing raw materials, zoning laws that would need to be negotiated or circumvented, and so on. This is too much for the "expert academic" to handle, and the professor finally reprimands Dangerfield and states that what the lecture is about is the "legitimate business world." After the professor regains his composure, he asks the class to choose a name for the site of this enterprise. From the back we hear Dangerfield's classic response: "How 'bout Fantasy Land?" The class cracks up.

I am a diagnostician, and trained to be extremely careful in arriving at a diagnosis. I cannot help this. I cannot, and will not, turn away from the proverbial elephant in the living room; I am aghast at the silence of the American Muslim activist scene in its lack of support of 9/11 truth. The first step in accurate diagnosis is always to build as thorough a database as possible, and maintain what in medical diagnostics is called a "broad differential"—which means a full range of possible diagnoses to explain a given phenomenon (symptom complex). If you walk into my ER with a severe headache, it can be a spontaneous intracranial hemorrhage, or a simple tension headache, and until I am sure it is not the former, you are not leaving my ER. Going to an Islamic scholar for a diagnosis of what happened on 9/11 and why is quite absurd. It is less absurd to walk into the ER with a crushing headache and ask to be seen by a neuroscience professor instead of a trained emergency physician. The neuroscientist may be able to explain a little, and even offer some answers and potential remedies, but as an academic, this neuroscientist cannot and should not try to offer definitive diagnoses nor attempt to find what is wrong based on a theoretical expertise that covers a limited knowledge base (neuroscience) when it comes to headaches (remember, head-aches can be caused by non-neurological disorder that can be just as deadly as a neurological one).

The Defective Package

When you build on a flawed foundation, the structure is always unsound.

We begin with what is offered by our mainstream (corporate-sponsored) media as to the etiology of 9/11. All such explanations can be boiled down to the following equation:

[Muslims gone bad] + [incompetent/overwhelmed surveillance] = 9/11

Based on the overwhelming amount of evidence, pulled from mainstream sources, investigative journalism, and foreign mainstream press, the 9/11 truth thesis maintains the following critical differences:

[Maybe Muslims gone bad, or persons impersonating them] + [facilitation by members of our own national security apparatus] = [9/11 blamed on "militant Islam"]

The massive impact of 9/11 in the daily life of the world cannot be overstated. Specifically, for American Muslim activists, its distal effects (such as the PATRIOT Act) have been quite devastating, and these folks work tirelessly and for the most part fruitlessly to alleviate the symptoms produced by 9/11, without ever addressing the cause. I find it astounding that they are so silent about questioning the legitimacy of the mainstream thesis—for it is from this very thesis that all the misery for the American Muslim activists began.

Covering the evidence contradicting this thesis is beyond the scope of this essay; however, the following general lines of inquiry will aid a truth seeker in trying to make an accurate diagnosis as to the why and what of 9/11. In addition, sources for further reading will be listed at the end of this section.

Required Topics for Understanding the Background of 9/11

• Wall Street/corporate America/the banking industry. All the directors and highest-ranking officials of the national security apparatus (e.g., the CIA) are from this sector. The CIA is a creation of Wall Street/corporate America, designed specifically to ensure a fiscal inertia securing a one-way flow of cash, labor, and resources. It is cosmetically presented and conceived of as looking out for national security, but functionally speaking, it behaves as described. If you have no understanding of the difference between cosmetic and functional definitions, then don't bother with the topic of 9/11. You may happily go on believing the mainstream thesis.

• Violent modalities used (past and present) in sustaining our US economy. The implication is that violence may be sanctioned on US soil because the drive for fiscal inertia cannot logically be constrained by loyalties based on citizenship; when fiscal logic dictates that livelihoods or actual lives must be sacrificed, then they must be sacrificed, whether in Indonesia, Iraq, Chile, Nicaragua, or in the World Trade Center. For those who question whether anyone would so betray their loyalty to their fellow citizens, ask the employees of ENRON or the thousands who have lost their pension funds, or the tens of thousands whose share of Social Security or health benefits have literally disappeared. Or ask the surviving crew of the *USS Liberty*, or the sufferers of Gulf War Syndrome, or the families of the victims of the *USS Lusitania* or Pearl Harbor.

• Related to the aforementioned: one must also consider the inherent instability of fiat money (paper currency whose fabrication is divorced from any traditional store of value, such as gold), which culminated in the rise of fractional reserve banking and a blatantly usurious financial system. Sustaining the supremacy of the US dollar in terms of exchange, as well as the global reserve currency, has been linked to many geopolitical and domestic criminal actions and loss of life.[2]

• The hydrocarbon industry and interests in the Caspian Basin. The Afghans were explicitly warned in July 2001 by US officials that by October 2001, they were either going to receive carpets of gold or carpets of bombs, depending on the degree of their cooperation with various geostrategic corporate-driven agendas. Troops had already mobilized into Uzbekistan, and other allied military were scrambled, headed toward Central Asia prior to 9/11.

• The geopolitical implications of post–peak production of oil (peak oil).

• The $500 billion, if not more, inflow of liquid cash per year laundered through correspondent US banks by the heroin industry, of which Afghanistan is largest proximal supplier. 2002— after the US invasion—was the biggest export year ever.

• The rise of militant Islamic networks, of Salafi/Wahhabi ideology, and their empowerment, both financial and military, with particular emphasis on Afghanistan, the Pakistani ISI, and its liaison with US covert operations that are themselves always governed by corporate, industrial, and banking interests.

• The use, frequency, and utility of false-flag operations (see David Ray Griffin's essay in this volume).

• The petrodollar relationship—the prototypical example being the ruling elite of Saudi Arabia.

• The ISI (the Pakistani equivalent of the CIA). The ISI is a creature of the CIA, and the head of ISI has to be approved by our security apparatus. It is well known that all of the backing for the militant Islamic networks in the '80s and '90s went from the CIA to the ISI to the militants—most notably the mujahideen and thereafter the Taliban.

• The State of Israel—its crime syndicates, secret service, and false-flag operation history and capability.

• Our American mainstream media and its egregious conflicts of interests between honest journalism and the corporate-sponsored mainstream agenda. The absence of a thesis from the mainstream media cannot be taken as a sign of its illegitimacy; if anything, absence of a thesis is probably an indication of its authenticity.

• The Binladin Group, and the Saudi elite's relationship to our economy. Investigations of Saudi elites are continuously thwarted from within our own security apparatus. (The bin Ladens lived in Falls Church, VA—next door to CIA headquarters.) Clinton's regime specifically mandated that the FBI back off from investigating anything that involved the bin Ladens or the Saudi elite. They were quickly flown out of the country several days after 9/11, while private air flight was suspended.[3]

• Reports in the mainstream foreign press that Osama bin Laden met with CIA officials in July 2001 during his hospitalization in the American hospital in Dubai. This is when he was supposedly wanted dead or alive. The press has not retracted the story to this day.

• FBI agent complaints and accusations that some of their superiors suppressed action based on terrorist leads; many of these complaints and the persons issuing them have been silenced or gagged (Coleen Rowley, Sibel Edmonds, and others).

• That the 50 or so documented warnings of terrorists' strikes scheduled for the week of 9/11 were not heeded, including those from the intelligence services of Israel, Egypt, and four other nations.

Required Knowledge: The Disturbing Questions and Anomalies Surrounding 9/11 Proper, All Based on Mainstream Press Reports

• Who were the hijackers, given that at least six of the nineteen alleged hijackers are still alive and had their identities stolen? How was their continued entry into the US allowed if they were on security risk lists? How are we to explain the debaucheries in their behavior if they were Islamists? Why were some reported to be at two different ends of the US at the same time?[4]

• Why, according to cell phone conversations, did the seat numbers not match the names of the hijackers?[5] Why haven't the original flight passenger manifests been made public record? Why were the cell phone calls allegedly made from distressed passengers considered anomalous, and how is that there were extended conversations flowing smoothly from altitudes greater than 8000 feet?[6] Why weren't any hijack signal codes, or radio communications, relayed to ground control? What about the fact that based on what is recorded of their alleged flight training (some of which was received in US military schools), none of the hijackers could functionally fly a Boeing commercial airliner?[7] (Hani Hanjour allegedly piloted a Boeing 757 through a 270-degree spiral during a steep dive, followed by an over-400-miles-per-hour cruise parallel to the ground so low that it clipped lamp posts 500 feet from the Pentagon—yet he was so incompetent at the alleged flight school he attended that he was not allowed to fly. Some expert pilots reviewing the trajectory data declared it near impossible, or flat out impossible, to conduct such a maneuver.)

• Why did different US grade-school students (of foreign descent) proclaim the WTC was going to be bombed the week of the tragedy while our intelligence agencies were allegedly taken by surprise?[8] Why did top Pentagon officials stop flying commercial flights the week of 9/11?[9]

• Why did investigators not pursue the massive, record-breaking dump of United and American airline stock during the week before 9/11 during the activity (monitoring real-time suspicious activities of stock trades is standard procedure), or after the event of 9/11? Why did the SCC stop the investigation after it discovered the transactions were carried out through Deutsche Bank, whose head is A. K. Krongard, ex–deputy director of the CIA? Why did Mayo Shattuck (CEO of Deutsche Bank) abruptly retire following 9/11?[10]

• What about the Israelis in the white van who were arrested in New Jersey on 9/11? They were seen taking celebratory photographs and videos with the WTC burning in the background; they were reported to the police, arrested, and interrogated. They were suspected to be Mossad agents, yet released without investigation.[11] And why were there forty Mossad agents literally living within hundreds of yards of some of the hijackers, in the tiny town of Hollywood, Florida?[12] Why were all the witnesses who knew the hijackers in Florida either silenced by the FBI or made to disappear to "the island of lost witnesses" as reported in Daniel Hopsicker's *Welcome to Terrorland*? Why were the "hijackers" apparently being run by a CIA-linked drug cartel that owned the "flight schools"—actually fronts for drug smugglers—where they were posing as Muslims learning to fly? Why the attempted cover-up of the fact that the "hijackers" were brought to the US by the CIA and trained at US military facilities?[13]

• Why the scores of documented accounts of foreknowledge of this event from a diverse source base? To assume "we were taken by surprise" is ludicrous. For example, one New York–based military communications operator left his post, phoned his brother who was in WTC 2, and told him to leave immediately. It seems that he knew a second plane attack was imminent, yet no one was sounding any alarms to evacuate the thousand or so people who were alive at the time.[14]

• What hit the Pentagon? As this book is going to press, five years after the tragedy, there is still zero evidence it was a Boeing. The place is sprawling with video surveillance, yet no video is available, except for the few frames from a parking lot surveillance camera that do not suggest a commercial airplane hit the Pentagon.[15] Why were there so many contradictory eyewitness statements as to the physical appearance and other characteristics of the alleged plane? Why was there no mention of the White House Annex fire that was broadcast on network television that morning?[16]

• Why did Mr. Bush behave so oddly that day? Why had the president apparently been removed from the chain of command, and the vice president put in his place, that day? Why have the vice president and the 9/11 Commission apparently lied about evidence reflecting this unconstitutional and deeply damning shift in the chain of command? Specifically, why have they apparently lied in inventing a nonexistent phone call between Bush and Cheney, and by making up a false story about Cheney's whereabouts—lies whose apparent purpose is to conceal the fact that Cheney was in command throughout the 9/11 operation?[17]

• Why does the wreckage from Pennsylvania (Flight 93) indicate that the "fourth plane" was indeed shot down, or suffered a mid-air explosion?[18] Why did Mr. Rumsfeld say that Flight 93 was shot down, and then quickly correct himself?[19]

• Why did WTC 7 collapse? This happened long after the strikes, and in a manner that suggested it was demolished. Why did its owner say on TV, "they told me they had to 'pull the building'"—which is an expression for demolishing a building? Who were "they"? Why did the fire rescue personnel also state that WTC 7 was demolished? If this happened, when were the explosives planted?[20]

• Why have so many civil engineers, including one that worked for the steel company that built the WTC, stated there was no way such a crash could have caused the whole structure to fall without any teetering or sign of partial collapse? Why does video analysis of the collapse suggest that the towers could not have "pancaked down" with such speed? The fires were dying down, and never has fire ever caused the collapse of a reenforced steel skyscraper. Why was the steel whisked away without a forensic analysis (the one conducted was called "a half-baked farce" by the editor of *Fire Prevention Engineering*[21])? What of the credible reports that the black boxes had been found—not unlikely, since black boxes almost always survive crashes, and that a "hijacker's passport" of paper and plastic supposedly survived the crash and fire?

• What of the completely contradictory official versions of what transpired in the sky around Washington[22]—and why hasn't anyone inquired why the air-defense response took so long, since Vice President Cheney has revealed that the Secret Service, FAA, and NORAD keep the lines of communication open 24/7?

• How do we explain the complete incapacitation and stand-down of standard air-space defense protocols (which functioned effectively over 60 times the previous year) and the lies and contradictions between NORAD, the FAA, Secret Service, and the Air Force? How is it that there were "war game" scenarios based on hijacked Boeings going on as the real events were taking place?[23] When asked about these issues, General Eberhardt's response was simply "no comment."[24]

• Why has the current regime obstructed any serious attempt to investigate the circumstances that led to 9/11? Why was known war criminal and cover-up specialist Henry Kissinger Bush's first choice to lead the investigation? Why was the Kean commission comprised of members who had egregious conflicts of interest by their presence on such a panel? Philip Zelikow, who exerted near-total control over much of the investigation as well as the final report, is a crony of Secretary of State Rice and a White House staff appointee—was he expected to oversee an impartial critique of the performance of the administration?[25] Why did one member, Max Cleland, resign from the commission after accusing it of incompetence and lack of dedication, saying "The Warren Commission blew it... I will not be part of that"?[26]

• Why have all pressing inquiries been completely ignored, and inquirers gagged? Sibel Edmonds (a former FBI employee, presently under several gag orders) posited relations between illicit drug profiteering, the flight schools, and the "terrorists" themselves, as indicated by the fact that 43 pounds of heroin were found at one "flight school"—and records of operations of that school were moved out of the country, as per orders of governor Jeb Bush.[27] The 9/11 family steering committee has explicitly stated their dismay at the incompetence and inability of the Kean commission to even address these serious questions.[28]

• Why was an FAA supervisor found destroying evidence of flight patterns and other data that was crucially relevant to any investigations?[29]

These are just a few leads; there are so many more, any one of which causes serious doubts or completely disproves the mainstream 9/11 thesis. It is the job of authentic journalism to chase these leads, and these are quite simply the tips of many, many icebergs. The mainstream corporate press did not just drop the ball, it hid the ball. The only arena where these leads are pursued is by intrepid independent media outlets and journalists— who often don't have the training or funding to produce analyses that would reach and penetrate the public mind.

9/11 truth seekers are, from the global perspective, in the majority. Reports from the Islamic world indicate that the majority reject the official theory.[30] Domestically, a 2004 Zogby poll demonstrated that 49 percent of New York City residents and 41 percent of New York state residents believe that members of the federal government were complicit in the 9/11 attacks in that they consciously failed to act to prevent them; more than 56 percent of New York state residents (66 percent of NYC residents) believe an independent investigation should be re-opened.[31] A more recent Scripps-Howard poll shows that 36 percent of Americans think it "very likely" or "somewhat likely" that federal officials either participated in the attacks on the World Trade Center and the Pentagon or took no action to stop them because they wanted the United States to go to war in the Middle East.[32] And they are right. For there is no doubt that the official version of 9/11 does not stand up to even the most elementary scrutiny.[33]

Now, we turn to an analysis as to why the "American Muslim academic/activist scene" has been grossly negligent in their lack of support for 9/11 truth.

Why The Silence?

Incompetence and mediocre analysis are, by definition, more common than excellence, high intelligence and penetrating analysis. When the former dominate the discourse, it results in an impotent response that falls prey to underlying agendas. The forms of mediocrity and incompetence come in the following guises:

• Not accumulating data before arriving at a conclusion. This is synonymous with getting the story from FOX or CNN or the *New York Times* and then assuming one is ready to effectively respond and discuss 9/11.

• Confining the analysis to allegiance based on nation-states. When it comes to geopolitics, the concept of the nation-state is largely superfluous. The governing dynamics of geopolitical conflict transcends allegiances based on the idea of nation-states. Indeed, the concept of nation-state is more of a public relations tool at this level than anything else. Simply looking at fiscal flow, how else can you explain the unbelievable sums of taxpayer money (and now jobs) that flow to other lands and peoples, while the "citizens of this country" often live in poor conditions, especially in rural and inner-city areas? From this perspective alone, the nation-state based on geographical borders has very little meaning. The architects of the agendas that cause geopolitical conflicts are rarely seeking above all to serve the nation-state.

Without digressing into a historical account of the concept of the nation-state, it is necessary to observe that this concept functions as little more than an effective propaganda tool with relation to the geostrategic ploys that we examine, and that allegiance to the nation-state is subordinate to other agendas in relation to global conflict, both low-intensity and overt, and hence has no effective meaning in analyzing the basis for conflicts of the magnitude under discussion.[34] In this model, agendas that require conflict are initiated, and subsequently one or multiple nation-state apparatus—executive, military, judiciary, legislative—are often co-opted to effectuate the necessary policies. In this manner, many of the heads of state and other government officials become, in reality, middle management or public relations personnel for the agendas that trickle down through their orders or words. The lower-level human resource and labor for conflict (soldiers, grassroots activists, functionaries, technocrats) may be galvanized through the psychology of allegiance to the nation-state. If the public of a given nation benefits from effectuating such policies, great; but if a policy calls for harm to some, tough luck. Much of the American public does benefit from the global policies of financiers and corporations that act via co-option of government. Thanks to the greed of financiers and the multinationals, standards of living for the middle classes and above are high, and retirement funds stay nice and plump.

The reason the meaninglessness of nation-state needs to be emphasized is that some who are critical of the 9/11 truth thesis ask, "Do you really believe that America attacked itself?" To this question, which suffers from the delusional error of misapplying the notion of nation-state to an arena where it has no meaning, we can only respond, "Can you please define America?" Or, we can say that we, part of America, are blaming another part of America for allowing harm to come to yet another part of America. So to those who cannot see past this idea of the nation-state, we say "America attacked itself, and America is looking for that cancerous part of itself that was complicit." Assuming the 9/11 truth thesis is correct, we may ask, "Which party is America? Those complicit in the attacks or the truth seekers?"

Rejection of the 9/11 Truth Thesis: The Etiologies

The 9/11 truth thesis often meets with *a priori* disbelief. This disbelief is irrational at best; its roots have far less than to do with lack of evidence contradicting the mainstream explanation and more to do with the psychological obstructions that exist in those facing these difficult truths. This disbelief has the following etiologies:

Disbelief etiology A: "You don't expect me to believe in this conspiracy theory, do you?"

It's fine if you want to call me a conspiracy theorist, as long as I can call you a coincident theorist.
—9/11 researcher John Judge

We are dealing less with conspiracy theory than with conspiracy facts. Moreover, many conveniently overlook the fact that the mainstream explanation of 9/11 is a conspiracy theory. The data documented above, and in the numerous works available, are facts that any twelve-year-old with sufficient mental capabilities can put together in an effort to formulate a diagnosis of what happened, or at least realize that the mainstream thesis is utterly false. The term "conspiracy theory" is often used to discredit valid lines of inquiry— and the uninformed usually are dissuaded from using their intelligence in evaluating data they believe relates to "conspiracies." But conspiracies are all around us. Any time more than one party act in concert and without publicity for a given agenda it is conspiracy. And if the actions or agenda involve any activities that are against the law, the behavior fits the legal definition of criminal conspiracy. Conspiracy is actually one of the most common criminal legal terms used in this country. To believe that such behavior is nonexistent or uncommon at high levels of power is the height of naïveté.

Along the same lines of naïve *a priori* rejectionism, we hear: "How can this be so hidden, I mean—wouldn't it take far too many people to pull this thing off?" The short answer is no. Brigham Young University physicist Steven Jones has pointed out that ten men carrying ten forty-pound loads each could easily place the 4,000 pounds of explosives necessary to bring down the Twin Towers.[35] As for conspirators in government agencies, bureaucracy and hierarchies are structured in such a way that there are key nodal positions, which are akin to a narrow part of a funnel. If you imagine a funnel upside down, narrow side up, there is a gatekeeper, usually the superior, who sits at this nodal position, and all activity/information goes through this node to the next layer. It was severe criticism of people in such positions that characterized the complaints by such FBI field officers as Coleen Rowley, who used such words as "obstruct," and "sabotage," and "undermine" to describe the behavior of certain personnel involved in concealing terrorist activities, and pointedly mentioned FBI field agents joking that al-Qaeda must have a mole at FBI headquarters. FAA, NORAD, NSA, CIA, and other organizations are structured in the same manner.[36]

Disbelief etiology B: How could a group of people actually do this to others? This type of reaction is sheer sentimental naïveté. Anyone who asks this question has been distracted by the spectacular and horrifying drama of the attacks. In essence, this was a murder of almost 3,000 people and the destruction of an infrastructure closely related to US covert operations. (The WTC possessed many departments related to such activities—including building 7, which was not hit by a plane, and whose collapse cannot be rationally explained except as a controlled demolition with explosives.) In order to overcome this naïve sentimentality, which keeps so many minds from arriving at an accurate diagnosis, one must understand that we are exposing a faceless, cold mentality that operates as necessary.

Most folks cannot handle associating the faces of our leaders as seen on TV with committing wrong. The idea that they may be in tacit approval of, cooperation with, or actually design policies which involve harming other human beings, let alone their fellow citizens, is unimaginable. First, let me reiterate that those leaders seen in the media are best thought of as middle management or public relations folk for such policies. Moreover, I dealt with the mistake of introducing the idea of allegiance to the nation-state above. We are then forced to examine a cold, pragmatic, dispassionate mentality that invariably justifies its actions to itself and other like-minded individuals. These actions may be of omission or commission. They may involve the following behavior: looking the other way in the face of suspicious, anomalous, or criminal activities; passively or actively cooperating with enacting a harmful policy in order to preserve or secure one's sociopolitical or financial position[37]; or designing policies that actively harm other human beings. I speak of a mentality and behavior pattern that can co-opt the psyche of humans once, recurrently, or chronically. It often takes possession of individuals and collectivities devoted to maintaining financial or political hegemony.

One must understand that this same faceless mentality promoted the nuclear incineration of hundreds of thousands of human beings; it sponsored the genocide of literally millions of people in Asia and hundreds of thousands in Europe and on this continent. This mentality has been around for millennia, and in truth has its origin in metaphysical realms described in the ontological precedents of all faith traditions—and has expressed itself through people of all skin colors, ethnicities, times, climes, and colors. Loyalties and allegiances (least of all to fellow citizens of any nation-state) are not in the mindset of this mentality. It is eminently practical.

If need be, it will express itself on US soil. It does so all the time in the form of looting taxpayers and honest citizens who are victimized by financial scams and deceptive accounting practices that ruin livelihoods and destroy lives. Most Arab and South Asian nations are impoverished because of these practices, which lead to suffering and loss of life in so many ways. If, for this mentality, maintaining hegemony means absorbing losses of life on US soil—so be it. Pearl Harbor provides an excellent example, and may have provided a model for the perpetrators of the 9/11 operation.[38]

One of the driving forces of the mentality that we are describing is the desire for sustained material wealth—securing a net one-way flow of cash, resources, or labor. We may term this drive "fiscal inertia"—and this inertia is a compulsion of such weight and might that all of the world's prophets, saints, and scriptures have warned about it over and over and over again. There is a reason for such dire warning of what happens to the human psyche dominated by pursuit of material wealth. Unguarded, the human psyche, collective or individual, falls prey to the criminal mentality of which we speak. And this is what is behind so many events of mass killing and destruction. Let us not make the mistake of pointing fingers. The criminal mentality lurks in most of us, and expresses itself often in different forms. Put another way: If we found ourselves in the same position as the perpetrators, we too might well succumb to this mentality. Humans do remarkably dishonorable things when getting or staying ahead financially is at stake.

Ironically, fiscal inertia was a great peacekeeper in many traditional civilizations. Such fiscal inertia, used for honorable ends, was the basis of the "blood penalty" that kept the peace in traditional societies. In many tribal societies, if a member of one clan was slain wrongfully, the aggrieved clan had the right to forego instituting punitive measures and demand hefty financial compensation. This option was often taken, and since the desire to stay fiscally sound was powerful, manslaughter and murder were extremely rare in such societies, because would-be perpetrators knew that acting on their impulses would bring their families great hardship—and often cost the perpetrator a falling out with his clan, a social connection that provided critical support for individuals.[39]

Fiscal inertia is terribly real. I witness the aforementioned mentality, and people succumbing to it, day in and day out, harming and betraying the people of this nation, through increasing morbidity and mortality, in a field that I know intimately—health care. Parasitic folks with a corporate mentality have assaulted what was once a sacred relationship between healers and healed—and because of the "worship" of fiscal inertia, this mentality wreaks havoc by consciously forcing decisions by handcuffed and cowardly policy makers that result in sustaining sickness, and even loss of life—be this through hospital policies that prioritize profits over patient care, or through stamping out medical progress that would threaten profits for industries that have entrenched themselves in health care, or through promoting the pharmaceutical industry based on flimsy or even fraudulent data. This is one of the reasons why the 9/11 truth thesis was not too surprising for me to grasp. Health care is ridden by forces promoting sickness and slow loss of life and suffering for the sake of fiscal inertia; 9/11 exemplified the same process in acute form.

Disbelief etiology C: Are we still naïve outsiders?
The American Muslim community has been unable to come to grips with 9/11, and speak out for truth, for a variety of reasons. The whole American Islamic culture is based on the residues of the flavor and mentality brought to these shores by the immigrant generation hailing mainly from the Arab world and Indian Subcontinent. The major exceptions are the African-American and white American converts, whose role in the build-up and maintenance of mainstream American Islamic sentiment and ethos is (unfortunately) at best marginal or contained in a separate subculture.

These immigrant residues are just beginning to wear off from the second generation, the immigrants' children—most of whom are slowly improving their understandings not only of Islam but of the dynamics of Western foreign policy.[40] Though there are many areas of understanding that still need improvement, we will focus on a few that have enormous bearing on understanding the silence and lack of vigorous support for 9/11 truth by American Islam.

The first and dominant factor is fear. The great majority of American Muslim immigrants came to this country looking to better their lives through opportunities afforded by American society. Thankfully, many have found success. For them, the reality is that the US is the best place on earth in terms of opportunity, returns on hard work, honesty, and the rule of law. They see that the blatant nepotism, corruption, bribery, and cut-throatedness necessary to ascend socioeconomically in their home countries are relatively absent here. This is true—and as an American, I am proud of this. However, this feeling of gratitude does not absolve anyone from his or her spiritual responsibility to speak out against crime. This gratitude, this "thank God I'm here and not there" mentality has led to an "I don't care to rock the boat by sticking up for justice in the manner My Prophet would ask of me" mentality, or an "I am not going to bite at the hand that feeds me" mentality. The logical unsoundness of this position is obvious, so I won't bother exposing it. The hand that feeds us is not the same hand that killed almost 3,000 people on 9/11. The reason why the immigrants are doing so well is thanks to a nation-state which some intrepid, bright men and women set into motion circa the late 1700s—and those same men and women would be crying bloody murder at the attitudes "American" Muslims display in their avoidance of 9/11 truth. "Don't call yourself American," they would tell us. "Don't call yourself Muslims, either" may be a voice some of us hear in our hearts when we realize what transpired and our lack of response.

The second psychological complex some of the Muslim immigrants suffer from—which has left its residues on the American Muslim response, or rather lack of response, to 9/11 truth—has to do with a naïveté and inferiority complex that most of this group feels before the "shiny, modern white man's world." What people who are in the grip of such a complex (the majority) need to do is to talk to those of us who have had access to the arenas where the maintenance of fiscal inertia is the only guiding precedent—and if fiscal inertia dictates the creation of a false-flag operation that sacrifices some lives on US soil for "a greater good," so be it. In the context of the world of health care, if it means keeping certain beneficial breakthroughs or beneficial knowledge away from the public markets—so be it, let some lives be sacrificed, let some people remain sick. Such arenas, where fiscal inertia demonstrably reigns supreme over the public welfare, and where policies dictating such inertia originate, are accessible to those of us who have had the distinct pleasure to sit in on board meetings at the top of the hierarchies of a given institution that has a for-profit component.

Most folks have no such experience. Such folks suffer from a delusional perception that confuses the "glitter" of living in a society with functional infrastructure and institutions, with a guarantee of ethical conduct when fiscal inertia is at stake. Indeed, there are scores of examples showing that within large bureaucracies and hierarchical organizations, some individuals, groups, and agendas can quite literally get away with murder. Those of us who have witnessed the functioning of this dynamic need no further proof that it is possible for groups to be so sociopolitically and financially insulated and manipulated that tacitly approving and getting away with even mass murder and hiding within the blitz of hierarchy, bureaucracies, plausible deniability, excuses of incompetence, and so on is certainly a plausible scenario. Remember, fiscal inertia is a most powerful compeller.

It is an interesting paradox, because in the developing world, the corruption and criminality that have leeched into policy-making institutions, be they governmental or corporate, is so much more transparent and intuitively expected by those who live there. But in the West, this immigrant Muslim generation that influences the tone of American Islam somehow believes all of that has magically disappeared. In short, most folks who have been imprisoned in this thought pattern need to learn that there are indeed cracks and cobwebs in the walls at Disneyland, and underneath, Mickey and Goofy are not Mickey and Goofy—they are two guys getting paid $10 an hour, and they do take their masks off once they are in the sub-basement underneath the Magic Kingdom. Such folks ought to listen to those who have been to the sub-basement.

The last harmful residue left upon an American Muslim struggling to understand the nature of 9/11 is an "outsider" mentality (transposed onto our psyches from an immigrant generation), which leads to the notion that the way to combat terrorism is to "clean up our own backyard"—as though our backyard were not also the United States of America. Ironically, this alienating mentality is expressed by many who claim they are emancipated from "backward traditional mentalities" and integrated into modern American culture while still in retention of their Islamic identity. Such folks want to rid the Islamic World of "the baddies." "This should be our priority," so the proponents claim, "We should have the courage to criticize our own." Indeed we should—when the criticism is justified. But if you have been paying attention, I hope you are open to the fact that when it comes to 9/11 and many other such events, to assume that the Islamic community is solely responsible for these crimes is false. These crimes are the stuff of covert operations involving parties that cannot be neatly categorized. To speak of a community's responsibility for its own in the above fashion when it comes to such events as 9/11 is sheer nonsense.

What is the Islamic backyard anyway? Since I am an American Muslim, my backyard is just as much the halls of the American executive branch, Congress, the judiciary, the NSA, the Pentagon, and the CIA (all sustained by my tax dollars) as it is the ideological trends within Islamic thought.

If we are going to be intelligent about addressing the problems within our own communities, we must recognize that our communities do not divide along the ethnic, religious, or political lines we traditionally recognize, but are formed by people's moral choices. There are those among us who are willing to go to great lengths—even to commit murder—for financial, political, or social gain. There are others who would never do so and whose lives are defined by their concern for their fellow man. This first, malignant element includes folks in suits, in robes, in thawbs, clean shaven or shariah-bearded—as does the second, virtuous element. The first includes people who speak English, who speak Arabic, who speak just about every language there is; so does the second. The phrases "Allahu akbar," "jihad," and "sunna" are heard in each, as are the phrases "God bless America," "national interest," "democracy," and "freedom." Both elements include people from all socioeconomic classes and all religious backgrounds. It is no longer possible to say that terrorism or violence, or any problem, belongs then to one community, whether Islamic or American; it must belong to all. Our problems must be addressed by attending to our common human virtues, and addressing our common human failings.

Disbelief Etiology D: Can we afford to acknowledge this 9/11 truth?
Many individuals who consider themselves activists, academics, or commentators have found a niche for themselves. There is a great deal of personal energy, egoistic pride, and even financial interest invested into the niche within which they operate. Suppose a thesis comes along and exposes the very basis of your activist, academic, or analytic platform as misdirected, diluted in comparison to an alternative path of activism, or patently false. The whole construct of your work is pulled out from beneath you. This does not take away from any of the good work that you may do, but the very basis of your perceptions and diagnosis of a given problem that you are trying to remedy has been found to be profoundly lacking, and it may be time to face the facts and re-organize if you are sincerely committed to dealing with the issue (in this case, 9/11). The problem for a given activist may be that he/she has so many material and non-material factors (or other psychological obstructions—see below) invested in sustaining a given misdiagnosis, a misdiagnosis that yields the coveted opportunities to soapbox, pontificate, lead, organize, rally, dialogue, or be the spokesperson in the limelight.

The moderate Muslim response to terror has become an industry of its own—an offspring of the movement to bring healing between "Islam" and "the West." This industry has grown exponentially due to 9/11. After all, the mainstream thesis, which 9/11 truth exposes as false, is based on a terrible thing done to the West by angry Muslims. "Please, let us try to understand each other's grievances," cry the darling moderates, be they Muslim, Jewish, or Christian American activists, clergy, or academics. On their proverbial soapboxes, in the spotlight, and at times seduced by the notoriety and ego massage, you can hear the American Muslim activist: "Shame on those bad Muslims.... Islam means peace... damn those Wahhabis.... We have got to clean out our own house and take dar al-Islam back from these bad apples, or else nasty terror attacks will keep on happening, to Shias, and Sunnis, and Americans, and Hindus, and Jews, and us!"

There is a tremendous amount of secondary gain to be had if one successfully assumes this position. One enters the world of lecture tours, book contracts, TV interviews, financial incentives, meetings with prominent officials (middle management), and of course a national and even international celebrity-type notoriety and acceptance. From a psycho-spiritual perspective, these are very potent intoxicants and pitfalls (extremely attractive, their gravity underestimated, habit-forming, and difficult to reject), which quite often muddy the vision and determination to pursue truth. From the criminally strategic perspective of those who actually designed 9/11, one engaged in this moderate position becomes a duped (or, if they do realize the truth, complicit) disinformation and propaganda agent who serves to keep the truth concealed. The moderate Muslims' impulse to "shame those bad Muslims," as if 9/11 occurred solely by the hands of Muslim extremists, ignores the fact that the very existence of these alleged extremists—as Muslims and as hijackers—is in serious doubt, and that Muslim fundamentalism can by no means be seriously considered responsible for the success of the 9/11 attacks.[41]

Many such activists do not engage in the the profound reassessment that ought to occur to a sincere, lucid mind when confronted with the arguments of the 9/11 truth movement. This is not because of their lack of intelligence, nor the lack of evidence. Rather, the obstruction is likely more than anything psycho-social or socio-economic in etiology and based on losing any one of the aforementioned, coveted fruits of being labeled "a true, moderate Muslim." But at a certain point, we all have to ask, "Do I care about what comes with my role, being seen as a leader, being seen as having the right answers? Or do I care about the truth?" I have been vulnerable to being cast in a negative light as an MD for refusing to subscribe to much of what is and what is not considered standard medical practice (usually influenced by industry). My resolve has always been fueled by the same sort of self-examination: Do I care more about the truth of what heals or harms my patient, or do I care about what others perceive as the proper roles and protocols of an MD?

The good Muslim–bad Muslim dialectic that supposedly moderate Muslim commentators use is a direct result of uncritically swallowing the mainstream thesis. When moderate Muslims adopt this dialectic, they are letting the devil win: By defining themselves in relation to the very religious extremist stance they wish to reject, they in fact legitimize it. On the other hand, Muslims prone to a simplistic jihadist geopolitical view that sees the Western–Israeli–Arab puppet regime alliance as a monolithic implacable enemy to Islam and its adherents, and as an entity that has murdered millions of Muslims over the past five decades, are liable to feel some degree of justice in the success of the attacks. For them, 9/11 was a kick to the groin of the Great

Satan. This political view may at first seem completely opposed to the moderate Muslim stance that sees 9/11 resulting simply from an ideological aberrancy within the Muslim world. The moderate Muslims would indeed condemn the jihadist view. What is tragically ironic is that these two stances are actually flawed in precisely the same way, and in effect are two opposite sides of a profoundly counterfeit coin. They both inject religious discourse into the discussion because they both accept the element of mainstream thesis that uses religious discourse as a false flag and motive. The only argument between them is on the subject of whether the alleged perpetrators were martyrs or condemned to burn in hell.

The jihadists may be categorized as belonging to two types. The first is convinced that since the Western–Israeli–Arab puppet regime is an implacable enemy to Islam, false-flag terror ops may be part of their game. To this perspective, it matters little that 9/11 may not truly have been committed by martyrs; it was still a providential payback for dar al-Islam. The second type may actually believe that 9/11 was indeed a successful martyrdom operation as the mainstream thesis posits. Either way, whether the response be moderate or either version of jihadist, religion stays in the foreground and there is no impetus to get to 9/11 truth; this is precisely what the true criminals prefer.

I must explicitly state that both categories of jihadists stand condemned from an Islamic doctrinal perspective. It is categorically sinful and punishable by death deliberately to target non-combatants during armed conflict. Interestingly enough, this categorical forbiddance calls into serious question the permissibility to participate in modern warfare period, which as a rule uses tactics and weaponry that by necessity kill indiscriminately. I wonder why the moderate Muslims remain silent on this matter.

The mainstream thesis must be rejected, and 9/11 must be seriously rethought as a crime perpetrated for strategic reasons, in which religious discourse was not in fact a motive but a false flag, a scapegoat, a smokescreen to which both so-called extremist and moderate Muslim responders have fallen victim. As has been stated, and bears repeating: to proceed with a discussion when its premise is an outright lie is in this context to do nothing more than spread disinformation.

Being moderate does not mean we must use only a moderate amount of intelligence. Nor does being moderate mean compromising the truth of things, or neglecting the facts of a case. Being moderate means politely presenting one's thoughtfully considered view, and condemning all forms of aggression. What is needed is a platform of intelligent moderation. Such a platform rejects the good Muslim–bad Muslim dialectic as distracting, and instead considers the evidence against the official story.

It is necessary to reiterate that the proponents of 9/11 truth dutifully acknowledge the existence of the phenomenon known as the "militant Islamic networks" and the ideologies that espouse such a phenomenon—"the bad Muslims." We also realize the real need to re-educate those that have been mentally conditioned by the various covert operations–funded *madrassas*. But assigning full blame to them for the attacks of 9/11 is patently false.

I am not suggesting that we should stop defending the religion of Islam from the slanderous implications that spring directly from the mainstream thesis; even pre-9/11, clarifying the Islam of Muhammad from its counterfeit forms and the various misperceptions promoted, whether ignorantly or deliberately, by various actors with agendas has been mandatory for anyone who loves Muhammad. It is important to heal the relationship between Islam and the typical modern Western psyche.

Many activists choose to use their limited resources to address the symptoms of 9/11. But if you feel compelled to address symptoms, why do you not care about the cause? It makes no therapeutic sense to dilute resources by treating only symptoms, without exposing the actual perpetrators and their agenda—what in the world of pathology is known as etiology. Not only will chasing after symptoms while allowing the etiology to thrive waste and further consume your precious resources, but striking at the etiology will most definitely cure the symptoms, not just alleviate them. Heightened Islamaphobia is a symptom. Public embrace of the so-called PATRIOT Act is a symptom. Public willingness to allow detention camps to hold those arrested without charges, trial, or elementary rights is a symptom. Public pro-war sentiment is a symptom. These are all linked directly to the false 9/11 mainstream thesis. The 9/11 truth thesis cures the disease. And the 9/11 truth movement is out there, alive and inexorably gaining ground. Ironically, the 9/11 truth movement is led almost entirely by non-Muslim Americans. They are doing almost all the work—certainly the hardest part—and they badly need our support.

It is both pathetic and tragic that so many activists, especially Muslim activists, ignore the vast positive potential of the 9/11 truth movement.

Disbelief etiology F: Disinformation patterns
The most useful kind of disinformation is that which is full of accurate information, but contains just the right amount of falsehood, either by omission of key facts or addition of wrong information, such that perpetrators may continue their course. The best counterfeit is that which best mimics the real thing. In this light, we need to look at the phrase formerly used to swear in witnesses in a court of law: "I promise to tell the truth, the whole truth, and nothing but the truth, so help me God." This phrase protected against the basic forms of disinformation. First, the promise to tell the truth. Next, this was qualified by a request to reveal the truth in its entirety, because it is possible to misinform through telling the truth, but not the whole truth. Moreover, it is possible to tell the whole truth while embellishing it in a way that misinforms a jury about a given situation; hence the additional pledge of telling nothing but the truth. There you have the basic forms of misinformation: to not tell the story, or not tell the whole story, or tell the whole story while embellishing it with the aim of keeping people in the dark.

In the context of 9/11, let us just mention two misinformation patterns that have arisen. In bringing these up, I am not accusing their proponents of consciously disseminating disinformation; what I am stating is that in light of the corpus of data found by the 9/11 truth movement, the following explanations must be seen as misinformation.

Misinformation pattern #1—The "blowback" hypothesis: This essentially acknowledges that the US government, under the influence of US corporations, did help to create and sustain militant Islamic networks, and that the US should be ashamed of its one-time ties to these "Muslim rogues." This hypothesis acknowledges that the US trained, financed, and armed these militants, and argues that now they, like Frankenstein's monster, have turned against us. This position has been proven false by evidence showing widespread foreknowledge of 9/11 among US officials, evidence of continued liaisons and support of so-called militant Islamic networks, and the obstructive behavior of the present regime and various oversight committees toward investigations of 9/11.[42]

2) *Misinformation pattern #2—"Damn those Saudis!"*: This was one of the recurrent themes of Michael Moore's "Fahrenheit 911."[43] I am not accusing Mr. Moore of consciously purveying misinformation—but not telling the whole story can be misleading. Mr. Moore stuns the audience in exposing just how deep the US corporate–Saudi ties run, and how much of our economy the Saudis influence. Typical American viewers are thus led to believe that their country has been economically invaded by the Saudis.

Mr. Moore was partially describing the US–Saudi petrodollar relationship. The crux of this relationship lies in a dynamic that commands the Saudis to sell oil to the Western corporate sector at massively subsidized prices; the cash the Saudis get from this is re-invested back into Western banks and Wall Street. These petrodollars play a large role in keeping our economy afloat. Corporations and banks need the Saudis to re-invest the cash they get from selling us oil back into our economy. The corporate/banking element needs petrodollars and uses our government to ensure that only regimes willing to perpetuate this system occupy seats of power (i.e., the Saudi royals, whose petrodollars finance much of our economy).[44] Yet, as in Moore's film, the Saudis are often depicted as an autonomously imposing threat.[45] In actuality, it is a rigged game, rigged to ensure that hydrocarbons, and cash, keep flowing in a one-way fashion into Wall Street, with the Saudi regime taking a cut for its own use. If US corporations and banks get even a slight inkling that the Saudis are planning to take the cash from oil sales and proceed to some other market, or direct them toward developing local Arab educational systems and infrastructures, it will be bye-bye for that particular regime and hello to another "friendlier" one. The leaders of US client regimes are never allowed to forget that we have the guns to enforce this, and use them with regularity. This "regime change" for the sake of keeping profit margins plump and our economy afloat makes complete business sense, and has been implemented plenty of times.[46]

The last thing to realize is that these dynamics have nothing to do with America or Saudi Arabia. People who describe situations in terms of nation-states often get thrown off by believing that at this level, the nation-state, or the citizens of a particular nation-state, have any authority. To say the behavior of Western corporate interests has anything to do with Americans is quite wrong. To say the behavior of the Saudi regime has anything to do with the Arabs that live in the Arabian Peninsula is equally wrong. What we are dealing with are corporations, sleazy profiteers, and those willing to "play ball" with them. For such agendas, there is no essential allegiance to nation-states, except as a tool to increase profit margins.

Disbelief etiology E: If 9/11 really was an inside job, isn't the situation hopeless? What difference can we make?
The psychological need to maintain some feeling of control, to believe one possesses the ability to effect change, is quite powerful in those who answer the call of activism and address 9/11. This need is so strong that in light of the obvious evidence that suggests 9/11 was an inside job coordinated through our own US security apparatus, many still cannot admit that yes, perhaps there are rogue elements in our own US covert operations and security apparatus who helped make 9/11 happen, and that it is pressure from these same rogues that is squashing attempts at bringing 9/11 truth into the mainstream discourse.

The implications of the 9/11 truth thesis are very psycho-logically disempowering, for they imply perpetrators within the US, and indeed the world, who are above the law. People are notorious for avoiding a feeling of disempowerment at all costs—even to the extent that they are willing to look away from evidence that may break the "idol" of their delusional construct.[47] People are so terrified of feeling disempowered that often they would prefer to cling to delusional constructs rather than face facts. The truth does indeed sometimes hurt. Even in individual social relationships, if we may use this as a microcosmic example, the capacity of individuals to delude themselves into maintaining dysfunctional relationships is astounding, when the alternative is facing a feeling of disempowerment. Those who avoid the issue of 9/11 truth have a similarly dysfunctional relationship with the topic.

So, how do our efforts, whether our symptomatic relief efforts or more etiology-focused efforts measure up in this case? As activists, do we have the courage to understand what we are up against? Or will we continue clinging to our delusion that things will get better if we just keep on writing, lecturing, sloganeering, marching, shouting, and chasing symptoms, convincing others that these were bad Muslims, but we are good Muslims because Islam is good.

The way to face this correctly, from the spiritual perspective, is fully to assimilate (not just mentally understand) one of the maxims taught in slightly different words by all of the great prophets and saints, be they in the Hindu, Parsi, Buddhist, Jewish, Christian, or Islamic traditions. Since I try my best to adhere to the Islamic tradition, the words I always keep in mind are: *La Hawla wa La Quwataa illa billahil Aleeyul Adheem* ("There is no Power or Might Save through God the Most High and Magnificent"). That is, any temporal authority, command, or advantage is only possible through God's Leave; it is borrowed, on loan—which means in the end, His Will is always Manifested. Sooner or later, Justice Cometh. In the face of such powerful perpetrators, then, our response can never be a feeling of disempowerment, and its attendant hopelessness or avoidance of facing facts. Rather, a rise to Holy Struggle against criminality ensues in the heart of one who is conscious of the Sacred. This call to righteous struggle is accompanied by a feeling of firmness, resolve, yet at the same time pity for the perpetrators, who have necessarily deluded themselves into thinking their schemes are leading them to success. The Divine Scheme (Makr-Allah) necessarily outdoes any scheming. They abuse the dominion and authority that is granted them, erroneously believing that they are the beneficiaries of nothing but their own cunning and devices. Ultimately this will be their ruin, whether we witness it or not, whether in this temporal life or not. While we work against their scheming, both by "relieving symptoms" that their actions cause, and trying to expose them directly (and thus cure the cause of the symptoms), we know that the effort, no matter how small or negligible the result here in the mortal phase of our existence, is always exalted in the Eyes of the Divine Audience, and bears fruit no matter what. I am reminded of the words of perhaps the most brilliant western Muslim metaphysician of the twentieth century, Rene Guenon (Abdul Wahid Yahya), who wrote:

> Those who might be tempted to give way to despair should realize that nothing accomplished in this order can ever be lost, that confusion, error and darkness can win the day only apparently and in a purely ephemeral way, that all partial and transitory disequilibrium must perforce contribute towards the great equilibrium of the whole, and that nothing can ultimately prevail against the power of truth.[48]

Our response to the criminals who perpetrated 9/11 is at first stern warning and pleading for them to stop their behavior and policies. If they persist in their crimes, we persist in opposing them by all legitimate means, while never stooping to the tactics which they use—tactics that promote lies, fear, terror and harm to innocents. We struggle while continually purifying our intentions, and mustering our actions of the heart, tongue (pen), and limbs, and say: "Wait then.... and we shall wait with you, for the Last Day" (Qur'an 6:158).

Hence, from the theistic perspective there can be no feeling of disempowerment. Being free of this feeling allows us to face the facts of the situation. (From the perspective of secular humanistic activism, ways to avoid disempowerment also exist, but this is beyond the scope of our discussion.) In the words of Frithjof of Schuon, another great expositor of traditional doctrines:

> ...that an affirmation of truth, or any effort on behalf of truth, is never in vain, even if we cannot from beforehand measure the value or outcome of such an activity. Moreover, we have no choice in the matter. Once we know the truth, we must needs live in it and fight for it, but what we must avoid at any price is to let ourselves bask in illusions. Even if, at this moment the horizon seems as dark as possible, one must not forget that in a perhaps unavoidably distant future the victory is ours, and cannot but be ours. Truth, by its nature, conquers all obstacles. *Vincit omnia Veritas.*[49]

Verily is Truth Hurled against Falsehood, and Falsehood withers
away, for Falsehood is ever bound to vanish.
—(Qur'an, 21:18).

To live [indifferently] in co-existence with a zaalim[50] *is sinful.*
—the grandson of Muhammad, the Saint Imam Hussain,
who died in an act of state-sponsored terror

14

A CLASH BETWEEN JUSTICE AND GREED

Enver Masud

THE APPARENT CLASH BETWEEN ISLAM AND THE WEST IS NOT A CLASH OF civilizations. It is a mirage deliberately created after the collapse of the Soviet Union in order to justify US "defense" spending, and to provide a pretext for controlling the world's resources and markets through military aggression against Muslim-majority countries. This fabricated clash between Islam and the West may be summed up in three words: justice versus greed.

Muslims, Christians, and Jews

Islam teaches that "the most excellent jihad is for the conquest of self." It teaches Muslims to speak out against oppression, and to fight if necessary for justice. This is jihad. The Qur'an—the Word of God for Muslims—states:

> O mankind! We created you from a single soul, male and female, and made you into nations and tribes, so that you may come to know one another. Truly, the most honored of you in God's sight is the greatest of you in piety. (49:13)

Thus, Islam, perhaps like no other religion, declares to Muslims the sanctity of all "nations and tribes." What may surprise Christians and Jews, and even many Muslims, is that the Qur'an refers to members of all three traditions as "muslim." Muhammad Asad, born Leopold Weiss in Poland in 1900, wrote in his interpretation of the Qur'an:

> When his contemporaries heard the words islam and muslim, they understood them as denoting man's "self-surrender to God" and "one who surrenders himself to God," without limiting himself to any specific community or denomination—e.g., in 3:67, where Abraham is spoken of as having "surrendered himself unto God" (kana musliman), or in 3:52 where the disciples of Jesus say, "Bear thou witness that we have surrendered ourselves unto God (bianna musliman)."[1]

In Arabic, this original meaning has remained unimpaired, and no Arab scholar has ever become oblivious of the wide connotation of these terms.

The three faiths share the Abrahamic heritage, the same values, and revere many of the same prophets. The prophets of Judaism and Christianity are also Islam's prophets.

Muslims, Christians, and Jews once lived in peace in Palestine, with all three referring to God using the same Arabic word, Allah. The three faiths thrived in Muslim Spain until its fall to Christian armies. Maimonides, highly revered among Jews, studied and practiced in Muslim Spain. With the fall of Muslim Spain to Christian armies in 1492, Muslims and Jews were expelled or forced to convert to Christianity. The Jews who chose to convert and remain in Spain were called *maranos* (pigs) by the Christians.

Coerced conversions are banned by the Qur'an and largely absent from Islamic history. From the very earliest Arab conquests more than 1,300 years ago, when conquered Jews and Christians were encouraged to retain their faiths and allowed self-governance under Muslim protection, forced conversions have been anathema to Muslims. And for the past 1,000 years, Islam has spread mainly through conversion-by-example, with little help from conquests by Muslim rulers. Indonesia has more Muslims than any other country, yet no Muslim armies ever invaded Indonesia. Indeed, Christianity has spread with the help of conquest far more than Islam has, especially during the past 500 years of European global imperial-colonial domination.

Following the still-mysterious events of September 11, 2001, virtually every Muslim country supported the US "war on terrorism" until it degenerated into an excuse for a crackdown on Muslims by governments across the world. Once it became clear that 9/11 had been a pretext for repression, tyranny, and pre-planned wars of aggression, voices of morality from all backgrounds and traditions began to speak out for justice. While leading Christian evangelicals, and the hawks in US government, pushed for war on Iraq, predominantly Christian Europe opposed it. Church leaders including the new Archbishop of Canterbury, Rowan Williams, questioned the legality and morality of an American-led assault on Iraq. And because of Likkud-governed Israel's increasing repression of Palestinians, which could not have happened without the so-called war on terrorism that 9/11 seems to have been designed to trigger, Presbyterians are divesting from

Israel, and Anglicans have called for sanctions on Israel. Jews, Christians, Muslims, and others around the world have demonstrated together against the wars on the Iraqi and Palestinian people. More recently, as this volume shows, religious people from widely varying traditions have been speaking out for 9/11 truth and global justice.

It is important for Muslims and others to understand that many honorable Jewish voices, representing an extremely broad diversity of viewpoints from pro-Zionist to anti-Zionist, have joined the call for peace and justice in the Middle East. Many Jews support statehood for the Christians and Muslims in Palestine. "Britain's chief rabbi, Jonathan Sacks, head of the Jewish community in the U.K. and the Commonwealth for 11 years, warned that Israel's stance towards Palestinians is incompatible with Judaism," reported BBC News.[2] The moral misgivings of much of the world's Jewish population toward Israeli policy extends, in some cases, to forthright Jewish anti-Zionism. Jews Not Zionists is one well-known group, while Naturei Karta International, an Orthodox Jewish organization, has printed on its stationery: "Pray for the peaceful dismantling of the Zionist State."[3]

Clashes Between Peoples and Nations, and within Civilizations

But there have been, and perhaps there always will be, clashes both among and between peoples and nations, and within civilizations. The clash between the Dalits—the lowest Hindu caste in India—and the upper castes is a clash that has persisted for centuries. Europe, throughout its history, has been ravaged by clashes within Christianity. Muslims have fought wars with Muslims.

For the most part, the underlying reason for these clashes is economic. Economics, more specifically greed, is the primary reason for the clash between Islam and the West. This is not surprising, since it is usually the major factor in wars between developed countries and developing countries. The current American wars of aggression fit the pattern. The US desire to control the world's resources and markets, its abject surrender to the Zionist agenda, and the virtual exclusion of dissenting voices from the national dialogue were key factors that led to the US war on Iraq. September 11 merely provided the pretext.

Control of the World's Resources and Markets

Following the fall of Muslim Spain in 1492, Europeans spread out over the world—to the Americas, Africa, Asia, and Australia.[4] Millions of natives in those continents were brutalized, enslaved, or killed. By some accounts, 15 million natives of North America, 50 million natives of South America, and 100 to 200 million Africans perished, since ten people had to be killed for one to be taken alive during capture by the slave-dealers. By the end of the eighteenth century, the Spanish, Portuguese, Dutch, British, and French ruled much of the world. In the mid-twentieth century, when the British empire was crumbling, as the colonial powers pulled out of Asia and Africa, they drew up national boundaries for their continuing benefit, and the US empire began to take shape.

The US has fought for control of the world's resources and markets while keeping the true reasons for war from Americans. Major General Smedley D. Butler, recipient of two Congressional Medals of Honor, described his experience in the US Marine Corps:

> War is just a racket... I helped make Mexico, especially Tampico, safe for American oil interests in 1914. I helped make Haiti and Cuba a decent place for the National City Bank boys to collect revenues in. I helped in the raping of half a dozen Central American republics for the benefit of Wall Street. The record of racketeering is long. I helped purify Nicaragua for the international banking house of Brown Brothers in 1909... I brought light to the Dominican Republic for American sugar interests in 1916. In China I helped to see to it that Standard Oil went its way unmolested.[5]

George Kennan, recipient of the Albert Einstein Peace Prize, chairman of the Policy Planning Staff at the State Department, wrote in the top-secret *Policy Planning Study No. 23*:

> We have about 50% of the world's wealth, but only 6.3% of its population.... Our real task in the coming period is to devise a pattern of relationships which will permit us to maintain this position of disparity.[6]

While US policy advisors may differ on the specific timing and means, this militant foreign policy—often backed up by assassination of opponents (a.k.a. "regime change"), military coups, terrorism—has powerful proponents.[7] Zbigniew Brzezinski, former national security advisor to President Carter, writes in *The Grand Chessboard* (1997):

A power that dominates Eurasia [the territory east of Germany and Poland, stretching all the way through Russia and China to the Pacific Ocean—including the Middle East and most of the Indian subcontinent] would control two of the world's three most advanced and economically productive regions. A mere glance at the map also suggests that control over Eurasia would almost automatically entail Africa's subordination.... About 75 per cent of the world's people live in Eurasia, and most of the world's physical wealth is there as well, both in its enterprises and underneath its soil. Eurasia accounts for 60 per cent of the world's GNP and about three-fourths of the world's known energy resources.[8]

The key to controlling Eurasia, says Brzezinski, is controlling the Central Asian Republics. He adds:

The three grand imperatives of imperial geostrategy are to prevent collusion and maintain security dependence among the vassals, to keep tributaries pliant and protected, and to keep the barbarians from coming together.[9]

According to the *Los Angeles Times*:

Behind a veil of secret agreements, the United States is creating a ring of new and expanded military bases that encircle Afghanistan and enhance the armed forces' ability to strike targets throughout much of the Muslim world... Since Sept. 11, according to Pentagon sources, military tent cities have sprung up at 13 locations in nine countries neighboring Afghanistan.[10]

Chalmers Johnson, author of *Blowback: The Costs and Consequences of American Empire* and *The Sorrows of Empire*, writes: "the Pentagon currently owns or rents 702 overseas bases in about 130 countries."[11] It is reported that the US is constructing 14 new bases in occupied Iraq.

Uncritical Support of the Apartheid State of Israel

The unresolved issue of Israel helps keep Zbigniew Brzezinski's "barbarians," presumably the Muslim nations of the Middle East, Africa, and Central Asia, from coming together. The US—which displayed exceptional zeal in implementing UN Security Council resolutions against Iraq—has displayed the same zeal in blocking implementation of UN Security Council resolutions against Israel. UN Security Council Resolution 242 of 1967, which emphasizes "the inadmissibility of the acquisition of territory by war," and requires the "withdrawal of Israeli armed forces from territories occupied in the recent conflict," has yet to be implemented.

While the US pushed for war on Iraq, and maintained no-fly zones in northern and southern Iraq, under the US interpretation of UN Security Council Resolution 687 (an interpretation with which most other nations disagreed), the US ignored Article 14 of the same resolution, which has "the goal of establishing in the Middle East a zone free from weapons of mass destruction and all missiles for their delivery and the objective of a global ban on chemical weapons" for all the nations in the region—including Israel, which is known to possess chemical and biological weapons, as well as 200 to 400 nuclear weapons and the missiles to deliver them.[12]

The United States, which claims to promote democracy around the world, continues its uncritical support of the apartheid state of Israel and the unlawful occupation of Palestine.[13] Israel has cost the US about $1.6 trillion since 1973, estimates Thomas Stauffer, a consulting economist.[14] A survey conducted by the *Guardian* of 500 people from each of the European Union's member nations included a list of 15 countries with the instruction, "tell me if in your opinion it presents or not a threat to peace in the world." Israel was reportedly picked by 59 percent of those interviewed as a threatening nation.[15]

Poll: US Greatest Danger to World Peace

Now the "barbarians" and most of the "civilized" world appear to be standing on the side of justice and against not just Israel, but its American sponsor as well. A poll conducted by *Time* magazine's Europe edition asked: "Which country really poses the greatest danger to world peace in 2003?" With 673,027 responses received by March 10, 2003, the results were: North Korea 5.6 percent; Iraq 6.5 percent; the US 87.9 percent.[16]

BBC World (April 9, 2004) asked 1,500 viewers of its news and international channel for the biggest problems in the world. Fifty-two percent said the US and globalization.[17]

The *Independent* (October 18, 2004) reported the findings of a new survey of African attitudes, thought to be the biggest-ever of its kind. Fifty-four percent of the interviewees—not just among Muslims—saw the US as a threat.[18]

US "Defense" Spending

According to the Center for Defense Information (February 3, 2003), "the United States and its allies account for two-thirds of world military expenditures." Not counting the $200 billion for the war on Iraq, the $399 billion US "defense" budget is equal to that of the next fifteen biggest spenders combined—six times bigger than Russia's (the third biggest spender), eight times bigger than China's, and 52 times bigger than Canada's! The defense spending of the "rogue states," or "axis of evil," pales in comparison. In 2001, Iran spent $4.8 billion; North Korea 2.1; Iraq 1.4; Libya 1.2; Syria 1.0; Cuba 0.8; Sudan 0.6—a total just under $12 billion.

Former Defense Secretary McNamara, in his 1989 testimony before the Senate Budget Committee, said US military spending could safely be cut in half.[19] This "peace dividend" was unacceptable to powerful entrenched interests. With the demise of the Soviet Union, it became necessary to find or create new enemies. The choice was between the Yellow Peril (East Asia) and the Green Peril (Islam). Islam was selected. Over the next decade this evolved into the "war on terrorism."[20]

International Outlaw

Multibillionaire George Soros writes in *Open Society: Reforming Global Capitalism*: "The United States has become the greatest obstacle to establishing the rule of law in international affairs."[21] According to a survey done for the Chicago Council on Foreign Relations and the German Marshall Fund of the US, "a majority of people in six European countries believe American foreign policy is partly to blame for the Sept. 11 attacks." The US stands virtually alone against the world in efforts to build a safer, better world. For example:

—International Covenant on Economic, Social, and Cultural Rights (1966): unanimously approved by the UN General Assembly but not ratified by the US;

—Anti-Ballistic Missile Treaty (1972): signed and ratified by the US and USSR, but overturned by President Bush;

—Convention on the Elimination of Discrimination Against Women (1979): ratified by more than 150 governments but not the US;

—UN Convention on the Law of the Sea (1982): supported by 130 governments but never ratified by the US;

—Convention on the Rights of the Child (1989): ratified by 187 governments but not the US;

—Comprehensive Test Ban Treaty (1996): signed by President Clinton, ratified by all NATO allies and Russia, voted down by the US Senate, and opposed by President Bush;

—Kyoto Protocol (1997): sets targets for emissions that cause global warming; awaits ratification by the US;

—Chemical Weapons Convention (1998): crippled by the US, which limits what may be inspected in the US;

—Biological Weapons Convention (2001): signed by 144 countries, but the US rejected the "verification protocol;"

—Nonproliferation and Test Ban Treaties (2002): jeopardized by the US by its announced intention to build and use small, tactical, nuclear weapons;

—International Criminal Court (July 1, 2002): backed by 74 countries, signed by President Clinton, but fiercely opposed by the US unless American citizens were given immunity from war crimes prosecutions.

The opposition by a signatory to the treaty undermines the entire system of international law. Meanwhile, the US continues to develop new nuclear weapons, microbes to wipe out entire cities, genetically engineered fungus, genetically engineered materials-eating bacteria, and to test warheads containing live microbes. The US "government has been planning to test warheads containing live microbes in large aerosol chambers at the US Army's Edgewood Chemical Biological Centre in Maryland," wrote George Monbiot in the *Guardian* (March 19, 2002).

September 11, 2001: America Attacked

The 110-story towers of the World Trade Center were obliterated. The Pentagon suffered massive damage. This much is clear. Much else remains a mystery.

According to the official story: On September 11, 2001, American Airlines Flight 11, a Boeing 767 out of Boston and headed for Los Angeles, crashed into the north tower of the World Trade Center in New York at 8:48AM. Eighteen minutes later, United Airlines Flight 175, a Boeing 767, headed from Boston to Los Angeles, crashed into the south tower. American Airlines Flight 77, a Boeing 757 from Washington's Dulles International Airport bound for Los Angeles, crashed into the western wall of the Pentagon at 9:40AM. United Airlines Flight 93, a Boeing 757 flying from Newark to San Francisco, crashed near Pittsburgh.

Europol's director Jürgen Storbeck stated: "It's possible that he [bin Laden] was informed about the operation; it's even possible that he influenced it; but he's probably not the man who steered every action or controlled the detailed plan."[22] President Bush, however, ignored Europol's doubts, reneged on Secretary of State Colin Powell's pledge to provide evidence, and named Osama bin Laden and al-Qaeda as the perpetrators.

As for the nineteen alleged hijackers, their names do not appear on the Associated Press September 17, 2001 "partial list of victims" on the hijacked flights—the final list has not been made public.[23] On September 23, 2001, the BBC reported that four of the suspected hijackers were alive, and that "FBI Director Robert Mueller acknowledged on Thursday that the identity of several of the suicide hijackers is in doubt."[24]

The 9/11 Commission Report

On July 22, 2004, the Commission charged with investigating the events of 9/11, released its final report, which "provides a full and complete account of the circumstances surrounding the September 11th, 2001, terrorist attacks, including preparedness for and the immediate response to the attacks."[25]

The report is an egregious failure.[26] Among its many short-comings, the conspiracy theory set forth in *The 9/11 Commission Report* makes no attempt to clear up questions surrounding the alleged hijackers' identities, its explanation of the collapse of the Twin Towers and WTC 7 fails to answer the issues raised, and it appears to contradict publicly available evidence regarding the Pentagon crash site.

In the Pentagon crash site photos, there is little or no evidence of the airliner that allegedly struck the Pentagon. I live about one-half mile from the Pentagon. The first question that I asked other onlookers as we viewed the crash site was, "Where's the plane?" Indeed, early reports claimed that a truck bomb had exploded, and the damage was similar to that inflicted on the *USS Cole* in Yemen. The gash in the hull of the *USS Cole* was reported to be about 30 feet by 40 feet.

The Pentagon crash may be the only commercial airline crash in modern history for which so much of the available video evidence has been withheld from the public. Five video frames from Pentagon cameras raise more questions than they answer—no Boeing 757 is visible.[27]

In the publicly available photos, the hole in the Pentagon wall—prior to the collapse of the roof—appears much too small to accommodate a Boeing 757. If only the fuselage penetrated the Pentagon, then the wings would have remained outside. But no large debris—anything resembling the wings and Boeing 757 engines—is visible on the Pentagon lawn, and the lawn itself shows no sign that a Boeing 757 skidded across it or struck it.[28]

How does one reconcile the relatively minor damage to the Pentagon by a Boeing 757 (the Pentagon's reinforced concrete walls are eighteen inches thick), with the total destruction of the World Trade Center by two Boeing 767s (each tower was built with 236 exterior columns and 47 core columns—all made of steel and connected to each other by steel trusses)?

Though a majority of eyewitnesses do report having seen a large plane hit the Pentagon, and a few are reported to have seen a commuter plane, one eyewitness account should take precedence over those of passersby. Arlington County Fire Chief Ed Plaugher—at a Department of Defense news briefing with Assistant Secretary Victoria Clarke on September 12, 2001—when asked, "Is there anything left of the aircraft at all?", said, "There are some small pieces of aircraft... there's no fuselage sections and that sort of thing."[29]

Didn't Chief Plaugher see the plane's engines? The engines would have survived the impact and heat. An engine from a plane that struck the World Trade Center was shown on network television, and so was an engine from American Airlines Flight 587, which crashed shortly after takeoff from New York on November 12, 2001. A photo from the Pentagon crash site shows what could be an engine part about 30 inches in diameter outside the Pentagon—but a Boeing 757's engines are eight or nine feet in diameter. Another photo shows what could be an engine part (its size is difficult to determine) inside the Pentagon. Were these parts, and another piece of debris on the Pentagon lawn, traced to Flight 77? We don't know.

Another question put to Chief Plaugher at the briefing was: "Chief, there are small pieces of the plane virtually all over, out over the highway, tiny pieces. Would you say the plane exploded, virtually exploded on impact due to the fuel...?" Plaugher responded: "I'd rather not comment on that."

How did "small pieces of the plane" end up "out over the highway" when the plane is reported to have disintegrated inside the Pentagon after it crossed the highway? If it disintegrated outside the Pentagon, why is there nothing that looks like a Boeing 757 on the Pentagon lawn? If it disintegrated either inside or outside the Pentagon, what caused the hole in the third ring? The landing gear or some other part?

It is curious that at this news briefing, held approximately 24 hours after American Airlines Flight 77 departing from Dulles airport is said to have crashed into the Pentagon, the words "Boeing," "Dulles," "flight," and "passengers" were not even mentioned. The word "plane" was mentioned once, but Chief Plaugher would "not comment on that." It is even more curious that national news media failed to follow up on Chief Plaugher's comment that "there's no fuselage sections and that sort of thing" when dozens of onlookers, relatives, and firefighters were interviewed on network television about the planes that crashed into the World Trade Center.

Photos and videos of the Pentagon reveal yet more curious sights: one apparently shows about 50 men, dressed like FBI officers, walking shoulder to shoulder in line apparently looking for small items; another shows office furniture and a computer monitor which survived the fire that is alleged to have vaporized the Boeing 757, but left human bodies in good enough condition to be identified (highly improbable, if not impossible).[30]

The issue of whether or not a Boeing 757 crashed into the Pentagon could be settled by examining the photos and videos taken between 9:35AM and 10:15AM on September 11, 2001, by cameras located inside and outside the Pentagon, the cameras at the nearby gas station and the Sheraton, and the Department of Transportation cameras. These have not been made public. And we still require an explanation for the "complex maneuver" made by the alleged Arab pilot of the Boeing 757, Hani Hanjour. The *New York Times* quoted his flight instructor as saying, "He could not fly at all,"[31] while CBS News reported:

> Radar shows Flight 77 did a downward spiral, turning almost a complete circle and dropping the last 7,000 feet in two-and-a-half minutes. The steep turn was so smooth, the sources say, it's clear there was no fight for control going on. And the complex maneuver suggests the hijackers had better flying skills than many investigators first believed. The jetliner disappeared from

radar at 9:37 and less than a minute later it clipped the tops of street lights and plowed into the Pentagon at 460 mph.[32]

Were We Deceived?

Is it possible that the US government, or rogue elements within the government, were in some degree responsible for the events of 9/11? Were others involved?

Professor David Ray Griffin, in his book *The New Pearl Harbor: Disturbing Questions about the Bush Administration and 9/11*, and former investigative producer for ABC's World News Tonight James Bamford, in his book *A Pretext for War*, make a convincing case that the Bush administration was looking for a pretext for toppling Iraqi president Saddam Hussein.

Indeed, neoconservatives within the Bush administration were following a script first drafted by them for Israeli Prime Minister Benjamin Netanyahu, and later rewritten for the Bush administration as a report of the Project for the New American Century.[33]

On the day of the attack on America, the *Washington Times* quoted a paper by the Army School of Advanced Military Studies, which said that the Mossad, the Israeli intelligence service, "has capability to target US forces and make it look like a Palestinian/ Arab act."[34] Dozens of Israelis were reported to have been arrested during 2001 both before and after 9/11, but the role played by this "huge Israeli spy ring that may have trailed suspected al-Qaeda members in the United States without informing federal authorities" remains unclear, and "it is no longer tenable to dismiss the possibility of an Israeli angle in this story."[35]

Field reports by the Drug Enforcement Administration agents and other US law enforcement officials on the alleged Israeli spy ring have been compiled in a 60-page document. John F. Sugg of the *Weekly Planet* reported that "DEA agents say that the 60-page document was a draft intended as the base for a 250-page report. The larger report has not been produced because of the volatile nature of suggesting that Israel spies on America's deepest secrets."[36]

James Bamford, who has written investigative cover stories for the *New York Times Magazine*, the *Washington Post Magazine*, and the *Los Angeles Times Magazine*, describes an operation which suggests that even the US armed forces may be suspect. Mr. Bamford's book, *Body of Secrets: Anatomy of the Ultra-Secret National Security Agency from the Cold War Through the Dawn of a New Century*, reveals that the US Joint

Chiefs of Staff (JCS) drew up and approved plans for "launching a secret and bloody war of terrorism against their own country in order to trick the American public into supporting an ill-conceived war they intended to launch against Cuba."

Mr. Bamford writes:

> Codenamed Operation Northwoods, the plan... called for innocent people to be shot on American streets; for boats carrying refugees fleeing Cuba to be sunk on the high seas; for a wave of violent terrorism to be launched in Washington, D.C., Miami, and elsewhere. People would be framed for bombings they did not commit; planes would be hijacked. Using phony evidence, all of it would be blamed on Castro, thus giving Lemnitzer [Chairman JCS] and his cabal the excuse, as well as the public and international backing, they needed to launch their war.[37]

Windfall for the Military-Industrial Complex

9/11 was a godsend for the US military-industrial complex. It led to an open-ended "war on terrorism," which helped justify enormous increases in "defense" and "security" spending, and the passage of "anti-terrorism" legislation long desired by some in the Justice Department. A $48 billion increase in the defense budget sailed through both houses of Congress, bringing US military spending to $379 billion. This, according to the *Washington Post* (January 27, 2002), represents "the biggest one-year rise since the Reagan buildup two decades ago and a suspension of 'the peace dividend.'" The post-9/11 US military budget now matches the combined military spending of the fifteen countries with the next biggest defense budgets, and the proposed increase alone is about the same as the entire defense budget of the next biggest spender—Japan. It would roughly match, in inflation-adjusted terms, the US defense budget in 1967, at the height of the Vietnam War.

By 2005 the defense budget had reached $419 billion. Congress approved $350 billion to fight terrorism and for combat and reconstruction in Iraq and Afghanistan—an amount that matches the total cost of the Korean War in today's dollars.

Agreement for Afghan Pipeline

The events of 9/11 led to the US war on Afghanistan—a war apparently planned prior to 9/11, and possibly after US negotiations with the Taliban for a pipeline broke down. According to the BBC, Niaz Naik, a former Pakistani Foreign Secretary, was told by senior American officials in mid-July that military action against Afghanistan would go ahead by the middle of October.[38]

The invasion secured the pipeline deal for the US. According to the *Irish Times* (February 11, 2002), "The Pakistani President, Gen. Pervez Musharraf, and the Afghan interim leader, Mr. Hamid Karzai, agreed yesterday that their two countries should develop 'mutual brotherly relations and cooperate in all spheres of activity'—including a proposed gas pipeline from Central Asia to Pakistan via Afghanistan."

It's curious that these two leaders, who only later vowed to "bury the recent history of poisonous relations" between their nations (*Washington Post*, April 3, 2002), could agree so quickly to the pipeline. Afghanistan's interim president Hamid Karzai, as well as Zalmay Khalilzad, the Bush-appointed special envoy to Afghanistan, may have facilitated the agreement.

The American invaders of Afghanistan made little or no attempt to capture Osama bin Laden. Their real objective was to secure Central Asian oil reserves. According to George Monbiot: "Both Hamid Karzai, the interim president, and Zalmay Khalilzad, the US special envoy, were formerly employed as consultants to Unocal, the US oil company which spent much of the 1990s seeking to build a pipeline through Afghanistan."[39] Zalmay Khalilzad drew up Unocal's risk analysis on its proposed trans-Afghan gas pipeline, according to the *Irish Times*. The Taliban, after initially negotiating with Unocal, had begun showing a preference for Bridas Corporation of Argentina. Could this possibly be the reason why the Bush administration has let Argentina's financial crisis spiral out of control?

While relevant questions regarding 9/11 went unanswered, without the benefit of UN resolutions, and despite the fact that the Taliban stated their willingness to give up Osama bin Laden for trial to an international court, the US launched its war on Afghanistan— one of the world's poorest countries, already devastated by 23 years of war and civil strife following the Russian invasion of 1979.

The war in Afghanistan created a million new refugees (adding to the existing five or six million) and caused the death of 4,000 civilians (about 2,800 civilians were killed in the 9/11 attack).[40]

Infinite Justice

President Bush seems intent on continuing his father's crusade. Former President Bush is reported to have told US troops in

Kuwait that they were "doing the Lord's work."[41] With his post-9/11 endless war that began as Operation Infinite Justice, President Bush vows to save civilization itself. He expanded his "crusade" to the brutally repressed Moros of the Philippines. Yet five years after the US launched its "war on terrorism," hard evidence regarding the 9/11 attacks remains scarce. FBI Director Robert S. Mueller, III, in his April 19, 2002 talk at the prestigious Commonwealth Club of California, said: "In our investigation, we have not uncovered a single piece of paper—either here in the United States, or in the treasure trove of information that has turned up in Afghanistan and elsewhere—that mentioned any aspect of the September 11 plot."[42]

The absence of convincing evidence for the "nineteen Arabs" conspiracy theory, and abundance of evidence for the competing "inside job" theory, has grown more obvious with each passing year. George Nelson, Colonel USAF (ret.), wrote on April 23, 2005:

> Every military and civilian passenger-carrying aircraft [has] many parts that are identified for safety of flight.... These parts are individually controlled by a distinctive serial number and tracked by a records section of the maintenance operation and by another section called plans and scheduling... The government alleges that four wide-body airliners crashed on the morning of September 11, 2001, resulting in the deaths of more than 3,000 human beings, yet not one piece of hard aircraft evidence has been produced in an attempt to positively identify any of the four aircraft. With all the evidence readily available at the Pentagon crash site, any unbiased rational investigator could only conclude that a Boeing 757 did not fly into the Pentagon as alleged. Similarly, with all the evidence available at the Pennsylvania crash site, it was most doubtful that a passenger airliner caused the obvious hole in the ground and certainly not the Boeing 757 as alleged. Regarding the planes that allegedly flew into the WTC towers, it is only just possible that heavy aircraft were involved in each incident, but no evidence has been produced that would add credence to the government's theoretical version of what actually caused the total destruction of the buildings, let alone proving the identity of the aircraft...
>
> As painful and heartbreaking as was the loss of innocent lives and the lingering health problems of thousands more, a most troublesome and nightmarish probability remains that so many Americans appear to be involved in the most heinous conspiracy in our country's history.[43]

Dissent and Dialogue Needed

The voracious US appetite for resources and markets, the desire to control those resources and markets, uncritical US support of Israel, and the need to justify military spending drive US wars. These are bound to create more "terrorists," who may, with or without help from US leaders and intelligence agencies, succeed in inflicting substantial damage. The terror myth could become a self-fulfilling prophecy.

Those who stand to benefit by war have characterized opposition to US domination as a "clash of civilizations." The "war on terrorism" is a cover for far more destructive state-sponsored terrorism—the US war on Iraq.

Fortunately, due to an increasingly multicultural society, and to the internet, the world is waking up. Many see the apparent clash between Islam and the West for what it is: a clash between justice and greed. Dialogue, and national and international forums for dissenting views, are urgently needed so that we may not succumb to the official lies, fear-mongering, and mythologizing that followed the attacks of September 11, 2001. As Thomas Jefferson, third president of the US, who at age thirty-three drafted the Declaration of Independence, said: "I have sworn upon the altar of god, eternal hostility against every form of tyranny over the mind of man."[44]

15

THE REMAKING OF ISLAM IN THE POST-9/11 ERA

Yasmin Ahmed

WHEN I WAS GROWING UP, I THOUGHT MY PARENTS WERE CRAZY. I WATCHED my friends attend church camps and youth groups, but for me it was different. We were Muslim, so my parents were afraid. In their paranoia, they thought if we attended a Muslim youth camp— where Muslim teens gather to talk about God and go boating—we would be added to an FBI watch list for being too "actively involved" with our faith. That was before 9/11. At that time, their fear was madness.

In the post-9/11 era, simple adherence to the faith of Islam has become a punishable crime. This is almost entirely due to the impact of the 9/11 attacks, which were portrayed as the act of "fundamentalist," "hyper-religious" Muslims.

What is most ironic, however, is the fact that the accused hijackers were themselves not at all religious. According to many reports, a number of them drank heavily and frequented strip clubs, nude bars, and porn shops.[1] On September 10, 2001, three of the accused hijackers reportedly spent $200 to $300 each on lap dances and drinks in a Florida strip club.[2] Following that, two of them were seen with strippers at a bar in Palm Springs where they spent another $1,000 on Krug and Perrier-Jouet champagne.[3]

More importantly, one could not kill innocents and then claim to be a strict follower of a religion that teaches its followers that killing a single innocent is like killing all of humanity, and saving a single innocent is like saving all of humanity.[4] And as it turns out, those who knew the accused hijackers report that they were indeed non-practicing Muslims. According to *Newsweek*, the mayor of Paterson, New Jersey, says of the six hijackers who stayed there: "Nobody ever saw them at mosques, but they liked the go-go clubs."[5] According to Richard Foltz, religion professor at the University of Florida, "It is incomprehensible that a person could drink and go to a strip bar one night, then kill themselves the next day in the name of Islam..."[6]

Given this description of the notorious "Islamic terrorists," and the fact that Islam prohibits the slaughter of innocents, it would follow that any successful strategy for fighting terrorism committed by such so-called Muslims should strive to increase their Islamic piety—not decrease it. Unfortunately, the current strategy has been just the opposite. Today, there is a fierce propaganda war, driven by the underlying assumption that Islam itself is the problem—not just some extreme version of it. As a result, seriousness about Islam has been criminalized, and abandonment of the faith has been presented as the solution for the problem of terrorism.

As a result, a devout Muslim who has broken no laws can be considered a criminal simply by virtue of practicing his faith. In December 2004, 39 American citizens learned this lesson well. At the US border with Canada, these citizens were detained, photographed, and fingerprinted. The detainees, ranging in age from an infant to men and women in their fifties, were told that at the border they had "no rights." One woman in her seventh month was even forced to lift her shirt to prove that she was pregnant—an extreme indignity to Muslims, who consider the belly to be among the body's private parts.[7]

What crime did these 39 US citizens commit? Their only offense was that they all returned from the same spiritual conference—an Islamic spiritual conference. These citizens were all Muslims, and therefore targets of groundless investigation and harassment. By simply practicing their faith—because that faith was Islam—these Americans were automatically considered suspects.

The next year, 2005, was no different. In December, a prominent national Islamic civil rights and advocacy group issued a travel advisory for Muslim citizens attending this same conference or participating in the Hajj (pilgrimage to Mecca). According to US Newswire, "The Washington-based Council on American-Islamic Relations (CAIR) [was] concerned that American Muslim travelers returning to the United States [would] be singled out by US Customs and Border Protection (CBP) officials for special security checks and fingerprinting based solely on their attendance at both religious events."[8]

In what way could a religious pilgrimage to a holy city—during which a pilgrim is forbidden from even hurting a fly—be associated with terrorism? Why are images of prostrating Muslims, in a completely helpless position, so often linked to violence? Why would a woman who chooses to wear the headscarf or a man who prays at the mosque become symbols of militancy?

The answer lies in the hidden assumptions. If Islam is assumed to be radical by definition, anyone who adheres to it is automatically a militant. If Islam as a faith is deemed criminal, any adherence to it is a crime.

Mona Mayfield understood these rules well when she defended her husband Brandon, wrongfully accused of participating in the March 2004 Madrid bombing. To prove his innocence, Mayfield tried to downplay her husband's commitment to Islam. She even felt the need to justify his conversion—as if that were his crime. "We have a Bible in the house. He's not a fundamentalist—he thought it was something different and very unique," Mayfield told the Associated Press of her husband's conversion to Islam.[9]

Mosque administrator Shahriar Ahmed took a similar approach to defend Mayfield. "He was seen as a moderate," Ahmed told reporters. "Mayfield showed up for the Friday ritual of shedding his shoes, washing his bare feet and sitting on the carpets to hear services. He did not, as some devout Muslims do, pray five times a day at the mosque."[10] The implication here is that Brandon Mayfield's guilt or innocence was somehow related to how many times he prayed at the mosque—and that praying more would be a sign of guilt. Ahmed even went on to assert in Mayfield's defense, "He was on the less religious side if anything."[11]

For most Muslims, who know that facing God five times a day makes it that much harder to contemplate evil actions, such twisted logic is nonsensical. That Muslims are forced to invoke this absurd "devotion equals criminality" paradigm to defend themselves against false charges of terrorism is tragic and humiliating.

Nonetheless, these "less religious" examples of what an "acceptable" Muslim should look like are relentlessly trumpeted by the media. Since Islam is deemed by definition problematic, the ones who have won the much-coveted title of a "moderate Muslim" are actually just those who are only moderately Muslim, and therefore only moderately bad.

In a column entitled "Coulter Wars," Steve Kellmeyer explains: "There are essentially two kinds [of Muslims]: good Muslims who do their best to be orthodox and follow all the precepts of their faith (whether Sunni, Shiite, etc.), and bad Muslims who do not follow all Muslim precepts... No one has a quarrel with bad Muslims. It is the good Muslims that pose the problems."[12]

Ignoring the undisputed fact that the alleged 9/11 hijackers were entirely un-Islamic, the media has succeeded at defining the only acceptable kind of Muslim as a non-practicing one. Irshad Manji, media entrepreneur and author of *The Trouble with Islam*, is one of the most celebrated of these "moderate" icons. Manji is widely published and has appeared in all the top media outlets. She even received Oprah's Chutzpah Award for "gutsiness."

Although Manji refers to herself as a "Muslim refusenik," the media constantly touts her as an ideal model of what a "practicing Muslim" should be. Daniel Pipes, a former board member of the United States Institute of Peace, calls her a "courageous, moderate, modern Muslim." But Manji's ideas have less to do with Islam than do Pipes's ideas with peace. A *Washington Post* article describes Manji's epiphany about prayer (*salaat*), the cornerstone of the Islamic faith:

> Instead [of *salaat*], she said, she began praying on her own. After washing her feet, arms and face, she would sit on a velvet rug and turn toward Mecca. Eventually, she stopped this as well, because she did not want to fall "into mindless submission and habitual submissiveness."[13]

Manji is welcome to her opinion about the sacred religious practice of 1.5 billion people worldwide. She is also free to abandon any and all of these practices. But in the media's ongoing propaganda war, Manji is not simply depicted as what she is—an insignificant woman who decided not to pray. Her personal decision to abandon the central tenet of her faith—so long as that faith is Islam—is portrayed as a fight for freedom, a heroic struggle against tyranny. She is "courageous" and "gutsy," a model for other not-*too*-Islamic Muslims to follow.

Making this the model is like asking someone not to be "too black" or "too Jewish," as if these were essentially bad or violent, and then going on to portray anyone who struggled only to be "moderately black" or "moderately Jewish" as a freedom fighter. The *Washington Post* admiringly quoted Manji, describing her struggle to change Islam: "The violence is going to happen, then why not risk it happening for the sake of freedom?" Of course. Freedom is good, so the "they" who supposedly "hate our freedoms"—the Muslims—must be bad. Manji sugarcoats her message, but a business management professor at California's Imperial Valley College says bluntly how he really feels: "The only way to end Islamic terrorism is to eliminate the Islamic religion."[14]

This misunderstanding of Islam is not just genocidal, but deeply ironic.[15] In actuality, Islam calls its followers to stand up firmly for justice and oppose all evil. The Qur'an describes the believers as those "enjoining what is good, opposing what is evil, and believing in God."[16] Moreover, Islam as a faith calls for moderation in all things. The Qur'an states: "Thus, have We made you a people of the middle path."[17] A key Islamic concept is *tawazzun*, translated as "balance" or "harmonious equilibrium." The very word Islam comes from a root meaning "peace."

Since Islam is moderate in its very essence, it would follow that the more one adheres to its fundamentals, the more moderate one will be. It is, therefore, not surprising that those accused of committing such evil acts as the 9/11 attacks were in fact those who have abandoned the precepts of their faith. Unfortunately, despite this fact, *The 9/11 Commission Report* completely ignores the abundant evidence that the nineteen hijackers were utterly un-Islamic.[18]

Even more unfortunate, the mass media has played along, originally reporting on the alleged hijackers' un-Islamic lifestyles, then consigning those stories to the memory hole and continuing to blame 9/11 on "Islamic extremists."

This insistence on a nonexistent religious connection to the crime of the century is unusual to say the least. In ordinary news coverage religious affiliation is never reported in a crime. It is considered irrelevant. Nobody knows—or cares—that Jeffrey Dahmer was raised in a born-again Christian home or that Timothy McVeigh was a strong Catholic who talked about defending Christian America. Religion remains irrelevant—except of course if the criminal happens to be Muslim. In that case it is relevant enough to appear in the headline. Even when so-called Muslim criminals commit a crime, and never claim their crime had anything to do with their religion, that claim is made for them by the media. When the sniper in Washington, DC turned out to be a member of the Nation of Islam (a religion distinct from Islam) CNN reported in the headline that he was an "Islam convert."[19] Notice that although the sniper himself never claimed his crime had anything to do with his religion, CNN felt that it did. He wasn't a criminal armed with a gun. He was a man armed with a criminal religion.

When a Christian gunman walked into a church meeting and killed seven people last year, the headlines didn't read: "Christian Suicide Shooter Kills Seven." And when Baruch Goldstein, a Jewish settler from New York, walked into the Ibrahimi Mosque in Hebron and gunned down 29 Muslims while they prayed, no one in the mainstream media blamed Judaism.[20] And no one even expected Christians and Jews all over the world to condemn these acts of terrorism. It was assumed that they were committed in spite of Christianity and Judaism—not because of them. Islam, however, is not afforded this same good will. When a Muslim commits a crime, it is Islam that goes on trial.

And so after 9/11, many people turned to the Qur'an to see what could have motivated those heinous acts. Yet, I doubt anyone opened the Bible to find out what motivated Jeffery Dahmer to kill and eat seventeen people. Dahmer was just a crazy man. But Mohamed Atta, we are falsely told, was a sane man following a crazy religion.[21]

And so it follows that if Islam itself is the problem, and perceived as "militant" by definition, it would follow that anyone who chooses to actually adhere to it is automatically labeled a "militant Islamist" and considered an enemy. Suddenly, praying and wearing a headscarf becomes tantamount to terror.

Just last week I opened a magazine only to see the unfortunately familiar image of a man praying with a gun at his side. This connection is so deeply ingrained that there have been numerous incidents of people calling the FBI because they saw a Muslim praying.

But as it turns out, this irrational fear of Muslims has proven to be quite unsubstantiated. Although thousands of Muslims have been profiled, detained, and questioned since 9/11, an FBI report obtained by ABC News admits flatly that "to date, we have not identified any true 'sleeper' agents in the US." The report goes on to say: "US Government efforts to date also have not revealed evidence of concealed cells or networks acting in the homeland as sleepers."[22]

But America is undeniably at war. And so the obvious question is: if we've found no US terror cells and Iraq had no connection to

9/11 and harbored no WMDs, what exactly are we at war against? James Schall, professor of government at Georgetown University, tells us what: "I always thought it was a mistake not to say what Iraq really was, that is, a war against an expanding Islam." Schall is the author of policy papers for Hoover Institute, one of the largest and most influential US think tanks.[23] Daniel Pipes, director of the Middle East Forum, agrees. Pipes told *FrontPage* magazine that he would advise President Bush to "announce that the 'War on Terror' has been redefined as the 'War on Militant Islam.'"[24] When asked to define his version of a "militant" Muslim, Pipes told an audience at the University of Wisconsin-Madison that a "militant" Muslim was anyone who believed "Islam is the solution."[25] It is crucial to note that Pipes' definition had nothing to do with violence or extremism. Rather, it was simply anyone who took Islam seriously enough to think it could actually solve problems in his or her life. The question is, if someone did not believe Islam could solve their problems, why would they bother being Muslim at all?

While Pipes is careful to use the euphemistic prefix "militant," Lawrence Auster of *FrontPage* magazine is more blunt. Auster writes: "The problem is not 'radical' Islam but Islam itself, from which it follows that we must seek to weaken and contain Islam."[26] Ann Coulter elaborates: "We should invade their countries, kill their leaders, and convert them to Christianity."[27]

But those who know you can't "convert them to Christianity," as suggested by Coulter, have taken a more subtle approach to solving the "problem" of Islam. If you can't convince people not to practice their "problematic" religion, launch a stealth campaign to alter that religion and make it less "problematic."

In a four-month *US News & World Report* investigation of more than 100 interviews and a dozen internal government reports and memorandums, a "previously undisclosed effort was identified." According to an April 25, 2005 *US News & World Report* article: "Washington is plowing tens of millions of dollars into a campaign to influence not only Muslim societies but Islam itself."[28] The article continues: "Although US officials say they are wary of being drawn into a theological battle, many have concluded that America can no longer sit on the sidelines as radicals and moderates fight over the future of a politicized religion with over a billion followers." As a result, "the White House has approved a classified new strategy, dubbed Muslim World Outreach, that for the first time states that the United States has a national security interest in influencing what happens within Islam."

Does it matter that the First Amendment reads: "Congress shall make no law respecting an establishment of religion, or prohibiting the free exercise thereof; or abridging the freedom of speech, or of the press; or the right of the people peaceably to assemble, and to petition the government for a redress of grievances?" Our government doesn't seem to think so. And neither does RAND, the influential think tank that receives $140 million a year from the government to define US policy. In the RAND report *Civil Democratic Islam: Partners, Resources, Strategies,* Cheryl Benard writes:

> There is no question that contemporary Islam is in a volatile state, engaged in an internal and external struggle over its values, its identity, and its place in the world. Rival versions are contending for spiritual and political dominance. This conflict has serious costs and economic, social, political, and security implications for the rest of the world. Consequently, the West is making an increased effort to come to terms with, to understand, and to influence the outcome of this struggle.[29]

The key word here is "influence." RAND and the White House seem to both agree that when it comes to Islam, they can no longer afford to abide by the constitutional separation of church and state. Instead Washington is taking a leading role in defining what Islam should mean to Muslims. Benard writes:

> Modernism, not traditionalism, is what worked for the West. This included the necessity to depart from, modify, and selectively ignore elements of the original religious doctrine... There are definite indications that change can be effected in Islam. In fact, some explicit and quite major departures from Quranic norms have historically already taken place. (37)

Note the blatant egoism and ethnocentrism. Benard does not seem to fathom the possibility that what worked for the West may not necessarily work best for the rest of humanity. To claim that the West knows better how all others should practice religion is arrogant at best. Worse yet, such supercilious self-righteousness precludes dialogue or any hope of effective policy.

And yet RAND openly calls for such a strategy. To further this policy, Benard suggests supporting the so-called modernist

Muslims against other Muslims. Benard says, "The modernist vision matches our own" (37). She also explains, "The modernists find concepts within Islamic orthodoxy that support the right of Muslims, as individuals and as communities, to make changes and revisions even to basic laws and texts" (7).

Who Are the "Modernists"?

Under the heading "Modernism Has Respected Intellectuals and Leader" Benard refers to Khaled Abou El Fadl, a professor of Islamic law at UCLA, whom she describes as "a well-regarded modernist scholar and author, [whose] writings criticize the 'rampant apologetics' of traditionalists and the 'authoritarian, puritanical' approach of the fundamentalists alike" (38). Abou El Fadl is known to represent the views of a group that calls themselves "progressive Muslims." His essay on tolerance appears in the book *Progressive Muslims*, edited by Omid Safi. On November 15, 2004—just eight months after the release of the first RAND report—the Progressive Muslim Union (PMU) was created with Aiman Mackie, a previous employee of RAND, on the board of directors.

Why RAND Supports the Modernists

Abou El Fadl admits that there may be an "irresolvable conflict" between the literal Qur'anic text and contemporary (Western) values—which he calls "the individual conscience." In such a conflict, Abou El Fadl argues that so long as one has exhausted all ways of explaining away the text, one should disregard the Qur'anic "determination" in favor of one's "conscience." In his book *Speaking in God's Name*, he writes:

> It is also possible that an adequate resolution would not be found, and that the individual conscience and the textual determination continue to be pitted in an irresolvable conflict. I argue that as long as a person has exhausted all the possible avenues towards resolving the conflict, in the final analysis, Islamic theology requires that a person abide by the dictates of his or her conscience.[30]

Abou El Fadl's position has very dangerous implications. If a distraught "individual conscience" cries out for revenge, is the individual then free to ignore Islamic injunctions against the slaughter of innocents? Does not such "modernism" open the door to terrorist acts, as well as other evil actions prohibited by Islamic scripture and tradition?

But as a result of the modernists' willingness to change Islam to fit dominating Western sensibilities, Benard calls for the US to "support the modernists first, enhancing their vision of Islam over that of the traditionalists by providing them with a broad platform to articulate and disseminate their views." She continues: "They, not the traditionalists, should be cultivated and publicly presented as the face of contemporary Islam."[31] Benard also suggests that the US should "use popular regional media, such as radio, to introduce the thoughts and practices of modernist Muslims to broaden the international view of what Islam means and can mean."[32]

What Exactly Does This "Support" Entail?

In order to redefine Islam and make the "modernist" version of Islam dominate, Benard suggests the following strategies:

> The modernists and secularists are closest to the West in terms of values and policies. However, they are generally in a weaker position than the other groups, lacking powerful backing, financial resources, an effective infrastructure, and a public platform. The secularists, besides sometimes being unacceptable as allies on the basis of their broader ideological affiliation, also have trouble addressing the traditional sector of an Islamic audience... That role falls to the Islamic modernists, whose effectiveness, however, has been limited by a number of constraints, which this report will explore. To encourage positive change in the Islamic world toward... compatibility with the contemporary international world order, the United States and the West need to consider very carefully which elements, trends, and forces within Islam they intend to strengthen; what the goals and values of their various potential allies and protégés really are; and what the broader consequences of advancing their respective agendas are likely to be. A mixed approach composed of the following elements is likely to be the most effective:
>
> • Support the modernists first:
>
> —Publish and distribute their works at subsidized cost.
>
> —Encourage them to write for mass audiences and for youth.
>
> —Introduce their views into the curriculum of Islamic education.
>
> —Give them a public platform.

—Make their opinions and judgments on fundamental questions of religious interpretation available to a mass audience in competition with those of the fundamentalists and traditionalists, who have Web sites, publishing houses, schools, institutes, and many other vehicles for disseminating their views.

—Position secularism and modernism as a "counterculture" option for disaffected Islamic youth.

—Facilitate and encourage an awareness of their pre- and non-Islamic history and culture, in the media and the curricula of relevant countries.

—Assist in the development of independent civic organizations, to promote civic culture and provide a space for ordinary citizens to educate themselves about the political process and to articulate their views. (xi)

Benard goes on to say:

Whichever approach or mix of approaches is chosen, we recommend that it be done with careful deliberation, in knowledge of the symbolic weight of certain issues; the meaning likely to be assigned to the alignment of US policymakers with particular positions on these issues; the consequences of these alignments for other Islamic actors, including the risk of endangering or discrediting the very groups and people we are seeking to help; and the opportunity costs and possible unintended consequences of affiliations and postures that may seem appropriate in the short term. (xii)

Following Benard's prescription almost to the letter, the media has indeed provided a platform for only one view of Islam: the view RAND calls "modernist," Abou El Fadl calls "progressive," and Daniel Pipes calls "moderate."

Muslim media stars such as Asra Nomani, Irshad Manji, and Amina Wadud represent a view of Islam that in no way characterizes the beliefs of the majority of Muslims in the United States and around the world. And yet, these same people represent the only voice of mainstream Islam conveyed by the media. Why is this? Because, according to Benard, these are the icons who present a face of Islam that is closest to a certain Western sensibility. It doesn't seem to matter whether that face is true to Islam or not. Still less does it matter whether such "modernism" would open the door to heinous acts, including terrorism, that are clearly prohibited by Islamic scripture.

A quick perusal of major US newspapers and media outlets will make very clear which brand of Islam is being sold. More importantly, it will become clear that this is the only brand being sold. There is only one Muslim voice being heard, and oddly enough that voice is the voice of a small and unrepresentative minority. Tragically, this misleading monologue is precluding the possibility of honest dialogue between Muslims and non-Muslims.

Toward Finding a Real Solution

In order to solve any problem, one must first understand its true cause. Attempting to solve a problem without understanding its roots will be futile at best. At worst, such misguided "solutions" tend to backfire and worsen the very problems to which they were addressed. Prior to the current "war on terrorism," the US was still moderately popular in most of the Islamic world. Since then, US policies in the Muslim world have only fueled more hatred and resentment, and the RAND attempt to give Islam a facelift will certainly contribute to the further alienation of Muslims.

Terrorism must be correctly understood before it can be prevented. Until now, terrorism has been perceived and portrayed as a problem of "Islamic fundamentalism." As a result, the current strategy to solve this problem has amounted to a campaign against full adherence to Islam. However, a simple look at the profiles of those who actually engage in such violence suggests that it is *disengagement* from Islam that has led to violence. The accused 9/11 hijackers were in no way practicing Muslims and lived their lives in ways that contradict the teachings of Islam. It should therefore be of no surprise that such people would also disregard Islam's forceful prohibition with regards to killing innocents. From the devastating events that occurred on 9/11 and after, one clear and inarguable fact emerges: The violence committed today by so-called Muslims is being committed in spite of Islam—not because of it.

In fact, a look at the profiles of those who even support violence makes clear that such support is not driven by religion at all. The *Washington Post* reported that a recent Gallup poll of 8,000 Muslims throughout the Muslim world found "supporters of terrorism—defined as those who applauded the 9/11 attacks— were no more religious than other Muslims and tended to be better-educated and more affluent." Muslims who agreed that religion "was an important part of your daily life" and Muslims who attended regular prayer services were no more likely to back terrorism than those who did not, according to surveys in eight Muslim countries.

However, the same Gallup poll found that one factor did distinguish supporters of terrorism from non-supporters. That factor was "belief in self-determination." According to the poll, "Extremists were only half as likely as moderates to believe that the United States would allow people in the Middle East to fashion their own political future."[34] The poll shows that it is political grievances that drive the deep-seated anger. Whether it is the bombing and occupation of Iraq and Afghanistan, unbridled US support for Israel, or US backing for dictatorships in the Arab world, one thing is very clear: The grievances are political, not religious.

Therefore, in order to address the real causes of terrorism, we must address these political grievances and defuse their ability to transform a potential friend into a bitter enemy. Furthermore, we must step away from the ethnocentric view that whatever worked for the West must by definition be what is best for all of humanity. We must stop believing and acting according to the notion that we know best how the rest of the world should live and believe.

So far, the US engagement with Islam has been nothing more than a blatant attempt to redefine and mold beliefs and practices that are not ours to define or mold. By imposing our own Western frame of reference, we presume that our way of life is superior and therefore must be enforced upon all others. At best, this is arrogance; at worst, oppression. Moreover, such a strategy simply won't work. It has not solved, and will not solve, the problem of terrorism. Indeed, it has only worsened it. This type of self-righteous imposition of "our way of life" on the rest of the world only perpetuates a climate of resentment and anger.

Until we can begin to understand Islam on its own terms and stop trying to mold it into what we think it ought to be given our own unique perspectives and experiences, we will continue to misunderstand the problem and miss the solution. Honest dialogue, peace, and coexistence will only be possible when we extend to others what we insist upon for ourselves: the right to determine one's own destiny.

CONTRIBUTORS

Nafeez Mosaddeq Ahmed is executive director of the Institute for Policy Research and Development in Brighton, England, and the best-selling author of *The War on Freedom: How and Why America was Attacked, September 11, 2001*, which won him the Naples Prize, Italy's most prestigious literary award, and *The War on Truth: 9/11, Disinformation, and the Anatomy of Terrorism* (Olive Branch Press, 2005). A regular political commentator on BBC Radio, Ahmed has been named a Global Expert on War, Peace, and International Affairs by The Freedom Network of the International Society for Individual Liberty, based in California. He is the author of many internationally acclaimed research papers and reports on human rights practices and Western foreign policy. His latest book is *Behind the War on Terror: Western Secret Strategy and the Struggle for Iraq*.

Kevin Barrett has taught English, French, Arabic, American civilization, humanities, African literature, folklore, and Islam at colleges and universities in the San Francisco Bay Area, Paris, and Madison, Wisconsin. He is serving as president of Khidria, a nonprofit corporation dedicated to Islamic socio-environmental awareness, writing and editing for the Muslim magazine *al-Jumuah*, and spearheading MUJCA-NET, the Muslim-Jewish-Christian Alliance for 9/11 Truth.

John B. Cobb, Jr., is professor emeritus of the Claremont School of Theology. He is founding director of the Center for Process Studies and co-founder of Progressive Christians Uniting, for which he edited *Progressive Christians Speak* (2003). He is an ordained minister of the United Methodist Church. Among his books are *The Liberation of Life* with Charles Birch (1984) and *For the Common Good* with Herman Daly (1989), as well as *Christ in a Pluralistic Age* (1975) and *Postmodernism and Public Policy* (2001).

Marc H. Ellis is University Professor of American and Jewish studies at Baylor University, where in 2000 he founded and became the first director of the Center for American and Jewish Studies. In 1980, Dr. Ellis joined the faculty of the Maryknoll School of Theology where he founded the Institute for Justice and

Peace. From 1995 to 1998 he was a Senior Fellow at the Center for the Study of World Religions and a Visiting Scholar at the Center for Middle Eastern Studies at Harvard University, as well a Visiting Professor in Religious Studies at Florida State University. Among his books are *Toward a Jewish Theology of Liberation: The Challenge of the Twenty-first Century* (2004); *Israel And Palestine—Out Of The Ashes: The Search for Jewish Identity in the Twenty-first Century* (2002); *Revolutionary Forgiveness: Essays on Judaism, Christianity, and the Future of Religious Life* (2000); *A Year at the* Catholic Worker*: A Spiritual Journey Among the Poor* (2000); and *Unholy Alliance: Religion and Atrocity in Our Time* (1997).

Tamar Frankiel is Dean of Students and professor of comparative religion at the Academy for Jewish Religion in California. She holds a PhD in the history of religions from the University of Chicago and is the author of *The Gift of Kabbalah* (2001); *The Voice of Sarah: Feminine Spirituality and Traditional Judaism* (1990); co-author of *Minding the Temple of the Soul* and *Entering the Temple of Dreams* (1997 and 2000, with Judy Greenfeld), as well as four other books and numerous scholarly articles on comparative religion in America.

Roger S. Gottlieb is professor of philosophy at Worcester Polytechnic Institute in Massachusetts. He is the author of *A Spirituality of Resistance* (2003); *Joining Hands: Politics and Religion Together for Social Change* (2002); *Marxism: Origin and Betrayal* (1992); and editor of *Liberating Faith: Religious Voices for Justice, Peace, and Ecological Wisdom* (2003) and *This Sacred Earth: Religion, Nature, Environment* (1995).

David Ray Griffin is professor of philosophy of religion and theology, emeritus, at Claremont School of Theology and Claremont Graduate University in Claremont, California, where he remains a co-director of the Center for Process Studies. His 30 books include *God, Power, and Evil: A Process Theology* (1976); *Process Theology: An Introductory Exposition* (1976); *Two Great Truths: A New Synthesis of Scientific Naturalism and Christian Theology* (2004); and *Deep Religious Pluralism* (2005). He has also written *The New Pearl Harbor: Disturbing Questions about the Bush Administration and 9/11* (2004) and *The 9/11 Commission Report: Omissions and Distortions* (2005), both published by Olive Branch Press.

Carter Heyward is Howard Chandler Robbins Professor of Theology Emeritus at the Episcopal Divinity School in Cambridge, Massachusetts. One of the first women ordained to the Episcopal priesthood, in 1974, she is the author or editor of over a dozen books, including most recently *God in the Balance: Christian Spirituality in Times of Terror* (2002) and *Flying Changes: Horses as Spiritual Teachers* (2005). A lesbian feminist theologian of liberation, she has been involved over the years in the struggles for justice and peace, at home and abroad. She is also founder and board chair of a therapeutic horse-back riding center in western North Carolina, where she and her companions live in a small intentional community.

Catherine Keller has taught at the Theological School of Drew University since 1986, where, as a professor of constructive theology, she teaches courses in systematic, process, ecological, postcolonial, and feminist theology. Her books include *From a Broken Web: Separation, Sexism and Self* (1986); *Apocalypse Now and Then: A Feminist Guide to the End of the World* (1996); *The Face of the Deep: A Theology of Becoming* (2003); *Postcolonial Theologies: Divinity and Empire* (2004); and *God and Power: Counter-Apocalyptic Journeys* (2005).

Faiz Khan is a Muslim scholar and educator as well as an M.D. with a dual specialty in emergency and internal medicine. He has been living and working in New York City since 1969. A 9/11 first responder, he has been in the forefront of post-9/11 peace and education efforts in New York and elsewhere. He is well known as a staunchly outspoken opponent of terror in all its guises, and has participated in two memorial services for the victims of 9/11, as well as the New York group Muslims Against Terrorism. Dr. Khan is the author of "9/11: An Islamic Perspective" published by Belief Net in their selection of essays on religion and 9/11. An Assistant Imam at two New York area mosques, Dr. Kahn has discussed subjects related to Islam, politics, and 9/11 at numerous speaking engagements as well as in numerous publications. Dr. Khan is a co-founder of MUJCA-NET, the Muslim-Jewish-Christian Alliance for 9/11 Truth.

Rabbi Michael Lerner is editor of *Tikkun*, co-chair with Cornel West and Sister Joan Chittister of the Network of Spiritual Progressives (www.spiritualprogressives.org), and author of eleven books, most recently *The Left Hand of God: Taking Back our Country from the Religious Right* (2006).

Sandra B. Lubarsky is professor of religious studies and director of a graduate program on "sustainable communities" at Northern Arizona University. She is author of *Tolerance and Transformation: Jewish Approaches to Religious Pluralism* (1990), co-editor with David Ray Griffin of *Jewish Theology and Process Thought* (1996), and author of numerous essays on Jewish theology.

Enver Masud is an engineering management consultant and has worked for the US Department of Energy, the World Bank, EBRD, and USAID in Albania, Egypt, Ethiopia, Ghana, Indonesia, Latvia, Pakistan, Russia, and Tanzania. He is the founder and CEO of The Wisdom Fund, a think tank and information outlet based near Washington, DC, dedicated to advancing social justice and interfaith understanding through presenting the truth about Islam.

Rosemary Radford Ruether, one of America's foremost Christian theologians, has been a leader in many areas. Her many books include *Liberation Theology: Human Hope Confronts Christian History and American Power* (1972); *Sexism and God-Talk: Toward a Feminist Theology* (1983); *Gaia and God: An Ecofeminist Theology of Earth Healing* (1992); *Religion and Sexism: Images of Woman in the Jewish and Christian Traditions* (1998); *To Change the World: Christology and Cultural Criticism* (2001); and *Goddesses and the Divine Feminine: A Western Religious History* (2005). Having long taught at Garrett-Evangelical Theological Seminary in Evanston, Illinois, she has most recently taught at Pacific School of Religion in Berkeley.

NOTES

INTRODUCTION

1 See Shadia Drury's work on the Strauss cult. A good place to start is Danny Postel's interview of Drury, "Noble Lies and Perpetual War: Leo Strauss, the Neo-cons, and Iraq" (www.informationclearinghouse.info /article5010.htm).

2 For a sobering view of the prospects for climate collapse, see James Lovelock, *The Revenge of Gaia: Why the Earth is Fighting Back—and How We Can Still Save Humanity* (London: Allen Lane, 2006). For civilizational collapse in general, see Jared Diamond, *Collapse: How Societies Choose to Fail or Succeed* (New York: Viking, 2004). For an exploration of prospective collapse due to peak oil, see James Kunstler, *The Long Emergency: Surviving the Converging Catastrophes of the Twenty-First Century* (New York: Atlantic Monthly Press, 2005).

3 David Ray Griffin, "9/11 and American Empire: How Should Religious People Respond?" (www.911truth.org/article.php?story= 20050521102328420).

4 See Faiz Khan's essay in this volume.

TWO: GRIFFIN

1 On the Mukden incident, see Walter LaFeber, *The Clash: U.S.-Japanese Religions throughout History* (New York: Norton, 1997), 164–166; Louise Young, *Japan's Total Empire: Manchuria and the Culture of Wartime Imperialism* (Berkeley: University of California Press, 1999), 40; "Mukden Incident," *Wikipedia* (en.wikipedia.org/wiki/Manchurian_Incident); "Mukden Incident," *Encyclopedia Britannica*, 2006 (www.britannica.com/ eb/article-9054193).

2 The question of responsibility for the Reichstag fire had long remained controversial—but the dominant view, that the fire was set by the Nazis themselves, was confirmed in 2001 with the publication of *Der Reichstagbrand: Wie Geschichte Gemacht Wird*, by Alexander Bahar and Wilfried Kugel (Berlin: Edition Q, 2001). This book presents ample evidence of Nazi responsibility, including the testimony of a member of the SA, who said that he was in the subterranean passageway that night and saw other SA members bringing explosive liquids from one building to the other. Bahar and Kugel have, accordingly, substantiated the position contained in William Shirer, *The Rise and Fall of the Third Reich* (New York: Simon and Schuster, 1990), 191–193.

3 Wilhelm Klein, "The Reichstag Fire, 68 Years On" (review of Alexander Bahar and Wilfried Kugel, *Der Reichstagbrand*), World Socialist Website, July 5, 2001 (www.wsws.org/articles/2001/jul2001/reic-j05.shtml).

4 Ibid.

5 See Ian Kershaw, *Hitler: 1936–45: Nemesis* (New York: Norton, 2001), 221; "Nazi Conspiracy and Aggression, Vol. II: Criminality of Groups and Organizations" (www.nizkor.org/hweb/imt/nca/nca-02/nca-02-15-criminality-06-05.html); and "Gleiwitz Incident," Wikipedia (en.wikipedia.org/wiki/Gleiwitz_incident#References). Although there was only one dead man at the scene, the incident is often said to have involved several men. This idea evidently originated with the Germans themselves, as the BBC said, in a bulletin broadcast later that evening: "There have been reports of an attack on a radio station in Gleiwitz, which is just across the Polish border in Silesia. The German News Agency reports that the attack came at about 8:00PM this evening when the Poles forced their way into the studio and began broadcasting a statement in Polish. Within [a] quarter of an hour, says reports, the Poles were overpowered by German police, who opened fire on them. Several of the Poles were reported killed, but the numbers are not yet known" (www.bbc.co.uk/history/worldwars/wwtwo/countdown_ 390831_thur_05.shtml).

6 Howard Zinn, *A People's History of the United States* (New York: HarperCollins, 1980), 150. Richard Van Alstyne, *The Rising American Empire* (1960; New York: Norton, 1974), 143.

7 Van Alstyne, *The Rising American Empire*, 146.

8 Walter LaFeber, *The American Age: U.S. Foreign Policy Since 1750*, 2nd ed. (New York: Norton, 1993), 83.

9 Philip S. Foner, *The Spanish-Cuban-American War and the Birth of American Imperialism*, 2 vols. (New York: Monthly Review, 1972), Vol. I: xv–xvi, xxviii.

10 Ibid., 145, 179–187.

11 Ibid., 213, 229, 248.

12 Ibid., xxx, 209, 229, 258.

13 Stuart Creighton Miller, *"Benevolent Assimilation": The American Conquest of the Philippines, 1899–1903* (New Haven: Yale University Press, 1982), 11.

14 Geoffrey Perret, *A Country Made by War: From the Revolution to Vietnam—The Story of America's Rise to Power* (New York: Random House, 1989), 280 n.

15 Foner, Vol. I: 304, 309; Van Alstyne, *The Rising American Empire*, 132, 188; and Thomas McCormick, *China Market: America's Quest for Informal Empire, 1893–1901* (Chicago: Quadrangle Books, 1967).

16 Miller, *"Benevolent Assimilation,"* 57–62.

17 Quoted in Zinn, *A People's History* (New York: Harper, 1990), 307.

18 Gabriel Kolko, *Anatomy of a War: Vietnam, the United States, and the Modern Historical Experience* (New York: Pantheon Books, 1985), 124; George McT. Kahin, *Intervention: How American Became Involved in Vietnam* (Garden City: Anchor Press, 1987), 217–19.

19 Kahin, *Intervention*, 221; Marilyn B. Young, *The Vietnam Wars 1945–1990* (New York: HarperCollins, 1991), 116–117.

20 Kahin, *Intervention*, 221.

21 Ibid., 222–23. Young, *Vietnam Wars*, 118–119.

22 Kahin, *Intervention*, 220.

23 Young, *Vietnam Wars*, 119.

24 Daniele Ganser, *NATO's Secret Armies: Operation Gladio and Terrorism in Western Europe* (New York: Frank Cass, 2005), 53–54.

25 Ibid., 27–29.

26 Ibid., 16.

27 Ibid., 2, 13, 16, 91–97, 227, 241, 245–246.

28 Ibid., 119.

29 Ibid., 3.

30 Ibid., 5.

31 Ibid., 3, 119–120.

32 Ibid., 7, quoting Casson on *Newsnight*, BBC1, April 4, 1991.

33 Ibid., quoting the *Observer*, June 7, 1992.

34 Ibid., 9–11.

35 Ibid., 82, 120. On the evidence linking NATO and the United States to the Bologna massacre, see ibid., 25, 81.

36 Ibid., 234–235.

37 Ibid., 234–235.

38 US Department of State, "Misinformation about 'Gladio/Stay Behind' Networks Resurfaces: Thirty-Year-Old Soviet Forgery Cited by Researchers," USINFO, Identifying Misinformation, Jan. 20, 2006 (usinfo.state.gov/media/Archive/2006/Jan/20-127177.html).

39 Allan Francovich, "Gladio: The Foot Soldiers," BBC2, June 24, 1992, cited in Ganser, *NATO's Secret Armies*, 235.

40 The only other support the State Department provides for its claim is this statement: "In April 1992, journalist Jonathan Kwitny wrote in *The Nation* that, 'evidence so far hasn't supported initial allegations that the secret armies used their hidden CIA-supplied caches of weapons and explosives to carry out political violence that killed civilians." It is interesting that this was evidently the strongest evidence the State Department could find, especially given the fact that Kwitny's statement, about what evidence has emerged "so far," was made thirteen years before Ganser's well-researched book appeared.

41 Former CIA agent Philip Agee, describing the CIA's attempt to prevent any participation of Communists in the executive branch of government, wrote: "For the CIA this is evidently the priority of priorities" (Philip Agee and Louis Wolf, *Dirty Work: The CIA in Western Europe* [Secaucus: Lyle Stuart, 1978], 182; quoted in Ganser, *NATO's Secret Armies*, 85).

42 Ganser, *NATO's Secret Armies*, 86.

43 Ibid., 88; this is Ganser's summary statement.

44 Ibid., 90.

45 Ibid., 98.

46 Ibid., 115–118.

47 Ibid., 225–230.

48 Ibid., 239.

49 Ibid., 241–243.

50 Ibid., 241.

51 Ibid., 138–139.

52 Ibid., 144–147, citing Allan Francovich, "Gladio: The Foot Soldiers," BBC2, June 24, 1992.

53 Ibid., 142–143, 146.

54 Ibid., 143, quoting Phil Davison, "A Very Right-Wing Coup Plot Surfaces in Belgium," *Independent*, Jan. 24, 1990.

55 Ibid., 27, quoting the Portuguese newspaper *Expresso*, Nov. 24, 1990. According to the Spanish newspaper *El Pais*, Nov. 26, 1990, Wörner added that SHAPE's coordination of Gladio had been confirmed by US General John Glavin, who was then the SACEUR (Supreme Allied Commander Europe).

56 Ibid., 21, 22.

57 This memorandum can be found at the National Security Archive, April 30, 2001 (www.gwu.edu/~nsarchiv/news/20010430). It was revealed to US readers by James Bamford in *Body of Secrets: Anatomy of the Ultra-secret National Security Agency* (2001: New York: Anchor Books, 2002), 82–91.

58 Paul O'Neill, who was secretary of the treasury and hence a member of the National Security Council, has stated this in Ron Susskind, *The Price of Loyalty: George W. Bush, the White House, and the Education of Paul O'Neill* (New York: Simon & Schuster, 2004), and in an interview on CBS's "60 Minutes" on Jan. 11, 2004. The main topic within days of the inauguration, O'Neill says, was going after Saddam, with the question being not "Why Saddam?" or "Why now?" but merely "finding a way to do it." Susskind, whose book also draws on interviews with other officials, says that in its first weeks the Bush administration was discussing the occupation of Iraq and the question of how to divide up its oil (www.cbsnews.com/stories/2004/01/09/60minutes/main592330.shtml). Richard Clarke, who had been the national coordinator for security and counterterrorism, has confirmed O'Neill's charge, saying: "The administration of the second George Bush did begin with Iraq on its agenda" (*Against All Enemies: Inside America's War on Terror* [New York: Free Press, 2004], 264).

59 See David Ray Griffin, *The 9/11 Commission Report: Omissions and Distortions* (Northampton, MA: Olive Branch Press, 2005), chap. 10.

60 *The 9/11 Commission Report: Final Report of the National Commission on Terrorist Attacks upon the United States*, authorized edition (New York: W. W. Norton, 2004), 116.

61 "Terrorist Stag Parties," *Wall Street Journal*, October 10, 2001 (www.opinionjournal.com/best/?id=95001298).

62 *The 9/11 Commission Report*, 248.

63 I have summarized 115 such problems in "The 9/11 Commission Report: A 571-Page Lie," 9/11 Visibility Project, May 22, 2005 (www.septembereleventh.org/newsarchive/2005-05-22-571pglie.php).

64 The flight manifest for AA 11 that was published by CNN can be seen at www.cnn.com/SPECIALS/2001/trade.center/victims/AA11.victims.html. The manifests for the other flights can be located by simply changing that part of the URL. The manifest for UA 93, for example, is at www.cnn.com/SPECIALS/2001/trade.center/victims/ua93.victims.html.

65 Associated Press, Oct. 5, 2001; *Boston Globe*, Sept. 18, 2001; *Independent*, Sept. 29, 2001.

66 *The 9/11 Commission Report*, 1–2.

67 Ibid., chap. 1, n. 1.

68 The trip likewise provided the opportunity for security video frames showing Mohamed Atta and Abdullah al-Omari, also said to have been on Flight 11, at the Portland airport. Strangely, however, there were no photos of them at Boston's Logan airport, which, as a major international airport, surely was better equipped with security cameras. Both issues are discussed in Rowland Morgan and Ian Henshall, *9/11 Revealed: The Unanswered Questions* (New York: Carroll & Graf, 2005), 180–183.

69 Richard Labeviere, "CIA Agent Allegedly Met Bin Laden in July," *Le Figaro*, Oct. 31, 2001. This story was also reported in Anthony Sampson, "CIA Agent Alleged to Have Met Bin Laden in July," *Guardian*, Nov. 1, and Adam Sage, "Ailing bin Laden 'Treated for Kidney Disease,'" *London Times*, Nov. 1, 2001.

70 See Labeviere, "CIA Agent Allegedly Met Bin Laden in July," and Craig Unger, "Unasked Questions: The 9/11 Commission Should Ask Who Authorized the Evacuation of Saudi Nationals in the Days Following the Attacks," *Boston Globe*, April 11, 2004. For more on the "black sheep" issue, see Nafeez Ahmed, *The War on Freedom: How and Why America was Attacked, September 11, 2001* (Joshua Tree, CA: Tree of Life, 2002), 178–179.

71 *Telegraph*, Feb. 23, 2002; Griffin, *The 9/11 Commission Report: Omissions and Distortions*, 60.

72 "White House Warns Taliban: 'We Will Defeat You'" (CNN.com, Sept. 21, 2001). Four weeks after the attacks began, a Taliban spokesman said: "We are not a province of the United States, to be issued orders to. We have asked for proof of Osama's involvement, but they have refused. Why?" (Kathy Gannon, AP, "Taliban Willing To Talk, But Wants U.S. Respect" [www.suburbanchicagonews.com/focus/terrorism/archives/1001/w01taliban.html]).

73 See "The Fake bin Laden Video" (www.whatreallyhappened.com/osamatape.html).

74 "High-Rise Office Building Fire One Meridian Plaza Philadelphia, Pennsylvania," FEMA (www.interfire.org/res–file/pdf/Tr-049.pdf); "Fire Practically Destroys Venezuela's Tallest Building" (www.whatreally happened.com/venezuela_fire.html).

75 Chief Thomas McCarthy of the FDNY said that while the firefighters "were waiting for 7 World Trade to come down," there was "fire on three separate floors" (Oral History of Thomas McCarthy, 10–11). Emergency medical technician Decosta Wright said: "I think the fourth floor was on fire... [W]e were like, are you guys going to put that fire out?" (Oral History of Decosta Wright, 11). These quotations are from the 9/11 oral histories recorded by the New York Fire Department at the end of 2001 but released to the public (after a court battle) only in August 2005, at which time they were made available on a *New York Times* website (graphics8.nytimes.com/packages/html/nyregion/20050812_WTC_GRAPHIC/met_WTC_histories_full_01.html).

76 A photograph taken by Terry Schmidt can be seen on page 63 of Eric Hufschmid's *Painful Questions: An Analysis of the September 11th Attack* (Goleta, CA: Endpoint Software, 2002). According to Schmidt, this photo was taken between 3:09 and 3:16PM, hence only a little over two hours before Building 7 collapsed. It shows that on the north side of the building, fires were visible only on floors seven and twelve. Therefore, if there were more fires on the south side, which faced the Twin Towers, they were not big enough to be seen from the north side.

77 Some of the witnesses testifying to the existence of molten steel have reported that the ends of some of the steel beams were molten—which would be the case if explosives had been used to slice them. Joe O'Toole, a Bronx firefighter, said about a beam that was lifted from deep below the surface: "It was dripping from the molten steel" (Jennifer Lin, "Recovery Worker Reflects on Months Spent at Ground Zero," *Knight Ridder*, May 29, 2002 [www.messenger-inquirer.com/news/attacks/4522011.htm]). A company vice president reported that "sometimes when a worker would pull a steel beam from the wreckage, the end of the beam would be dripping molten steel" (Trudy Walsh, "Handheld APP Eased Recovery Tasks," Government Computer News, 21/27a, Sept 11, 2002 [www.gcn.com/21_27a/news/19930-1.html]).

78 See David Ray Griffin, "Explosive Testimony: Revelations about the Twin Towers in the 9/11 Oral Histories," 911Truth.org, January 18, 2006 (www.911truth.org/article.php?story=20060118104223192).

Fire Captain Dennis Tardio, for example, said: "I hear an explosion and I look up. It is as if the building is being imploded, from the top floor down, one after another, *boom, boom, boom*" (Dennis Smith, *Report from Ground Zero: The Story of the Rescue Efforts at the World Trade Center* [New York: Penguin, 2002], 18). Another firefighter said: "It seemed like on television [when] they blow up these buildings. It seemed like it was going all the way around like a belt, all these explosions" (Oral History of Richard Banaciski, 3–4).

79 Stephen E. Jones, "Why Indeed Did the WTC Buildings Collapse?" In David Ray Griffin and Peter Dale Scott, eds., *9/11 and American Empire: Intellectuals Speak Out* (Northampton, MA: Olive Branch Press, 2006). See

also David Ray Griffin, "The Destruction of the World Trade Center: Why the Official Account Cannot Be True," Paul Zarembka, ed., *The Hidden History of 9-11-2001*, vol. 23 of *Research in Political Economy* (Amsterdam: Elsevier, 2006); also available at 911Review.com, Dec. 9, 2005 [911review.com/ articles/griffin/nyc1.html]).

For videos of the WTC collapses, see "9/11/01 WTC Videos" (911research.wtc7.net/wtc/evidence/videos/index.html).

80 Griffin, *The 9/11 Commission Report: Omissions and Distortions*, 31–32.

81 Another problem with this story is that there were at least two versions of it. One said that the passport was found in the rubble the day after 9/11, the other that it was found minutes after the attack (see Morgan and Henshall, *9/11 Revealed*, 68).

82 "PAVE PAWS, Watching North America's Skies, 24 Hours a Day" (web.archive.org/web/200109270624554/www.pavepaws.org).

83 Russ Wittenberg, who flew large commercial airliners for 35 years after serving in Vietnam as a fighter pilot, says that it would have been impossible for Flight 77 to have "descended 7,000 feet in two minutes, all the while performing a steep 270-degree banked turn before crashing into the Pentagon's first floor wall without touching the lawn." It would, he adds, have been "totally impossible for an amateur who couldn't even fly a Cessna to maneuver the jetliner in such a highly professional manner" (Greg Szymanski, "Former Vietnam Combat and Commercial Pilot Firm Believer 9/11 Was Inside Government Job," Lewis News, Jan. 8, 2006 [www.lewisnews.com/article.asp?ID=106623]). Hanjour's incompetence was reported by the *New York Times*, May 4, 2002, and CBS News, May 10, 2002. *The 9/11 Commission Report* sometimes acknowledges in places that Hanjour was known to be a "terrible pilot" (225–226, 242), but it elsewhere calls him "the operation's most experienced pilot" (530 n. 147).

84 Won-Young Kim and Gerald R. Baum, "Seismic Observations during September 11, 2001, Terrorist Attack" (www.mgs.md.gov/esic/publications/download/911pentagon.pdf).

85 Karen Kwiatkowski, who was then an Air Force lieutenant colonel employed at the Pentagon, writes of "a strange lack of visible debris on the Pentagon lawn, where I stood only moments after the impact.... I saw... no airplane metal or cargo debris" ("Assessing the Official 9/11 Conspiracy Theory," in David Ray Griffin and Peter Dale Scott, eds., *9/11 and American Empire: Intellectuals Speak Out*). For a more technical discussion of the debris, see "The Missing Wings" (www.physics911.net/missingwings.htm), in which A. K. Dewdney and G. W. Longspaugh argue that the absence of wing debris alone is sufficient to disprove the claim that an airliner hit the Pentagon. With regard to debris *inside* the building, both Ed Plaugher, the county fire chief, and Lee Evey, the head of the renovation project, reported seeing, immediately after the strike, no big pieces from an airplane (DoD News Briefings, Sept. 12 and 15, 2001).

86 Photographs show that the façade of the west wing remained standing for 30 minutes after the strike and that, during this time, the hole in this façade was too small to have accommodated a 757. See Eric Hufschmid, *Painful Questions*, Chap. 9, and Dave McGowan, "September 11, 2001 Revisited: The Series: Act II," Center for an Informed America (www.davesweb.cnchost.com/nwsltr68.html).

87 Ralph Omholt, "9-11 and the Impossible: Part One of an Online Journal of 9-11" (www.physics911.net/omholt.htm).

88 Karen Kwiatkowski, who was working at the Pentagon that morning, reports that "any physical remains of the aircraft that hit the Pentagon were quickly carted away to some unknown location, so we have no physical evidence that the aircraft really was Flight 77 or even a Boeing 757" ("Assessing the Official 9/11 Conspiracy Theory"). Photographic evidence of this removal can be seen on Eric Hufschmid's video, "Painful Deceptions" (available at www.EricHufschmid.net).

89 A photograph showing this literal cover-up can be seen in Ralph Omholt, "9-11 and the Impossible: Part One of an Online Journal of 9-11" (www.physics911.net/omholt.htm).

90 On the confiscation of the film from the Citgo gas station and a nearby hotel, respectively, see Bill McKelway, "Three Months On, Tension Lingers Near the Pentagon," *Richmond Times-Dispatch*, Dec. 11, 2001 (news.nationalgeographic.com/news/2001/12/1211_wirepentagon.html) , and Bill Gertz and Rowan Scarborough, "Inside the Ring," *Washington Times*, Sept. 21, 2001.

91 Scott Bingham, who has tried to get videos of the Pentagon strike released under the Freedom of Information Act, has his lawsuit and the official response posted on his website (www.flight77.info). See also "Government Responds to Flight 77 FOAI Request," 911Truth.org, Aug. 2005 (www.911truth.org/article.php?story=20050824131004151). Further evidence of a cover-up is provided by investigative journalist Wayne Madsen, who reports that he learned from both a senior Pentagon official and a US Army employee that after 9/11 the Pentagon enacted a strict anti-leak policy, which forbade all employees to discuss the Pentagon strike and the FBI's confiscation of the security video tapes (Wayne Madsen Report, Jan. 15, 2006 [www.waynemadsenreport.com]).

92 Richard A. Horsley, *Jesus and Empire: The Kingdom of God and the New World Disorder* (Minneapolis: Fortress, 2003), 197.

93 Tacitus, *Agricola* 14.1; quoted in Horsley, *Jesus and Empire*, 31.

94 Susan P. Mattern, *Rome and the Enemy: Imperial Strategy in the Principate* (Berkeley: University of California Press, 1999), 117, 172.

95 Mattern, *Rome and the Enemy*, 22, 117.

96 Ibid., 27.

97 Pseudo-Quinteilian, *Declamations*, 274.

98 Mattern, *Rome and the Enemy*, 90.

99 Andrew J. Bacevich makes this point in *American Empire: The*

Realities and Consequences of U.S. Diplomacy (Cambridge, MA: Harvard University Press, 2002), 30, 218–219.

100 Charles Krauthammer, "The Unipolar Moment," in *Foreign Affairs* 70/1 (1990–91): 295–306, at 304–305.

101 Krauthammer, "A Second American Century?" *Time*, Dec. 27, 1999 (www.cnn.com/ALLPOLITICS/time/1999/12/20/american.century.html).

102 Quoted in Bacevich, *American Empire*, 219.

103 Krauthammer's statement is quoted in Emily Eakin, "All Roads Lead To D.C.," *New York Times*, Week In Review, March 31, 2002.

104 Krauthammer, "The Bush Doctrine," *Time*, March 5, 2001.

105 Jonathan Freedland, "Is America the New Rome?" *Guardian*, Sept. 18, 2002.

106 Ben Wattenberg, *The First Universal Nation: Leading Indicators and Ideas about the Surge of America in the 1990s* (New York: Free Press, 1991), 202.

107 Robert Kagan, "The Benevolent Empire," *Foreign Policy*, Summer 1998: 24–35 (www.carnegieendowment.org/publications/index.cfm?fa=view&id=275).

108 Krauthammer, "A Second American Century?" *Time*, Dec. 27, 1999 (www.cnn.com/ALLPOLITICS/time/1999/12/20/american.century.html).

109 Max Boot, "What Next? The Foreign Policy Agenda beyond Iraq," *Weekly Standard*, May 5, 2003 (www.weeklystandard.com/Content/Public/Articles/000/000/002/606hotoc.asp?pg=2).

110 Bacevich, *American Empire*, 242 (quoting Charles Beard, *Giddy Minds and Foreign Quarrels* [1939], 87).

111 Ibid., 244.

112 Ibid., 4, 133.

113 Ibid., 4, 52, 133.

114 Ibid., 17.

115 Chalmers Johnson, *The Sorrows of Empire: Militarism, Secrecy, and the End of the Republic* (New York: Henry Holt, 2004), 4, 33.

116 "Resisting the Global Domination Project: An Interview with Prof. Richard Falk," *Frontline*, 20/8 (April 12–25, 2003).

117 Noam Chomsky, *Hegemony or Survival: America's Quest for Global Dominance* (New York: Metropolitan Books, 2003).

118 Bacevich, *American Empire*, 44.

119 "The National Security Strategy of the United States of America", Sept. 2002 (www.whitehouse.gov/nsc/nss.html). See Duncan E. J. Currie, "'Preventive War' and International Law after Iraq," Globelaw, May 22, 2003 (www.globelaw.com/Iraq/Preventive_war_after_iraq.htm#_ftn15).

120 Richard Falk, *The Great Terror War* (Northampton, MA: Olive Branch Press, 2002), xxvii.

121 Jack Hitt, "The Next Battlefield May Be in Outer Space," *New York Times Magazine*, Aug. 5, 2001.

122 Lawrence Kaplan, *New Republic* 224 (March 12, 2001), quoted in

Bacevich, *American Empire*, 223.

123 "Rebuilding America's Defenses," 51. This apparent hope for a "new Pearl Harbor" had already been articulated in Zbigniew Brzezinski, *The Grand Chessboard: American Primacy and Its Geostrategic Imperatives* (New York: Basic Books, 1997), as can be seen by reading together pages 24–25 and 212.

124 Henry Kissinger, "Destroy the Network," *Washington Post*, Sept. 11, 2001 (washingtonpost.com).

125 This according to the *Washington Post*, Jan. 27, 2002.

126 "Secretary Rumsfeld Interview with the New York Times," *New York Times*, Oct. 12, 2001.

127 K.C. Hanson and Douglas E. Oakman, *Palestine in the Time of Jesus: Social Structures and Social Conflicts* (Minneapolis: Augsburg Fortress, 1998), 67.

128 Horsley, *Jesus and Empire*, 29.

129 Horsley, *Jesus and Empire*, 6, 15, 28; Richard A. Horsley and Neil Asher Silberman, *The Message and the Kingdom: How Jesus and Paul Ignited a Revolution and Transformed the Ancient World* (New York: Grosset/Putnam, 1997), 84–86.

130 Horsley and Silberman, *The Message*, 26–29.

131 Quoted in Horsley, *Jesus and Empire*, 23–24.

132 Horsley and Silberman, *The Message*, 17; Horsley, Jesus and Empire, 32, 85.

133 Horsley and Silberman, *The Message*, 83.

134 Horsley, *Jesus and Empire*, 41, 99.

135 Horsley and Silberman, *The Message*, 129.

136 Richard Horsley, *Jesus and the Spiral of Violence: Popular Jewish Resistance in Roman Palestine* (San Francisco: Harper & Row, 1987), 170.

137 Ibid., 174–175; Matthew 21:33–46; Mark 12:1–12; Luke 20:9–19.

138 Horsley, *Jesus and the Spiral*, 307–314 (referring to Mark 12:13–17 and Luke 23:2).

139 Ibid., 282.

140 Ibid., 299; E. P. Sanders, *Jesus and Judaism* (Philadelphia: Fortress, 1985), 69–70, 302.

141 Horsley, *Jesus and Empire*, 132.

142 Horsley and Silberman, *The Message*, 227.

143 Rev. 12:9, 13:2, 20:2.

144 Horsley and Silberman, *The Message*, 11.

145 Deborah L. Madsen, American Exceptionalism (Jackson: University Press of Mississippi, 1998); Anders Stephanson, Manifest Destiny: American Expansion and the Empire of Right (New York: Hill and Wang, 1995); Ivan Eland, "American Exceptionalism," Antiwar.com, October 26, 2004 (www.antiwar.com/eland/?articleid=3847).

146 "The Theological Declaration of Barmen" (www.creeds.net/ reformed/barmen.htm).

147 I have developed the idea of making resistance to the empire a matter of faith more fully in David Ray Griffin, John B. Cobb, Jr., Richard Falk, and Catherine Keller, *The American Empire and the Commonwealth of God* (Louisville: Westminster John Knox, 2006).

Three: Heyward

1 Carter Heyward, *Saving Jesus From Those Who Are Right: Rethinking What It Means to Be Christian*, (Minneapolis: Fortress, 1999), 86–87.

2 This term is a gift from Marvin Ellison, Sylvia Thorson-Smith, and other justice-loving Presbyterians. See Ellison and Smith, eds., *Body and Soul: Rethinking Sexuality as Justice-Love* (Cleveland: Pilgrim, 2003).

3 According the Iraq Body Count project, at www.iraqbodycount.net. Viewed August 10, 2006.

4 David Ray Griffin, *The New Pearl Harbor: Disturbing Questions About the Bush Administration and 9/11* (Northampton, MA: Olive Branch Press, 2004) and *The 9/11 Commission Report: Omissions and Distortions*, (Northampton, MA: Olive Branch Press, 2005).

5 In Nafeez Mosaddeq Ahmed, *The War on Truth: 9/11, Disinformation, and the Anatomy of Terrorism*, (Northampton, MA: Olive Branch Press, 2005), 359.

6 Ibid, 361.

7 See Ahmed, *The War on Truth*, as well as his essay in this volume.

8 *Saving Jesus*, 181.

9 Since the early 1980s and the administration of Ronald Reagan, Elie Wiesel has increasingly sounded like a "neocon" in his uncritical endorsement of Israel's behavior as well as US foreign policy. But his early works, such as the powerful autobiographical testimony *Night* (1958, trans. 1969), followed by several novels—*Dawn (1960), The Accident* (1961), *The Town Beyond the Wall* (1964), and *The Gates of the Forest* (1966)—resonate with an urgent quest for God in the midst of human courage and the struggle against oppression.

10 Especially important to me have been Soelle's *Christ the Representative: An Essay in Theology After the "Death of God"* (Philadelphia: Fortress, 1967); *Creative Disobedience* (originally, *Beyond Mere Obedience*, 1971) (Cleveland: Pilgrim, 1995); and *Suffering* (Philadelphia: Fortress, 1975); her autobiography *Against the Wind* (Minneapolis: Fortress, 1996); and *The Silent Cry: Mysticism and Resistance* (Minneapolis: Fortress, 1997).

11 I have developed these ideas more fully in *Saving Jesus*.

Special thanks to Janet Surrey and Steve Bergman for many discussions of these matters. If any wisdom is found in these pages, they helped shape it.

FOUR: KELLER

1 Andrew Bacevich, *The New American Militarism: How Americans are Seduced by War* (Oxford and New York: Oxford University Press, 2005), 146.

2 Mt 22:37–39; Lk 10:27; Mk 12:29–31.

3 David Ray Griffin, *The New Pearl Harbor: Disturbing Questions About the Bush Administration and 9/11* (Northampton, MA: Olive Branch Press, 2004).

4 Quoted in Max Blumental, "Onward Christian Soldiers," Salon.com., 15 April 2003. Cited in Bacevich 143, 249.

5 For instance, among the brave voices who publicly articulated both grief and hope in the immediate aftermath of the 2004 election, were the authors of a couple of wise articles posted on the Nov. 11 Alternet. Both reached into a love-discourse unfamiliar among progressive secular venues. One asked "What's our job? To dedicate our lives to preserving and passing on what we love, so that if things ever get sane again there'll be something left" (Michael Ventura, "Dancing in the Dark," *Austin Chronicle*). Another argued that while many "God-fearing" individuals are outside our range, "religious Americans who believe in a loving God share many of our values." To reach them, we have to "reach into our hearts, as we slowly recover from the heartbreak of Nov. 2, and rediscover our own capacities to appreciate people who, as things stand, really do threaten what we most value: our planet's health, our civil liberties, our commitment to a government that cares for its people." (Vivan Dent, "From the Heart"). A "love of the enemy" as outreach to the swing-vote?

6 Michael Hardt and Antonio Negri, *Multitude: War and Democracy in the Age of Empire* (New York: Penguin, 2004), 351.

7 Michael Hardt and Antonio Negri, *Empire* (Cambridge, MA: Harvard University Press, 2001).

8 February 26, 2005, cited in Martin E. Marty, "Fun for Christian Soldiers?" *Sightings*, March 7, 2005.

9 For a groundbreaking feminist challenge to the Christological tradition of atonement by blood sacrifice, see Rita Nakashima Brock, *Journeys by Heart: a Christology of Erotic Power* (New York: Crossroads, 1984/1999); also Delores Williams, *Sisters in the Wilderness: The Challenge of Womanist God-Talk* (Maryknoll, NY: Orbis Books, 1995). For the intensely readable follow-up, see Rita Nakashima Brock and Rebecca Ann Parker, *Proverbs of Ashes: Violence, Redemptive Suffering, and the Search for What Saves Us*, 2nd ed. (Boston: Beacon, 2002).

10 Hardt and Negri, *Multitude*, 16.

11 Ibid., 19.

12 Ibid.

13 Catherine Keller, *God and Power: Counter-Apocalyptic Journeys* (Minneapolis: Fortress, 2005).

14 Rev. 2:6.

15 "They may love all that he has chosen and hate all that he has rejected." Community Rule of Qumran. See Robert J. Miller, ed., *The Complete Gospels Annotated Scholar's Edition* (Sonoma: Polebridge Press, 1992), 67.

16 Hardt and Negri, *Multitude,* 356.

17 Ibid.

18 Ibid., 351–352.

19 The theological polarity of agape as divine self-giving vs. eros as human desire has been most forcefully developed in Anders Nygren's now classic *Agape and Eros,* (Philadelphia: Westminster, 1953).

20 Hardt and Negri, *Multitude,* 192.

FIVE: RUETHER

1 See Chalmers Johnson, *The Sorrows of Empire: Militarism, Secrecy and the End of the Republic* (New York: Henry Holt and Co., 2004), 154.

2 For this citation of Winthrop, as well as the general inspiration of this article, see Tom Barry, "El complejo de poder: se acabo 'el gringo bueno'" in *Envio: Revista Mensual de la Universidad Centroamericana,* no. 248 (November 2002), 45–50.

3 The Project for the New American Century, *Rebuilding America's Defenses: Strategy, Forces, and Resources for a New Century* (www.newamericancentury.org).

4 See David Ray Griffin, *The 9/11 Commission Report: Omissions and Distortions* (Northampton, MA: Olive Branch Press, 2005).

5 See Ed Harriman, "Where has all the Money Gone?" in *London Review of Books* 27, no. 13 (July 7, 2005), 3.

SIX: LUBARSKY

1 Cited in Collin Hanson, "Why Some Jews Fear 'The Passion,'" *Christianity Today,* 2004 (www.christianitytoday.com/ct/2004/107/51.0.html).

2 For an excellent discussion and examination of Jewish and Christian master stories, see Michael Goldberg, *Jews and Christians: Getting Our Stories Straight* (Nashville: Abingdon Press, 1985). "Master stories," writes Goldberg, "...offer us both a model for understanding the world and a guide for acting in it. By providing us with a paradigm for making sense of our existence, master stories furnish us with a basis for answering some of the most fundamental questions that we human beings can have: Who are we? What is our world like? And given who we are and what our world is like, what then is the best way for us to respond to such a world as this? The answers to those questions often constitute our most deep-seated convictions about our identity, responsibility, and destiny over the course of our existence. Hence, master stories not only *inform* us, but more crucially, they *form* us" (13).

3 Nikki Stern, "Our Grief Doesn't Make Us Experts," *Newsweek,* 13 March 13, 2006.

4 Emil Fackenheim, *God's Presence in History: Jewish Affirmations and Philosophical Reflections* (New York: Harper Torchbooks, 1972), 8–11. Fackenheim adds the proviso that the experience remain vivid to the consciousness of future generations, something to which we are not yet privy.

5 See "Unraveling Anti-Semitic 9/11 Conspiracy Theories," Anti-Defamation League, a publication of the Gorowitz Institute, 2003 (www.adl.org/anti_semitism/9-11conspiracytheories.pdf).

6 The Middle East Media Research Institute (MEMRI), "Leading Egyptian Journalist: The Jews are Behind Every Disaster or Terrorist Act," Special Dispatch Series, no. 750, April 23, 2004 (memri.org/bin/opener.cgi?Page=archives&ID=SP70004).

7 See the Quoman, "Serving One Flag," posted March 4, 2006 (planetquo.blogspot.com/2006/03/serving-one-flag.html); see also www.planetquo.com

8 William Kittredge, "Home," in *New Writers of the Purple Sage: An Anthology of Contemporary Western Writers*," Russell Martin, ed. (New York: Penguin Books, 1992), 6–7. Kittredge's full statement is "Storytelling and make-believe, like war and agriculture, are among the arts of self-defense and all of them are ways of enclosing otherness and claiming ownership." His point is that stories are a way of making ourselves "at home" in the world.

9 B. A. Robinson, "Aftermath of the 9-11 Terrorist Attack: Attacks on Muslims," Religious Tolerance.org (copyright 2001 by Ontario Consultants on Religious Tolerance), October 25, 2001 (www.religious tolerance.org/reac_ter1.htm).

10 Susannah Heschel, writing of her father in the introduction to *Moral Grandeur and Spiritual Audacity*, Abraham Joshua Heschel, essays edited by Susannah Heschel (New York: the Noonday Press, 1996), vii.

11 Ibid.

12 Jonathan Rowe, "The Demand for the Common Good," *Yes!* magazine (online), Summer 2004 (www.yesmagazine.org/article.asp?ID=868).

13 Carol Rittner and Sondra Myers, *Courage to Care: Rescuers of Jews during the Holocaust* (New York University Press, 1989), 102.

14 Claudia Deane and Darryl Fears, "Negative Perception Of Islam Increasing: Poll Numbers in U.S. Higher Than in 2001," *Washington Post*, March 9, 2006.

15 Aldo Leopold, *A Sand County Almanac* (New York: Oxford University Press, 1949).

16 Wendell Berry, lecture at Northern Arizona University, 1999.

SEVEN: ELLIS

1 On this subject see Adi Ophir, *The Orders of Evil: Toward an Ontology of Morals* (Brooklyn, NY: Zone Books, 2005).

2 I have written a number of books exploring this theme. For a summation of these ideas see my *Toward a Jewish Theology of Liberation: The Challenge of the 21st Century* (Waco, TX: Baylor University Press, 2005).

3 The academic variant of this attempt to transcend Holocaust and Israel can be found in the textual reasoning movement. For an example see Steven Kepnes, Peter Ochs, and Robert Gibbs, *Reasoning After Revelation: Dialogues in Post-Modern Jewish Philosophy* (Boulder, CO: Westview Press, 1998) and Robert Gibbs, *Why Ethics?: Signs of Responsibilities* (Princeton, NJ: Princeton University Press, 2000).

4 I develop this thought at some length in *Israel and Palestine: Out of the Ashes* (London: Pluto Press, 2002).

5 Unfortunately, the charismatic leadership of Lerner and Waskow over the years has, at least in my opinion, severely disrupted the capacity of Jews to think through the questions of Holocaust and Israel because of their Judeo-centric bias and their inability to confront our history critically without a religio-mystical foundation. That their power has been enhanced by the recognition of non-Jewish thinkers such as Cornel West is unfortunate. In this case West seems unable to think through the pretense of Lerner and Waskow and therefore helps legitimate self-appointed leaders of the Jewish progressive movement. For a discussion of this topic in the academy, with special attention to feminist thinkers, including Heyward and Schussler-Fiorenza, see my "Post-Holocaust Jewish Identity and the Academy: On Traveling the Diaspora and the Experience of the Double-Standard," in Jose Ignacio Cabezon and Sheila Greeve Davaney, ed., *Identity and the Politics of Scholarship in the Study of Religion* (London: Routledge, 2004), 163–182.

6 The theme of the "new" or "real" anti-Semitism is a recurring one, beginning in the 1970s and reemerging after 9/11. For one example of the post-9/11 take on anti-Semitism see Phyllis Chesler, *The New Anti-Semitism: The Current Crisis and What We Must Do About It* (San Francisco: Jossey-Bass, 2003).

7 One only needs to look at the maps of the settlements, their projected size in Jerusalem and the West Bank to see the obvious. For a good sense of this see Jeff Halper, *Obstacles to Peace: A Re-framing of the Palestinian-Israeli Conflict*, 3rd ed. (Jerusalem: Al Manar Printing Press, 2005).

8 The way Jews think, speak and write about Palestinians is an unexplored but important area of research. One place to look is commentary over the years on Yassir Arafat. My own sense is that the Jewish discourse on Palestinians, including progressive Jewish discourse, has been essentially racist. See my own take on the death of Arafat—and the proposal to bury Sharon with him—in "After Arafat: Mapping a Jewish/Palestinian Solidarity," *Journal of Church and State* 47 (Winter 2005): 5–18.

9 Rafi Segal and Eyal Weizman, eds., *A Civilian Occupation: The Politics of Israeli Architecture* (London: Verso, 2003).

EIGHT: FRANKIEL

1 One report among many was Abraham Foxman's in the *International Herald Tribune*, April 22, 2005: In April 2002, "more than 100 academics demanded a moratorium on European funding of Israeli universities. Cases of discrimination in Britain have included two Israeli academics' firing from the editorial board of a translation journal and an Israeli postgraduate who was refused doctoral supervision because he had served in the Israeli Army."

2 David Ray Griffin, *Reenchantment Without Supernaturalism: A Process Philosophy of Religion* (Ithaca, NY: Cornell University Press, 2001), 185.

3 Ibid., 257.

4 Eliyahu Dessler, *Strive For Truth*. Rabbi Dessler is not from a Hasidic school of thought, but rather of what is known as Mussar, an approach to ethics and self-improvement generally regarded as the work of Rabbi Israel Salanter in the nineteenth century, though based on earlier writers. Mussar literally means "rebuke" in the sense of instructions for correcting a flaw, as in "Rebuke your neighbor frankly so you will not share in his guilt" (Leviticus 19:17). However, the sages warned against rebuking others except in certain specific circumstances; and this school of thought is founded on deep self-understanding rather than trying to correct the flaws of others.

5 Inter-inclusion is a concept based on teachings of the Baal Shem Tov (1700–1760), the founder of Hasidism. For this quotation, in one of many applications, see Rabbi Yitzchak Ginsburgh, "Anxiety Relief: Kabbalah Approach to Mental Health," part 13, www.inner.org/mental/mental13.htm, accessed August 28, 2006.

6 These concepts are also from the Baal Shem Tov; see ibid., part 12: "Submission refers to the humbling of the ego effected by silencing the inner turbulence of thought. Separation is the process through which evil is isolated, severed from the good, and discarded. Sweetening is the reevaluation of reality in the positive light of the liberated kernel of good that had been trapped inside the evil."

7 As with many of the famous Jewish sages, an acronym was used for his name: ARI stands for Elokei Rabbi Yitzchak, "the Godly Rabbi Isaac." He is the only one of the rabbis over two thousand years to have the name "Godly" attached to his title. In Hebrew, the word *ari* also means "lion."

8 Griffin, *Reenchantment Without Supernaturalism*, 73.

9 In process philosophy, this relates to the doctrine of pan-experientialism. See Griffin's discussion in chapter three of *Reenchantment*, especially pp. 103–108.

10 For deeper understanding, refer to Abraham Joshua Heschel's book, *The Prophets*, as well as many of his essays.

11 This may sound similar to the Quaker ideal of the "inner voice," that gathered in silence, people would experience God's direction. It also

seems to be the aim of the newly popular "spiritual direction" movement in American Christianity and Judaism. My experience, however, is that it is not silence as such but deep, ego-free listening to the other, combined with joy, that gives rise to the quality of vision that approaches prophecy.

NINE: GOTTLIEB

1 I am aware that some other authors in this volume believe that 9/11 was the work of the US government. For a variety of reasons, I am not convinced. For one thing, I am much more attracted to the idea that simple incompetence and the cover-up of that incompetence was the US government's role in the matter. Second, even if there were some tacit agreements between the US government, eager to have reasons to pursue an aggressive foreign policy, and the terrorists, this does not mean the US was not assaulted on that day. Agreements between Krupp and DuPont during WWII do not mean that Germany and the US were not also at war. Third, whatever one may say about 9/11 in particular, examples of fundamentalist Islamic violence, as well as theoretical justification of that violence and praise of it, are all too common.

2 For a cogent and frightening account of what militant Islamic fundamentalists say about their goals and reasons, see David Cook, *Understanding Jihad* (Berkeley: University of California Press, 2005).

3 There are tens of millions of "refugees from development" whose lives, cultures, and health are adversely affected. There have been millions of deaths from the effects of handling pesticides alone. In many Indian reservations in the American west the cancer rate (from uranium extraction) is ten to fifteen times the national average. And so on.

4 The literature on the negative effects of globalization is enormous. For a start: Manfred B. Steger, *Globalism: The New Market Ideology* (Lanham, MD: Rowman and Littlefield, 2001); Vernonia Bennholdt-Thomsen, Nicholas Faraclas, and Claudia Von Werlhof, eds., *There is an Alternative: Subsistence and Worldwide Resistance to Corporate Globalization* (London: Zed Books, 2001); Jackie Smith and Hank Johnston, eds., *Globalization and Resistance: Transnational Dimensions of Social Movements,* (Lanham, MD: Rowman and Littlefield, 2002); William F. Fisher and Thomas Ponniah, eds., *Another World is Possible: Popular Alternatives to Globalization at the World Social Forum* (London: Zed Books, 2003); International Forum on Globalization, *Alternatives to Economic Globalization: A Better World is Possible* (San Francisco: Berrett-Koehler Publishers, 2002).

5 A variety of terms have been applied to the many manifestations of this movement: fundamentalist Islam, radical Islam, Islamo-fascism, etc. More important than the label is what I have in mind as the movement's central ideological characteristics. 1. Fundamentalism arises in response to a perceived threat to established forms of meaning and power. 2. That threat is identified with some features of modernity; e.g., religious and

cultural pluralism, equal rights for women, consumerism, sexual freedom, religious freedom, skepticism toward traditional religious claims. 3. As an alternative to modernity, fundamentalism offers what it claims to be the one true version of a religious faith. 4. Since it is the one true version, different religions and competing versions of its own religion must be denounced and often violently suppressed. 5. The absolute truth of this one true version, combined with a sense of threat (from a secular government, mass culture, feminists, homosexuals, the West, etc.) justifies violent actions on behalf of the threatened community and the threatened truth. In various forms, fundamentalism is now common among the Christian right in the US, the Hindu nationalist movement in India, right-wing Jews in Israel and the US, and in various movements throughout the Muslim world. It appears in its most frightening guise when it takes state power (as in Iran or Afghanistan under the Taliban), but it is also deeply destructive when it has powerful influences on a government (as in India or Israel) or when it engages in terrorist actions. My view of fundamentalism is indebted to: Mark Juergensmeyer, *Terror in the Mind of God: The Global Rise of Religious Violence* (Berkeley: University of California Press, 2001); Malise Ruthven, *Fundamentalism: The Search for Meaning* (Oxford: Oxford University Press, 2004); Karen Armstrong, *The Battle for God: Fundamentalism in Judaism, Christianity and Islam* (New York: HarperCollins, 2000); Martin Riesebrodt, *Pious Passion: The Emergence of Modern Fundamentalism in the United States and Iran* (Berkeley: University of California Press, 1993); Charles Kimball, *When Religion Becomes Evil: Five Warning Signs* (San Francisco: Harper San Francisco, 2002). It should be clear from what I am saying that I am not addressing Islam as a religion, Muslims as people, or Arabs as an ethnic/national group.

6 For both Buddhism and Plato, we cannot do evil knowingly. If we truly understand our own nature, we will see that selfishness, greed, injustice, etc. damage ourselves.

7

"Why have we fasted," they say,
"and you have not seen it?
Why have we humbled ourselves,
and you have not noticed?"
"Yet on the day of your fasting, you do as you please
and exploit all your workers.
Your fasting ends in quarreling and strife,
and in striking each other with wicked fists.
You cannot fast as you do today
and expect your voice to be heard on high.
Is this the kind of fast I have chosen,
only a day for a man to humble himself?
Is it only for bowing one's head like a reed
and for lying on sackcloth and ashes?

Is that what you call a fast,
a day acceptable to the LORD?
"Is not this the kind of fasting I have chosen:
to loose the chains of injustice
and untie the cords of the yoke,
to set the oppressed free
and break every yoke?
(Isaiah 58:3–6)

8 By saying that this is the *first* question I do not mean to suggest that it is the *most important*. Rather, I believe that we should not get to more important critical analyses—of imperialism and patriarchy, violent mullahs, or soulless bureaucrats of the World Bank—until we have looked at ourselves.

9 This capacity for self-criticism is one of the great aspects of any serious religious tradition, and makes it (perhaps surprisingly) quite a bit like science, which also must use its own methods to criticize its own positions in order to find better ones.

10 Michael Lerner, *Jewish Renewal: A Path to Healing and Transformation* (New York: Harper Perennial, 1995).

11 Lawrence Troster, "Created in the Image of God," in Martin Jaffe, ed. *Judaism and Environmental Ethics* (Lanham, MD: Rowman and Littlefield, 2002).

12 As Jewish philosopher Emmanual Levinas puts it: "Our response to the face of the Other means we are responsible for everyone—everyone, that is, who is not Hitler". *Nine Talmudic Readings* (Bloomington, IN: Indiana University Press, 1990), 87.

13 See the cogent arguments (with which I actually disagree) in Michael J. Perry, *The Idea of Human Rights: Four Inquiries* (New York: Oxford University Press, 1998).

14 As John Cobb observed in regard to Christianity: "One can find within the Bible excellent grounds for overcoming anthropocentrism and for care for the earth. But Christians did not do so until the insights of persons outside the church led to accusations against them." John B. Cobb, Jr., *Reclaiming the Church* (Louisville, KY: Westminster John Knox Press, 1997), 64.

15 I have made the general argument for this claim in *Joining Hands: Politics and Religion Together for Social Change* (Cambridge, MA: Westview Press, 2004) and in *Liberating Faith: Religious Voices for Justice, Peace, and Ecological Wisdom* (Lanham, MD: Rowman and Littlefield, 2003). The way in which the connections between progressive politics and radical religion are particularly strong in religious environmentalism is described in Roger S. Gottlieb, *A Greener Faith: Religious Environmentalism and our Planet's Future* (New York: Oxford University Press, 2006).

16 The best example is probably the *Bhagavad Gita*.

17 One of those quotes which I have used for years but for which I cannot find the reference!

18 Rebbe Nachman of Bretzlov, *Likutei Moharan*, final edition, chapter 25.

19 The (much) longer version of my understanding of the connection between awareness, resistance, and spiritual joy was developed in *A Spirituality of Resistance: Finding a Peaceful Heart and Protecting the Earth* (Lanham, MD: Rowman and Littlefield, 2003).

20 I am indebted to John Sanbonmatsu for helpful and supportive comments and to Miriam Greenspan for much help in making sure I said what I meant and didn't say anything I didn't mean. Kevin Barrett did his best to help me see things I hadn't seen. Whatever confusions are left are my fault alone.

ELEVEN: BARRETT

1 Francis Fukuyama, *The End of History and the Last Man* (New York: Penguin, 1992).

2 The Zelikow quotes are from his article "Thinking About Political History" in Miller Center Report (Winter 1999). His prognostications of a watershed Pearl Harbor–style terrorism event may be found in Ashton B. Carter, John Deutch, and Philip Zelikow, "Catastrophic Terrorism: Tackling the New Danger," *Foreign Affairs*, Nov/Dec 1998 (www.foreignaffairs.org/ 19981101faessay1434/ashton-b-carter-john-deutch-philip-zelikow/ catastrophic-terrorism-tackling-the-new-danger.html).

3 For evidence that the Twin Towers and WTC 7 were destroyed by explosives, see Steven Jones, "Why Indeed Did the WTC Buildings Collapse?" (www.st911.org) and David Griffin, "The Destruction of the World Trade Center: Why the Official Account Cannot Be True" (www.st911.org). For evidence that the official account of Flight 93 is false, see Rowland Morgan, *Flight 93: What Really Happened On The Heroic 9/11 'Let's Roll' Flight* (London: Constable & Robinson, 2006).

4 One example: According to the footnotes to *The 9/11 Commission Report*, most of the information about the alleged hijackers' purported plot came from secret interrogations of one Khalid Shaikh Mohammed, or KSM. Yet the alleged arrest of KSM in early 2003 in Pakistan was a ludicrously transparent hoax, and there is no convincing evidence that KSM was ever captured or interrogated—or, even if he was, that his alleged confession was genuine. The video of KSM's alleged arrest that was shown to journalists was "openly mocked as a bad forgery" by those journalists (ABC News, Reuters, Paknews, Daily Times) cited in Paul Thompson, *The Terror Timeline* (New York: HarperCollins, 2004), 212. As Thompson proves in his thoroughly documented essay "Is There More to the Capture of Khalid Shaikh Mohammed Than Meets the Eye?" the story of KSM's arrest "is a mass of lies, cover-ups and contradictions" (cooperativeresearch.org/essay.jsp?article=essayksmcapture). Along with

this evidence that KSM's alleged arrest was a hoax, which makes the whole *9/11 Commission Report* a hoax, there is convincing evidence that KSM was not an Islamist extremist, but an intelligence asset (see Nafeez Ahmed's essay in this volume). In short, it seems that the mad "historian" Zelikow is about as reliable a transmitter of KSM's story as Nabokov's narrator was a transmitter of the story of John Shade.

5 David Ray Griffin's *The 9/11 Commission Report: Omissions and Distortions* (Northampton, MA: Olive Branch Press, 2005) proves beyond a reasonable doubt that the Kean Commission Report is mendacious. Griffin builds on the work of many other researchers, as well as his own *The New Pearl Harbor: Disturbing Questions About the Bush Administration and 9/11* (Northampton, MA: Olive Branch Press, 2004). For Griffin's summary of the best reasons to believe that the official story of 9/11 is a myth in the pejorative sense, i.e., a lie, see "9/11: The Myth and the Reality," (www.911podcasts.com/files/audio/20060330_David_Ray_Griffin_32k.mp3).

6 *Myth* is contrasted to legend, a monoepisodic narrative built around an explicit or implicit debate on belief, and folktale, a narrative that is told and received as fiction. See Eliot Oring, "Folk Narratives" in *Folk Groups and Folklore Genres: An Introduction* (Logan, UT: Utah State University Press, 1986).

7 As co-founder of the Muslim-Jewish-Christian Alliance for 9/11 Truth (mujca.com) I am constantly being asked by secularist 9/11 skeptics how religious people, who are presumed to be driven by faith rather than reason, could be expected to examine the 9/11 myth, or anything else, lucidly and critically. The question reflects an abysmal ignorance of the history of thought, with its complex interplay of religion and rational criticism, as well as a tendency toward secularist fundamentalism that projects its own ignorance of worldviews it does not understand.

8 The oft-exaggerated thematic and stylistic differences between the Meccan and Medinan suras are plainly the result of changed social and historical circumstances.

9 On the CIA's purchase of the rights to *Animal Farm*, see Michael P. Rogin, "When the CIA Was the NEA," *The Nation*, June 12, 2000 (www.thenation.com/doc/20000612/rogin). On Howard Hunt, see Gore Vidal, "The Art and Arts of Howard Hunt," *The New York Review of Books*, Dec. 13, 1973 (www.nybooks.com/articles/article-preview?article_id=9660).

10 See Wendy Doniger, *Other Peoples' Myths: The Cave of Echoes* (Chicago: University Of Chicago Press, 1995).

11 On dialogism versus monologism, see Mikhail Bakhtin, *Problems of Dostoevsky's Poetics* (Minneapolis: University of Minnesota Press, 1984).

12 For a Christian analysis of idolatry that runs parallel to the Muslim one, see John Cobb's essay in this volume.

13 René Girard, *Violence and the Sacred* (Baltimore: Johns Hopkins University Press, 1977).

14 Campbell's seminal work is *The Hero with a Thousand Faces* (New

York: Pantheon, 1949). For an evaluation of Campbell, see Robert A. Segal, *Joseph Campbell: An Introduction* (New York: Penguin, 1997).

15 "Resisting the Global Domination Project: An Interview with Prof. Richard Falk," *Frontline*, 20/8 (April 12–25, 2003).

16 David Ray Griffin, "9/11 and the American Empire: How Should Religious People Respond?," authorized, modified transcript of a speech delivered at the University of Wisconsin–Madison, April 18, 2005 (911review.com/articles/griffin/madison.html#ftnote).

17 The Project for the New American Century (PNAC), *Rebuilding America's Defenses: Strategy, Forces, and Resources for a New Century*, Sept. 2000 (www.newamericancentury.org), 51.

18 See Qur'an 79:20–25, among other passages.

19 Roland Barthes, "The Death of the Author," in *Image, Music, Text* (New York: Hill, 1977).

20 Thierry Mayssan has argued that Americans have come to see 9/11 as a religious event, and that this aura of sacrality has blinded them to the obvious falsity of the official story.

21 Brian W. Sturm, "The Storylistening Trance Experience," *Journal of American Folklore* 113.449 (2000): 287–304.

22 Normally I am not a fan of neologisms, but *perpetraitors* perfectly describes the authors of the 9/11 neocon job.

23 On misdirection and magic, see en.wikipedia.org/wiki/Magic_(illusion). For evidence that the alleged "cell phone calls" were a scripted hoax, see A. K. Dewdney, "The Cellphone and Airfone Calls from Flight UA93" (www.physics911.net/cellphoneflight93.htm) and "Project Achilles Report Parts One, Two and Three" (www.physics911.net/projectachilles.htm). For evidence that the Twin Towers and WTC 7 were destroyed by explosives, see Steven Jones, "Why Indeed Did the WTC Buildings Collapse?" (www.st911.org) and David Ray Griffin, "The Destruction of the World Trade Center: Why the Official Account Cannot Be True" (www.st911.org).

24 Alfred McCoy, *A Question of Torture: CIA Interrogation, from the Cold War to the War on Terror* (New York: Metropolitan Books, 2006).

25 See Douglas Rushkoff's book *Coercion: Why We Listen to What "They" Say* (New York: Riverhead, 1999). Reviewed by Kevin Barrett in the context of 9/11 in the article "Apocalypse of Coercion," *Global Outlook* 11, April 2006 (www.mujca.com/apocalypse.htm).

26 An apropos expression I first heard from Pete Creelman.

27 Fukuyama, *The End of History and the Last Man*.

28 See John Ralston Saul, *The Collapse of Globalism and The Reinvention of the World* (Toronto: Viking Canada, 2005).

29 For a frank admission from a Zionist historian that the Palestinian historians as well as popular memory were right all along, and that the 1948 expulsion of Palestinians was clearly an episode of ethnic cleansing, see Benny Morris, *Righteous Victims: A History of the Zionist-Arab Conflict*,

1881–2001 (New York: Vintage, 2001). For an ongoing dialogue involving this volume's editors and contributors on the discomfort provoked by our widely differing views on Zionism and the question of Palestine, see mujca.com/newbook.htm.

30 PNAC, *Rebuilding America's Defenses.*

31 Charles Kupchan, *The Vulnerability of Empire* (Ithaca, NY: Cornell University Press, 1996).

32 Everett Fox translation.

33 Sidney Blumenthal, "One Gulp, and Bush Was Gone: Behind the Scenes at the Clinton Library, We Saw America's Future," *Guardian*, Nov. 25, 2004 (www.guardian.co.uk/usa/story/0,12271,1358966,00.html).

34 Remarks by the president at the signing of H.R. 4613, the Defense Appropriations Act for Fiscal Year 2005, Room 350, Dwight D. Eisenhower Executive Office Building (www.whitehouse.gov/news/releases/2004/08/20040805-3.html).

35 David Enger, *The God That Failed* (New York: Columbia University Press, 2001).

36 Roland Barthes, "L'effet du réel," *Communications* 11, 1968.

37 PNAC, *Rebuilding America's Defenses.*

38 *The 9/11 Commission Report* is palpably the product of a single (mendacious) mind—apparently that of its executive director, Philip Zelikow. The 9/11 operation itself, however, bears the stamp of too many minds fumbling and jumbling, unable to pull it off cleanly.

39 Pearl Harbor was a staged pretext for war, in that it was intentionally provoked and made inevitable by a strangling blockade. Convincing revisionist accounts suggest that the attack probably arrived not by surprise, but with the full foreknowledge of the US high command, which intentionally allowed thousands of Americans to die needlessly in order to provoke the war hysteria that enabled the US to join the slaughter. Such murderous mendacity clearly provided a model for PNAC's "new Pearl Harbor" of 9/11. See Robert Stinnett, *Day of Deceit: The Truth About FDR and Pearl Harbor* (New York: Simon and Schuster, 2001).

40 Tom Robbins, *Fierce Invalids Home from Hot Climates* (New York: Bantam, 2000), 22.

41 In an October 2003 debate on al-Jazeera's program *Opposing Viewpoints*, Thierry Meyssan roundly thrashed a Pentagon spokesman. Al-Jazeera's accompanying survey showed that 89 percent of its audience believed that the US government had perpetrated the 9/11 attacks, while only 11 percent blamed al-Qaeda.

42 Zbigniew Brzezinski makes it clear that this is the overriding US geostrategic imperative in *The Grand Chessboard: American Primacy and its Geostrategic Imperatives* (New York: Basic Books, 1997). See Griffin, *The New Pearl Harbor* 95–96, and Nafeez Mosaddeq Ahmed, *The War on Truth: 9/11, Disinformation, and the Anatomy of Terrorism* (Northampton, MA: Olive Branch Press, 2005), 336–340.

43 Ron Suskind, *New York Times Magazine* (Oct. 17, 2004), quotes an unnamed aide to George W. Bush:

> The aide said that guys like me were "in what we call the reality-based community," which he defined as people who "believe that solutions emerge from your judicious study of discernible reality." ... "That's not the way the world really works anymore," he continued. "We're an empire now, and when we act, we create our own reality. And while you're studying that reality—judiciously, as you will—we'll act again, creating other new realities, which you can study too, and that's how things will sort out. We're history's actors... and you, all of you, will be left to just study what we do."

44 "The vice president bluntly said: 'It is different than the Gulf War was, in the sense that it may never end. At least, not in our lifetime.'" Bob Woodward, "CIA Told to Do 'Whatever Necessary' to Kill Bin Laden," *Washington Post*, Oct. 21, 2001 (www.washingtonpost.com/ac2/wp-dyn?pagename=article&contentId=A27452-2001Oct20).

45 See Victor Turner, *The Ritual Process: Structure and Anti-Structure* (Ithaca, NY: Cornell University Press, 1969).

46 T. S. Eliot, *The Waste Land* (New York: Boni and Liveright, 1922); Bartleby.com, posted 1998 (www.bartleby.com/201/1.html).

47 James Kunstler, *The Long Emergency* (New York: Atlantic Monthly Press, 2005).

48 Unity (*tawhîd*) is the most central characteristic of God according to Islamic tradition. The created cosmos, or "multiverse," is also undergirded by a principle of unity according to various scientific, mystical, and religious traditions. Humanity, of course, stems from a common ancestor not many generations ago, which is why we all share over 99 percent of our DNA. And humanity's current challenge is to recognize and act on the unity of planet earth, both at the level of the noosphere (Teilhard de Chardin) and Gaia (James Lovelock). For a bottom-up, democratic movement for deep planetary unity see Planetization: www.planetization.org/membership.htm.

TWELVE: AHMED

1 BBC News, "Islam 'Hijacked' by Terror," Oct. 11, 2001 (news.bbc.co.uk/1/hi/world/americas/1591024.stm).

2 Ziauddin Sardar, "Islam Has Become Its Own Enemy," *The Observer*, Oct. 21, 2001 (observer.guardian.co.uk/islam/story/0,1442,577943,00.html).

3 Remarks by the President to the United Nations General Assembly, "President Bush Speaks to United Nations," UN headquarters (New York), Nov. 10, 2001 (www.whitehouse.gov/news/releases/2001/11/20011110-3.html).

4 Nafeez Mosaddeq Ahmed, "9/11 'Conspiracies' and the Defactualisation of Analysis: How Ideologues on the Left and Right Theorise Vacuously to Support Baseless Supposition," Media Monitors Network (Los

Angeles), June 28, 2002 (www.mediamonitors.net/mosaddeq37.html).

5 Jay Kolar, "What We Know About the Alleged 9/11 Hijackers," in Paul Zarembka, ed., *The Hidden History of 9-11-2001*, vol. 23 of *Research in Political Economy* (Amsterdam: Elsevier, 2006).

6 Don Kirk, "Filipinos Recall Hijack Suspects Leading a High Life," *International Herald Tribune*, Oct. 5, 2001 (www.intellnet.org/news/2001/10/05/7357-1.html).

7 Kevin Fagan, "Agents of Terror Leave Their Mark on Sin City: Las Vegas Workers Recall the Men They Can't Forget," *San Francisco Chronicle*, Oct. 4, 2001 (www.sfgate.com/cgi-bin/article.cgi?file=/chronicle/archive/2001/10/04/MN102970.DTL).

8 Jody A. Benjamin, "Suspects Actions Don't Add Up," *South Florida Sun Sentinel*, Sept. 16, 2001.

9 Terry McDermott, "Early Scheme to Turn Jets into Weapons: Philippines: Police Say Khalid Shaikh Mohammed Led a Cell Aiming to Blow up Planes in '95," *Los Angeles Times*, June 24, 2002.

10 Quintan Wiktorowicz and John Kaltner, "Killing in the Name of Islam: Al Qaeda's Justification for September 11," *Middle East Policy* X, no. 2, summer 2000 (www.blackwell-synergy.com/links/doi/ 10.1111/1475-4967.00107).

11 Michael Elliot, "Hate Club: Al-Qaeda's Web of Terror," *Time*, Nov. 4, 2001.

12 David Zeidan, "Radical Islam in Egypt: A Comparison of Two Groups," *Middle East Review of International Affairs* 3, no. 3, Sept. 1999 (meria.idc.ac.il/journal/1999/issue3/jv3n3a1.html).

13 Nicholas Hellen, "Ultra Zealots: If You Think Bin Laden is Extreme—Some Muslims Want to Kill Him Because He's Soft," *Sunday Times* (London), Oct. 21, 2001.

14 Anthony Barnett, et al., "London-based Terror Chief Plotted Mayhem in Europe," *Observer*, Sept. 30, 2001.

15 Giles Foden, "The Hunt for 'Public Enemy No 2': Egyptian May Now be Running Terror Operations from Afghanistan," *Guardian*, Sept. 24, 2001 (www.guardian.co.uk/international/story/0,3604,556872,00.html).

16 Douglas Waller, "Was Hijack 'Ringleader' in Bin Laden Orbit?," *Time* magazine, Oct. 5, 2001 (www.time.com/time/nation/article/0,8599,178228,00.html).

17 "Turkey arrests al Qaeda suspects," BBC News, Aug. 10, 2005 (news.bbc.co.uk/2/hi/europe/4140210.stm).

18 "A 'Strange' Al Qaeda Leader: 'I Don't Pray, I Drink Alcohol,'" *Journal of Turkish Weekly* [contributions from Turkish dailies, *Zaman* and *Hurriyet*], Aug. 14, 2005 (www.turkishweekly.net/news.php?id=17778).

19 Ercun Gun, "Sakra: I Dispatched Men to US and UK for Terrorist Activity," *Zaman*, Aug. 15, 2005 (www.zaman.com/?bl=national&alt=&trh=20050815&hn=23056).

20 Gun, "Interesting Confession: I Provided 9/11 Attackers with

Passports," *Zaman*, Aug. 14, 2005 (www.zaman.com/?bl=national&alt=&trh=20050815&hn=23006).

21 Gun, "Sakra: I Dispatched Men to US and UK for Terrorist Activity."

22 Gun, "Al-Qaeda: A Secret Service Operation?" *Zaman*, Aug. 14, 2005 (www.zaman.com/?bl=national&alt=&trh=20050815&hn=22982).

23 Andy Beckett, "The Making of the Terror Myth," *Guardian*, Oct. 15, 2004 (www.guardian.co.uk/terrorism/story/0,12780,1327904,00.html).

24 Andrew Sike, "Profiling Terror," *Jane's Police Review*, Aug. 7, 2003 (www.janes.com/security/law_enforcement/news/pr/pr030807_1_n.shtml).

25 For further discussion see Nafeez Mosaddeq Ahmed, "Terrorism and Statecraft: Al-Qaeda and Western Covert Operations after the Cold War," in Paul Zarembka, ed., *The Hidden History of 9-11-2001*, vol. 23 of *Research in Political Economy* (Amsterdam: Elsevier, 2006).

26 Philip Paull, *"International Terrorism": The Propaganda War*, San Francisco State University, California, June 1982 (Thesis submitted in partial fulfillment of the requirements for the degree Master of Arts in International Relations), 9–10. I would like to thank the Arab American Institute for kindly sending me this thesis within a matter of days, and journalist Roger Trilling for alerting me to it in the first place.

27 Ibid., 18–20.

28 Ibid., 48–52.

29 Ibid., 59–91.

30 Ibid., 95, 99–100.

31 Ibid., 96–98.

32 Ibid., 8.

33 Ibid., 9–17.

34 Diana Ralph, "Islamophobia and the War on Terror: The Continuing Pretext for US Imperial Conquest," in Paul Zarembka, ed., *The Hidden History of 9-11-2001*, vol. 23 of *Research in Political Economy* (Amsterdam: Elsevier, 2006).

35 Cited in Ruth Blakely, "Rhetoric and Reality: US Foreign Military Training Since 1945," Network of Activist Scholars of Politics and International Relations (NASPIR) (www.naspir.org/members/ruth_blakeley/rhetoricandreality1.htm), viewed Feb. 19, 2004.

36 Mark Curtis, *The Ambiguities of Power: British Foreign Policy since 1945* (London: Zed, 1995); *The Great Deception: Anglo-American Power and World Order* (London: Pluto Press, 1997); *Web of Deceit: Britain's Real Role in the World* (London: Vintage, 2002); *Unpeople: Britain's Human Rights Abuses* (London: Vintage, 2004).

37 Foreign Office (UK), "Russian Strategic Intentions and the Threat to Peace," *Documents on British Foreign Policy [DBFP]*, calendar to ser. II, vol. IV (Dec. 7, 1950), 9, 57.

38 Bureau of Near Eastern, South Asian and African Affairs, "Regional Policy Statement: Near East" (Dec. 28, 1950), *Foreign Relations*

of the United States [FRUS], vol. V, 271–272.

39 Bureau of Near Eastern, South Asian and African Affairs, "Regional Policy Statement on Africa South of the Sahara" (Dec. 29, 1950), in *FRUS* vol. V, 1587.

40 Summary of remarks by McGhee (Oct. 25, 1950), in *FRUS*, vol. V, 1570, 1572. 41 Minutes of a Policy Planning Staff meeting (Oct. 11 1950), in *FRUS* (1949), vol. I, 400.

41 Minutes of a policy planning staff meeting (Oct. 11, 1950), in *FRUS* (1949), vol. I, 400.

42 Report of the Mutual Defence Assistance Programme Mission to Southeast Asia (Dec. 6 1950), in *FRUS*, vol. VI, 168.

43 *Guardian*, January 1, 1999. Also see the introduction to my *Behind the War on Terror: Western Secret Strategy and the Struggle for Iraq* (Gabriola Island: New Society, 2003).

44 In W. Strang to T. Lloyd, *British Documents on the End of Empire [BDEE]*, June 21 1952, ser. A, vol. 3, part I (June 21, 1952), 13–19.

45 Mary Kaldor, *The Imaginary War: Understanding the East-West Conflict* (Oxford: Blackwell, 1990). Also see William Blum, *Killing Hope: US Military and CIA Interventions Since World War II* (Monroe, ME: Common Courage Press, 1995); Noam Chomsky, *Deterring Democracy* (Cambridge, MA: South End Press, 1991, 1992); Gabriel Kolko, *The Politics of War: The World and United States Foreign Policy, 1939–1945* (London: Vintage, 1970); Kolko, *Confronting the Third World: United States Foreign Policy, 1945–1980* (New York: Pantheon, 1988).

46 Cited in Daniele Ganser, *NATO's Secret Armies: Operation Gladio and Terrorism in Western Europe* (London: Frank Cass, 2005), 40.

47 Ibid., 41.

48 Ibid., 42.

49 Ibid., 234, 297. The field manual was published in the 1987 parliamentary report of the Italian parliamentary investigation into the terrorist activities of P2, the CIA–MI6 sponsored Italian anti-communist network. See *Commissione parlamentare d'inchiesta sulla loggia massonica* P2. *Allegati alla Relazione* Doc. XXIII, n. 2-quarter/7/1, serie II, vol. VII, tomo I (Roma, 1987), 287–298.

50 Agence France Presse (AFP), Dec. 12, 2000.

51 Rahul Bedi, "Why? An Attempt to Explain the Unexplainable," *Jane's Defence Weekly*, September 14, 2001. Cited in Michel Chossudovsky, "Who is Osama bin Laden?", Center for Research on Globalization (Montreal), Sept. 12, 2001 (www.globalresearch.ca/articles/CHO109C.html).

52 Richard Labévière, *Dollars for Terror: The United States and Islam* (New York: Algora Publishing, 2000), prologue.

53 Chossudovsky, "Osamagate," Center for Research on Globalization, Oct. 9, 2001 (www.globalresearch.ca/articles/CHO110A.html).

54 Peter Dale Scott, "9/11 in Historical Perspective: Flawed Assumptions—Deep Politics: Drugs, Oil, Covert Operations and Terrorism,

A Briefing for Congressional Staff," in *The 9/11 Report: One Year Later—A Citizen's Response* (congressional briefing, Washington, DC, July 22, 2005). Available at ist-socrates.berkeley.edu/~pdscott/911Background.htm.

55 Ahmed Rashid, *Taliban: Militant Islam, Oil and Fundamentalism in Central Asia* (New Haven, CT: Yale University Press, 2000).

56 Ibid., 179.

57 Nafeez Mosaddeq Ahmed, *The War on Truth: 9/11, Disinformation and the Anatomy of Terrorism* (Northampton, MA: Olive Branch Press, 2005).

58 M. Boudjemaa, "Terrorism in Algeria: Ten Years of Day-to-Day Genocide" in Jakkie Cilliers and Kathryn Sturman, ed., *Africa and Terrorism: Joining the Global Campaign*, Institute for Security Studies Monograph no. 74 (Pretoria, July 2002). Available at www.iss.co.za/PUBS/MONOGRAPHS/No74/Chap6.html.

59 Colin Robinson, "Armed Islamic Group a.k.a. Groupement Islamique Arme," Center for Defense Information (Washington, DC), Feb. 5, 2003 (www.cdi.org/terrorism/gia_020503.cfm). See Ahmed, *The War on Truth*.

60 ABC Asia Pacific, "Cause & Effect: Terrorism in the Asia Pacific Region," 2004.

61 Rohan Gunaratna and Phil Hirschkorn, et al., "Blowback," *Jane's Intelligence Review* 13, no. 81 (Aug. 2001).

62 *Guardian*, April 8, 2004.

63 "Armed Islamic Group: Algeria, Islamists" in *Terrorism: Questions & Answers*", Council on Foreign Relations (Washington, DC), 2004 (cfrterrorism.org/groups/gia.html).

64 Cited in Betsy Hiel, "Algeria Valuable In Hunt For Terrorists," *Pittsburgh Tribune*-Review, Nov. 18, 2001.

65 John Sweeney, and Leonard Dolye, "Algerian Regime Responsible for Massacres: Algerian Regime Was behind Paris Bombs," *Manchester Guardian Weekly*, Nov. 16, 1997.

66 See Ahmed, *The War on Truth*, 68, 74.

67 Richard Norton-Taylor, "Terrorist Case Collapses after Three Years," *Guardian*, March 21, 2000.

68 Ibid.

69 Derrick Jensen, "Nothing to Lose but our Illusions: An Interview with David Edwards," *The Sun* magazine, June 2000.

70 HRW, World Report 2000, op. cit.

71 See "Algeria," United States Energy Information Administration, Feb. 1999 (www.eia.doe.gov/emeu/cabs/algeria.html).

72 John K. Cooley, *Unholy Wars: Afghanistan, America and International Terrorism* (London: Pluto Press, 1998), 205–206.

73 Labévière, *Dollars for Terror*, 182–189. See Ahmed, *War on Truth*, 74, 75–77.

74 Paul Joseph Watson, *Order Out of Chaos: Elite Sponsored Terrorism and the New World Order* (AEJ Productions, 2002).

75 Martin Bright, "MI6 'Halted Bid to Arrest bin Laden'," *Observer*, Nov. 10, 2002 (observer.guardian.co.uk/print/0,3858,4543555-102279,00.html). See Ahmed, *The War on Truth*, op. cit.

76 David Shayler, "MI6 Plot to Assassinate Colonel al-Qadhafi: Police Enquiries Confirms Plot is Not 'Fantasy'," press release, November 11, 2001 (www.cryptome.org/shayler-gaddafi.htm).

77 David Shayler, "Don't Shoot the Messenger," *Observer*, Aug. 27, 2000 (www.guardian.co.uk/Archive/Article/0,4273,4055752,00.html).

78 Mark Hollingsworth, "Secrets, Lies and David Shayler: The Spy Agencies Are Pursuing the Press Because They Are Afraid," *Guardian*, March 17, 2000 (www.guardian.co.uk/comment/story/0,3604, 181807,00.html).

79 Patrick McGowan, "Calls for Secret Shayler Trial," *Evening Standard*, Oct. 7, 2002 (www.thisislondon.co.uk/news/articles/ 1488303). A detailed review of the Shayler affair can be found in the book by his partner, former MI5 officer Annie Machon, *Spies, Lies and Whistleblowers: MI5, MI6 and the Shayler Affair* (Brighton: Book Guild, 2005).

80 The Federal Bureau of Investigation, Most Wanted Terrorists, "Anas al-Liby" (www.fbi.gov/mostwant/terrorists/teralliby.htm). Viewed June 11, 2004.

81 Martin Bright, "MI6 'Halted Bid to Arrest bin Laden'," *Observer*, Nov. 10, 2002, (observer.guardian.co.uk/print/0,3858,4543555-102279,00.html). See Ahmed, *War on Truth*, 113–117.

82 See Ahmed, *The War on Truth*.

83 See Ahmed, "Terrorism and Statecraft."

84 William M. Arkin, "The Secret War: Frustrated by Intelligence Failures, the Defense Department is Dramatically Expanding its 'Black World" of Covert Operations," *Los Angeles Times*, Oct. 27, 2002.

85 Pamela Hess, "Panel Wants $7bn Elite Counter-terror Unit," *United Press International*, Sept. 26, 2002.

86 Bill Berkowitz, "Hellzapoppin' at the Pentagon: Rumsfeld's Defense Science Board Proposes 'Prodding' Terrorists to Terrorism," *Working For Change* (online magazine), Nov. 13, 2002 (www.workingfor change.com/ article.cfm?ItemID=14076).

87 Chris Floyd, "Into the Dark: The Terrorist Plan to Provoke Terrorist Attacks," *Counterpunch*, Nov. 1 2002 (www.counterpunch.org/ floyd1101.html).

88 Correspondents in Dubai, "Iraq Extremists Threaten Attacks," *The Australian*, Nov. 24, 2004.

89 Marie Colvin, "Al-Qaeda Directs Iraqi Hit Squad," *Sunday Times* (London), Aug. 10, 2003. Excerpts available online at watch.windsof change.net/03_0804_0810.htm#directs.

90 Syed Saleem Shahzad, "US Fights Back Against 'Rule by Clerics,'" *Asia Times*, Feb. 15 2005 (www.atimes.com/atimes/Middle_East/ GB15Ak02.html).

91 "Cleric says al-Zarqawi died long ago," Al-Jazeera News, Sept. 17, 2005 (english.aljazeera.net/NR/exeres/73570F02-EA07-492F-9E04-C080950DF180.htm).

THIRTEEN: KHAN

1 A *fasiq* in this context is a person or thing that is untrustworthy or vicious. The term in its original sense meant a person or thing that is non/ungodly. Persistent lying or hiding the truth for secondary gain is a sign of ungodliness. To say the mainstream media and temporal rulers (politicians) of the day are caught in cover-ups or persistent lies is an understatement.

2 For more on the subjects of the petrodollar, peak oil, fiat money, and dollar hegemony, please consult the following works: *The Creature from Jekyll Island* by G. Edward Griffin (American Media, 1994); *Man and Money* by Elgin Groseclose (Fredrick Ungar, 1961); *Money: Understanding and Alternatives to Legal Tender* by Thomas H. Greco (White River Junction, VT: Chelsea Green, 2001); *Man and Money: Toward Understanding and Alternative Basis of Credit* by Shaikh Mahmud Ahmad (New York: Oxford Univ. Press, 2002); *Gold Wars: The Battle Against Sound Money as Seen From a Swiss Perspective* by Ferdinand Lips (Foundation for Monetary Education, 2001); *When Corporations Rule the World* by David C. Korten (Kumarian Press, 2001); *Tragedy and Hope* by Carrol Quigley (GSG & Assoc., 1966), and *Traditional Economics and Liberation Theology* by Rama Coomaraswamy, published in *In Quest of The Sacred: The Modern World in the Light of Tradition* by S. H. Nasr and Ken O'Brien (Suhail Academy, 2001); Franklin Sanders' Moneychanger.com; *Petrodollar Warfare: Oil, Iraq and the Future of the Dollar* by William R. Clark (New Society, 2005); *A Century Of War: Anglo-American Oil Politics and the New World Order* by F. William Engdahl (London: Pluto Press, 2004).

3 Mike Ruppert, "Oh Lucy!—You Gotta Lotta 'Splain' To Do: A Timeline Surrounding September 11—If the CIA and the Government Weren't Involved in the September 11 Attacks, What Were They Doing?" From the Wilderness Publications (www.fromthewilderness.com), 2001, expanded and revised Sept. 4, 2004; Paul Thompson, *The Terror Timeline* (New York: HarperCollins, 2004), 287.

4 Daniel Hopsicker, *Welcome to Terrorland: Mohamed Atta and the 9/11 Cover-up in Florida* (Eugene, OR: Mad Cow Press, 2004).

5 Thompson, *The Terror Timeline*, 363.

6 911research.com, "Analysis: Cell Phone Calls" (911research.com/planes/analysis/phonecalls.html); Michel Chossudovsky, "More Holes in the Official Story: The 9/11 Cell Phone Calls," (www.globalresearch.ca); Webster Tarpley, *9/11 Synthetic Terror: Made in USA* (Joshua Tree, CA: Progressive Press, 2006), 321–324. Thompson, *The Terror Timeline*, 404.

7 Tarpley, *9/11 Synthetic Terror*, 172–217.

8 Ruppert, "Oh Lucy!"; *The Journal News*, Oct. 11, 2001; Thompson,

The Terror Timeline, 63.

9 Ruppert, "Oh Lucy!"; Thompson, *The Terror Timeline*, 99.

10 Ruppert, "Oh Lucy!"; Tarpley, 319.

11 Thompson, *The Terror Timeline*, 310.

12 Ruppert, *Crossing the Rubicon: The Decline of the American Empire at the End of the Age of Oil* (Gabriola Island, British Columbia: New Society Publishers, 2004), 259–264; Tarpley, 332.

13 Hopsicker, op. cit.

14 Ruppert, *Crossing the Rubicon*.

15 Tarpley, 249–259.

16 Thierry Meyssan, *9/11: The Big Lie* (New York: Carnot USA, 2002).

17 See "Part II" in David Ray Griffin, *The 9/11 Commission Report: Omissions and Distortions* (Northampton, MA: Olive Branch Press, 2005).

18 Tarpley, 260–271.

19 Jamie McIntyre, "Pentagon: Rumsfeld Misspoke on Flight 93 Crash," CNN.com, Dec. 27, 2004.

20 "9/11 Firefighters: Bombs and Explosions in the WTC," Michael Rivero's What Really Happened (website), June 7, 2006 (www.whatreally happened.com/911_firefighters.html); "Larry Silverstein, WTC 7, and the 9/11 Demolition," Aug. 14, 2005 (www.whatreallyhappened.com/ cutter.html). See also Alex Jones's prisonplanet.com.

21 "Ground Zero: Talk of Rescue Used to Mask Destruction of Evidence," 911Research.org, Aug. 8, 2006 (911research.wtc7.net/ wtc/groundzero/index.html).

22 Ruppert, *Crossing the Rubicon*, 308–330; Thompson, *The Terror Timeline*, 353–368; David Ray Griffin, "Disturbing Truths About 9/11," lecture in New York City, 2003 (I was preliminary speaker and moderator).

23 Ruppert, *Crossing the Rubicon*, 333–357; see also preface to Tarpley, *9/11 Synthetic Terror*.

24 Michael Kane, "The Final Fraud: 9/11 Commission Closes its Doors to the Public; Cover-Up Complete," From the Wilderness (website), July 9, 2004 (www.fromthewilderness.com/free/ww3/071204 _final_fraud.shtml).

25 Tarpley, 49–58. Michael C. Ruppert, presentation to the first Citizens' 9/11 Truth Commission, September 2003, New York City (presented to me as one of the commissioners); Sander Hicks, *The Big Wedding* (New York: Vox Pop, 2005), 75–85.

26 Tarpley, 55.

27 Hicks, 38; Daniel Hopsicker, "The 9/11 Heroine Connection," Mad Cow Morning News, September 2006.

28 Kyle Hence, "Open Letter from 9/11 Family Steering Committee Challenging 9/11 Commissioners: Commentary," 911citizenswatch.org June 14, 2004 (www.911citizenswatch.org/ modules.php?op=modload& name=News&file=article&sid=302&mode=thread&order=0&thold=0). The Family Steering Committee Statement and Questions Regarding the 911

Commission Interview with President Bush, Feb. 16, 2005 (www.ratical.org/ratville/CAH/FSCstmtQs.html).

29 Sara Kehaulani Goo, "FAA Managers Destroyed 9/11 Tapes: Recordings Contained Accounts of Communications With Hijacked Planes," *Washington Post*, May 6, 2004 (available at portland. indymedia.org/en/2004/05/287757.shtml).

30 On June 22, Pew Global Attitudes Project 2006 released the results of a survey that asked Muslims if they thought Arabs carried out the September 11 attacks. Only 17 percent of British Muslims, 48 percent of French Muslims, 16 percent of Indonesians, 32 percent of Egyptians, 16 percent of Turks, 39 percent of Jordanians, and 15 percent of Pakistanis answered "yes."

31 Poll conducted by Zogby International, released August 30, 2004 (www.zogby.com/search/ReadNews.dbm?ID=855).

32 Thomas Hargrove and Guido H. Stempel III, "One in 3 Americans Say US Aided 9/11: Survey Shocker," *New York Post*, Aug. 3, 2006 (www.nypost.com/news/nationalnews/one_in_3_americans_say_u_s__aid ed_9_11_nationalnews_thomas_hargrove_and_guido_h_stempel_iii.htm).

33 I would like to offer some helpful references for those who are beginning their search. Websites: st911.org, 911research.wtc7.net, 911truth.org, unansweredquestions.org, physics911.ca, mujca.com, copvcia.com, cooperativeresearch.ca, whatreallyhappened.com.

Books: David Ray Griffin, *The New Pearl Harbor: Disturbing Questions about the Bush Administration and 9/11* and *The 9/11 Commission Report: Omissions and Distortions* (Northampton, MA: Olive Branch Press, 2004 and 2005, respectively); Nafeez Mosaddeq Ahmed, *The War on Truth: 9/11, Disinformation, and the Anatomy of Terrorism* (Northampton, MA: Olive Branch Press, 2005); Michael Ruppert, *Crossing the Rubicon* (op. cit.); Paul Thompson, *The Terror Timeline* (op. cit.); Thierry Meysan, *The Big Lie* (op. cit.) and *Pentagate* (New York: Carnot USA, 2003); Daniel Hopsicker, *Welcome to Terrorland* (op. cit.); Webster Tarpley, *9/11 Synthetic Terror Made in USA* (op. cit.); Sander Hicks, *The Big Wedding* (op. cit.).

Videos: 911 Eyewitness (www.911eyewitness.com); "The Truth and Lies of 9/11" (copvcia.com); "The Great Deception" (Barry Zwicker); "9/11 Revisited: Scientific and Ethical Questions" (Steven Jones); "Truth and Politics and 9/11 and the American Empire" (David Ray Griffin); "Confronting the Evidence" (reopen911.org); "Loose Change" (Louder Than Words Productions 2005).

34 These ideas are essential to grasp and are effectively illustrated in Webster Tarpley's *9/11 Synthetic Terror*, G. Edward Griffin's *The Creature from Jekyll Island: A Second Look at the Federal Reserve*, fourth ed. (Thousand Oaks, CA: American Media, 2005), and Carrol Quigley's magnum opus, *Tragedy and Hope: A History of the World in Our Time* (San Pedro, CA: GSG & Assoc., 1975).

35 Steven Jones, *9/11 Revisited: Scientific and Ethical Questions*. DVD of lecture at Utah Valley State College, February 1, 2006.

36 "Coleen Rowley's Memo to FBI Director Robert Muller" (edited), *Time* magazine, May 21, 2002 (www.time.com/time/nation/article/ 0,8599,249997,00.html).

37 Catherine Austin Fitts—former director of housing and urban development, and a candidate to be on the board of governors for the federal reserve—informed me of the routine use of control files, whereby sensitive and embarrassing information about government officials are used to blackmail them into complying with the desired role they need to maintain during the operation of a given agenda.

38 The case that the Roosevelt administration intentionally sacrificed 2,476 American lives at Pearl Harbor has grown ever stronger with time. See Robert Stinnett, *Day of Deceit: The Truth About FDR and Pearl Harbor* (New York: Simon and Schuster, 2001). The fact that the neoconservative Project for the New American Century openly yearned for a "new Pearl Harbor" in a document released in September 2000 is the source of the title of David Ray Griffin's first book on 9/11, *The New Pearl Harbor*, op. cit.

39 Conversation with traditionalist author Charles Le Gai Eaton, author of *Islam and The Destiny of Man*, (Albany, NY: SUNY Press, 1986) and *Remembering Allah: Reflections on Islam* (Chicago, IL: Kazi Publications, 2001).

40 This discussion is drawn from the proceedings of the international conference sponsored by the American Society for Muslim Advancement, Copenhagen, Denmark, April 2006, and from the Imam's session in dialogue with Islamic Scholars Feisal Abdul Rauf and Kecia Ali.

41 On 9/11 as a false-flag attack, see David Ray Griffin's essay in this volume. For some of the extensive evidence that the alleged 9/11 hijackers were not the Muslim extremists of the official myth, see Nafeez Ahmed's and Yasmin Ahmed's essays in this volume, as well as Hopsicker (op. cit.). For overwhelming evidence that the alleged Muslim extremist hijackers could not possibly have been responsible for the success of the 9/11 attacks, see the works cited earlier in this essay.

42 For evidence of continued interpenetration of Western intelligence and the so-called militant Islamic networks, see Nafeez Ahmed's essay in this volume. For an analysis of the farcical official non-investigation of 9/11, see Griffin, *The 9/11 Commission Report: Omissions and Distortions*. Evidence that US officials had extremely specific advance knowledge of 9/11 is cited in Griffin, *The New Pearl Harbor*, 69–74. Additionally, Hicks (*The Big Wedding*, 10) quotes FBI informant Randy Glass, who learned from various sources before and during the summer of 2001 that the Twin Towers were going to be destroyed, and was directed to then–State Department counterterror official Francis X. Taylor, who told him "we know all about the planes being flown into the World Trade Center" and told Glass to remain silent for reasons of national security. (Glass had said nothing to Taylor about planes, nor had he known that planes would be used). Glass frantically contacted Senator Bob Graham (D-Florida) during the summer of 2001, speaking to

Graham aide Charles Yonts more than six times, and providing information about the plan to fly planes into the World Trade Center. Graham stated he turned over Glass's information "to the appropriate intelligence agency."

43 Released in 2004 by Lion's Gate Entertainment.

44 That Saudi money is heavily invested in Wall Street is a well-known fact; see *Petrodollar Warfare: Oil, Iraq, and the Future of the Dollar* by Clark, William R. (Gabriola Island, British Columbia: New Society Publishers, 2005). The assassination attempts and ultimate deposition and arrest of Iranian Prime Minister Muhammad Mossadegh and the installation of the Shah of Iran is documented as a CIA/British-backed operation with the intent of foiling popular favorite Mossadegh's assertion of control of the oil revenue and resources of Iran. When the Shah was initially overthrown by a clearly populist (non-Mullah) movement led by the intellegentsia, Wall Street immediately froze Iran's assets. See, for instance, the *Telegraph*'s summary of events at www.telegraph.co.uk/news/main.jhtml?xml=/news/campaigns/iran/irankey.xml.

45 Following the post-9/11 discourse on mainstream media, one often heard occasional pushes for "bombing Saudi Arabia" because it was seen as the home of many of the hijackers. Lawsuits were leveled against the Saudi government by victims' relatives. At the New York City 9/11 Truth Breakthrough Conference (Cooper Union, Grate Hall, 2006), my friend and fellow 9/11 truth activist former Lt. Colonel Bob Bowman, democratic Florida congressional candidate, mentioned that if the mainstream 9/11 truth thesis was true, the military invasion should have been targeted at Saudi Arabia.

46 The escalating violence of American imperial pressure on client/debtor states is vividly described in John Perkins, *Confessions of an Economic Hit Man* (San Francisco: Berrett-Koehler, 2004).

47 Islam holds idolatry (*shirk*) to be the most unforgivable and ontologically central sin. Clinging desperately to a comforting lie or illusion can make that illusion into a false god, turning the person into a *mushrik* or idolator. One of the highest names of the one true God is al-Haqq, "absolute truth" or "reality." For a parallel Christian interpretation of idolatry, see John Cobb's essay in this volume.

48 See Rene Guenon's *Crisis of the Modern World*, fourth ed. (Sophia Perennis, 2004).

49 Frithjof Schuon. See *Understanding Islam* (London: Mandala, 1976) and www.frithjof-schuon.com/start.htm.

50 A criminal tyrant or oppressor.

FOURTEEN: MASUD

1 Muhammad Asad, *The Message of the Quran* (The Book Foundation, 2004).

2 Jonathan Sacks, "Rabbi Warns of Israel's 'Tragic Path'," BBC News, August 27, 2002 (news.bbc.co.uk/1/low/uk/2218571.stm). Accessed

September 8, 2006.

3 For an ongoing dialogue involving this volume's editors and contributors on the discomfort provoked by our widely differing views on Zionism and the question of Palestine, see mujca.com/newbook.htm.

4 For a broad and nonjudgmental account of the genocidal and ecocidal European colonization of most of the world's temperate zones—the most salient feature of the past 1,000 years of history—see Alfred Crosby's *Ecological Imperialism*. Crosby argues that Europeans could only successfully colonize lands that were sparsely populated, temperate, and very far away; all European settler-colonial ventures in other areas (with the perhaps temporary exception of the Zionist effort in Palestine) have failed.

5 Smedley Butler, "War is a Racket," The Wisdom Fund, September 11, 2001 (www.twf.org/News/Y2001/0911-Racket.html).

6 Thomas H. Etzold and John Lewis Gaddis, *Containment: Documents on American Policy and Strategy, 1945–1950* (1978), 226–227. From "Memo PPS23 by George Kennan," Wikisource, the Free Library (en.wikisource.org/w/index.php?title=Memo_PPS23_by_George_Kennan&oldid=204558).

7 For a recent description of this policy from the viewpoint of a former ground-level operative, see John Perkins, *Confessions of an Economic Hit Man* (San Francisco: Berrett-Koehler Publishers, 2004).

8 Zbigniew Brzezinski, *The Grand Chessboard: American Primacy and Its Geostrategic Imperatives* (New York: Basic Books, 1997), 31.

9 Ibid., 40

10 William Arkin, *Los Angeles Times*, Jan. 6, 2001.

11 Chalmers Johnson, "America's Empire of Bases," published by TomDispatch.com, Jan. 15, 2004 (available at www.commondreams.org/views04/0115-08.htm).

12 Michael Barletta and Eric Jorgensen, "Israel: Weapons of Mass Destruction Capabilities and Programs," the Center for Nonproliferation Studies, May 1998 (cns.miis.edu/research/wmdme/israel.htm). Accessed September 8, 2006.

13 On Israeli apartheid, see Uri Davis, *Israel: An Apartheid State* (London: Zed Books, 1987). On Israeli violation of UN Resolutions, see www.un.org/Depts/dpi/palestine/.

14 David R. Francis, "Economist Tallies Swelling Cost of Israel to US," *The Christian Science Monitor*, December 9, 2002 (www.csmonitor.com/2002/1209/p16s01-wmgn.html).

15 "Israel Outraged as EU Poll Names It a Threat to Peace." *Guardian*, November 2, 2003 (www.guardian.co.uk/israel/Story/0,2763,1076084,00.html).

16 The numbers posted as this book is going to press (September 2006) are almost identical, with 86.9% saying the US is the greatest threat to peace. See "The Biggest Threat to Peace," *Time Europe* (www.time.com/time/europe/gdml/peace2003.html).

17 "Globalisation 'Bigger Threat than Terror,'" *BBC News*, April 9,

2004 (news.bbc.co.uk/2/hi/uk_news/3613217.stm).

18 "Us and Them," *Independent*, October 18, 2004.

19 Michael Klare, "In Pursuit of Enemies: The Remaking of US Military Strategy," *Third World Traveler* (online) (www.thirdworldtraveler.com/ Book_Excerpts/InPursuit_RSNO.html).

20 See Nafeez Ahmed's essay in this volume for a discussion of how the Cold War–era state-sponsored "leftist" terrorism of Operation Gladio and its epigones has morphed into the state-sponsored "Islamist" terrorism of al-Qaeda, as part of a "strategy of tension" aimed at facilitating Western and especially American access to geostrategic resources.

21 George Soros, *Open Society: Reforming Global Capitalism* (New York: Public Affairs Press, 2000), 333.

22 Ambrose Evans Pritchard, "Europol has doubts on bin Laden conspiracy," *Daily Telegraph* (London), September 15, 2001.

23 "Partial list of victims," Associated Press, Sept. 17, 2001 (www.boston.com/news/daily/13/victims_list.htm#aa77).

24 "Hijack 'Suspects' Alive and Well," BBC News, Sept. 23, 2001 (news.bbc.co.uk/2/hi/middle_east/1559151.stm).

25 See www.9-11commission.gov.

26 See David Ray Griffin, *The 9/11 Commission Report: Omissions and Distortions* (Northampton, MA: Olive Branch Press, 2005).

27 See 911research.wtc7.net/talks/pentagon/video.html.

28 www.rense.com/general29/penta.htm.

29 www.defenselink.mil/transcripts/2001/t09122001_t0912asd.html.

30 A good place to start looking at the Pentagon photos controversy is: www.scholarsfor911truth.org/Resources.html.

31 Jim Yardley, "A Trainee Noted for Incompetence," *New York Times*, May 4, 2002.

32 CBS News, Sept. 20, 2001 (www.cbsnews.com/stories/2001/ 09/11/national/main310721.shtml).

33 The Netanyahu-commissioned *A Clean Break: A New Strategy for Securing the Realm*, whose authors included neoconservatives and PNAC members Richard Perle and Douglas Feith, called for Israel to institute the principle of pre-emption and overthrow the government of Iraq: "This effort can focus on removing Saddam Hussein from power in Iraq—an important Israeli strategic objective in its own right—as a means of foiling Syria's regional ambitions." In this it eerily foreshadowed PNAC's *Rebuilding America's Defenses* as well as Bush's unprovoked invasion of Iraq. See: www.information clearinghouse.info/article1438.htm; www.iasps.org/ strat1.htm.

34 Rowan Scarborough, "Army Study Suggests U.S. Force of 20,000," *Washington Times*, Sept. 11, 2001.

35 "French Reports: US Busts Big Israeli Spy Ring," Reuters, March 5, 2002 (available at www.commondreams.org/headlines02/0305-05.htm).

36 John F. Sugg, *Weekly Planet* (Tampa, FL), April 22, 2002.

37 James Bamford, *Body of Secrets: Anatomy of the Ultra-Secret National*

Security Agency (New York: Anchor Books, 2002).

38 BBC, Sept. 18, 2001.

39 George Monbiot, *Guardian*, Feb. 12, 2002.

40 Geov Parrish, "Who Counts? New Estimates of Afghanistan's Civilian Dead," *In These Times*, Dec. 26, 2001 (available at www.alternet.org/story.html?StoryID=12143).

41 *Agence France Presse*, Jan. 19, 2000.

42 Transcript available at www.commonwealthclub.org/archive/02/02-04mueller-speech.html.

43 George Nelson, Colonel, USAF (ret.), "911 and the Precautionary Principle: Aircraft Parts as a Clue to their Identity" (www.physics911.net/georgenelson.htm).

44 Thomas Jefferson, letter to Dr. Benjamin Rush, Sept. 23, 1800 (available at etext.virginia.edu/jefferson/quotations/).

FIFTEEN: AHMED

1 Kevin Fagan, "Agents of Terror Leave their Mark on Sin City: Las Vegas Workers Recall the Men They Can't Forget," *San Francisco Chronicle*, Oct. 4, 2001 (www.sfgate.com/cgi-bin/article.cgi?file=/chronicle/archive/2001/10/04/MN102970.DTL); Evan Thomas, "Cracking the Terror Code," *Newsweek*, Oct. 15, 2001.

2 Shelly Murphy and Douglas Belkin, "Hijackers Said to Seek Prostitutes," *Boston Globe*, Oct. 10, 2001.

3 Eric Bailey, "It Was A Little Strange. Most People Want To Do Take-Offs And Landings. All They Did Was Turns," *Daily Mail*, Sept. 16, 2001.

4 Qur'an, 5:32.

5 Thomas, "Cracking the Terror Code."

6 Jody A. Benjamin, "Suspects' Actions Don't Add Up," *Sun-Sentinel*, Sept. 16, 2001.

7 Carolyn Thompson, "Muslims Claim Unfair Treatment at Border," Associated Press, Dec. 30, 2004.

8 "CAIR Issues Travel Advisory for US Muslims; 'Civil Rights Hotline' Created for Hajj Pilgrims, Canada Conference Attendees," US Newswire, Dec. 20, 2005 (releases.usnewswire.com/GetRelease.asp?id=58451).

9 Associated Press, "Mayfield's Wife Denies Leaving Country for 10 Years," King5 Seattle News, May 7, 2004 (www.king5.com/sharedcontent/northwest/specialreport/stories/NW_050704ORK mayfieldwifeLJ.19bfe14a3.html).

10 Ibid.

11 Ibid.

12 Steve Kellmeyer, "Coulter Wars," Nov. 30, 2004 (www.renewamerica.us/columns/kellmeyer/041130).

13 "She's Got Chutzpah," *O: The Oprah Magazine*, May 2004 (www.oprah.com/spiritself/omag/slide/ss_o_slide_200405_chutzpah_04.jhtml).

14 DeNeen L. Brown, "'Muslim Refusenik' Incites Furor With Critique of

Faith: Canadian's Book Challenges Treatment of Women Under Islam," *Washington Post* Foreign Service, Jan. 19, 2004 (www.muslim-refusenik.com/news/washingtonpost-040118.html).

15 Bill Gay, news release, Imperial Valley College, Oct. 22, 2004 (www.imperial.edu/current_issues/NewsRelease10-22-04.pdf).

16 The contested term *genocide* can refer to any effort to obliterate a religious or ethnic group. An effort to "eliminate the Islamic religion" would be the largest genocide attempt in history, since that religion has well over a billion adherents.

17 Qur'an, 3:110.

18 Qur'an, 2:143.

19 National Commission on Terrorist Attacks Upon the United States, "The 9-11 Commission Report," 2004 (www.gpoaccess.gov/ 911/index.html).

20 "Muhammad a Gulf War Vet, Islam Convert," CNN, Jan. 26, 2004 (archives.cnn.com/2002/US/10/24/muhammad.profile/).

21 Patrick Cockburn, "Mass Killer Given Status of a Saint," *Independent,* June 19, 1998 (www.al-bushra.org/Truth/mass.htm).

22 http://en.wikipedia.org/wiki/Mohammed_Atta.

23 ABC News, March 9, 2005 (http://abcnews.go.com/WNT/print?id=566425).

24 John Vinocur, "Politics: Bush might be heading for tangle with neocons," International Herald Tribune, January 11, 2005.

25 Jamie Glazov, "Frontpage Interview: Daniel Pipes," FrontPageMagazine.com, Dec. 16, 2003 (www.danielpipes.org/ article/1358).

26 Daniel Pipes, "Three Wars: Iraq, Terrorism and the Arab-Israeli Conflict," Madison, WI: University of Wisconsin–Madison, 2003.

27 Lawrence Auster, "The Search for Moderate Islam," FrontPageMagazine.com, Jan. 28, 2005 (www.frontpagemag.com/Articles/ReadArticle.asp?ID=16798).

28 Ann Coulter, "This Is War," Sept. 13, 2001 (www.national review.com/coulter/coulter.shtml).

29 David E. Kaplan, "Hearts, Minds, and Dollars," *U.S. News & World Report*, April 25, 2005.

30 Cheryl Benard, "Civil Democratic Islam: Partners, Resources, Strategies," RAND-National Security Research Division (Santa Monica: RAND Corporation, 2003; available at www.rand.org/pubs/monograph_reports/2005/MR1716).

31 Khaled Abou El-Fadl, *Speaking in God's Name: Islamic Law, Authority and Women* (Oxford: Oneworld Publications, 2001), 94.

32 Benard, 47.

33 Ibid., 48.

34 Richard Morin, "A Terrifying Truth About Terrorism," *Washington Post,* May 11, 2006 (www.washingtonpost.com/wp-dyn/content/article/2006/05/10/AR2006051001912.html).

INDEX